Becoming Free

Becoming Free

Autonomy and Diversity in the Liberal Polity

Emily R. Gill

 University Press of Kansas

© 2001 by the University Press of Kansas

Published by the University Press of Kansas (Lawrence, Kansas 66049), which
was organized by the Kansas Board of Regents and is operated and funded by
Emporia State University, Fort Hays State University, Kansas State University,
Pittsburg State University, the University of Kansas, and Wichita State
University

Library of Congress Cataloging-in-Publication Data

Gill, Emily R., 1944–
   Becoming free : autonomy and diversity in the liberal polity / Emily
R. Gill.
        p. cm.
Includes index.
   ISBN 0-7006-1075-8 (cloth : acid-free paper)—ISBN 0-7006-1094-4
(pbk. : acid-free paper)
   1. Liberalism.   2. Individualism.   3. Liberty.   4. Multiculturalism.
I. Title.
   JC574 .G56   2001
   320.51—dc21   00-010958

British Library Cataloguing in Publication Data is available.

Printed in the United States of America

10 9 8 7 6 5 4 3 2 1

The paper used in this publication meets the minimum requirements of the
American National Standard for Permanence of Paper for Printed Library
Materials Z39.48-1984.

To the memory of my parents,

Oliver Arthur Gill (1904–1997) and
Josephine Bates Gill (1913–1989)

Contents

Preface

The inspiration for this book stems from my young adulthood and even perhaps from my childhood, although I certainly did not recognize this at the time. My parents, to the memory of whom the book is dedicated, afforded me wonderful opportunities for education and travel, but they each at times seemed to focus on one conception of the person I should be to the exclusion of other capacities. As it became evident that I was a good student and that I had broad intellectual interests, my father periodically remarked that any woman could marry and have children but not everyone could do what I was doing. Although my mother, on the other hand, was proud of my scholarly accomplishments, she was also somewhat ambivalent, hoping that these would not be off-putting to young men. In particular, I recall a dinner I was to give for my tenth reunion class from my preparatory school for girls in California. She enthusiastically supported my plans, remarking as I was setting the table that all these girls had husbands now, and I had a Ph.D. The implication was that I had a Ph.D. as a sort of consolation prize, and I began to wonder whether I should perhaps put a place card beside me for my Ph.D.! Although they were supportive in every way, both my parents sometimes lost sight of the idea that I might want it *all*, and that if I were truly living my life from the inside, all is what I intended to have.

I also recall a conversation with a family friend when I was about ten years old. I was playing with my dolls, and she remarked that in a year or so I would probably no longer be interested in dolls. I started to cry, and, startled, she reassured me that I could play with dolls as long as I wanted. I tried to explain to her that I knew that, but that I didn't want *not* to be interested in dolls. In my own way, apparently I was trying to explain that I thought a life that included interest in dolls was preferable to one bereft of that interest. In other words, I was experiencing a second-order desire about what my first-order desires should be. The absence of a preferred first-order desire would constitute false consciousness, as it were. The issues raised by these two incidents certainly have bearing on the subject of autonomy and on how this is defined and achieved.

I have looked forward to writing this preface, because it is my opportunity to thank a number of people without whose input this book would not have been written. Ron Terchek and Suzanne Jacobitti each read the first incarnation of the proposal for the book in 1993, making valuable suggestions along the way. When I finished writing the manuscript, it was nearly twice as long as it should have been. Patrick Neal valiantly offered to read the entirety, suggesting a number of areas where I might cut the text while minimizing damage to the overall argument. Suzanne Jacobitti read the resulting product, making detailed comments about sections that were not clear or that might be cut still further. Later she read the manuscript once again, offering more suggestions where she thought I still did not have matters quite right. Donald Lutz and Rogers Smith, formal and informal reviewers for the University Press of Kansas, offered constructive comments on the completed manuscript.

Although he never saw the manuscript until it was finished, Rogers Smith in informal conversations through the years acted as the proverbial dutch uncle, proffering encouragement and support in difficult times, and his own work has greatly influenced my thinking. Sam Marcosson, a good friend whom I am proud to claim as a former student, critiqued a number of articles and papers over the years containing ideas that ended up in this book. Clifford Scott, a former student, discussed with me in depth many of the issues addressed in chapter 3. I owe special thanks to Mike Briggs, editor in chief of the University Press of Kansas, who in 1989 first started encouraging me to think about writing a book of my own. Willie Heberer and Tracy Anderson at Bradley University prepared the manuscript. Their diligence, care, and good cheer have rendered even the mechanical aspects of this project a pleasure. I am deeply grateful to the Earhart Foundation in Ann Arbor, Michigan, for a grant that enabled me to take a leave from teaching during the 1997–1998 academic year. I also benefited from a sabbatical leave from Bradley University in spring 1996. Finally, I want to thank my husband, James Temples, and my son, Robert Temples. Together they have provided the ideal mixture of support that allowed me to work along with distractions that lightened my task.

I conclude with a couple of points about mechanics. Emphases that appear within quotations are original ones unless otherwise indicated. First references to a source in any portion of the text appear in an endnote, but subsequent references to the same source that immediately follow without intervening references are indicated parenthetically in the text itself.

Introduction

This book is devoted to an exploration of the tension that often exists between autonomy and diversity as core commitments of liberalism. The liberal polity has characteristically championed background conditions for individual choice, autonomy, and self-development. It has also traditionally been hospitable to diversity, which has provided a plurality of options among which individuals may choose. Together, these commitments have provided a context within which individuals may become free. That is, individuals in a liberal polity should possess a variety of external resources that afford choice and an array of internal resources that enable them to engage in critical reflection on the options with which they are confronted. Ideally, then, individual autonomy and conditions of diversity should complement one another. Autonomy should allow individuals to make the best possible use of their options, while the existing diversity of options provides the raw material, as it were, on which individuals bring to bear their capacities for autonomy.

Autonomy and diversity are not always as compatible, however, as this sketch suggests. Individuals with certain cultural or religious affiliations, for example, may view unquestioning obedience to traditional authority as primary. They do not necessarily value critical reflection, and they may see its promotion as a threat to rather than as an enhancement of their children's lives. The promotion of the capacity for autonomy, then, may appear to exclude individuals and groups who do not value autonomy, thus threatening liberal hospitality to diversity. Alternatively, we may encourage or allow cultural or religious groups and families to inculcate their own values in individuals who are their members. This process may implicitly or explicitly denigrate the importance of critical reflection on a variety of options. But the accommodation of these groups and families who do not value autonomy denies the development and/or exercise of the capacity for critical reflection to those who might value it highly, if they were given the opportunity. Such an accommodation thus lessens the liberal commitment to autonomy.

Either way, individual citizens of the liberal polity lose out. In the first case, the promotion of the capacity for critical reflection forecloses ways of life that discount or even devalue this capacity, thereby eliminating a range of options and commitments eschewing critical reflection that would otherwise be available. In the second case, hospitality to diversity in effect forecloses to some people ways of thinking or inner resources that could assist them in reflecting on their options and possible commitments. In this book I shall explore some of the ways in which this tension plays out in several different issue areas. Although a number of books and articles are directed to the subject of autonomy, or to the manner in which diversity contributes to or detracts from the liberal polity, none that I know of addresses the manner in which autonomy and diversity intersect with one another, particularly with regard to specific issues that confront the liberal polity. My interest is neither in the maximization of choice independent of the framework within which it exists, nor in the maximization of the number of options, regardless of their nature. Rather, I focus on the context within which choice exists and options present themselves. I argue that we should attend to this context or framework and that we should structure it in ways that both preserve a broad range of options and encourage the development and use of the capacity for critical reflection as individuals survey and make use of these options.

Chapter 1 is devoted to an exploration of the meanings of autonomy and diversity as I understand them and to establishing the framework for my commitment to the development of the capacity for autonomy. Moral autonomy implies the capacity to govern oneself, including both the freedom to pursue what one judges to be good and the ability to define this good in one's own manner. Personal autonomy requires rational scrutiny of and critical reflection on our projects and goals. The presence of autonomy, then, must be judged not by the projects and goals we select, but by the way we form our preferences. We can act in *accordance* with habit and custom and still act autonomously, as long as we do not act simply from *force* of habit, unthinkingly taking the path of least resistance, as it were.

As autonomous persons, I argue, we not only have desires, but we also care what those desires are. The critical reflection in which we engage focuses both on what desires we actually have, or first-order desires, and on discerning what desires we *want* to have, or second-order desires, and on what desires we wish to govern our wills and move us to action, or second-order volitions. This attention increases the degree of our self-understandings, the continuity of our agency over time, and our integrity or wholeness as persons.

Early liberals such as John Locke and John Stuart Mill defended individual freedom and autonomy but did so within the context of comprehensive liberal doctrines that included an account of the good life. Such an account is often called perfectionistic, as it specifies an ideal toward which we should strive as we direct our lives. Contemporary liberals, such as Ronald Dworkin and John Rawls, on the other hand, have suggested that the liberal polity must be independent of or neutral toward rival conceptions of the good if individuals are truly to make their own unbiased choices. I argue, however, that even the liberal polity is nonneutral, sometimes by default. Although an emphasis on the capacity for autonomy appears perfectionistic to some scholars, *any* theory that holds out a range of desirable outcomes could be labeled perfectionistic, although some theories are of course more perfectionistic than others. The liberal polity can achieve a degree of neutrality, but this degree must be measured or judged by a standard independent of neutrality itself. For me, that standard should be that of the promotion of the capacity for autonomy, and the goal should be autonomy-based neutrality.

Autonomy-based neutrality does not abandon the ideal of neutrality among rival conceptions of the good but treats it as a derivative value that serves the goal of the development of the capacity for autonomy. This means, in the words of Will Kymlicka, that we must live our lives "from the inside," ordering them in accordance with our own beliefs about value rather than in accordance with others' beliefs, even if the beliefs of these others purport to represent some set of transcendent values. Moreover, the capacity for autonomy requires the ability to question, examine, and revise or reaffirm our beliefs about value as a result of critical scrutiny and reflection. The life that is good for each of us as individuals is not a fixed object, like a Holy Grail, to be discovered either through good luck or good management and to be adhered to forever. The liberal polity is *nonneutral* in the sense that it embraces autonomy as a necessary means to the good life. It should, in my view, encourage in all individuals the development of the capacity for autonomy as rational deliberation, critical scrutiny, and reflection on the projects and goals that we adopt. It is *neutral*, however, as to the choices of values and projects that individuals make, as long as these choices do not interfere with the capacity for autonomy or rule out its development in others. Values and projects carry meaning only for individuals who can choose or affirm them for themselves. And doing this requires, once again, the capacity to question, examine, and either revise or reaffirm one's current projects and goals.

If the liberal polity's neutrality requires that it encourage individuals to form and revise their own values, its corresponding nonneutrality requires that, despite its support for diversity, it not allow choice among all conceivable preferences and practices. Any espousal of core commitments acts to produce one range of preferences rather than others. Autonomy-based neutrality requires a diversity of values or options on which to reflect. Yet, as we have seen, accommodation of diversity cannot, I believe, include the right to limit the development of others' capacities to engage in critical reflection on and possible revision of their projects and goals. One solution to the challenge of diversity, Rawls's attempt to construct an overlapping consensus by getting citizens to abstract from their comprehensive doctrines about the good life when they engage in political dialogue, delivers less than it promises. Rather than opening new possibilities or offering new interpretations of what might be politically possible, it depoliticizes public dialogue, too often confirming the status quo, or the dominant consensus on the limits of the reasonable. A greater reliance on comprehensive doctrines, on the other hand, suggested by some scholars like William Galston and Michael Sandel as a means of broadening the range of options, also too often strengthens the dominant consensus as individuals become subject to majoritarian interpretations of these doctrines.

I defend greater attention to an intrasubjective conception of the self, according to which a range of options is available *within* and thus for each individual who surveys and reflects on them, makes choices, and then reflects anew. This process again requires the capacity for critical reflection on our projects and goals. Moreover, on the collective level it is through debate and discussion that we decide what is compatible with the liberal ideal. Although some ways of life and certain values will necessarily be excluded, the resulting consensus is both authoritative and provisional, authoritative because it results from dialogue, and provisional because it is never finally settled but will again be the object of question, examination, deliberation, and possible revision. The fact that these activities occur both in the public arena and within the individual once more emphasizes the necessity for developing the capacity to engage in critical reflection on both public and private projects and goals.

Chapter 2 focuses on national citizenship in the liberal polity. I believe that political communities must be bounded and control their membership if individuals are to possess a space within which they can express their communal identities, or the ties and values they share with others. Yet the value of the political community is not intrinsic but lies in the forum it provides for individual self-expression. Moreover, communities, like individuals, are free over time to question, examine, and revise or reaffirm their collective projects and goals, engaging in deliberation and critical reflection as they survey their options. Our collective identity, like our individual identities, is not a fixed or static one.

In this context, I examine a number of Supreme Court decisions over the past generation for their interpretation of the notion of political community. Although my focus is the United States, the principles I discuss may apply elsewhere as well. Any political community, even a liberal one, must exercise some control over its boundaries if it is to remain an entity within which it may practice its principles, in this case liberal ones. Yet liberalism's traditional inclusivity increases the difficulty of justifying the difference between members and strangers. I argue that the traditional distinction between the economic functions of government, in which aliens have often been included, and the sovereign or political functions of government, from which aliens traditionally have been excluded, is generally too unclear to justify the exclusion of resident aliens from participation in the collective destiny of which, by their very presence, they are already a part. Whatever their formal status, aliens who are geographically present interact with citizens and exert an impact on the polity as a whole. Therefore, I consider the political community as a type of expressive association, or as an association the existence of which creates and perpetuates a distinctive voice or message. I argue that although a political community that desires to preserve a distinctively liberal way of life may exclude some strangers, those whom it admits or allows to remain it must treat as members or eventual members. The liberal polity must be bounded externally if its members, actual or potential, are to control their destinies. But it cannot be bounded internally if all are to have the opportunity to examine, question, and revise or reaffirm their projects and goals.

In chapters 3 and 4, I examine two sorts of cultural membership that may exist in the liberal polity. Chapter 3 focuses on national minorities who may be incorporated into a larger nation-state. Although this contingency is exceptional rather than common in the United States, my discussion is motivated by the way divergent responses to separatist versions of cultural membership illuminate the tension between autonomy and diversity when the latter is magnified. Kymlicka, for example, would privilege cultural membership by according group-differentiated rights to cohesive national minorities within larger liberal states, on grounds that cultural membership is an unchosen feature of identity. Chandran Kukathas, however, would offer no special legal protection to minorities against the larger culture but would support the authority of leaders within a culture to enforce traditional practices, such as religious ones, on its members. These members in effect choose cultural membership as long as they possess freedom to exit. Still others, like Yael Tamir, would accord legal protections and exemptions to cultural minorities because they are minorities, whether members were born to this status or subsequently chose this affiliation. Finally, Jeff Spinner argues that although culture may or may not be chosen by its adherents, the liberal polity should accord some internal autonomy to cultural communities without equating them with private associations.

After consideration of ways these arguments intersect, I maintain that although membership in some culture is a precondition of human agency, membership in any particular culture for mature adults is not a precondition of autonomy but should instead be regarded as an expression of autonomy. In a liberal polity, then, our focus should be on ensuring the existence of a context of choice maximizing the probability that cultural membership will indeed proceed from critical reflection and thus function as an expression of autonomy.

Therefore, I support prima facie neither the external protection of cultural structure against the larger society through group-differentiated rights nor the internal protection of cultural content against dissident individuals or groups, because both kinds of protection may narrow the range of options of individual members or thwart their capacity to engage in critical reflection on these options. Although some cultural options may disappear without protection, even cultures that remain are changed by their interaction with the larger society. Indeed, their very continuation depends on the willingness of the larger society to leave them alone. Moreover, many theorists who would protect cultural structure or content want indirectly to protect choice, which for me requires the developed capacity to engage in critical reflection on our projects and goals.

Chapter 4 continues the discussion of many of these issues, but the focus is on ethnic groups and gender. Ethnic minorities and women typically wish to be full members of the larger society yet retain and seek recognition of certain features of their identity that may diverge from what is considered typical of the majority or of what is considered to be the norm. Ethnic groups are not national minorities but still resist giving up their cultural allegiances to assimilate totally into a cosmopolitan culture. How much protection do they merit against the thrust of the dominant culture? To the extent that they must accommodate the latter, to what extent should members of the dominant culture engage in some accommodation of their own? In the case of gender, are women who are treated like men being asked to assimilate into a "male" culture? Or is the dominant culture an androgynous one that until recently has been dominated by males? With respect to both ethnicity and gender, I argue, addressing specific examples, that individuals should be self-interpreting and should decide for themselves the meaning of their unchosen identities in the context of their own lives. Although they cannot choose their ethnicity or gender at birth, they do have a choice as to how they want ethnicity or gender and its purported attributes to function in their own lives. Throughout, I shall bear in mind relationships between cultural membership and the capacity for autonomy.

Chapter 5 treats religious belief, an instance of diversity that has traditionally been privileged in the liberal polity. I maintain that despite honorable intentions, civil law cannot be neutral with respect to religion, because policies that appear neutral given one set of assumptions seem nonneutral when premised on a different set of assumptions. In this context I discuss first Locke's classic view of toleration and its functions and then move on to consider two contemporary models of toleration, one based on freedom of conscience that encompasses the right to choose one's beliefs, and one rooted in group rights that protects the right to adhere to one's beliefs but not the right to subscribe to new ones.

I argue that the liberal polity must adhere to freedom of conscience as the right to choose. Although some individuals suggest that religious belief should be respected as an unchosen constituent of identity, I suggest, instead, that we take responsibility for our ends even in the area of conscience. Conscientious belief represents the expression of autonomy when its affirmation or revision results from rational deliberation and critical reflection. Where public policies of toleration or accommodation are appropriate, individuals' practices merit protection, not because they are unchosen but because they are features that are central to identity and expressive of autonomy. In other words, they represent constitutive choice. Persons who view their religious practices as duties and constitutive of identity have still made a choice, and the obligations incurred by this choice have then become constitutive. To illustrate, I apply this model to specific individuals like St. Paul. Not all beliefs are expressions of autonomy, as they may be arrived at or sustained unthinkingly, and we do not always know which is the case. But when we tolerate beliefs and the practices that flow from them, we are honoring and respecting the possibility or potential they possess for the expression of autonomy.

Despite the liberal polity's support from freedom of conscience, it must still determine which specific practices should be protected and which should not. Generally, I argue that the protection of the broadest possible scope for the expression and practice of religious belief enhances both autonomy and diversity. As an example of the harder sort of case in which these values conflict, however, I discuss the Boy Scouts of America and its policies confining membership to theists and heterosexuals. As an expressive association that publicly affirms the centrality of theism in the Boy Scout Oath, the Boy Scouts is entitled to restrict its membership to theists. Without a similarly clear public affirmation favoring heterosexuality, the Scout stance regarding sexual orientation is, I argue, on shakier ground. Overall, I would have to support the rights of organizations like the Boy Scouts to set the qualifications for their own members, although public aid to or public bodies' sponsorship of organizations that discriminate in a manner contrary to public policy should cease. I would need to rethink the issue, on the other hand, if most organizations were exclusive in the same way. If few organizations of any kind wanted to admit agnostics, atheists, or homosexuals, the combined effect would be to curtail drastically the context of choice within which individuals exercise their autonomy.

In chapter 6, on the topic of sexuality, I argue that just as the liberal polity cannot be strictly neutral, despite good intentions, regarding culture and religious faith, neither can it be neutral with regard to sexuality. Whether it privileges one sexual orientation, that of heterosexuality, over others or accords equal consideration and respect to people of all sexual orientations, it will appear nonneutral to some. As I maintain in chapter 1, any neutrality that the liberal polity achieves among rival conceptions of the good must be measured in terms of an admittedly nonneutral criterion, and in my view this criterion should be that of autonomy-based neutrality. As with culture and religious affiliation, I argue that persons of all sexual orientations should be accorded equal respect, not because these orientations are unchosen constituents of identity but because they may be expressions of autonomy. Although one's basic sexual orientation, like the culture or faith into which one is born, is indeed an unchosen constituent of identity, how one handles or responds to this orientation is a matter of choice.

Although some theorists, like Steven Kautz, for example, argue that grudging permission for unpopular ways of life satisfies the requirements of liberal toleration, I argue that, too often, this stance implies that such individuals and their supporters are expected simply to be grateful for this modicum of toleration and to withhold potential demands for measures that might end public discrimination and prevent private discrimination. Silence from any minority and/or supporters in the face of the dominant consensus goes against the core liberal values of rational deliberation and critical reflection, impoverishing both individuals and the community by foreclosing debate on and possible revision of the community's shared understandings. I therefore disagree with the stance of private tolerance combined with public disapproval taken by a number of conservatives. If we are willing to respect individuals with unpopular religious practices as long as the practices that flow from them are not banned as illiberal, we ought also, I believe, to respect individuals with unpopular sexual practices and protect these practices as expressions of autonomy, as long as these involve only consenting adults. By the same token, however, I would respect those who undergo conversion therapy to "cure" their homosexuality; the specific choice is less important than the imperative that it proceed from critical reflection.

I also disagree with libertarians who believe that the state need only end public discrimination against homosexuals, terminating the military ban and marriage prohibition, leaving civil society to work out its own accommodation. Homosexuals, like heterosexuals and members of minority cultures and ethnic groups, must be self-interpreting. They must be accorded the same liberty as heterosexuals to pursue the projects and goals that critical reflection has impelled them to choose or affirm. Therefore, civil rights legislation that protects sexual orientation does not constitute a special right but instead provides a context of choice that enables persons of all sexual orientations to pursue their projects and goals. In the course of this argument I examine two Supreme Court decisions as a means of elucidating my argument.

My final chapter addresses civic education in the liberal polity. Some liberal theorists, such as Rawls and Galston, believe that the civic education of citizens can eschew education for autonomy and individuality, as these are comprehensive values that comprise a vision of the good for the whole life and are therefore too exclusive to be publicly fostered in citizens, many of whom do not value critical reflection. I believe, however, that the civic respect necessary for liberal democratic citizenship requires sympathetic and imaginative engagement with other ways of life, and that this activity in turn requires the capacity to engage in critical reflection on our projects and goals. Because the liberal polity should not, I believe, exert pressure at the first-order level of actual choice, its role at the second-order level of how choices are made becomes crucial. It cannot instruct citizens *what* to choose, but it can and should provide instruction in *how* to choose. I disagree, however, with theorists like Stephen Macedo who think when the intolerant need to "mend" their views, the only critical reflection necessary is by individuals who liberals think are illiberal. I maintain that self-examination and critical reflection are appropriate for all citizens of the liberal polity.

I then discuss two court cases in which parents have sought to withdraw their children from the threat they perceive public education to pose for freedom of conscience. The decision in one champions the claims of diversity; the other can be interpreted to support the claims of autonomy. In the first, *Wisconsin v. Yoder,* I reluctantly agree with the Supreme Court that Amish parents should be allowed to curtail their children's schooling, but I also suggest that the larger society's decision to accommodate them means that we should now accord full respect to the Amish, rather than considering them as lesser citizens of the liberal polity. In the second, *Mozert v. Hawkins,* I agree that the fundamentalist parents involved should not be able to exempt their children from a basic reading series that was integrated into the overall curriculum. I am sympathetic, however, to the argument that students who are required in school to become aware of alternative ways of life may come to hold their faith in a qualitatively different manner than do those who adhere to faith unself-consciously. After considering two different possible compromises or types of accommodation that I think inadequate, I conclude that in a liberal polity, public education nevertheless must be able to expose students to ways of life and points of view that "threaten" them with the prospect of developing the capacity for rational deliberation and critical reflection if they are to be prepared for the option of active citizenship.

Finally, I suggest that although the development of the capacity for autonomy is desirable for all citizens of the liberal polity, liberals must recognize the particularity of their own moral stance. Liberals are persons who value autonomy, on my interpretation. But if we who are liberals truly espouse the value of critical reflection, we must also be reflective about the strengths and weaknesses of that commitment itself. Some critics would say that an emphasis on self-examination and critical reflection on our own projects and goals betokens an inappropriate self-centeredness, for example. We need to recognize this possibility. More generally, we need to develop the imagination to envision ourselves as committed to different ideals, projects, and goals from the ones that we in fact espouse. This sympathetic and imaginative engagement with other ways of life broadens our openness to diversity yet also enhances our capacities for autonomy by promoting our ability to question, examine, deliberate, and possibly to revise our conceptions of the good or our projects and goals, both individually and collectively. An understanding of the contingent character of any particular commitment should be sought not only by those whose liberal credentials appear questionable but also by the liberals doing the questioning.

Overall, I want to retain both the liberal self or moral individual who reflects upon his or her projects and goals and also the diversity that I view as a major strength of liberalism. I realize that the thicker moral core I attribute to liberalism may undermine some of this diversity, despite efforts to prevent this outcome. To readers who may view this possibility as a major flaw in my interpretation of liberalism, I would simply reply that it is a risk a liberal polity must take. Both individual and collective choices produce new manifestations of diversity over time; the disappearance of certain current manifestations need not result in complete homogenization. More important, however, I believe that to deemphasize the importance of the capacity for autonomy is to betray the liberal birthright, as it were, for the sake of a diversity that cannot be valued indiscriminately. Diversity is valuable not for its own sake but for the way it may function in individual lives as an expression of autonomy.

Although I do not want to discuss the potentially exhaustive topic of what might ground a common human nature, for present purposes I shall take the position that the development of the capacity for autonomy is more likely than any other single capacity to promote human flourishing. In defining this capacity and in applying it to the resolution of specific controversies, I should like to persuade both citizens whose beliefs undergird liberal institutions and also those who make and apply public policy of the centrality of autonomy. If the development of the capacity for autonomy and the preservation of diversity cannot bear equal weight because they are incommensurable, liberals should not shrink, nevertheless, from identifying and promoting the core values of liberalism as they understand them. I am attempting to do so in this book.

1. Neutrality, Autonomy, and Diversity

This book is about the relationship between autonomy and diversity as they bear on citizenship in the contemporary liberal polity. My perspective is grounded in a commitment to the individual integrity or wholeness that may emerge from rational deliberation and critical reflection and to conditions that will promote these qualities. The liberal polity has characteristically championed the background conditions for individual choice, autonomy, and self-development. Liberalism has traditionally espoused, in addition, a culture of diversity, providing a plurality of options among which individuals may choose. A good life requires both the exercise of choice and a reasonable basis for making choices among options that are often incommensurable. Ensuring this requires both a variety of possibilities and "a sufficiently developed imagination" for us to envision what these possibilities entail.[1]

These requirements, however, may not intersect as neatly as this description suggests. Classical liberals were committed to rationality, progress, and the liberty of humankind, which seemed to them unproblematic. The championing of reason as a core human attribute grounded the rights-claims characteristic of the Enlightenment and of the American and French Revolutions. In turn these claims and their historical outcomes were defined as moral progress and were interpreted as universal in their application. All humans could potentially make legitimate claims on these rights, which would expand both individual human autonomy and collective self-determination. In this constellation, liberty functions as a central value, and the freedom of some individuals does not appear to conflict with the freedom of others.

These assumptions were challenged by the rise of romanticism and nationalism. On the individual level, conventional interpretations of rationality and progress appeared to promote homogeneity and to threaten personal self-expression. On the collective level, prevailing definitions of rationality and progress by particular nation-states threatened the self-definition of communities of ethnicity, culture, or belief existing within many of those national states. Either way, the loss of belief in a universalistic grounding for morality and politics became apparent, accompanied by increasing doubt about the value of conventional rationality and the existence of progress. Since the dissolution of the former Soviet Union and Yugoslavia, conflicts emanating from ethnic, religious, and historical differences have come into sharp focus on the international scene. Simultaneously, the plight of displaced persons has attained new prominence as many national states have incorporated new residents within their borders, both voluntarily and involuntarily. Many of these newcomers have differed culturally, both in beliefs and practices, from the existing populations. This situation has exacerbated existing tensions and created new ones.

As the United States itself has become an increasingly multicultural polity, the nature of the background conditions for both autonomy and diversity and the ways these are best promoted have become subjects of increasing controversy. The autonomy of some individuals or groups appears to threaten the autonomy of other individuals or groups, especially when the liberal polity accommodates subgroups that do not themselves value individual autonomy. Thus, the values of autonomy and of the liberal toleration of diversity may themselves conflict. Yet these values are also interdependent: autonomy gives rise to diversity as individuals make disparate choices, and diversity reinforces autonomy by providing a range of alternatives among which individuals may choose. Moreover, individual citizens are not merely passive reflectors of the larger community and its subgroups. They also enjoy an active role in which their practices in turn shape these entities in a relationship of reciprocity. From my own perspective, the larger community and its constituent subgroups can both engender and endanger individual autonomy.[2] The question informing this book, then, is that of how the liberal polity may most effectively integrate the values of autonomy and diversity to promote the background conditions for individual integrity or wholeness in its citizens.

My thesis is that although a liberal polity must by definition be receptive to diversity and accommodate it, it must do more than this. It must also be dedicated to achieving conditions that aid the development in all individuals of capacities for rational deliberation, critical judgment, and reflective self-direction. The relationship between the liberal polity and the individuals or subgroups with which it interacts may itself contribute to individual autonomy. The task for liberals, then, is to ensure that the collective is a source of autonomy and not simply a danger to it. The pursuit of this goal will result in a society of considerable diversity, because a developed capacity for autonomy will produce different choices by different individuals. But the diversity thus produced must be bounded diversity. Ways of life that prevent or severely inhibit the development of individual capacities for autonomy will not be supported, and in extreme cases they may be circumscribed or banned. My purpose here is to establish the framework for my commitment to the development of the capacity for autonomy.

Liberal Neutrality

Two broad strategies can be used to justify the liberal state, one based on distinctively liberal values and the other on neutrality among different ways of life. Each of these justifications has enjoyed periods of ascendancy, and much of the current debate within liberal theory centers on the relative value of these strategies and on how each might be implemented. Although early liberals such as Locke were committed to individual liberty, the values of popular governance, religious tolerance, the rule of law, and other liberties were means to the specific ends of peace, prosperity through economic growth, and intellectual progress. On this view, argues Rogers Smith, representative government is not simply a vehicle for the transmission of popular consent but should also enhance government's pursuit of properly liberal ends. Among these is the capacity for rational deliberation and self-determination, which "is the distinctive feature of human nature and also the essential element of moral responsibility."[3]

Yet because Locke views law as an expression of both free choice and transcendent standards (69), the exercise of reason may not always promote congruence between our desires and the proper ends of liberalism (36–39, 68–71). Even in his arguments for religious toleration, Locke eschews neither persuasion nor the conviction that moral virtues can be rationally known. Moreover, religious toleration does not imply that conscience is inviolable, and civil authority is dispositive in cases of conflict.[4] Locke's advocacy of toleration, then, does not extend to arguments that would threaten the benefits of his moral principles, to which he accords "the decidedly non-skeptical status of natural rights."[5]

Modern liberal theorists, by contrast, tend to hold that the liberal state must be neutral among rival conceptions of the good. This claim has rested sometimes upon moral skepticism, the idea that no rational basis exists for choosing among different ways of life, and sometimes upon moral autonomy, the idea that each individual must define the good to be pursued in his or her own manner. On a standard liberal account like Ronald Dworkin's, "Political decisions must be, so far as is possible, independent of any particular conception of the good life. Since the citizens of a society differ in their conceptions, the government does not treat them as equals if it prefers one conception to another," either because of its seeming intrinsic value or the strength of its support.[6] According to Dworkin's interpretation of the constitutive political morality of liberalism, "Government must treat those whom it governs with concern, that is, as human beings who are capable of suffering and frustration, and with respect, that is, as human beings who are capable of forming and acting on intelligent conceptions of how their lives should be lived."[7]

Other contemporary liberals, however, argue that even a liberal polity cannot espouse neutrality among rival conceptions of the good. Although William Galston, for example, agrees with Dworkin as to the rational purposiveness of human beings, calling the liberal conception of the good that of rationalist humanism, he maintains that "liberalism is the theory, not of the neutral state, but of the minimally committed state. . . . The liberal state rests solely on those beliefs about the good shared by all its citizens, whereas every other state must coercively espouse some controversial assumptions about the good life."[8] A liberal commitment to moral and practical rationality, he says, requires extensive moral education that may verge on the characteristic of a tutelary or perfectionist state (95). Moreover, the liberal state, like others, must make binding determinations of public policy that are implicitly grounded in specific assumptions about human nature, proper conduct, well-ordered institutions, and just practices. "In such cases, neutrality is never violated, because it is never possible. Every polity, then, embodies a more than minimal conception of the good that establishes at least a partial rank-order among individual ways of life and competing principles of right conduct" (96–97).

Similarly, John Rawls seeks to avoid public coercion in a culture of social diversity through the terms of an overlapping consensus, the content of which "is expressed in terms of certain fundamental ideas seen as implicit in the public political culture of a democratic society."[9] This consensus aims at a public basis of justification grounded in the fundamental intuitions of the political culture but abstracted from comprehensive doctrines, which encompass religious, philosophical, and moral aspects of life in a coherent framework (59). But although his conception of justice seeks the common ground of an overlapping consensus, this common ground is not procedurally neutral. The priority of procedural principles of right over substantive conceptions of the good dictates that individuals and groups advance only permissible conceptions of the good, and the state may not favor some permissible conceptions over others. Nevertheless, "It is surely impossible for the basic structure of a just constitutional regime not to have important effects and influences as to which comprehensive doctrines endure and gain adherents over time, and it is futile to try to counteract these effects and influences" (193). In fact, justice as fairness may even endorse the moral superiority of certain virtues and forms of character, such as civility, tolerance, reasonableness, and fairness. "The crucial point is that admitting these virtues into a political conception does not lead to the perfectionist state of a comprehensive doctrine" (194).

It is evident that both Galston's commitment to rationalist humanism and Rawls's advocacy of an overlapping consensus justified through public reason are incompatible with a neutrality rooted in moral skepticism, or in the idea that no rational basis exists for choosing among different ways of life. Even if citizens themselves believe that no rational basis exists for choosing among rival conceptions of the good, their sociopolitical institutions and the principles grounding them will exert influences that are not neutral. That is, common principles mean ones that are shared, not ones that are neutral. I shall consider next one distinctively liberal value on the basis of which the liberal polity can be justified, that of autonomy. I shall argue that although the liberal state cannot embrace neutrality in the sense of avoiding appeal to any moral values whatsoever, the range of options within which it can be neutral should be defined to serve the development of the capacity for autonomy. Within this context, neutrality among rival conceptions of the good is not itself a constitutive liberal value but is a secondary or derivative value that serves the goal of the development of this capacity for autonomy.

Liberal Autonomy

AUTONOMY DEFINED

Moral autonomy, simply put, means the capacity to govern oneself. In the liberal context, this capacity implies not only the freedom to pursue what one judges to be good but also the ability to define this good in one's own manner. Even certain knowledge of the good life would not justify the breach of individual freedom represented by the state's imposing this knowledge on its citizens.[10] The concept of moral autonomy typically incorporates three features. First, the individual must be free to act without compulsion or threat from external forces. Second, the individual must be "a rational free chooser," undriven by mind-altering substances or irresistible urges that would color his or her choices. Finally, the individual must prescribe for himself or herself the law to be followed, rather than allowing his or her will to be determined by customs, practices, or the will of other individuals.[11] We may believe that we are governing ourselves even when we are unwittingly acting with reference to others' conceptions of the good rather than our own. To be truly free or rational choosers, then, individuals must stand apart from and undefined by the particularities that are contingent features of their lives or situations. In the words of Michael Sandel, the liberal self is "an unencumbered self . . . prior to and independent of purposes and ends," because only a self beyond the reach of experience and without constitutive ends and interests is free as an independent agent to *choose* its ends.[12]

Determining whether an individual's actions are devoid of external compulsion, internal and irresistible urges, or unthinking conformity to contemporary custom and practice is a matter not simply of observing the behavior of the agent but also of understanding the agent's motivation. First, the presence of autonomy must be assessed historically, by an examination of the way desires and values are formed.[13] Second, autonomous persons engage in rational scrutiny of and self-reflection on their opinions and tastes, forming or altering them for their own reasons.[14] In assessing autonomy, we must beware of what Jon Elster terms adaptive preference formation, which may impel us to tailor our ideals, goals, and values to fit the particular contingencies of our existence, even as we appear free.[15] Third, we assess autonomy in the context of a life that links individual identity with personal projects and goals. When persons identify with what motivates them and view themselves as wishing to be so moved, they are autonomous actors.[16] Finally, choices must be self-justified, both over time and by their role in shaping the sort of person who evolved from them.[17] Autonomy, then, is more than freedom. The latter is a quality manifested in our given, discrete actions, but autonomy manifests itself in and as a developmental process, wherein we strive for congruence between these discrete actions and the goals and values we would like our lives as a whole to espouse.

Even the autonomous person, however, is not completely self-made,[18] a point emphasized by critics of the liberal notion of the self. To Sandel, for example, deontological theorists, who view the individual as an unsituated, autonomous chooser, impoverish the self by emphasizing the voluntarist dimension of human agency, "in which the self is related to its ends as a willing subject to the object of choice," at the expense of the cognitive dimension, "in which the self is related to its ends as a knowing subject to the objects of understanding."[19] Because we are "subjects constituted in part by our central aspirations and attachments" (172), human agency requires the self not only to choose but also to reflect, "to turn its light inward upon itself, to inquire into its constituent nature, to survey its various attachments and acknowledge their respective claims . . . to arrive at a self-understanding less opaque if never perfectly transparent, a subjectivity less fluid if never finally fixed, and so gradually throughout a lifetime, to participate in the constitution of its identity"

(153). Because the self is made up of past reflections and experiences, it cannot experience freedom from constitutive ends and interests without being disempowered and actually dissolved.

Although we are not self-made, this simply means, however, that we cannot constantly start afresh as we approach each life decision, uninfluenced and unencumbered by past reflections and experiences. Rational reflection requires the application of accepted principles and settled convictions to new situations. We need these as a basis for further reflection.[20] But past reflections and experiences are not dispositive in our decisions. Rational scrutiny may lead autonomous persons to affirm their past convictions in the light of current developments, or the latter may induce them to revise their long-standing convictions and to act differently. Either way, they are acting for reasons of their own, from reasons that are authentically *theirs*. In fact, when the self in Sandel's description looks inward, surveys its constituent attachments, and acknowledges their respective claims, this also is rational scrutiny performed by a self with a reality apart from its apparently constitutive ends. Otherwise, its attachments would be fixed and unable to be ranked and ordered. Thus, even Sandel's self is itself autonomous.

We may act *in accordance* with custom and habit, then, and still act autonomously if we have subjected our decision to rational scrutiny, rather than acting unthinkingly or from *force* of habit. An individual may appear, for example, to act from force or compulsion when this is not really the case. As Harry Frankfurt notes, in some cases people act in accordance with paths along which others stand ready to compel them, when they have already decided on their own to follow these paths. The threat of compulsion is irrelevant, then, to the actions performed. On this interpretation, "It is incorrect to regard a man as being coerced to do something unless he does it *because* of the coercive force exerted against him."[21] Alternatively, if we act for reasons of our own, and would have acted thus even in the absence of the threat of coercion, known or unknown to us, we are uncoerced and therefore morally responsible for our actions. "A person is not morally responsible for what he has done if he did it only because he could not have acted otherwise" (10). But even in the absence of options, we are morally responsible for pursuing a path if we would still have pursued that option even in the presence of other options. The range of available options, then, is less important than the mental state of the agent in determining whether the agent is acting freely or autonomously. Having more options is preferable to having fewer or no options, but the number of options takes second place to whether or not we have subjected our putative options to rational scrutiny and critical reflection and have acted on the basis of that scrutiny.

The distinctive vision of the early liberals included the establishment of background conditions for individual choice, autonomy, and self-development. For Rogers Smith, they were committed to individual liberty not only as a means to certain goods but also as an intrinsic end, in that rational deliberation could raise the mind's "level of desire for the greatest good available to the point where that desire determines the will."[22] In his estimation, "Their advocacy of rational liberty, of the preservation and enhancement of human capacities for understanding and reflective self-direction, was the core of the liberal political moral vision." On this account, rational liberty functions both as a procedural and a substantive ideal of conduct, concerned with both processes and outcomes. According to this imperative, "If we value rational self-direction, we must strive to maintain in ourselves, and to respect in others, these very capacities for deliberative self-guidance and self-control. Correspondingly, we must see the habitual exercise of these capacities as constituting morally praiseworthy action" (200).

AUTONOMY AND SECOND-ORDER VOLITIONS

An account of autonomy that identifies it with rational scrutiny or rational self-direction, and that also treats neutrality as a derivative value that serves the goal of the development of autonomy, can be found in the work of Will Kymlicka. In his view, humans possess an "essential interest" in leading a good life. But a good life is not a fixed object, like a Holy Grail, which individuals and communities can discover, once and for all, if only they are clever enough to surmount the obstacles that may hide it from view. Leading a good life, on the contrary, may be "different from leading the life we *currently believe* to be good."[23] There are, according to Kymlicka, two preconditions for fulfilling our essential interest in leading a good life. First, we must "lead our life from the inside, in accordance with our beliefs about what gives value to life," rather than in accordance with others' beliefs about the "correct" account of value. Second, we must "be free to question those beliefs, to examine them in the light of whatever information and examples and arguments our culture can provide," and free implicitly to revise them as a consequence of this scrutiny. Because each individual possesses this essential interest in leading a good life, Kymlicka follows Dworkin in asserting that a liberal state "treats people as equals, with equal concern and respect, by providing for each individual the liberties and resources needed to examine and act on these beliefs" (13). That is, all must enjoy this opportunity to engage in critical reflection and to act on this basis.

On this interpretation, liberals are not skeptics and their goals are not arbitrary. "Some projects *are* more worthy than others, and liberty is needed precisely to find out what is valuable in life—to question, re-examine, and revise our beliefs about value. . . . Liberty is important not because we already know our good prior to social interaction, or because we can't know about our good, but precisely so that we can come to know our good" (18). Although critics sometimes suggest that liberals advocate freedom for its own sake, Kymlicka instead suggests, and I agree, that freedom is "a precondition for pursuing those projects and practices that *are* valued for their own sake" (48). We do not value given projects because their pursuit affords us freedom; we value freedom, rather, because of the opportunity it affords us to pursue projects or goods that we value. Liberals, then, on this view, do espouse a theory of the good, but what is good is a matter decided by individuals, each for himself or herself, over time.

Moreover, although we are partly constituted by prior attachments and experiences as we make judgments about what is the good life for us, "no particular task is set for us by society, and no particular cultural practice has authority that is beyond individual judgement and possible rejection. . . . Nothing is 'set for us,' nothing is authoritative before our judgement of its value" (50–51). Although I can imagine myself with different interests and motivations, or different ends, from those I now espouse, "this doesn't require that I can ever perceive a self totally unencumbered by any ends—the process of ethical reasoning is always one of comparing one 'encumbered' potential self with another 'encumbered' potential self" (52–53). Liberals need not be skeptics for whom the good is unknowable, but neither need they be creatures of their circumstances for whom the good is unquestionable. They may affirm projects and goals, but "*no end or goal is exempt from possible re-examination*" (52). Or, as Kymlicka says, "moral independence" is the key to a good life "not because our goals in life are fixed, nor because they are arbitrary, but precisely because our goals can be wrong, and because we can revise and improve them" (18).

Central to Kymlicka's account and mine is not only the fact that we make judgments about the value of our current projects and goals but also the idea that we realize that our judgments are fallible. Otherwise, living a good life would be synonymous with leading whatever life we currently believe is good. Instead, we affirm projects and goals not simply because they are what we desire to pursue but also because, upon evaluation, they are what we *want* to desire to pursue. In other words, the rational scrutiny to which we subject our projects and goals involves the formation of second-order desires. More specifically, humans possess both the capacity to want to have a certain desire or to form second-order desires and the capacity to wish, on critical reflection, for a certain desire to be one's will and to govern one's actions. This involves what Frankfurt calls second-order volitions.[24] Even addicts experience second-order volitions when they are unwilling addicts; although they may be unable to overcome their too-powerful desires for some substance, they may have conflicting first-order desires, and they then care about which desire wins out and finally constitutes their wills.

Having second-order volitions or caring about the desirability of one's desires, then, is key in the fulfillment of the essential human interest in living a good life. First, we cannot lead our life from the inside if we do not care what our desires are. But when we care about something, we invest ourselves in and identify with it over time, and this in turn implies a continuity in the subject itself as well as in the desires that the subject affirms. This continuity in turn impels us to prefer leading lives in accordance with our own beliefs rather than according to the beliefs of others. Second, having second-order volitions is crucial if we are to question, examine, and possibly revise our beliefs as a result of rational scrutiny. Caring about the desirability of our desires brings us closer to our beliefs when we invest ourselves in them to live life from the inside, but it also allows us to separate ourselves from our beliefs when we wonder if the life we currently believe to be good is really the good life for us. We can draw back and imagine ourselves with different projects and goals, motivations and ends, from those we now espouse and decide whether another set of encumbrances more truly expresses who we are. We want to be moved by the will we want, not by one we do not want. But to be moved by either, we must first decide which is which.

This account of the way in which we question, examine, and revise our projects and goals to bring them into congruence with the best life for us resonates with Alasdair MacIntyre's view of human life as possessing "the unity of a narrative quest." This is "not at all that of a search for something already adequately characterized, as miners search for gold or geologists for oil. It is in the course of the quest and only through encountering and coping with the various particular harms, dangers, temptations and distractions which provide any quest with its episodes and incidents that the goal of the quest is finally to be understood. A quest is always an education both as to the character of that which is sought and in self-knowledge."[25] If we have an essential interest in leading a good life for us, our questioning, examination, and possible revision of our current beliefs, projects, and goals take on the character of a quest. When we inquire as to whether the life that we currently believe to be good is really the good life for us, we are examining possible alternatives and deciding whether these new possibilities are dangers, temptations, and distractions or whether they are part of the goal of our quest that has been hitherto unrecognized. This seems to describe our essential interest in leading a good life, which may or may not be the life that we currently believe to be good. But as individuals we must determine this question for ourselves, whether we reaffirm our current projects and goals, whether we amend them, or whether we commit ourselves to new ones.

OBJECTIONS

Development of the capacity for autonomy, I have argued, requires development of the capacity to engage in rational scrutiny of and deliberation about our projects and goals. The exercise of this capacity, in turn, will aid in promoting a life that is good as *we* see it. This conception of the liberal project is not, of course, an uncontroversial one. Therefore, I shall briefly discuss two key and interrelated objections. First, pursuit of conditions for the development of autonomy may interfere with the actual exercise of autonomy. I have argued that liberty as individual autonomy or self-determination will promote the improvement and refinement of our desires, causing us to ask ourselves not simply what we desire but also what we want to desire. Yet this procession from first-order to second-order desires, as Susan Mendus observes, poses a dilemma. When autonomy fails to promote moral improvement as liberals define it, critics may conclude that freedom has no intrinsic value. But when autonomy is itself identified with moral improvement, then they may deem inferior choices to be lacking in autonomy precisely because they are inferior, as in a case where an individual reared to value autonomy becomes a racist. "Either way, the conclusion is not one which liberals ought to be happy to espouse. For the first alternative renders freedom merely an instrumental good, whilst the second makes morally inferior choices by definition non-autonomous."[26] An optimistic view of human nature like that held by John Stuart Mill can save us from these disturbing implications. But reliance on moral progress or perfectibility only works to buttress autonomy when freedom does promote what we see as good (65).

The result of this dilemma is that liberal societies experience difficulty in showing tolerance toward certain ways of life. Although they will value all ways of life that are grounded in autonomy, on this criticism they cannot promote policies of toleration or inclusiveness toward ways of life that do *not* place a high priority on individual independence and self-determination. Whether liberals view a state of autonomy as itself a matter of choice, or as a preexisting basis on which choices are then made, a liberal society's diversity requires autonomy if individuals are to select among alternative options. Therefore, it appears that perhaps the liberty of those who cannot affirm that way of life should be restricted until they learn to act autonomously. And where necessary, "tolerance becomes not a virtue, but merely a temporary expedient against the day when all are autonomous" (108). Potential conflict exists, then, between the exercise or *practice* of autonomy, which requires maximal liberty for individual independence and self-determination, and the *development* of autonomy, which may require restrictions on liberty if autonomy is to be achieved.

If one objection to the liberal valorization of the capacity for autonomy is that it excludes those who do not value personal autonomy and openness to revision of their projects and goals,[27] a second objection is that championing the capacity for autonomy makes this priority a comprehensive doctrine and eventuates in a perfectionist state. This criticism is well illustrated in Galston's interpretation of Rawls. Rawls describes citizens as free and equal persons with two moral powers, the capacity for a sense of justice and the capacity for a conception of the good, in the development and exercise of which they hold higher-order interests.[28] From these moral powers Rawls extracts a political conception of the person, according to which citizens are free to change their personal conceptions of the good without changing their public identities, free to make valid claims on their institutions to promote their reasonable conceptions of the good, and free in the capacity of taking responsibility for their ends and desires (31–34, 186). Citizens value the limited autonomy necessary for the development and exercise of their moral powers and for the pursuit of determinate conceptions of the good that they individually form. The political conception of justice, however, does not mandate public policy that recognizes the ethical value of autonomy as a public goal superior to other values (98–99, 199), as in the "comprehensive liberalisms" of Kant and Mill (77–78). To put it differently, although the political conception recognizes our essential interest in pursuing our conceptions of the good, and thus in the autonomy necessary for this pursuit, it does not affirm an essential interest in autonomy as a goal of this pursuit, or as the preferred conception of the good that we should share. By distinguishing between the political and the ethical values of autonomy, Rawls seeks to render the political conception of justice as inclusive as possible and to avoid its evolution into the comprehensive doctrine that would characterize a perfectionist state.

Galston, however, argues that Rawls's formulation does constitute a kind of perfectionism, because "it prescribes, as valid for all, a single, substantive, eminently debatable ideal of moral personality that gives pride of place to the capacity for just action."[29] Our moral powers and our higher-order interests in their development and exercise may seem universalizable and unexceptionable, but not to everyone. "I wonder whether (for example) religious fundamentalists would regard the capacity to form and revise a conception of the good as a good at all, let alone a higher-order interest of human beings." Because on their view the highest goods are externally defined through revelation, not self-defined through reason, "Rawls's Kantian conception would strike them as a sophisticated, and therefore dangerous, brand of secular humanism" (130). Individuals construct principles of justice that allow them to realize their moral powers, and they appraise social institutions in terms of this self-authenticating standard.

On Galston's implication, then, Rawls's conception of moral personality is not part of the political conception but is itself a comprehensive doctrine, encompassing a particular view of religious, philosophical, and moral aspects of life in a coherent framework and balancing conflicting values within the standpoint of its own tradition. Emphasis upon the capacity to form and revise a conception of the good disadvantages those for whom this activity is not a value by implying that they are stunted in the development of their moral powers and are therefore less free than others who have developed these powers more fully. If emphasis on this capacity is in fact a comprehensive doctrine, its instantiation or institutionalization results in a perfectionist state. Although Rawls rejects comprehensive liberalisms that champion autonomy and individuality as ideals that permeate the whole of life, a focus on the formation and revision of one's conception of the good is also comprehensive in nature. Development of this capacity weakens or obliterates the capacity to discover or receive externally defined goods, in Galston's terms, and to adhere to them unquestioningly. Thus, a commitment even to the political value of autonomy in the context of Rawls's conception of the person is not necessarily shared by all citizens of the liberal state.

A DEFENSE OF LIMITED PERFECTIONISM

Although Galston's reasoning is understandable, I believe he is incorrect in his blanket rejection of perfectionism. On Kymlicka's interpretation, "A perfectionist theory includes a particular view, or range of views, about what dispositions and attributes define human perfection, and it views the development of these as our essential interest. Perfectionists demand that resources should be distributed so as to encourage such development."[30] Rawls is not a perfectionist on this formulation, because individuals in his theory are not bound to any *particular* complex of interests or set of final ends that defines human perfection overall but are always free to question and revise them. Because a good life is not a fixed object that is discovered once and for all, it cannot be held that the development of any particular dispositions and attributes is in our essential interest. Critics may suggest, however, that our essential interest in leading the life that is good for us does require the fulfillment of preconditions, of the ability to lead our life from the inside and the freedom to question and revise our convictions and goals. We may therefore be inclined to distribute resources to encourage the development of the capacity to fulfill these preconditions. Not only does Kymlicka's formulation fail to exculpate Rawls from the charge of perfectionism, then, but it also incriminates Kymlicka himself, and, by extension, my own adherence to the values of rational deliberation and critical reflection as core commitments of the liberal polity.

We may confront this sort of objection on several levels. First, any theory of the good that holds out a range of desirable outcomes could be defined as a perfectionist one. Or, conversely, in order to qualify as nonperfectionist, a theory of the good would have to define the latter as want-satisfaction, regardless of the nature of people's wants or of how they came to hold them.[31] But Galston as well as Rawls holds out a range of desirable outcomes for the liberal state, which "must by definition be broadly inclusive of diversity, yet it cannot be wholly indifferent to the character of its citizens."[32] Although I agree with Galston that this tension is central to liberalism, I do not believe that his solution is any less perfectionistic than Rawls's or Kymlicka's, and I believe that it is at least equally debatable.

We have seen that Galston's conception is of a minimally committed liberal state that can abjure public coercion because it rests on beliefs shared by all rather than on controversial assumptions about the good. Yet he also supports the inculcation and the fostering of specifically liberal virtues by authoritative social institutions, calling for a "functional" traditionalism that "rests its case on asserted links between certain moral principles and public virtues or institutions needed for the successful functioning of a liberal community." On this interpretation divorce would be discouraged not because it intrinsically violates divine law but because its economic and psychological effects on children reduce their chances of becoming independent and contributing citizens (280). Galston's approach has broad implications for the distinction between public and private aspects of life. Different family structures are not simply "alternative life-styles"; he exhorts us to "reject the thesis that questions of family structure are purely private matters not appropriate for public discussion and response. After all, the consequences of family failure affect society at large" (285). Overall, although a liberal society and state in particular should accommodate dissent and minimize moral coercion, the liberal state should not abandon its core commitments. In the end, "liberal social philosophy cannot get along without a conception of the good—if you will, a kind of minimal perfectionism" (299).

Although I shall reserve discussion of the substance of Galston's position for chapter 7, here I merely observe that even his minimally committed state seems to require, by his admission, at least a minimal perfectionism. Even a state committed to a minimal conception of the good includes a particular range of views about the dispositions and attributes that define our essential interest and that therefore should be developed with the help of public resources and authoritative institutions. Because he does not equate the good with mere want-satisfaction, Galston must ipso facto specify a range of desirable outcomes and a means by which they may be realized. He presumably believes that his "minimal perfectionism" is more inclusive than is Rawls's formulation, because his own is more minimal. Yet I believe that the way in which it is minimal renders it as debatable as the ostensible perfectionism of Rawls or Kymlicka.

First, Galston rejects rationalist stances that encourage the questioning of socially central beliefs in favor of civic education, which inculcates values supportive of our own particular political order (241–245). He is committed to stability, to a conception of the good that encourages a minimal amount of questioning and possible revision of citizens' conceptions of the good life, either individually or, by extension, collectively. But this orientation is as "eminently contestable" as the liberal humanism to which Galston applies this description (94). Those who identify their essential interest with the capacity to form, question, and revise their conceptions of the good may feel as little at home in Galston's liberal state as those who reject this capacity supposedly feel in Rawls's state. Galston is correct to perceive a tension between the claims of diversity and the core commitments of liberalism. The resolution he prefers is neither less perfectionistic nor more inclusive than that of Rawls or Kymlicka. It is simply different.

Second, if Galston's liberal state is not really grounded in beliefs about the good that are truly shared by all its citizens, it cannot eschew coercion in the affirmation of liberal virtues as readily as he supposes. Public policy may be designed to reward or positively reinforce those who refrain from questioning "structures of unexamined but socially central belief" (242), to the disadvantage of those inclined to question and possibly to revise their attitudes toward these structures. If we recognize, like Galston and Rawls, that public policy is never completely neutral in its effects, we cannot claim that it is still inclusive to the point that it never coerces. If or when dissent or divergent practices appear to threaten core liberal commitments, whether the development of the capacity for autonomy or the development and affirmation of particular liberal virtues, the specter of coercion may also appear, whether explicitly or implicitly. One set of commitments is no less conducive to coercion than is the other.

We must confront directly, then, the question of why a core commitment to the development of the capacity for autonomy might be preferable to other interpretations of the core commitments of liberalism. On Frankfurt's account, as we have seen, reflective self-evaluation or rational scrutiny of our projects and goals manifests itself in the formation of second-order desires and volitions, as we come to care about what desires determine our wills. But in order to evaluate our first-order desires and volitions and to arrive at the second-order level, we must first acquire the capacity to engage in rational scrutiny, deliberation, and critical reflection on them. Only thus can we decide whether leading a good life is the same as or different from leading the life we currently believe to be good. First, we cannot examine, question, and possibly revise or reaffirm our beliefs apart from such a process. Second, we cannot otherwise lead our lives from the inside, in Kymlicka's terms, to invest ourselves in and identify with our convictions as authentically ours. Whether we choose new projects and goals, or rediscover and reaffirm ones to which we have already been committed, the capacity to engage in rational scrutiny and critical reflection is a prerequisite. Even collective agreement on the virtues necessary to the sustenance of liberal societies first requires collective deliberation and reflection. Commitment to the development of the capacity for autonomy is therefore potentially inclusive of any projects and goals that we might select or affirm.

Moreover, rational scrutiny and critical reflection are, as I have implied, as compatible with the affirmation of current projects and goals as they are with the choice of new ones. The capacity to form and revise a conception of the good also entails the capacity to adhere to a conception of the good already formed, but one to which we recommit ourselves after an examination of alternatives. Although the development of the capacity for autonomy may weaken the capacity to receive externally defined goods such as those proceeding from religious revelation, as Galston fears, this possibility reinforces Mendus's point that an autonomous life may not itself be an object of choice but may instead be the basis or ground upon which choices are made. As Joseph Raz suggests, "The autonomous life depends not on the availability of one option of freedom of choice. It depends on the general character of one's environment and culture. For those who live in an autonomy-supporting environment there is no choice but to be autonomous: there is no other way to prosper in such a society."[33] In my view, however, this very fact renders it imperative that we develop the capacity to reflect self-consciously upon our options, so that if we act, for example, as we have habitually acted, we do so not from *force* of habit, but in *accordance* with habit after critical reflection on our options. In fact, insofar as an autonomy-supporting environment conditions us to subject our options to rational scrutiny, an autonomy-supporting culture seems more inclusive even of options that discourage the practice of autonomy than a culture that is *not* autonomy-supporting seems of options that do encourage the practice of autonomy.

In other words, an autonomy-supporting environment supports both the *development* of autonomy, or the capacity to subject our options to rational deliberation and critical reflection, and the *practice* of autonomy, or the capacity to lead our lives from the inside, in accordance with our own convictions about the good life or what gives value to life. The latter may eventuate in the actual pursuit of options that in some cases involve voluntarily abdicating the practice of questioning and revising some of our future options. Although this pursuit may appear nonautonomous from the outside, from the inside it reflects our own beliefs about what gives value to life. An environment that is not autonomy-supporting, however, allows us to live life from the inside but does not encourage us to question, examine, and revise our convictions unless we are able to do so against the current, as it were, of the dominant social consensus about values. We form first-order desires and volitions about what projects and goals we want to pursue, but we are less likely to form second-order desires and volitions about what projects and goals we want to *desire* to pursue. In an autonomy-supporting environment, on the other hand, we develop the capacity to engage in the rational scrutiny of our options, and even if we reaffirm those projects that we are presently pursuing, we do so because we have decided that what we currently believe to be good is truly the good life for us.

Along similar lines, David McCabe suggests that as we form and pursue our conceptions of the good, living life from the inside encompasses a large variety of projects and goals, corresponding to the diversity of human talents and interests. The claim is not that any self-endorsed life is a good one but that any life is more fulfilling if it is self-endorsed.[34] Autonomy cannot be instantiated by the authoritative endorsement of "any particular conception of the good, because what determines whether a life is autonomous is not the particular ideals one is committed to, but is instead the way in which one comes to choose those ideals and to affirm their value" (70). McCabe appropriately calls this conception one of autonomy-based neutrality because, contra Ronald Dworkin, neutrality can be effected even in a liberal polity only when it can itself be measured or judged in terms of some standard independent of neutrality itself. Autonomy-based neutrality emphasizes virtues that do not privilege a specific conception of the good but that still "commit the state to some minimal conception of autonomy not just as a potential ideal, but as an ideal that properly extends to the way individuals form and pursue their conceptions of the good" (77).

In the final analysis, I would argue that the development of the capacity for autonomy is a second-order concept. That is, it acts as a context or framework within which we may then pursue first-order options that may appear either autonomous or nonautonomous to others. As long as we possess the capacity to question, examine, and revise our beliefs, an apparent failure to do so cannot be taken as an actual failure to do so. We cannot determine whether an individual's conformity to custom and practice is unthinking, or the result of rational scrutiny of these and other practices, without plumbing the individual's motivations. But because we cannot know by outward observation, the importance of the promotion of conditions for the *development* of autonomy is heightened. To use Galston's example, I believe that when we subscribe to an externally defined good like that of religious revelation, our subsequent actions may in part be grounded in habit but in part proceed from judgment that this sort of submission is in greater accord with what is truly good for us than are other options that might appear more exemplary of the practice of autonomy. Development of the capacity for autonomy is a necessary condition for the practice of autonomy. It is inclusive of a wide variety of first-order options: we may affirm or rebel against custom unthinkingly, or we may affirm or rebel against custom as a result of critical reflection. But the development of the capacity for autonomy as a second-order value heightens the possibility that our first-order actions will be authentically ours.

Liberal Diversity

DIVERSITY DEFINED

The preceding section has explicitly been devoted to autonomy, but implicitly it has also been about diversity. The subtext to objections to an emphasis on the development of the capacity for autonomy is that the pursuit of this capacity functions like a straitjacket, curtailing the diversity that would otherwise exist. This fear is succinctly expressed by Galston. "Liberalism is about the protection of diversity, not the valorization of choice. To place an ideal of autonomous choice at the core of liberalism is in fact to narrow the range of possibilities available within liberal societies. It is a drive toward a kind of uniformity, disguised in the language of liberal diversity."[35] Yet as we have seen, he also believes that the liberal polity should not abandon its core commitments, although it should accommodate a greater range of dissent than other forms of social organization.

Many current liberals recognize the conflict between diversity and the core commitments of liberalism, and this conflict would exist no matter what core commitments might be emphasized. For Donald Moon, although any social order is going to frustrate some of our desires, "we may all agree that certain drives, certain desires, ought to be repressed, even while we strive to remain open to the possibility that our judgments in this regard are mistaken."[36] If we do rule out particular practices, what about those who disagree? For Charles Larmore, "A liberal political system need not feel obliged to reason with fanatics; it must simply take the necessary precautions to guard against them."[37] As Rawls puts it, "That there are doctrines that reject one or more democratic freedoms is itself a permanent fact of life, or seems so. This gives us the practical task of containing them—like war and disease—so that they do not overturn political justice."[38] The questions, then, are which desires should be repressed, who are the fanatics, which doctrines function like war and disease, and who should decide these questions. Although these comments present the issue starkly, they illustrate the conflict between adherence to core liberal commitments and the accommodation of diversity.

Beliefs and practices need not be threatening, fanatical, or undemocratic, on the other hand, to lose out under the terms of particular core commitments or overlapping consensuses. Although some conceptions of the good will disappear and others will barely survive, Rawls follows Isaiah Berlin in asserting that regardless of the fairness of principles of justice, "there is no social world without loss: that is, no social world that does not exclude some way of life that realizes in special ways certain fundamental values" (197). The dilemma thus presented is exemplified by Patrick Neal, for whom "although liberalism is neutral with regard to *conceptions* of the good, it has a very distinct *conceptualization* of what it means to have a conception of the good."[39] We possess conceptions of the good individually and share them contingently and aggregatively, rather than possessing them collectively and sharing them essentially (38). In the latter sort of case generally, as Sandel observes, the community thus created is neither simply instrumental, motivated by self-interest, nor purely sentimental, rooted in affection, but instead describes "a mode of self-understanding constitutive of the agent's identity." Community is not simply an object its members possess but part of what defines them as moral subjects. It is "not a relationship they choose . . . but an attachment they discover, not merely an attribute but a constituent of their identity."[40] Ends shared contingently evolve from an individuated self-conception, while ends shared essentially character-ize an intersubjective conception of the self, or a moral subject understood as comprising more than one biologically individuated human.

Neal's example of the limits of liberalism is an individual who believes he can only properly develop the moral virtues he affirms in the context of the small, homogeneous Athenian *polis*. Although the liberal state respects diver-sity in that I may become a professor and you a priest, *he* may not become part of a society constituted like the Athenian *polis*. He cannot even pursue his con-ception of the good privately, because it can be pursued "only insofar as this pursuit is collectively undertaken upon the basis of essentially shared ends which are understood by the participants to be definitive of themselves as selves."[41] Although the liberal may object that this hypothetical individual is trying to sat-isfy his own ends and to impose his own conception of the good on others, each is actually arguing for a conceptualization of conceptions of the good, Neal sug-gests, or a metatheory of the good, which each claims is universally applicable. Where the affirmation of a conception of the good within liberalism is viewed as a private choice, in the language of metatheory it "is not without public con-sequence; for if the good is a matter for private individual choice, then it is not a matter for public political determination" (45). Within a communitarian frame-work, however, our choices are not only bound up with others' choices but also dependent upon these for their very ability to exist.

To put this differently, a liberal polity allows choice within a range of pref-erences, that entailed by its core commitments. But it cannot allow choice among all preferences that might conceivably exist, because its very espousal of core commitments acts to produce one range of preferences and not others. This is why, on Neal's account, "the positive defense of liberalism cannot be that it is neutral amongst preferences; it must be a defense of the *kind* of pref-erences liberalism produces" (28). Within the context of this chapter, com-mitment to the complete range of possibilities for diversity is as unachievable for the liberal polity as is the realization of a thoroughgoing neutrality. That is, the metatheoretical perspective advanced by Neal reveals that liberalism and value pluralism can be incompatible. Although liberalism is often viewed as a response to the existing diversity of incommensurable goods, "liberalism, if it is to give itself any identity and content at all, has to argue for precisely such values that, in the case of conflict, trump others."[42] A defense of liberalism therefore cannot rest upon its hospitality to diversity across the board but must instead be grounded on the particular range of values or preferences that a given interpretation of liberalism puts forward. This range may include hos-pitality to diverse conceptions of the good, but it cannot include within that range conceptualizations that rely for their effectiveness upon an essential identification with only one conception of the good.

DIVERSITY ACCOMMODATED?

Rawls's solution to the accommodation of diversity delivers less than it promises. It rests, of course, on citizens' abilities to abstract from the religious, philosophical, and moral aspects of the reasonable but comprehensive doctrines that they espouse. By implication, Rawls recognizes second-order desires and volitions when he suggests that citizens are free in taking responsibility for their ends. They are not "passive carriers of desires" but are expected to adjust their aspirations and preferences in view of both their realistic expectations and the restrictions of the principles of justice.[43] That is, even if we have champagne tastes, we are responsible for adjusting our preferences to soda pop if the latter is what we can afford. This applies even when our preferences do not arise from our actual choices, a circumstance that "allows us to view as a special problem preferences and tastes that are incapacitating and render someone unable to cooperate normally in society. The situation is then a medical or psychiatric one and to be treated accordingly" (185).

But with this formulation, it is difficult for Rawls's political conception of the person to sustain variations in tastes and preferences that may be intimately connected with individuals' seemingly idiosyncratic conceptions of the good. Because citizens abstract from their particularistic allegiances, their public interaction, suggests Bonnie Honig, does not open new possibilities or offer new interpretations of what might be politically possible but instead depoliticizes public dialogue, confirming the dominent consensus on the limits of the reasonable.[44] Although Rawls treats individual talents and abilities as undeserved and therefore as common assets, he does not treat attributes that prompt individuals to act outside the law as also undeserved and therefore as common liabilities. They may be punished for seemingly antisocial behavior, whatever its source. Citizens who do not fit in are expected to privatize their disappointment and strive to adjust to the norm rather than to politicize it through political action or organization aimed at changing the norm. Even the rational deliberation that informs politics inoculates citizens by encouraging them to rationalize against regrets for prior decisions, which, after all, were arrived at rationally. Even the presence of "dissonant characters" consolidates citizens' allegiance to their prior self-orderings. "In short, Rawlsian justification has a performative dimension: it produces and consolidates the justifying subject it presupposes" (155).

Honig reminds us, then, that we can too easily define diversity, or some kinds of diversity, as abnormal or incapacitating when they offend the dominant consensus, even in a regime that prides itself on eschewing public commitments to comprehensive conceptions of the good. Rawls's response to reasonable pluralism is "to fix, once and for all, the content of certain political basic rights and liberties, and to assign them special priority. Doing this takes those guarantees off the political agenda and puts them beyond the calculus of social interests, thereby establishing clearly and firmly the rules of political contest."[45] But this move shapes and limits pluralism instead of accommodating it.

If theorists like Rawls would solve the challenge of diversity by requiring citizens to bracket or abstract from the moral, philosophical, and religious ideals in their comprehensive doctrines, Sandel, in contrast, would proceed by encouraging a greater, not a lesser, reliance on these doctrines. Political values, or those rooted in public reason, he argues, neither can nor should always outweigh nonpolitical or comprehensive values. First and historically, for example, the debates between Lincoln and Douglas in 1858 were not only over the morality of slavery and its spread but also about whether the question of morality should enter public debate, as abolitionists believed, or should be ignored for the sake of political agreement. Similarly, the current debate about abortion is also "about how reasonable it is to abstract from that question for political purposes."[46] Comprehensive doctrines are not truly bracketed by allowing individual choice. "No one denies that the state should prohibit murder. To permit abortion is therefore to determine (at least implicitly) that abortion is not murder."[47] Neutrality within the context of liberal theory is not neutral from the viewpoint of metatheory. The solution of "local option" enhances diversity as a range of first-order choices, but the decision to permit local option itself expresses a second-order choice that reflects particular comprehensive values.

Second and theoretically, disagreement about issues of justice such as immigration, affirmative action, gay rights, and income distribution is certainly as prevalent in modern liberal democracies, suggests Sandel, as disagreement about issues of morality, philosophy, and religion. Yet because differences about income distribution are not instances of natural, reasonable pluralism for those like Rawls, it appears that government need *not* be neutral here but may use state power to implement redistributive principles like the difference principle. Sandel wonders, however, if moral reflection reveals "that some principles of justice are more reasonable than others, what guarantees that reflection of a similar kind is not possible in the case of moral and religious controversy?

If we can reason about controversial principles of distributive justice by seeking a reflective equilibrium, why can we not reason in the same way about conceptions of the good?"[48] More specifically, "If government can affirm the justice of redistributive policies even in the face of disagreement by libertarians, why cannot government affirm in law, say, the moral legitimacy of homosexuality . . . ? Is Milton Friedman's objection to redistributive policies a less 'reasonable pluralism' than Pat Robertson's objection to gay rights?" (1788).

Sandel is suggesting that although religious, philosophical, and moral ideals may be nominally nonpolitical values, they implicitly inform political values. By limiting political discourse to arguments from political values, Rawls's ideal of public reason "severely limits the kinds of arguments that are legitimate contributions to political debate" (1789). These limitations restrict the kinds of arguments that may be deployed against the toleration of gay rights, abortion, and so forth, but they also limit arguments in *favor* of toleration of these practices. Sandel believes that the political values of toleration, civility, and mutual respect could be achieved and by implication strengthened under broader rules of public discourse than those adduced by Rawls and theorists like him. Fewer views would require containment, and diversity would be enhanced. Yet it is unclear to me that infusing substance into the ethical ideals from which Rawls asks us to abstract will promote the rational scrutiny and critical reflection, the developed imagination, that is a necessary condition for enjoying the benefits of a culture of diversity.

We have seen that Sandel posits the faculty of human agency in two dimensions, a voluntarist one in which the self is dispossessed of essential or constituent ends, and a cognitive one in which the self is constituted, at least initially, by many undifferentiated ends.[49] In the first dimension, the subject defines itself by appropriating or choosing ends with which it never completely identifies; in the second, the subject defines itself by reflecting on and ranking ends from which it is never completely separated. We might imagine the voluntarist dimension of agency as corresponding to the overlapping consensus that grounds Rawls's political liberalism. Both Rawls's conception of the self and his public discourse are circumscribed to maximize stability and to minimize unforeseen developments that might call individual or collective identity into question. Similarly, the cognitive dimension of agency corresponds to the broader basis for public discourse urged by Sandel. The boundaries of the self and of political debate are potentially more inclusive, and identity is defined through reflection upon and understanding of what projects and goals truly constitute the persons or communities that we are or want to become. The identification of the subject with the constitutive setting of which it is a part is completed by Sandel with an intersubjective conception of community, under which "the relevant description of the self may embrace more than a single empirically-individuated human being" (80), and the contribution of its assets to the common endeavor is a source of individual pride and fulfillment (143).

Although the intersubjectively defined subject is communitarian in nature, its identity must nevertheless be bounded if it is to be determinate. It is here that Sandel's ostensible inclusivity becomes problematic. As Honig notes, "The range of intersubjectivity is bounded by the inclusion only of those who identify with a particular community and who are identified by a particular community as its own. What criterion of identification governs the all-important standard of appropriateness here?"[50] We may reject some whose contribution to the intersubjective subject of which we are each a part engenders our discomfort, or we may perceive some of our assets as forcibly conscripted rather than voluntarily enlisted if we question some aspects of our communities or do not take unmitigated pride in them. The experience of rejection characterizes homosexuals, for example, when majorities wish to exclude them from participation in aspects of the public life or institutions of a community. The experience of forcible conscription could conceivably characterize anyone who resents the way in which his or her assets, in either talent or treasure, are devoted to common goals with which he or she cannot agree. In other words, Sandel recognizes the community's role only in the enrichment and empowerment of the intersubjective self, not in the limitation or circumscription of this self. "But the self's identity, talents, and attributes are at least as likely to be the products of its *resistances* to community constitution as they are to be the products of hothouse care" (172–173). Like Rawls's overlapping consensus, Sandel's intersubjective self consolidates citizens and subjects, limits the ability to imagine alternatives, and erroneously believes its inclusivity is universal or "without remainder" (141).

THE INTRASUBJECTIVE APPROACH

Neither Rawls's public reason nor Sandel's intersubjective self, then, is truly hospitable to diversity. In addition to the intersubjective conception of the self, Sandel also posits a second, less noted conception, however, that appears more promising. According to this alternative, intrasubjective conception, "The appropriate description of the moral subject may refer to a plurality of selves within a single, individual human being, as when we account for inner deliberation in terms of the pull of competing identities, or moments of introspection in terms of occluded self-knowledge."[51] We each have constituent ends, but these are not automatically identified with any given community. "Each of us moves in an indefinite number of communities, some more inclusive than others, each making different claims on our allegiance, and there is no saying in advance which is *the* society whose purposes should govern the disposition of any particular set of our attributes and endowments" (146). Whether as willing subjects who make choices or as knowing subjects who become self-aware, reflect, and understand, our task is to define our identity by arriving at what for us is the proper relationship between ourselves as subjects, on the one hand, and the objects to which we attend, on the other.

This perspective returns us to the rational scrutiny of our options that I have described as the hallmark of the autonomous person. The voluntarist and cognitive dimensions of agency are not competitive, as Sandel sometimes implies, but complementary, necessary both to individual self-definition and to an accurate conception of agency. Both individual choice and social experience shape the self. Projects and goals cannot be chosen in a vacuum. Yet "Critical reflection needs an anchor—an individual standpoint marked by a set of endorsed preferences, traits, and so forth. Thus, voluntarism without some degree of situation and critical reflection without an independent base of choice are equally untenable."[52] Moreover, the two dimensions of agency reinforce each other. If preferences and traits, projects and goals, have been endorsed or affirmed by an agent, they have in some sense been chosen. Yet once affirmed, they become constitutive of the agent, although potentially subject to reexamination, and thus become the ground or standpoint from which subsequent choices are made.

To put this differently, if a culture of diversity requires both a broad range of possibilities and a developed imagination, the latter requires the capacity both to choose and to reflect, to will and to understand. The intrasubjective conception of the self is a provocative one because it posits a self that is not a fixed or static entity. Rather, its boundaries are fluid over time as it reflects upon its current circumstances and chooses among the claims on its allegiance or, alternatively, makes choices among its current options and then reflects anew. True diversity requires, then, the imagination necessary to make use of the range of available options. These must be available within the culture, in the objective sense. But they must also be available within the individual, as it were, in the sense of becoming real possibilities that we can imagine as defining our identities. Whether it is choice, understanding, or an interactive combination of both that makes us who we are, the process is an intrasubjective one. And a culture of diversity is one in which we as individuals are permeated with a lively sense of the kinds of individuals it is possible to be.

True inclusivity of diversity, as Honig puts it, "turns on an affirmation of the impossibility of closure and the celebration of the . . . perpetuity of political contest and agonistic engagement with the other within and among us. It turns on a commitment to live life without the assurance that ours is the right, good, holy, or rational way to live."[53] The living out of this commitment requires the development of the capacity to engage in rational scrutiny and critical reflection that constitutes autonomy. Yet we have seen that any state must by definition be grounded on certain determinate principles and commitments. Collectively as well as individually, we must be able to live our lives from the inside. It follows that some ways of life or certain fundamental values will necessarily be excluded. Because what seems neutral as liberal theory is nonneutral from the standpoint of metatheory, "Leviathan requires a sword," as Neal puts it,[54] to instantiate some distinction between what is compatible with liberalism and what is not.

If we are to fulfill the liberal promise of diversity that individuals and groups will also be enabled to live *their* lives from the inside, we must avoid judgments that are too quick as to which desires should be repressed, which individuals or groups are fanatics, and which doctrines function like war and disease to threaten the community as a whole. In this determination as in my definition of autonomy, the outcome is enhanced by the process. Although there may be no social world without loss, it is through politics that we decide or define what will be lost. If we accede to the displacement of politics by accepting too much as settled and therefore beyond the reach of politics, we lose the chance to question, to examine, and possibly to revise our beliefs about what gives value to our common life. Leviathan still requires a sword, but what that sword will defend is subject to deliberation and revision. As Mark Warren suggests, "It is not that moral visions cannot have political authority, but rather that their authority depends on politics . . . since this is what allows people to be convinced."[55]

The question is how to achieve consensus sufficient for the practice of politics without suppressing the differences without which identity cannot even exist. Although identity is developed dialogically, through interaction and exchange with others,[56] diversity and opposition are by-products of this process as surely as are commonality and consensus. Too often, however, identity "converts differences into otherness in order to secure its own self-certainty."[57] It constitutes them "as *intrinsically* evil, irrational, abnormal, mad, sick, primitive, monstrous, dangerous, or anarchical—as other. It does so in order to secure itself as intrinsically good, coherent, complete or rational and in order to protect itself from the other that would unravel its self-certainty and capacity for collective mobilization if it established its legitimacy" (65–66).

Even when we do not constitute differences as "other," modern liberal theory, as Thomas Bridges explains, has portrayed individual particularistic, cultural, or *communitarian* identity as an obstacle to the development of *civic* identity rather than as a building block in its formation. "The process of developing a civic identity was therefore defined as a process of stripping away the culturally accidental in order to arrive at a supposedly culture-neutral, natural, and universal standpoint."[58] A viable "postmodernist" liberalism must reverse the relationship between civic and communitarian identity and culture. Civic culture is "a partial and countervailing culture," the single function of which is "to render intelligible the liberal democratic moral ideals of individual freedom and equality, and to motivate citizens to pursue these ideals." As such, it "presupposes and remains dependent upon communitarian culture. It cannot stand by itself" (156–157). Abstract ideals alone cannot motivate individuals, grounded in particularistic cultural identities, to develop civic ones. "Liberal political institutions can flourish only where the particularistic cultural communities subject to them can find a basis within their particular traditions for an affirmation of civic freedom and civic equality" (202).

Similarly, Brian Walker suggests that a public culture of common citizenship is built up or created "through the ingenuity of situated cultural agents who would draw connections between the diverse potentials for toleration scattered in various doctrines" or by "individuals who strive to open up a position of tolerance within whichever culture they find themselves."[59] Any overlapping consensus that emerges does not precede but instead results from this process, though "there may need to be a fair amount of activity involved in *creating* the conditions of tolerance required for the requisite overlapping consensus." In sum, "Fighting for toleration is not a matter of attempting to align other groups with a preexisting order, but a form of dialogue in the course of which the picture of what toleration is and requires gradually becomes clear. By attempting to build my idea of toleration on the terrain of the other, I am myself affected by new and alien ideas, and perhaps my own view is changed" (121). Melissa Williams defines this approach as a political rather than a juridical one: "Standards of justice can only avoid reproducing inequality if they are defined *within* a political process that provides the opportunity for marginalized groups' perspectives to be expressed and heeded."[60]

This approach to consensus may appear to do both too much and too little. It concedes too much to particularistic traditions and doctrines, beliefs and practices, which may have little if any potential for developing positions of tolerance or commitments that are compatible with the liberal ideal. Worse, it may allow for the inclusion of illiberal elements under the rubric of a broadened consensus. On the other hand, this approach concedes too little because whatever the overlapping consensus turns out to be, it will necessarily still exclude certain ways of life or fundamental values. For some, the liberal society and state will always function as a modus vivendi. And although the consensus to be defended will be broadened, it will still be defended by a Leviathan who wields a sword.

It is through politics, however, that we decide *what* is compatible with the liberal ideal. Although some ways of life and certain values will indeed be excluded, the overlapping consensus is both authoritative and provisional, authoritative because it results from dialogue and provisional because it is never finally settled but will again be the object of question, examination, deliberation, and possible revision. Neal suggests that when we agree to take certain matters off the political agenda, we assume the identity of political interests is a given. "But what if this assumption is wrong? What if political actors and interests are thought of not as entities pre-existing the process of political activity, but as properties which emerge and constitute themselves within and through that process?"[61] Neal's example is that of homosexual rights, which until recently would neither have been discussed nor included on the political agenda. "Commentators and activists, however, have *made* themselves and their interests *recognizable* . . . by engaging in various forms of political activity" (125). Another example would be the insistence by some that unborn persons possess rights as potential persons. What we want to avoid is "closing the channels through which 'free and equal persons' manifest themselves in ways recognizable by others" (124). We sometimes make errors in our decisions about what is or is not compatible with the liberal ideal. But the authoritativeness of our decisions is tempered by their provisionality.

In a best-case scenario, not only will liberal society as a whole exhibit diversity but so also will individuals internally, through their awareness of and thoughtfulness about various alternatives. This, I believe, is the potential larger meaning of Sandel's intrasubjective conception of the self. This way of thinking about diversity also illustrates once more, in my view, the critical importance of the development in liberal democratic citizens of the capacity for autonomy and also the importance of refraining from defining too rigidly the meaning of autonomy in terms of substance. If we are to live our lives from the inside according to self-endorsed conceptions of the good and also to engage in the examination and possible revision of our beliefs about the good, either individually or collectively, we must possess the capacity for rational deliberation and critical reflection.

The early liberals' goal of rational liberty, as Rogers Smith observes, is to some degree a substantive standard for human conduct. "If we value rational self-direction, we must always strive to maintain in ourselves, and to respect in others, these very capacities as constituting morally worthy character and their enhancement as constituting morally praiseworthy action."[62] Simultaneously, however, a commitment to rational self-direction need not imply, in Honig's terms, that "ours is the right, good, holy, or rational way to live." Instead, argues Smith, "It authorizes the liberal political community to decide, not what behavior the community finds truly good or rationally correct, but rather what conduct expresses a process of rational deliberation and, conversely, what actions endanger persons' continuing capacities for rational deliberation. Only the latter can rightfully be prohibited" (213). Just as we cannot, or at least should not, define the boundaries of diversity prepolitically, we should also refrain from doing this with the capacity for autonomy. Warren views autonomy as "a future-oriented capacity, since it allows for a distancing from entanglements that determine the self, opening up the possibility that they could be otherwise."[63] An application of this conception to our collective political determinations makes room for Neal's suggestion that political actors and interests do not exist prior to the political process but become constituted partly through this process. This constitution may occur intrasubjectively as well as intersubjectively.

Most provocatively, in my view, Bridges suggests that reconciliation of our particularistic commitments with the imperatives of liberal democracy "requires both a continuing commitment to a particularistic life ideal and, at the same time, an affirmation of its revocability, an affirmation of the purely voluntary nature of that commitment."[64] To the extent that one's identity is defined through a particular life narrative, "a capacity for civic freedom consists of a capacity to incorporate into every narratively constructed identity or self a recognition and affirmation of its own narratively constructed status" (181). Thus, narrative imagination recognizes the possibility of commitment to ideals different from those to which one is committed, or of giving different narrative readings to the same series of life events. In this context, rationality is "the capacity to examine critically the means and ends involved in the pursuit of a particularistic concept of the good" (188). In other words, individuals come to understand the possibility of other objects of desire than those they currently hold, whether individually or collectively, and they also recognize that "liberal democracy requires particularistic desire to examine itself critically" (209). As Connolly puts it, this involves an appreciation of contingency, "whereby each maintains a certain respect for the adversary, partly because the relationship exposes contingency in the being of both."[65]

Narrative imagination, then, impels us to understand how others may be constituted by other sorts of particularistic values and ideals than those that animate us. If MacIntyre characterizes the search for a good life as possessing the unity of a narrative quest, Bridges invites us to recognize that even the same quest may be interpreted differently by different searchers. We may understand how we ourselves might hold to different values and ideals if we interpreted our own life events within the framework of an alternative narrative structure. This stance then broadens our openness to diversity. Yet it also enhances our capacity for autonomy, allowing us to imagine alternative ways of living our lives from the inside and promoting our ability to question, examine, deliberate, and possibly to revise our conception of the good, both individually and collectively.

I am aware that my brief for the centrality of the capacity for autonomy will not seem dispositive to those who envision a strong case for the centrality of diversity or perhaps of other values. That is, overwhelmingly compelling philosophical foundations for the centrality of any particular value or values, to the exclusion of others, appear nonexistent. Nevertheless, I am attempting to demonstrate that because the liberal polity cannot be neutral ipso facto, it must be neutral in terms of some other value that is external to neutrality. The development of the capacity for autonomy is a strong candidate, and in my eyes it is the correct candidate, for the role of the value in terms of which neutrality may be measured. Those who believe that even liberalism cannot espouse perfect neutrality are entitled to work out the implications of their substantive or external values and to show how they believe their espousal promotes liberal values overall. And I am attempting to do so with regard to the development of the capacity for autonomy.

2. National Citizenship in the Liberal Polity

The concept of national citizenship at the close of the twentieth century is an amorphous one, carrying different meanings for different people. Rights or privileges that some people think should depend upon national citizenship are increasingly sought by or on behalf of aliens, both documented and undocumented, who reside in the United States. Controversy as to when citizenship should be a condition of the pursuit of certain activities or for the receipt of various benefits shows no sign of abating. Alexander Bickel, exemplifying one view, finds it "gratifying . . . that we live under a Constitution to which the concept of citizenship means very little, that prescribes decencies and wise modalities of government quite without regard to the concept of citizenship."[1] Michael Walzer suggests, however, that "admission and exclusion are at the core of communal independence. They suggest the deepest meaning of self-determination. Without them, there could not be *communities of character*, historically stable, ongoing associations of men and women with some special commitment to one another and some special sense of their common life."[2] Admission and exclusion refer not simply to one's presence in the territorial jurisdiction of a sovereign state but also to one's participation in various elements of this common life. "The theory of distributive justice begins, then, with an account of membership rights. It must vindicate at one and the same time the (limited) right of closure without which there could be no communities at all, and the political inclusiveness of the existing communities" (63). I agree with Walzer that membership must be defined; I also believe it is a status to which all present should be able to aspire.

According to Yael Tamir, "A group is defined as a nation if it exhibits both a sufficient number of shared, objective characteristics—such as language, history, or territory—and self-awareness of its distinctiveness." Objective similarities among members are by themselves insufficient. The drawing of boundaries "involves a conscious and deliberate effort to lessen the importance of objective differences within the group while reinforcing the group's uniqueness vis-à-vis outsiders."[3] National self-determination entails the public expression of this collective identity, or "the right of individuals to a public sphere, thus implying that individuals are entitled to establish institutions and manage their common life in ways that reflect their communal values, traditions, and history—in short, their culture" (70). For Tamir, the right to adhere to a particular culture is an individual right and interest; it is the individual to whom the value of membership accrues (42–48).

Yet the resulting shared public space, says Tamir, functions "not only as an arena of cooperation for the purpose of securing one's individual interests, but also as a space where one's communal identity finds expression" (74). Individuals enjoy a type of self-fulfillment in interacting with others who are similar that they cannot experience alone. The members of such an expressive association, as we might call it, experience special and seemingly constitutive ties and obligations, a shared culture, and perhaps a collective destiny, and view each other "as partners in a shared way of life" (115). Particularistic ties, then, are not parochial attachments to be transcended in the course of individual moral development but fulfill a need that is part of the human condition. "Individuals are better off when they are able to share their lives with some particular others they care about and see as their partners in a life-project."[4]

The claim that there is an individual human need to adhere to particularistic cultural ties supports the traditional emphasis on exclusive national citizenship that accompanied the rise of the nation-state. As we have seen, however, the liberal polity has characteristically championed both the background conditions for individual autonomy and self-development and a culture of diversity that contains a plurality of options. If diversity requires both a range of possibilities and the ability to envision what these possibilities entail, exclusionary policies clearly narrow the range of choices and also possibly the will to imagine alternatives. From these perspectives, the liberal commitment to individualism ill accords with an exclusivity that thwarts individual choice.

I shall examine some theoretical arguments both for and against bounded political communities. I believe that the existence of bounded entities can promote both individual autonomy and a cosmopolitan culture of diversity, but I also believe that the meaning of boundedness is not and should not be fixed or rigid. Next, I shall survey a number of Supreme Court decisions within the past generation for their interpretation of the notion of political community. I shall then consider the political community as a type of expressive association, arguing that a political community that desires to preserve a distinctively liberal way of life may exclude some strangers, but those whom it admits it must treat as members or eventual members. The liberal polity must be bounded externally; but it cannot be bounded internally, if its members and potential members are both individually and collectively to live their lives from the inside and also to have the opportunity to examine, question, and possibly revise their projects and goals.

Inclusion and Exclusion in the Liberal State

The case for open international borders will be considered idealistic by some critics and verging on the utopian by others. Nevertheless, a thorough and thoughtful case has been made by Joseph Carens that open boundaries can be justified in three types of liberal political theory. First, they can be justified on libertarian grounds, because the state is merely a monopoly that protects the preexisting rights of individuals within its territory. It is individuals who possess property and may exclude others from it, not the state. Libertarian theory "provides no basis for the *state* to exclude aliens and no basis for individuals to exclude aliens that could not be used to exclude citizens as well."[5] Second, open boundaries can be justified in Rawlsian liberalism by extending Rawls's conviction that natural and social contingencies are morally arbitrary and by taking a global rather than a national view of the original position. The right to migrate would be a basic liberty essential to individuals' projects and goals, not to be curtailed by the arbitrary fact of birth into one society instead of another. Even if immigration could be shown to reduce the economic well-being of current citizens below the present level of potential immigrants, the priority of liberty would preclude restrictions on immigration unless public order were threatened. Moreover, such restrictions "to preserve the unity and coherence of a culture" would be rejected in the original position, because "no one would be willing to risk the possibility of being required to forego some important right or freedom for the sake of an ideal that might prove irrelevant to one's own concerns" (262).

Third, a utilitarian approach would rank the maximization of overall economic gains engendered by the free mobility of labor over any privileged position for current citizens, rendering it unlikely that "a utilitarian calculus which took the interests of aliens seriously would justify significantly greater limits on immigration than the ones entailed by the public order restriction implied by the Rawlsian approach" (264). For all forms of liberalism, Carens suggests that the right to equal treatment in the public sphere should take precedence over freedom of association. Moreover, "On the whole, the history of liberalism reflects a tendency to expand both the definition of the public sphere and the requirements of equal treatment" (268). Respect for diversity does not require that liberals shrink from universalistic claims or from a critique of others' values, and

for Carens, "the general case for open borders is deeply rooted in the fundamental values of our tradition" (269). Opening membership to all who desire
it limits the ability of current members to shape their future, "but it does not
utterly destroy their capacity for self-determination" (271). In fact, it reaffirms
the communal character of a liberal community.

Frederick Whelan, by contrast, examines the case for the moral permissibility of exclusion of immigrants by those nation-states that might wish to do
so. Like Carens, he infers an open admissions policy from both Rawls's principles and utilitarian theory. But where Carens begins from liberal principles
and infers inclusive principles from these, Whelan proceeds from the realization that liberal principles themselves are espoused by a minority of the world's
peoples and that liberal institutions are "scarce, . . . hard-won and fragile."
Thus we might justifiably compromise liberal principles with restrictive immigration policies where failure to do so might compromise liberal institutions.
"A liberal's first concern should be to nourish and defend liberal beliefs and
institutions, even imperfect ones, where they presently exist, as a base from
which their influence may someday expand when more favorable circumstances
permit."[6] Protectionist policies benefit not only current liberal citizens but also
humanity in general. Inclusivity and exclusivity should be determined by their
respective effects on the perpetuation of liberal principles, so that in some circumstances, "the maximal diffusion of these values, or the conferral of their
benefits on as many people as possible, might dictate the highest possible rate of
absorption and assimilation of new members. Every immigrant, being a
prospective new convert to liberal principles, represents a step towards the goal
of their universal realization" (23).

Whelan defends the permissibility of exclusivity on both liberal democratic
and liberal communitarian grounds. Liberal democracy presupposes membership in a civically bounded group through which individuals collectively exercise
democratic rights. Procedurally, the group must control membership if it is to
maintain its self-determination; substantively, the group is entitled to maintain
its value consensus against external pressures. Although current citizens may
not "deserve" their membership in a meritocratic sense, the community's political resources constitute a distinctive heritage that citizens are obligated "to pass
on intact or improved to their successors" (31). Alternatively, a liberal communitarian perspective also upholds the distinction between members and nonmembers. First, cultural vitality on a cosmopolitan scale is facilitated once again
by the existence of a variety of communities with distinctive ways of life, a variety that would be homogenized by universal free movement (34). Second, echo-
ing Tamir's conception of an individual right to adhere to a particular culture,

"one could uphold the value of community membership for each individual as a necessary component of a fully satisfactory human life" (32). It is this second aspect of liberal communitarianism that I wish to pursue here.

An advocate of the liberal communitarian view of national citizenship must maintain both the necessity of membership in a bounded community to individual flourishing and its status as a right of or a good for individuals, rather than for the state. In Charles Taylor's view, patriotism carries an independent value somewhere between personal attachments and altruistic dedication to universal principles. "Patriotism is based on an identification with others in a particular common enterprise. . . . Particularity enters in because my bond to these people passes through our participation in a common political activity."[7] This bond is neither a *convergent* good like fire protection, provided in common but still an individual benefit desired as a matter of enlightened self-interest, nor a *mediately* common good like a concert, which provides enhanced enjoyment because it is shared rather than experienced alone. It is instead an "immediately" common good (168), the value of which derives centrally from the very existence of common actions and meanings. "The bond of solidarity with my compatriots in a functioning republic is based on a sense of shared fate, where the sharing itself is of value. This is what gives this bond its special importance" (170). Taylor's distinctions roughly parallel Michael Sandel's effort to distinguish the *instrumental* value of community, based on cooperation for the sake of purely private ends, and the *sentimental* value of community, engaging the feelings of individuals who collectively pursue shared ends, from its *constitutive* value as an actual way that its members understand themselves. For its members, constitutive "community describes not just what they *have* as fellow-citizens but also what they *are,* not a relationship they choose (as in a voluntary association) but an attachment they discover, not merely an attribute but a constituent of their identity."[8] In both the immediately common good and the value of constitutive community, the focus is less on what is shared and more on the actual fact of sharing, less on what the members possess and more on their identities *as* members.

In focusing on the value of membership in a bounded political community, however, we need not choose between individual rights and holistic values if the latter point the way to the enrichment of individual experience.[9] That is, political community may function as a forum for individual self-expression. As Amy Gutmann observes, "Participation cannot be consistently valued by a liberal theorist as a means to socialization or loyalty without further justification of the *value to the individual* of social integration."[10] Whatever notion of community we emphasize, it is as individuals that we experience it, even when it is shared with others or is the focus of a common identity. In Will Kymlicka's terms, if we are to live our lives from the inside and be free to question, examine, and revise our projects and goals, we do this in community when we set a collective agenda. But it is as individual agents that we cooperate. Moreover, even if we are grounded in constitutive attachments that we discover, from that ground we must make choices that set our future course, which in turn requires deliberation and reflection by and among individuals as to how these attachments will be played out.

We begin as individuals who are situated or embedded in actual communities with concrete and particularistic histories. Michael Walzer suggests that the conception and creation of distributive goods themselves are social processes; the same goods have different meanings in different societies. Individuals "take on concrete identities because of the way they conceive and create, and then possess and employ social goods."[11] Moreover, justice also receives its identity as the result of a common endeavor. "A given society is just if its substantive life is lived in a certain way—that is, in a way faithful to the shared understandings of the members" (313). Yet communities, like individuals, can and should live their lives from the inside. Hence communities, like individuals, are free to question, examine, and revise their collective projects and goals. As with individuals, experience need not be dispositive. The community's members may collectively survey their various and perhaps competing attachments, acknowledge their respective claims, and rank and order them in new ways. Kymlicka's statement to this effect about individuals applies as readily to communities. "No particular task is set for us by society, and no particular cultural practice has authority that is beyond individual judgement and possible rejection. . . . Nothing is 'set for us,' nothing is authoritative before our judgement of its value."[12] The community is never totally unencumbered by ends, projects, and goals, but these change over time, differing today from yesterday and tomorrow from today.

This point is apparent even in the work of communitarians like Alasdair MacIntyre. He suggests that although moral identity is bound up with community membership, this "does not entail that the self has to accept the moral *limitations* of the particularity of those forms of community. . . . It is in moving forward from such particularity that the search for the good, for the universal, consists. Yet particularity can never be simply left behind or obliterated."[13] That is, members may perceive moral limitations or may conflict in their shared understandings or in their objective values. They may question, examine, and revise their collective projects and goals. Yet both their original perceptions and their possible later resolutions of conflicting claims will be the perceptions and resolutions of that particular community with its traditions, and only within and because of that context can they be the perceptions and resolutions they are. In fact, conflict plays a major role for MacIntyre in the moral development of individuals and of communities. "It is through conflict and sometimes only through conflict that we learn what our ends and purposes are" (153). Specifically, "When an institution—a university, say, or a farm, or a hospital—is the bearer of a tradition of practice or practices, its common life will be partly, but in a centrally important way, constituted by a continuous argument as to what a university is and ought to be or what good farming is or what good medicine is. Traditions, when vital, embody continuities of conflict" (206).

This point can also be expressed in terms of Sandel's intrasubjective conception of the self. The liberal polity, like the individual, functions intrasubjectively when it moves among "an indefinite number of communities, some more inclusive than others, each making different claims on our allegiances, and there is no saying in advance which is *the* society or community whose purposes should govern the disposition of any particular set of our attributes and endowments."[14] We define our collective identity, like our individual ones, by engaging in rational scrutiny of and critical reflection on our options, using the capacities to choose and to will, to reflect and to understand. Our collective identity, like our individual ones, is not a fixed or static entity. We reflect upon our current circumstances and choose among the claims on our allegiance, just as we choose among our current options and then reflect anew. The liberal polity's existence as a bounded political community enables us continuously to construct a collective identity. But the nature of this identity is up to us.

Finally, even a tradition with a written constitution need not fix or harden its members' shared understandings. Sanford Levinson suggests that when individuals express adherence to the U.S. Constitution and its dictates as expressed by either the courts or the community, it is not automatically clear which Constitution they mean. Some may think of the 1787 text, others of that amended by the Bill of Rights, and still others of the post–Civil War document amended by the Thirteenth, Fourteenth, and Fifteenth Amendments. Some will add "aspects of the American experience which cannot be reduced to a text at all."[15] Levinson's point is that the Constitution is fluid, resisting "any kind of fixity or closure." Supporting the Constitution "commits me not to closure but only to a process of becoming and to taking responsibility for constructing the vision towards which I strive, joined, I hope, with others. It is therefore less a series of propositional utterances than a commitment to taking political conversation seriously" (193). In my own view, a political community must be a bounded one if it is to function for individuals as a locus of particularistic cultural ties. But it is not bound to particular tasks or practices prior to or apart from the judgments of its members.

The Value of Citizenship

We have seen that citizens of the liberal polity may in their own self-interest use either or both of two arguments for excluding nonmembers or for limiting the benefits of membership. First, liberal democracy presupposes a bounded group within which members exercise their democratic rights, and second, liberal community requires a bounded framework that serves as a forum for the pursuit of particularistic ties and the expression of shared values. These objectives are linked. Because the members of a democratic community assume collective responsibility for the perpetuation of its basic values and common interests, they must have control over the admission of new members. Without such control, as Whelan argues, "the democracy that existed would be seriously attenuated; it would not amount to self-determination."[16] The existence of a bounded political community allows then both for self-determination and for the use of this self-determination to maintain shared values against external pressures.

The historical diversity of the liberal polity as a political entity, however, complicates the traditional distinction between members and strangers. Moreover, on a theoretical level, liberalism's traditional inclusivity increases the difficulty of justifying this difference. Referring to John Rawls, Donald Moon suggests that because political liberalism focuses on politics or the organization and aims of public power rather than on the realization of a particular form of excellence, this liberalism is necessarily limited in scope. "The only requirement is that the various groups in society be able to recognize some significant aspect of their own self-understandings in the public or common model, so that they can see the point and value of the principles to which this model gives rise."[17] That is, the liberal strategy requires us to abstract from the full complexity or particularity of our lives in order to discover common elements that can function as the basis for political association. While providing space for moral diversity, this approach may lack the specificity or substance that attaches to more particular ideals of human excellence. As a result, adherence to or manifestation of specific ideals cannot serve as a litmus test for the purpose of distinguishing between members of and strangers to the political community. And the legal norms that govern inclusion in and exclusion from this community may lack a moral basis that is readily apparent.

International law allows a state to make distinctions between citizens and aliens, "as long as the distinctions bear a rational relationship to the different obligations and loyalties that a state might expect from its nationals, on the one hand, and its guests, on the other."[18] In the United States, all persons enjoy civil liberties, but "there remains a wide spectrum of rights and government services to which individuals become progressively entitled as they approach citizenship" (60). But what are these "rational" distinctions along the way? An examination of some Supreme Court decisions may help. Although my focus is the United States, the principles I discuss may apply elsewhere as well. Generally speaking, first, the Supreme Court has recognized that the political branches of the national government, unlike the states, possess "what amounts to plenary power over non-citizens" (46–47). Distinctions drawn by the states on the basis of alienage have been struck down where distinctions drawn by the national government have not. Second, the status of alienage has traditionally been accorded moral legitimacy as a basis for distinctions. The proposition that community members are entitled to decide the extent and terms of their relationships with nonmembers, suggests Michael Perry, "necessarily entails the view that a person, in some respects at least, is more deserving in virtue of his status as a citizen than a person who is not a citizen."[19]

As authoritative statements of current thinking about the nature and definition of the political community, Supreme Court opinions might be expected to contain reasoning about the moral relevance or irrelevance of the status of alienage to the legal disposition of particular disputes. With some notable exceptions, however, this type of reasoning is often lacking. *Graham v. Richardson* is one of the most prominent of several judicial decisions that refuse to distinguish between citizens and aliens in the allocation of legal rights and economic advantages. In striking down legislation in two states that limited welfare payments to citizens or to legally resident aliens of fifteen years or more, the Court ruled that alienage, like nationality and race, is a suspect classification, and that aliens are a "discrete and insular" minority for whom "heightened judicial solicitude is appropriate."[20] Because aliens contribute to a state's economic growth through their taxes, no special public interest justifies reserving these revenues for citizens (376). And although Congress has excluded indigent aliens from entry, states may not in effect "deny entrance and abode" to already-resident aliens who are indigent (380). Compared with earlier case law, write Peter Schuck and Rogers Smith, "in its refusal to regard citizenship as a special status entitling its holder to special advantages in the welfare state, *Graham* marks an important milestone in the devaluation of citizenship."[21]

Sugarman v. Dougall in some ways extended but in others diluted the inclusionary impact of *Graham*. Here the Court invalidated as too broad a New York law that confined to citizens employment in the competitive civil service, as it applied alike to sanitation workers, typists, and those who directly formu-late and execute state policy,[22] although no citizenship restriction applied to elec-tive and high appointive offices in New York. The Court did recognize, however, the legitimacy of a state's limiting participation in government "to those who are within 'the basic conception of a political community' " (642). Under what is referred to as the political community doctrine, the state may require citizenship, among other things, as a qualification for office in a more narrowly defined classification where a rational relationship exists between cit-izenship and the demands of a particular position. "Such power inheres in the state by virtue of its obligation . . . 'to preserve the basic conception of a polit-ical community.' " These qualifications might apply to voters as well as to "state elective or important nonelective . . . positions, for officers who partici-pate directly in the formulation, execution, or review of broad public policy perform functions that go to the heart of representative government" (647).

On the same day in 1973, in *In re Griffiths,* the Court also struck down a Connecticut law limiting admission to the state bar to citizens. Although Con-necticut argued that lawyers are quasi-public officials who might experience conflicting national loyalties, the Court majority, citing precedent, asserted that " 'it requires no argument to show that the right to work for a living in the com-mon occupations of the community is of the very essence of the personal free-dom and opportunity that it was the purpose of the [Fourteenth] Amendment to secure.' "[23] Individualized scrutiny of applicants to the bar, oaths taken by members of the bar, and the prospect of bar discipline lessen the possibility "that the practice of law offers meaningful opportunities adversely to affect the interests of the United States" (724). The two dissenters maintained, however, that "it is reasonable . . . for a State to conclude that persons owing first loy-alty to this country will grasp these traditions and apply our concepts more than those who seek the benefits of American citizenship while declining to accept the burdens" (733).

Although the Court majority did not view alien lawyers as policymakers and therefore as excludable from the profession to protect the integrity of the polit-ical community, they have reasoned differently with regard to several other professions. In *Foley v. Connelie,* the majority further developed the concept of political community as it affected a New York citizenship qualification for members of the state police force. Officers who participate in the formulation or execution of broad public policy may exercise more impact on citizens' lives "than even the ballot of a voter or the choice of a legislator." Restriction of such responsibilities to citizens, then, "represents the choice, and right, of the people to be governed by their citizen peers."[24] Police officers "are clothed with authority to exercise an almost infinite variety of discretionary powers" (297), and it is reasonable for the state to presume that citizens are "more familiar with and sympathetic to American traditions" (299–300). The dissenters, however, argued that state troopers do not set broad public policy as required for the *Sugarman* exclusion but simply apply policy to specific factual settings (304). Moreover, if aliens possess the integrity to practice law, they are also qualified to be policemen absent "good and relevant" reasons to the contrary (311).

The issue in both *Sugarman* and *Foley* turned on the extent to which state employees actually participated in the making or execution of public policy. In *Ambach v. Norwick*, the Court determined that public schoolteachers perform a function that goes to the heart of representative government and that therefore a New York law forbidding certification to resident aliens eligible for citizenship who have not at least "manifested an intention to apply for citizenship" was legitimate.[25] Through both teaching and example, "a teacher has the opportunity to influence the attitudes of students towards government, the political process, and a citizen's social responsibilities. This influence is crucial to the continued good health of a democracy" (79). Because teachers are obliged "to promote civic virtues and understanding in their classes," regardless of subject, they unquestionably perform a governmental function (80). The dissenters argued that the citizenship restriction applied neither to those ineligible for citizenship nor to private schoolteachers (86), that it was overbroad (87), that it was an irrational method for the selection of competent teachers (87–88), and that teachers, like equally influential lawyers, should be able to include resident aliens in their ranks (88–90).

Finally, in *Cabell v. Chavez-Salido*, the Court upheld the California requirement that deputy probation officers be citizens, characterizing its activity since *Graham* as that of distinguishing between the economic and sovereign functions of government. "Although citizenship is not a relevant ground for the distribution of economic benefits, it is a relevant ground for determining membership in the political community."[26] The political self-definition of the community requires the exclusion of aliens from self-government, which "begins by defining the scope of the community of the governed and thus of the governors as well: Aliens are by definition those outside of this community" (439–440). Although this particular classification of peace officer was arguably too broad, since it included cemetery sextons, furniture and bedding inspectors, and toll service employees, nevertheless, "the probation officer acts as an extension of the judiciary's authority to set the conditions under which particular individuals will lead their lives and of the executive's authority to coerce obedience to those conditions. From the perspective of the probationer, his probation officer may personify the State's sovereign power" (447). The dissenters argued that the statutes excluded aliens from a range of public jobs "in an unthinking and haphazard exercise of state power" (454) and that because aliens might play other roles in the criminal justice system, California's exclusion must stem "solely from state parochialism and hostility toward foreigners who have come to this country lawfully" (463).

These cases turn on how we should distinguish between what *Cabell* labels the economic and sovereign functions of government. The legacy of *Graham* calls for strict scrutiny when states exclude aliens from the economic functions of government, here the payment of welfare benefits. *Graham* in turn based its classification of aliens as a "discrete and insular" minority worthy of heightened judicial solicitude on circumstances when legislation infringed on specific constitutional rights, when political processes were too unrepresentative to be democratically responsive, and when laws "discriminated against 'discrete and insular' religious and ethnic minorities, whose interests might be duly overridden by a democratic majority."[27] The second and third criteria are for aliens one and the same. Because aliens do not vote, they cannot choose direct representation, and their interests are therefore more likely to be overridden by majorities. Although states may not bar aliens even from public employment in common occupations without strict scrutiny, "some state functions are so bound up with the operation of the State as a governmental entity so as to permit the exclusion from those functions of all persons who have not become part of the process of self-government."[28] To the *Cabell* Court, what must be determined is whether such restrictions "belie the State's claim that it is only attempting to ensure that an important function of government be in the hands of those having 'the fundamental legal bond of citizenship.' "[29] That is, the classification must be able to resist the interpretation that its true purpose is simply to prefer citizens over aliens and to prefer them in situations where it is not the sovereign but really the economic functions of government that are at stake.

The Court has in several cases found that the criterion of citizenship has been used too broadly, excluding where this has been unnecessary to preserve the integrity of the political community. In *Hampton v. Mow Sung Wong*, it ruled that the barring of resident aliens by the Civil Service Commission from the federal competitive civil service violated the due process clause of the Fifth Amendment. Considering the disadvantages to which aliens are already subject, "the added disadvantage resulting from . . . ineligibility for employment in a major sector of the economy . . . is of sufficient significance to be characterized as a deprivation of an interest in liberty,"[30] thereby deserving some scrutiny as a function of due process. Also in 1976 in *Board v. Flores de Otero*, the majority struck down a Puerto Rican statute denying resident aliens licenses as civil engineers. Although the territory desired to prevent an influx into the field of Spanish-speaking aliens, the desire to discriminate does not in itself justify discrimination. When an alien is lawfully admitted, "a State may not justify the restriction of the alien's liberty on the ground that it wishes to control the impact or effect of federal immigration laws."[31] Excluding aliens from lawful occupations is too broad to be an acceptable means of raising the overall living standard and is an insufficient means of providing accountability for negligent workmanship (605–606). Finally, in *Bernal v. Fainter,* the Court struck down a Texas law requiring citizenship of notaries public. Citing *Graham*'s requirement of strict judicial scrutiny of discrimination on the basis of alienage, with the exception of positions with political functions as in *Foley, Ambach, and Cabell,* it found that the duties of notaries "hardly implicate responsibilities that go to the heart of representative government."[32] They involve neither coercive force nor pedagogical discretion but are somewhat similar to the duties of lawyers, who were included even if noncitizens by *Griffiths* in the practice of law.

These three cases appeared to the Court to center on professions closer to the economic than to the sovereign functions of government. Two other cases, pertaining to the receipt of educational benefits, tend to blur the distinction between economic and sovereign functions. In *Nyquist v. Mauclet,* the Court ruled that a New York statute restricting state financial assistance for higher education to resident aliens who had either applied for citizenship or filed a statement of intent to apply when eligible was unconstitutionally discriminatory. The state argued that this limitation might encourage naturalization and that reserving assistance for future voters would enhance the educational level of the electorate, justifiable under preserving the political community as in *Sugarman.* The Court, however, declared the first concern a federal one only and the second misplaced; solicitude for the political community is narrower than imagined, comprising legal qualifications for voters or for officials who participate directly in public policy.[33] Moreover, as with welfare benefits in *Graham,* resident aliens pay taxes supporting the financial assistance programs that New York would deny them. Aliens may play important or even leadership roles in nonpolitical arenas. At the least, "The State is not harmed by providing resident aliens the same educational opportunity it offers to others" (12). In dissent, Chief Justice Warren Burger wrote, "I am concerned that we not obliterate all distinctions between citizens and aliens, and thus depreciate the historic values of citizenship" (14). William Rehnquist distinguished between this case and *Graham* by suggesting that here, because resident aliens need only apply for citizenship or declare such intent, "a resident alien has, at all times, the power to remove himself from one classification and to place himself in the other" (19–20).

Although *Nyquist* suggested that reserving assistance for those potentially eligible to vote was an insufficient justification for the restriction, it did not address the possibility that some of those unwilling to apply for citizenship or to declare such intent might in the future choose differently. Another case involving education, however, did address the possible future ties of aliens to the community. In *Plyler v. Doe,* the majority ruled that a Texas statute withholding funds for the education of undocumented alien schoolchildren violated the Fourteenth Amendment guarantee of equal protection of the laws to which all persons within the territorial jurisdiction of the United States are entitled. Although public education is not a constitutional right, this benefit nevertheless plays "a fundamental role in maintaining the fabric of our society. We cannot ignore the significant social costs borne by our Nation when select groups are denied the means to absorb the values and skills upon which our social order rests."[34] Many undocumented children will remain here even if uneducated, some becoming legal residents or citizens, at worst adding to the burden of unemployment, welfare, and crime and at best suffering "a lifetime of hardship" for which they themselves are not accountable. "By denying these children a basic education, we deny them the ability to live within the structure of our civil institutions, and foreclose any realistic possibility that they will contribute in even the smallest way to the progress of our nation" (223). Individuals have a fundamental interest in education, whereas "the State's denial of education to these children bears no substantial relation to any substantial state interest" (239). The dissenters argued that it is not irrational to withhold a benefit from those whose very presence is illegal. Even if one might not make the political choice of denying public education to illegal alien children, "that is not the issue; the fact that there are sound *policy* arguments against the . . . choice does not render that choice an unconstitutional one" (252–253).

These cases as a body present several recurring themes. First, the Court has displayed a more inclusive stance in the distribution of economic benefits than in the distribution of opportunities interpreted as participation in the political functions of government. Documented aliens, like citizens, must be able to support themselves or to receive support when necessary, and for such purposes they are members of the community. Even in a case upholding a federal provision restricting aliens from participating in a Medicare supplemental insurance program unless they were permanent residents of five years' duration, the Court suggested that the distinction between citizens and aliens was quantitative, not qualitative. The striking feature of *Mathews v. Diaz* is the Court's explicit acknowledgment not only that all aliens need not be classified identically but also that ties between the individual and the community strengthen and deepen over time, an interdependence that should take precedence over purely formal classifications. No alien has a constitutional claim on national resources. But "The decision to share that bounty with our guests may take into account the character of the relationship between the alien and this country: Congress may decide that as an alien's tie grows stronger, so does the strength of his claim to an equal share of that munificence."[35] A durational residency requirement is reasonable in presuming that those who qualify for benefits "have a greater affinity with the United States than those who do not" (83).

Second, however, the distinction between the economic and political functions of government and of the opportunities that derive therefrom is less clear than the *Cabell* Court implies. In several of the cases cited, disagreements between the majority and minority turn on whether the responsibilities of given occupations involve the exercise of administrative discretion consistent with the political or sovereign functions of government.[36] But this difficulty arises in a more complex context in the two cases addressing education. These initially appear to fall into the economic category, as education bestows economic advantages that are otherwise difficult to attain. On the other hand, education also promotes political socialization, often inculcating knowledge of and commitment to the nation's culture and institutions, that both fosters and justifies full political inclusion.

A democratic community presupposes an ability to maintain the integrity of its value consensus, which in turn requires some distinction between members and nonmembers. Yet in the case of benefits that promote socialization, like education, muting the distinction between members and nonmembers may eventually further a more inclusive or complete consensus than is possible if nonmembers are set apart. The *Nyquist* majority noted that resident aliens might play leadership roles in nonpolitical arenas. We could infer, then, that the nature of their values and interests is not irrelevant to the identity of the liberal community, both political and otherwise. Moreover, because those who do not now apply for citizenship or declare a future intent are not disqualified from doing so later, withholding financial assistance for higher education from resident aliens does not obviate the possibility that we are withholding it from future citizens as well. Similarly, of course, current citizens receiving financial assistance may be uninterested in political participation; we simply cannot predict in these matters. Overall, however, to the extent that education promotes a greater identity of goals, values, and interests among individuals, educational opportunities carry implications that are not only economic but also political.

The impact of both *Mathews* and *Nyquist* is to place the claims of aliens along a continuum, rather than together and removed from the claims of citizens. The continuum in *Mathews* is temporal, but that in *Nyquist* is ontological, in the sense that educational benefits enable aliens to become more like citizens, exerting nonpolitical if not political leadership. This trend continues with *Plyler*. This growing inclusivity is a subject of controversy. It may be argued on the one hand, as Elizabeth Hull does, that this decision affected undocumented children rather than adults, it mandated education alone among social services, it did not disallow other state efforts to discourage illegal immigration, and it did not preclude future congressional action to restrict public education to documented alien children.[37] On the other hand, however, Peter Schuck argues that *Plyler* "not only enlarged the national community to uncertain dimensions and on the basis of uncertain principles, but did so in the face of a congressional policy to exclude undocumented aliens from the country *altogether*." Although children are not accountable for their parents' infractions of immigration law, they indirectly suffer harm when their parents are denied welfare benefits, public or private employment, and public housing. Overall, the principle germinated by *Plyler* "seems to be that a state may not seek to discourage illegal entry by means of disincentives that may harm the children of those who, because the disincentives are ineffective, decide to enter anyway."[38] In "a seismic shift, the Court seems to have begun to redefine the community to include all those whose destinies have somehow, even in violation of our law, become linked with ours" (57).

Schuck perceives a fundamental tension in this approach. Classical immigration law emphasized consent as the source of aliens' rights and duties, but the crucial locus of consent was the government and the duties were the aliens' (34). As with Whelan, some essential difference between members and strangers must be assumed if the value of membership is not to be seriously attenuated. More recent immigration law, however, is communitarian, for its theme "is that the government owes legal duties to all individuals who manage to reach America's shores. . . . These new norms derive the government's legal obligations to individuals from the nature of their social interactions and commitments rather than from the government's consent to be bound" (21; also 46, 65). That is, the locus of consent is with the aliens, and the duties are the government's. Although these norms emerge from the traditional emphasis on universal human rights, they are still "grounded in a fundamental nonliberal intuition—the perception that individuals, societies, and nations are bound to each other by pervasive interdependencies . . . and that membership in our national community should depend not upon formalistic criteria but upon the functional social linkages actually forged between aliens and the American people" (50–51; also 60–61, 78–79). Although complete freedom of movement might ideally be desirable, immigration law is nevertheless central in any attempt "to define, mold, and protect the American community." Specifically, "It undertakes to answer the first questions that any society must put to itself: What are we? What do we wish to become? How shall we reach that goal? And most fundamentally, which individuals constitute the 'we' who shall decide these questions?" (76). In Whelan's terms, then, exclusivity is a precondition of liberal community.

On an interpretation like Schuck's, the economic functions of government ineluctably mingle with its political functions. In the distribution or withholding of public economic benefits, government engages politically in defining the "we" who will participate in collective decisions as to the projects and goals we will pursue as a political community. One response to the tension that Schuck describes would be to return to classical immigration law, with its emphasis on the dependence of alien rights upon the government's express consent. This approach would reaffirm the moral authority of the current political community to define and shape itself. A different response, and one that I suggest, would acknowledge that the political community comprises all who are physically within it. Although all may not participate in the political functions of government in the narrow sense, all affect, even if indirectly, the substance with which these functions deal and the manner in which these functions are carried out. Unless we expel every undocumented alien, it cannot be denied that they share with us the possibility of a common destiny and in this sense are potentially members of the political community. Resident aliens we have explicitly admitted to our collective destiny, and thus, again, to a broadened conception of membership. Even without explicit consent, the presence of aliens is an explicit fact, and as a political community we must define the terms of this membership.

The Meaning of Membership

THE PROBLEM

If citizenship formally denotes membership in the political community, what then does this membership itself connote? First, citizenship might indicate knowledge of national values and traditions, because application normally requires five years' prior residence. In *Ambach*, however, the individuals excluded from teaching had resided here over a dozen years each; both were spouses of citizens. Although they agreed to take oaths of allegiance in lieu of declarations of intention to become citizens, which would have been acceptable under New York law, neither this nor long residency was sufficient for the Court. "The status of citizenship was meant to have significance in the structure of our government. . . . The form of this association is important; an oath of allegiance or similar ceremony cannot substitute for the unequivocal legal bond citizenship represents."[39] The Court therefore implicitly rejected any test, as in *Mathews v. Diaz*, of "affinity with the United States" or any notion that length of association is significant, although it had emphasized this consideration with respect to the economic functions of government. By contrast, cases purportedly involving the sovereign functions of government apparently do not consider whether an alien's claim to participate in the political community grows stronger over time. Neither declarations of loyalty nor evidence of assimilation is sufficient; only actual naturalization counts.

Second, citizenship might indicate simply a deliberate and self-conscious decision to set oneself apart from others who are not citizens, irrespective of the values connoted by citizenship or of the projects and goals citizens might individually or collectively be expected to espouse. In addition to an oath of allegiance and a promise of service, the citizen being naturalized also swears "that I absolutely and entirely renounce and abjure all allegiance and fidelity to any foreign prince, potentate, state or sovereignty, of whom or which I have heretofore been a subject or citizen." Although commitment to the country's values and traditions is expected, it is the *act* of commitment itself that makes the difference. Resident aliens may be knowledgeable and loyal but lack "a willingness . . . to identify themselves with the country and its people and to give up once and for all their attachment to the countries in which they were born. The unnaturalized alien is perhaps holding something back."[40] The importance of self-conscious consent is illustrated by rules announced in 1997 governing the application of a 1994 law that, although it exempted seriously disabled immigrants from English proficiency and civic requirements for citizenship, nevertheless disallowed exemptions from taking the oath.[41] As in the preceding cases, those who either will not or cannot consent to membership are properly excluded, not because of lack of knowledge or of affinity with this country's values but because they have not undertaken the self-conscious commitment that citizenship represents.

An act of commitment that requires that one abjure prior loyalties is, of course, the paradigmatic case of consent, presupposing the existence of autonomy or self-governance. In contrast to the principle of consent, which grounds membership in free individual choice, is the principle of ascription, which attributes political membership to an objective circumstance like birth. Schuck and Smith would strengthen the consensual conception of citizenship by guaranteeing birthright citizenship only to the children of citizens and legally resident aliens, leaving to Congress the authority to define the extent of birthright citizenship for the native-born children of undocumented aliens and nonimmigrant visitors. Automatic citizenship for the children of those to whose presence the political community has not consented "represents an ascriptive infringement of the community's democratic authority to shape its own destiny."[42] Where political membership traditionally conferred mainly the rights to vote and to remain permanently, the growth of the welfare state, "by vastly increasing the resources that government allocates, . . . has significantly raised the stakes in obtaining the legal status that assures access to those resources" (108). On the consensual view, the attainment of citizenship is a clear and unambiguous indication that membership has been proffered and accepted. It is this identification, rather than any sort of affinity with the political community, that counts.

A contemporary version of the ascriptive conception, on the other hand, is offered by Carens. "Moral claims to citizenship in a state normally rest not on choices that individuals make but on facts about people's relationships with a society. People who have lived and worked throughout their lives in a particular society should normally be regarded as full members of that society."[43] If social ties are not viewed as creating moral claims, the community may be defined exclusively and by those holding political power. Membership is a matter not of will but of fact. Ascription "implies that people are *entitled* to citizenship in any state in which they have sufficiently powerful social ties. They cannot legitimately be deprived of such citizenship against their will" (426), although they may decide to reject it. As Sandel might say, the ascriptive conception emphasizes the cognitive dimension of human agency exercised by a knowing subject over the voluntarist dimension exercised by a willing subject. We survey our experiences and attachments, weigh their claims, and may affirm or not those to which we are entitled. On this interpretation, illegal immigrants themselves as well as their native-born children would hold ascriptive claims to citizenship on the moral basis of established social ties, a point acknowledged by Schuck and Smith when they favor an amnesty program for long-term resident illegal aliens and their families "who have forged significant ties to the American community."[44]

At bottom, the question is that of whether the status of citizenship creates communal ties, or whether the existence of communal ties constitutes the status of citizenship. In T. H. Marshall's classic statement, "Citizenship is a status bestowed on those who are full members of a community."[45] Citizenship in his view comprises three elements. The civil element includes civil liberties, with the right to property and contract. The political element bestows the right of participation in the exercise of political power, either directly or through representation. The social element means "the whole range from the right to a modicum of economic welfare and security to the right to share to the full in the social heritage and to live the life of a civilized being according to the standards prevailing in the society" (72). Generally speaking, in recent times we have accorded civil rights but denied political rights to aliens; currently at issue is the element of social rights. Although the right to acquire an education or to pursue a livelihood may initially appear to be a civil liberty, in another sense it becomes a social right. The right to pursue a livelihood is central to economic welfare, to a share in the social heritage, and to life as a civilized being in accordance with prevailing standards. Access to the resources of the welfare state if one cannot pursue a livelihood is central in the same way. But is citizenship a matter of will or of fact? If citizenship is bestowed on those who are full members of the community, does the community's decision to bestow citizenship render individuals members? Or does de facto membership in the community eventually earn individuals the de jure status of citizenship?

Among the judicial decisions we have surveyed, *Graham* and *Mathews* explicitly accord welfare rights to resident aliens. *Sugarman, Griffiths, Hampton, Board v. Flores,* and *Bernal* accord the right to participate in the community's common occupations, and *Nyquist* and *Plyler* accord educational support or education itself. All of these qualify as social rights on Marshall's definition. I believe that in these cases, the Court recognized that the individuals concerned were on some level community members, to whom as such these rights were due. The according of these rights made them fuller members than before, following the consensual model. But our consent was rooted in an ascriptive consideration, the fact of these individuals' presence among us. Although this development may represent the devaluation of citizenship as a formal, de jure status, it does not devalue citizenship or membership as an effective de facto condition. The achievement of citizenship may be a continuum along which participation in the economic and social life of the community is a way station. Anyone present is at least in an attenuated sense a member. That is, one's presence here exerts an impact, whether as a participant in our common life or as a detractor from it. With or without educations or occupations, all are members of the *social* community, either as contributors or dead weights. If the theory of liberal community affirms the moral authority of the current *political* community to define and shape itself, as we have seen, current citizens have an interest in co-opting those who are present at the other end of the continuum, in giving them a stake or vested interest in our full social heritage. Although only de jure citizens constitute the "we" who decide on the nature of this stake, all of us, though perhaps holding varying degrees of de facto membership, contribute to the nature of this heritage.

The other judicial decisions surveyed ostensibly involve the right to participate in the exercise of political power or to engage in the sovereign functions of government. Yet insofar as the denial of certain occupations to aliens narrows the field within which they may seek economic welfare and security, these decisions impinge upon social rights as well as on political ones. Moreover, the moral authority of the community to define and shape itself may be exercised in more than one way. On the one hand, current citizens may try to ensure that new members display knowledge of our national values and traditions. The formal status of citizenship may function as a proxy for these qualifications, signifying that new members have embraced these values. But because actual citizenship is neither a necessary condition for the possession of this knowledge, as we see with long-term resident aliens, nor a sufficient condition, as in birthright citizens with little interest in civic values, the emphasis devolves upon the act of commitment itself by which nonmembers become formal members of the community. Simply by setting themselves apart from others, naturalized citizens ensure that there *is* a distinction between citizens and aliens and that a unique political community in fact exists.

On the other hand, current citizens may define and shape the community by treating all who are legally present at least as nascent members. Their presence already exposes them, in Marshall's terms, to the social heritage of the community. Guarantees of economic welfare and security, including the "right to work for a living in the common occupations of the community," in the Court's frequent words, enable them to live as civilized beings, according to prevailing social standards. As put by Moon, this sort of membership "includes a concern with social integration, or social solidarity, with promoting enough commonality in the social experiences and ways of life of different sections of the society so that genuine equality of respect will be possible."[46] Schuck notes, as we have seen, that in the communitarian model of immigration law, the traditional liberal emphasis on human rights is grounded in a nonliberal intuition that de facto interdependencies are binding. I would reverse this observation to suggest that convictions about the binding quality of these interdependencies are grounded in a liberal intuition that human rights are universal, at least within a liberal polity. The possession of civil rights and of some measure of social rights is a necessary condition for the generation of a modicum of equality of respect among all, citizens or not, who live side by side and interact with one another on a frequent basis.

In a liberal political community, the conviction that all *persons* merit the equal protection of the laws represents a core value for many and functions as a basis for the distinctive way of life that liberal communitarianism seeks to protect. But how then do we protect the integrity of this heritage? Recognition of certain rights regardless of mutual consent may redeem core aspects of the liberal promise but at the expense of metaphorical boundaries or literal borders that define the distinctiveness of the liberal political community. Yet a single-minded focus on consent, while preserving distinctiveness, may hollow out core values within the liberal promise to the point of rendering it vacuous. Whereas the eighteenth-century assertion of the individual right to consent to authority was seen as congruent with the collective interest in self-determination of newly democratized nation-states, this link is now severed. Today, majority self-determination may be interpreted to entail the exclusion of some persons, either from admission within national borders or from full membership once within. Any solution to this dilemma must preserve a measure of distinctiveness but must do so without undue sacrifice of core liberal values.

TOWARD A SOLUTION

In *Roberts v. United States Jaycees,* the Supreme Court addressed a case involving sanctions imposed by the U.S. Jaycees on two Minnesota chapters who violated bylaws by admitting women as regular members rather than as associate members limited in their participation. Although the court of appeals had ruled that the Jaycees' advocacy of political and public causes entitled it to freedom of association in the selection of members, which outweighed any compelling interest by Minnesota in eradicating discrimination, the Supreme Court ruled unanimously against the Jaycees. Some of the reasons offered bear on the subject of political communitarianism. The Court argued that the right to associate is not absolute and that the commercial programs and business contacts promoted by the Jaycees were goods and advantages to which all should have equal access. Moreover, no evidence existed to show that allowing greater participation by women "will impede the organization's ability to engage in these protected activities or to disseminate its preferred views" or "will change the content or impact of the organization's speech" in ways that exceed the accomplishment of the state's legitimate purposes in eradicating sex discrimination.[47]

Justice Sandra Day O'Connor, however, disagreed with a part of the

Court's analysis although she concurred in its judgment. Rather than predicating the constitutional protection of an association's membership selection on a foreseeable alteration of its disseminated views, the relevant distinction is that between the expressive association, for which the very formation "is the creation of a voice, and the selection of members is the definition of that voice" (633), as in admission to a religious faith, and the commercial association, whose activity should enjoy only minimal protection. Although many associations are neither purely expressive nor commercial, "an association should be characterized as commercial . . . when, and only when, the association's activities are not predominantly of the type protected by the First Amendment" (635). O'Connor implies that even if regulation of its membership does alter the group's message, this regulation is legitimate in the case of a predominantly commercial association. A predominantly expressive association, however, should enjoy full autonomy in the selection of its members.

In the court cases discussed, then, those who argue that citizenship is a legitimate qualification for a given office or position are in fact suggesting that the political community in its sovereign functions is an expressive association. As the majority stated in *Cabell,* not only for the probationer but also "from the perspective of the larger community, the probation officer may symbolize the political community's control over, and thus responsibility for, those who have been found to have violated the norms of the social order."[48] As an expressive association, the political community's exclusivity of membership may be protected regardless of whether the content of its message would change with greater inclusiveness. There need be little or no distinguishable difference between citizen and alien in terms of the values they espouse. If the selection of members constitutes the definition of an expressive association's voice, a distinction grounded in legal status "represents the choice, and right, of the people to be governed by their citizen peers."[49] To the extent, however, that the occupations at issue exemplify the economic functions of government, I submit that the political community is a commercial association. Jobs represent goods and advantages that should be open to all, and formal membership carries no protected status.

At the heart of the controversy over membership, then, is the question of the extent to which the political community is an expressive association as opposed to the extent to which it functions as a commercial association. It may function as an expressive association in at least two ways. First, it serves as a forum for self-expression, as we saw with Tamir, fulfilling a need that is part of the human condition. Participation in what are considered the sovereign functions of government might be regarded as a means of individual self-expression and self-determination in a pluralist context.[50] Such self-expression represents not only the living out of personal values but also the added value of doing so in concert with other, like-minded individuals in a collective setting. Membership represents a bond of solidarity, in Taylor's terms, based on a sense of shared fate in a particular common enterprise. The existence of an identifiable political community with expressive functions renders this bond of solidarity determinate in ways that would be impossible if the community simply included every person legally within the country's territory. And this concreteness may in turn promote the conviction among citizens that the political community is well-defined enough to be representative of their interests and aspirations. This sort of political community, then, while hospitable to diversity, simultaneously requires boundaries within which individual self-expression may be concentrated and have some effect.

Second, political community as an expressive association functions as a locus for discussion of what type of community this forum is or should be and of what the meaning of membership is or should be. This formulation is captured by Nancy Rosenblum in the concept of latent community. Some individuals discover community not in groups or in ideological agreement but "in liberal society as a whole, hidden beneath the surface of pluralism and legal formalism." Genuine community "is 'latent' in our deep shared meanings and in our faithfulness to common practices. The task of these communitarians is reclamation" (165). Walzer's account of complex equality exemplifies latent community: "A given society is just if its substantive life is lived in a certain way—that is, in a way faithful to the shared understandings of the members."[51] The concept of latent community in some ways appears vague and problematic. It is difficult to fix the substance and breadth of shared meanings, as well as the degree of permissible conflict before latent community is lost.[52] For example, for Walzer, disagreements about how shared values are to be applied in particular contexts are not simply conflicts but instead "are, at the deepest level, interpretations of that union."[53] Moreover, latent community ostensibly requires a pursuit of civic education and conditioned virtue that is often at odds with liberalism. Theorists simultaneously desire membership that is constitutive of the self, suggests Rosenblum, but "reject the hard politics that has always been necessary to produce and maintain community. They suggest that latent community is a force that is expressed in practices and somehow 'penetrates' selves to create members,"[54] as Sandel's constitutive community encumbers yet transforms us through revised self-understandings.

The purpose of the ideal of latent community is not to transcend the self "through identification with a group or nation" but to recover strong expressive selves, to make 'thin' selves 'thick'" (218). It is here that this concept bears on the function of the political community as an expressive association. As we have seen, there is no reason to conclude that resident aliens, particularly long-term ones, share less than do citizens in the country's values and traditions. Moreover, the substantive content of these values and traditions is itself indeterminate. The unity or self-identity that any shared values might supply, argue John Scanlan and O. T. Kent, "cannot plausibly be considered to imply basic agreement about what ethnically or ideologically constitutes 'our own way of life.' On the contrary, it more likely reflects an implicit moral agreement about how the nation's social and political institutions ought to be governed, *given the fact that individuals disagree* fundamentally over what that way of life is or ought to be."[55] But ironically, the relative indeterminacy of the substance of national values and traditions may heighten the importance of the notion of latent community, of the attempt to discover meanings and connections beneath a seemingly bland surface. Setting apart the political community as defined by formal membership in its sovereign functions may exemplify an attempt to "penetrate" selves to create members. The resident alien may symbolize the atomistic individual or antecedently individuated, "thin" self, whereas the naturalized citizen, by formally giving up former attachments and holding nothing back, has been penetrated to become the strong, expressive, or "thicker" self that seems desirable in fellow members of the political community.

Yet this straining for latent community can work toward inclusion as well as exclusion. As Rosenblum observes, "The distinction between members and strangers can be used critically to suggest that everyone is a potential member."[56] An example of this critical use occurs in Walzer's argument that all individuals present should at least potentially be citizens. Although special classes of guest workers are admitted to some countries to perform undesirable work and are often barred from the civil and economic protections of citizenship, "no contractualist argument can justify the creation of a caste of resident aliens."[57] Because any protections they do possess could be revoked at any time, "their material condition is unlikely to be improved except by altering their political status. Indeed, the purpose of their status is to prevent them from improving their condition; for if they could do that, they would soon be like domestic workers," unwilling to do hard and unpleasant work for low pay (59). Unless they may regard themselves as potential citizens, "their other choices cannot be taken as so many signs of their acquiescence to the economy and law of the countries where they work. And if they do have that choice, the local economy and law are likely to look different" (60). Thus, although the community may determine that some persons will be excluded from its territory, it should not decide that some within its territory will be permanently excluded from its politics.

On this interpretation, the political community is an expressive association but one that may only temporarily block membership by those present in the community who, once admitted, aspire to join. Yet insofar as the political status of documented aliens influences their material condition, we could argue that the political community also functions as a commercial association. Economic opportunities such as jobs represent goods and advantages that arguably should be open to all. If so, either the privileges of de facto membership should be available regardless of formal membership status, or formal citizenship should be readily accessible so that all may take advantage of these opportunities. I believe that redeeming the promised rights of both liberalism and democracy requires a stance like Walzer's, though many would disagree. My present point, however, is that the conception of latent community implies and indeed requires deliberation about the animating principles of the political community and of what their application means in practice. As Walzer states, disagreements represent not only conflict but also alternative interpretations of the union the political community represents. The critical potential of the concept of latent community appears in assertions that faithfulness to these animating principles requires change in the ways these principles are practiced.

To put this differently, the concept of latent community casts each of us in the role of what Walzer terms the connected critic, or the critic who assesses communal practices not from the outside, using an external standard of judgment, but from the inside, as one who shares certain understandings with his or her fellows and seeks to extend their application in new directions. The connected critic does not ask what the right course of action is in an absolute sense but asks, "What is the right thing *for us* to do?" within the context of a particular tradition of moral discourse.[58] Or, as we have seen in MacIntyre, traditions that are vital encompass not only agreement but also "continuities of conflict" about the goods the pursuit of which is central to such traditions. The underlying fear experienced by advocates of a broad interpretation of the political community doctrine, then, may be that inclusiveness expands the pool of connected critics, the universe of those who hold the moral authority, because they have the legal authority to enter into the debate about what is right *for us* to do. The political community functions as an expressive association because it can limit the potential universe of connected critics, minimizing the possibility that "latent" interpretations of political community will be exposed that might threaten or disturb the accepted interpretations or dominant consensus.

Recent and current debate over immigration policy exemplifies a continuity of conflict about how we ought to constitute ourselves as a national political community. Differences of opinion abound with regard to the empirical effects of immigration. Where Michael Lind asserts that a truly liberal immigration policy would reduce surplus labor by reducing immigration overall,[59] Robert Wright suggests that the incomes earned by highly skilled immigrants facilitate income equalization by promoting work in local services for lower-skilled workers in general.[60] Where Roger Waldinger argues that because immigrants constitute large majorities of those employed with less than high school diplomas or with solely elementary educations, low-skilled African Americans are especially hurt by immigration,[61] a National Academy of Sciences study reports that the latter suffer no more than other low-skilled workers and that the overall reduction in economic opportunities is slight in any case.[62] Where on some accounts illegal immigrants disproportionately affect financially particular states such as California, Arizona, Texas, Illinois, Florida, New York, and New Jersey,[63] other studies show that documented and/or undocumented immigrants often pay more in taxes than they cost in various welfare and educational services.[64] Finally, whatever the empirical data, public perceptions about the impact of immigrants differ widely. Many New Yorkers perceive immigrants as a source of economic growth and social vitality, whereas Los Angeles residents often blame immigrants for the greater part of the fiscal, educational, and law enforcement problems of California.[65]

Whatever the perceived dislocations posed by immigrants, both documented and undocumented, the decade from 1986 through 1996 saw three formal attempts to address some of them. The Immigration Reform and Control Act of 1986 established employer sanctions for the hiring of undocumented aliens and authorized the legalization of immigrants illegally residing in the United States prior to 1982.[66] The Immigration Act of 1990 addressed documented immigration by increasing, reducing, or creating various classes of visas (13–14). Unlike the 1986 law, the 1990 legislation aimed to reduce the undocumented population not by sanctions to discourage immigration but by measures to regularize to a degree the status of those already here. The Illegal Immigrant Reform and Immigrant Responsibility Act of 1996 targeted illegal entrants, covering increased border controls, stiffer penalties for alien smuggling and document fraud, more relaxed standards for detention and deportation, improved workplace verification systems for checking the status of potential employees, and provisions regarding public benefits, including reimbursement of states or localities for emergency medical care provided to illegal entrants.[67] This legislation more closely resembles the 1986 law, as it attempts to exclude illegal entrants at the start, deport them once here, or render their remaining here unattractive through hindrances to employment.

These provisions supplemented others in the Personal Responsibility and Work Opportunity Reconciliation Act of 1996, a comprehensive welfare reform law that addressed the status of both documented and undocumented entrants. This legislation denies a wide range of welfare services and benefits to both documented and undocumented aliens, although it also lists a number of exceptions. These include emergency medical services under Medicaid; short-term, noncash emergency disaster relief; immunization, testing, and treatment for communicable diseases; and certain noncash programs like soup kitchens and short-term shelter that are not means-tested and that are necessary to protect life or safety. Certain classes of documented immigrants may receive Supplemental Security Income and food stamps, but only after five years, which are calculated retroactively for those already here; resident aliens may enjoy such means-tested benefits indefinitely only if they have worked in the United States for ten years. Finally, the financial responsibility of sponsors for the welfare of immigrants has been increased.[68]

Several observations emerge from this litany. As Schuck observes, "The federal government has now made a clear, comprehensive policy choice . . . in favor of a national policy to discriminate against aliens in its federal programs, and to either require or permit the states to do so in their programs. This policy fundamentally reverses the recent law in this area."[69] But it also promotes an elision of the economic and the political functions of government. If the political community in its role as an expressive association determines that only members may have access to opportunities and benefits that we more typically attribute to a commercial association, individuals who might otherwise merely seek commercial association with the political community now seek political association as well. That is, they seek citizenship. Although most new immigrants must now wait five years to avail themselves of most means-tested benefits, that waiting period coincides with the five years of permanent residency after which individuals may become citizens. Even before the 1996 welfare or immigration legislation, the Immigration and Naturalization Service reported that during a four-month period of 1994–1995, citizenship applications increased by about 80 percent as compared with the same period a year earlier. In addition to legislation under discussion, declining economic conditions in Mexico, and the completion of residency requirements by many beneficiaries of an amnesty granted in the 1986 law, an Immigration and Naturalization Service (INS) spokesman also cited a climate of stigmatization of immigrants, both legal and illegal. In any case, the boom in citizenship applications derived not from increasing immigration but from increasing numbers of applications from those already here.[70]

The 1994 passage of Proposition 187 in California has undoubtedly fueled the boom in citizenship applications. This measure withheld welfare services, schooling, and nonemergency medical care from undocumented aliens; and although the recent federal legislation has overtaken it, its passage has promoted salutary debate about the meaning of membership in the political community.[71] Moreover, the backlash represented by Proposition 187 has in turn generated its own backlash. In 1994 2 million of California's 5 million adult Latinos were permanent resident aliens, but between 1992 and 1996 the number of citizenship applicants rose by 500 percent.[72] Toward the end of the fiscal year ending September 30, 1996, the INS reported that by that date, nearly 1.1 million immigrants would have become citizens, shattering the 1995 record of 445,853, which itself broke the previous record of 441,979 naturalizations established in 1944. More than 75 percent of these were concentrated in the vicinity of six cities in five states: New York, Chicago, Miami, Houston, Los Angeles, and San Francisco.[73]

The lesson of the naturalization boom is that many to whom citizenship appeared unimportant will become citizens if lack of citizenship functions as a disability. The social rights constituted by economic and welfare benefits converge with the political rights that accompany membership in the political community. Eligibility for and acceptance of membership in the expressive association, in other words, is a necessary condition of eligibility for membership in the commercial association. In theory, these developments should please current citizens. The polity has proffered formal membership to permanent residents who are already on the road to citizenship; they are accepting enthusiastically by seeking naturalization. The equation is balanced by consent on both sides.

Yet we like to think that immigrants seek citizenship because they espouse certain values that they share with others in the political community where they seek membership, not simply because they fear a denial of certain benefits. That is, we prefer that those seeking naturalization focus on the political community as an expressive association rather than on its commercial aspects. Immigration occurs, however, for a variety of reasons. These reasons are not always discrete and may be interconnected. For example, religious dissenters who came to the North American continent sought freedom from political and religious persecution. But the denial of economic opportunities *because* of one's religious affiliation is part of what constitutes religious persecution. And insofar as this denial precludes participation in the common occupations or common economic life of the community, it may also contribute to political marginalization, setting off what may become, if it is not already, a discrete and insular minority. Because of the difficulty of separating out the various motivations of immigrants, I believe that the seeking of naturalization is itself the ultimate test of affinity with the United States. A period of permanent residency plus the desire to become a citizen, after the experience of residence in the country, surely indicate some kind of affinity, and we need not inquire too closely into the grounds of that affinity.

Moreover, we do not always welcome too much affinity. Immigration throughout our history has contributed to a diversity that we claim to value. Yet the globalization of the economy and technological advances have devalued the importance of cultural capital, resulting in more homogenized cultures with less to offer each other, as Thurston Clarke suggests. "How much cultural capital, after all, does a young German or Indian who eats Big Macs, wears Nikes, adores Arnold Schwarzenegger movies and watches MTV bring to Los Angeles?"[74] From a self-interested standpoint, it is the differences between immigrants and current citizens that render the former willing to take jobs that the latter will not or cannot fill. Furthermore, though some immigrants display an affinity from the start, as in Clark's example, others may develop affinities about which even current citizens have reservations. A 1994 study demonstrated that although immigrant children initially surpass American children in their school performance, with respect to both grade point averages and homework time, "as immigrant children become Americanized they move in the direction of their American counterparts."[75] In sum, immigrants cannot win. Those who emulate the ideals of hard work and the drive for success are admired in theory but feared in reality for the jobs and resources they may take from current citizens. Those who do not seem to value these ideals arouse animosity from a different quarter if it is imagined they may *not* secure work and may therefore lay claim to welfare benefits, thus indicating an "affinity" with many unemployed American citizens.

Two other groups of noncitizens exist who are neither undocumented aliens nor documented, permanent residents who are eligible for and wish to take up citizenship. The first comprises those permanent residents eligible for citizenship who do not wish to forswear allegiance to their countries of origin. Some may be spouses of citizens, as in the case of the teachers in *Ambach*. Others may be reluctant to relinquish cultural ties that they perceive to be better maintained through retention of their original citizenship. Here I believe that the political community has the moral right to impose the legal obligation of citizenship on those who want to partake of the community's opportunities and benefits. But this is not because citizens are inherently better qualified to exercise opportunities normally reserved for full members of the political community. Rather, it is because the political community may legitimately require the self-conscious commitment that naturalization represents, if it is to reciprocate by proffering the benefits that citizens enjoy. I disagree, then, with the inclusivity of *Nyquist v. Mauclet* and agree with the state law limiting financial assistance for higher education to resident aliens who had either applied for citizenship or filed a statement of intent to apply when eligible. In both *Nyquist* and *Ambach*, aliens may alter their own classifications at will; therefore, the citizenship requirement does not seem unreasonable.

The second remaining category is that of documented aliens serving the period of permanent residency required before they may seek naturalization. The welfare reform law, as we have seen, creates a five-year durational residency requirement for most means-tested benefits. The denial of employment opportunities on the basis of alienage also affects this group adversely, as only the passage of time will enable these aliens to change their status by seeking naturalization. Here I believe we should err on the side of inclusivity. And it is here that the communitarian conception of immigration law, with its ascriptive model of citizenship, carries stronger claims than does the classical conception grounded in the consensual model. All individuals admitted to permanent residence in the United States are prospective citizens. Indeed, with the changes in current immigration law, more will probably become citizens than has been the case in the recent past. If we wish these prospective citizens to become full members of the community, not only politically but also economically and socially, we should afford them the opportunities and benefits of other residents who are citizens. Only thus will they participate in life as civilized beings in accordance with prevailing standards, in Marshall's terms. They are participants in our common life from the time they enter our borders. Insofar as citizenship involves more than a formal status, it is dynamic, something to which individuals become acculturated, rather than static, a discrete possession that individuals suddenly acquire through the oath of naturalization. Therefore, if we are willing to consent to their admission, we should also be willing to back up this consent with support in the form of opportunities and, where necessary, benefits. Thus, I agree with *Graham,* which struck down a durational residency requirement for welfare eligibility on the state level, over *Mathews,* which upheld such a requirement for Medicare supplemental insurance on the federal level.

One group of aliens I have not discussed is that of the children of undocumented aliens, both native-born children and children who, having as minors accompanied their undocumented parents here, are themselves undocumented.

It is the native-born children of undocumented aliens and nonimmigrant visitors to whom Schuck and Smith would allow Congress to deny birthright citizenship. Although they favor making the boundaries of the political
community a matter of self-conscious public choice, they do attend to the context, however, within which such choices are made. When such a proposal was
discussed in connection with the 1996 immigration reform, they noted that
effective control of illegal immigration is a crucial precondition for the elimination of birthright citizenship, because only such control will minimize the
number of children who could arrive here, yet perhaps forever be denied the
protection of citizenship. "Then—and only then—can Congress responsibly
consider eliminating birthright citizenship for illegal alien children." Meanwhile, Congress "'has an obligation to ensure that the . . . children, who
through no fault of their own are caught in a tragic statusless situation, can in
time become American citizens and truly join the society in which they will
have invested their pasts and are likely to invest their futures.'"[76]

I agree with Schuck's and Smith's qualification of their own position. It is
unclear either that a preponderance of undocumented mothers come to the
United States to take advantage of birthright citizenship or that they necessarily
secure an advantage in gaining legal status either for themselves or for other
family members. Stephen Chapman notes that nations like Germany do not provide at all for birthright citizenship, with the result that foreign nationals with
distant German ancestry may gain citizenship where third-generation ethnically
foreign residents who have never left the country may not. Denying birthright
citizenship here to the children of illegal immigrants would not discourage illegal entry but "would more likely fulfill the worst fears of the anti-immigration
forces—creating, out of people born within our borders, an unassimilable community of estranged aliens. It's hard to see how that could be an improvement
on a policy that, by treating them as Americans, makes them Americans." In
Schuck's testimonial words at a congressional hearing, "'Their children and
their children's children will continue to be outsiders mired in an inferior and
illegal status and deprived of the capacities of self-protection and self-advance-
ment.'"[77] This is a perfect recipe, in short, for the creation of a discrete and insular minority.

With respect to undocumented children, I agree with the Court's majority
in *Plyler* that given the fact that many will remain here indefinitely, often becoming documented residents and/or citizens, no rational basis exists for creating and perpetuating "a subclass of illiterates" who may contribute to social
problems and who at least will be marked with a lifelong stigma. As Schuck
and Smith argue with regard to birthright citizenship, only if we succeed much

better than we do now in preventing illegal entry in the first place will it make sense to deny public education to these children. Meanwhile, we should want those who remain here to develop the capacity to live according to the prevailing standards of life in the United States rather than, in Chapman's words, as "an unassimilable community of estranged aliens." In theory, the political community may choose whether to admit aliens to its territory and which ones to admit. But from a moral standpoint, once here, they are on the road to potential membership in the political community and ought to be treated as the potential members that they are.

Overall, I wish insofar as is possible to obliterate the existence of the range of different statuses held by individuals within the borders of the United States. Walzer suggests that "the rule of citizens over non-citizens, of members over strangers, is probably the most common form of tyranny in human history."[78] The nation-state can adopt in theory whatever principles of membership it might choose. But I believe that this choice is limited from the viewpoints of both liberal democracy and liberal communitarianism. With respect to liberal democracy, notes Walzer, we cannot argue that because aliens came to this country knowing what to expect and agreeing to the regulations governing their admission, they are therefore consenting in a kind of social contract. "But this kind of consent, given at a single moment in time, while it is sufficient to legitimate market transactions, is not sufficient for democratic politics. Political power is precisely the ability to make decisions over periods of time, to change the rules, to cope with emergencies; it can't be exercised democratically without the ongoing consent of its subjects. And its subjects include every man and woman who lives in the territory over which those decisions are enforced" (58). Although alien entrants need not immediately become full members, they must be regarded as potential members and respected as such. As Whelan suggests, liberal democracy presupposes membership in a civically bounded group through which individuals collectively exercise democratic rights. Although power over the admission of new members requires self-determination, these potential new members must be given educational and employment opportunities and benefits that will prepare them to share full membership in the political community. That is, all must have the opportunity to become part of the "we" who constitute this community.

With respect to liberal communitarianism, the political community will desire to preserve a way of life that is distinctively liberal, the integrity of which may require the exclusion of some individuals, this time on liberal rather than on democratic grounds. The members of the liberal political community, like the individual member, collectively possess autonomy, or the capacity to live life from the inside, and the capacity to question, examine, and revise their collective projects and goals. From a moral perspective, some of its choices may be better than others. If those persons inside the territorial boundaries of the community are to remain, however, they engage in interactions and build interdependencies with others, even when this is because the government failed to keep them out or to apprehend them once here. The presence of immigrants alters the political community by the fact of their presence, whether through formal membership, according to the consensual model, or through the influence of day-to-day living, according to the ascriptive model. In responding to their presence, we in the existing political community are forced to question, examine, and revise our collective projects and goals. Because ours is a *liberal* political community, we must enable the individuals within to develop their capacities for autonomy and to exercise this autonomy if they choose. This in turn means that *they* must be able to live their lives from the inside, and to question, examine, and revise their projects and goals, choosing among a range of possibilities as they do so. By giving them choices, we enable them to make their own choices.

The liberal tradition, in my interpretation, requires inclusiveness in our common life for those persons within our borders. Indeed, they are already included because they are already here. What is at issue is how we respond to their presence, and this response requires deliberation in the tradition of the concept of latent community. Chapman suggests that by treating aliens as Americans, we make them Americans. I suggest that for those who want to be here, by treating strangers as members, we make them members. As a "connected critic," I would argue that political rights are properly the culmination of community membership, not its start. In short, although liberal communitarianism requires a bounded political community vis-à-vis those outside, it can be both liberal and a community only if it is not bounded within.

3. Cultural Particularism in the Liberal Polity

We have seen that a bounded national community is required even for a liberal polity if its members are to possess a forum within which to construct and express shared values, projects, and goals, both collectively and individually. A national community, however, is seldom monolithic. In a liberal national entity, as Yael Tamir suggests, "its political system will reflect a particular national culture, but its citizens will be free to practice different cultures and follow a variety of life-plans and conceptions of the good."[1] I have argued that any state is necessarily based on some set of determinate principles and commitments; hence, legal neutrality among all possible conceptions of the good is impossible. I now advance the parallel argument that any state reflects a particular culture or cultural mixture; hence, the background conditions against which individuals and groups interact cannot reflect cultural neutrality. The question, then, is how we address the concerns of individuals and groups that do not share the dominant cultural background.

Because even liberal states typically contain implicit cultural norms, some practices will always fall outside these, although different liberal states will draw the boundaries in different places. As Deborah Fitzmaurice notes, "Even the minimal nightwatchman state proscribes lives of overt theft and violence."[2] But even if we accept some minimum as a matter of course and identify neutrality with a rejection of the superiority of particular conceptions of the good, neutrality is not self-explanatory. It may be understood either to permit a wide range of modes of life or, alternatively, to mandate the protection of "vulnerable modes of life from the erosive effects of public institutional arrangements" (5). In the first instance, ways of life that are permitted are tolerated as a matter of public policy, by default. In the second instance, ways of life for which protection is mandated are grounded in some decision as to which ways of life merit special protection if they are to exist on an equal footing with others. In both instances, decisions made in the public realm determine the scope of toleration or protection, which produces a tension well expressed by Maeve Cooke. "All proposals for structuring public life express some vision of human flourishing and human excellence, even when they explicitly strive not to do so. As such they inevitably exclude those who do not share the dominant vision."[3] Rather than focusing solely on the process of exclusion, however, we should also attend to the fact that some vision of human flourishing or human excellence is inevitable, trying to structure this vision in accordance with what we ourselves may believe about the conditions for flourishing or for excellence.

I have described the liberal polity as committed both to the background conditions for individual autonomy and self-development and to a culture of diversity containing a plurality of options. As we have seen, autonomy requires that we each develop the capacity to live our lives from the inside, and to question, examine, and revise our projects and goals. Cultural membership as a set of particular allegiances and commitments may function either to enhance or to inhibit this capacity. And if diversity requires a range of possibilities and the ability to envision what these possibilities entail, the existence of both a variety of cultural options and a variety of types of cultural affiliation will broaden this range. Attention to cultural particularism, then, is crucial to a focus on conditions for the development of the capacity for autonomy.

I shall outline the case for the value of cultural membership to the individual, particularly as this membership functions as a contribution to or an expression of individual autonomy. Then I shall examine the case for group-differentiated rights for members of national cultures who are effectively national minorities within a liberal nation-state. Although this contingency is the exception in the United States, my discussion is motivated by the way divergent responses to separatist versions of cultural membership illuminate the tension between autonomy and diversity when the latter is magnified. Some theorists would accord external protections against the larger society to the cultural *structure* of national minorities through group-differentiated rights. Others eschew external protections but would protect cultural *content* supporting the authority of cultural leaders to enforce traditional practices as a condition of membership. Some would accord legal protections and exemptions to individuals purely on the basis of minority status, and others would accord some internal autonomy to cultural communities without equating them with private associations. Each of these viewpoints is implicitly grounded on particular assumptions about the extent to which cultural membership is or is not a matter of choice. I maintain that although membership in some culture is a precondition of human agency, membership in any particular culture for mature adults is not a precondition of autonomy but should instead be regarded as an expression of it. The liberal polity should ensure the existence of a context of choice, maximizing the probability that cultural membership will indeed proceed from critical reflection and thus function as an expression of autonomy.

Cultural Membership

Even casual acquaintance with world events in the 1990s demonstrates the fact that individuals and groups are not assimilating into a common culture, despite the reciprocal interdependence supposedly promoted by global networks of information and transportation. Instead, individuals and groups are asserting or reasserting their particularist identities, be these ethnic, religious, cultural, or national. When diversity exists within a political entity, the thesis of the politics of multiculturalism, writes Charles Taylor, "is that our identity is partly shaped by recognition or its absence. . . . Non-recognition or misrecognition can inflict harm, can be a form of oppression, imprisoning someone in a false, distorted, and reduced mode of being."[4] The genesis of the human mind and of human agency is through interaction and interchange with others, giving human life "its fundamentally *dialogical* character" (32). That is, one's identity is defined and worked out in dialogue with others, even when the dialogue is hypothetical and internal. Individuality is developed, then, within a particular framework. For example, Tamir's concept of the contextual individual "portrays an autonomous person who can reflect on, evaluate, and choose his conception of the good, his ends, and his cultural and national affiliations, but is capable of such choices because he is situated in a particular social and cultural environment that offers him evaluative criteria."[5]

Too often, however, these evaluative criteria have been interpreted to minimize or suppress differences among individuals and groups. One major strain in modern liberal theory has premised the individual's civic identity as a free and equal individual on the dissolution of one's particularistic, cultural, or communitarian identity, when in reality civic culture "presupposes and remains dependent upon communitarian culture" and the particularistic building blocks that communitarian culture provides.[6] In this regard, I agree with Will Kymlicka and Tamir. For Kymlicka, cultural membership is a primary good, and its recognition contributes to and expands individual choice. "Cultural membership is not a means used in the pursuit of one's ends. It is rather the context within which we choose our ends, and come to see their value, and this is a precondition of self-respect, of the sense that one's ends are worth pursuing."[7] For Tamir, because the contextual individual is both a situated and a choosing self, "culture can be a precondition of reflective thinking and the exercise of choice, while in itself remaining an object of choice."[8]

Cultural particularism appears desirable in two respects. First, without a plurality of cultures, individuals cannot make choices among cultures. One's cultural context not only denotes a primary communal membership from within which one develops one's moral identity, but it also may provide a culturally plural environment from within which one may make cultural choices. Thus cultural pluralism benefits the members of or participants in given cultural groups, those who may borrow from or even assimilate into a particular culture from outside, and, finally, everyone else "for whom the existence of any culture enriches their own experience of what it means to be human" (32). Beyond its instrumental value, cultural pluralism's second claim to desirability lies in its intrinsic value. I believe that cultural communities as well as nations meet Tamir's test in which "recognition of fellow members, the drawing of boundaries between members and nonmembers . . . becomes a product of human imagination, contingent on the belief that there are similarities among members" (68). That is, feelings of similarity provide a sense of belonging. Although the right to adhere to a particular culture is an individual right and interest, culture also functions as a space for the expression of one's communal identity (42–48) with its special ties and obligations. Particularistic ties, once again, are not parochial attachments to be transcended in the course of individual moral development but fulfill a need that is part of the human condition.

I agree with Kymlicka that cultural membership functions as a primary good in the same way as self-respect. Both are preconditions of living good lives as we decide what has value in our lives, or as we question, examine, and possibly revise our projects and goals. Our cultural heritage determines the range of our options, and thus it functions as a precondition for lives that have meaning for us. Although particular cultural structures do not have moral status of their own, "it's only through having a rich and secure cultural structure that people can become aware, in a vivid way, of the options available to them, and intelligently examine their value."[9] Our cultural heritage provides a context in or background against which we may consider various life plans, projects, and goals. This heritage appears to play two roles. First, in James Nickel's words, it provides a range of choices that ground autonomy.[10] Second, it provides a means through which people test and confirm the value of choices they make.[11] For Kymlicka our beliefs about value depend upon the amalgam of values that constitute the cultural context. Our values, like our identities, are formed dialogically. We cannot evaluate their worth in isolation, but we require the presence and reactions of others. These form a mirror that reflects and clarifies our values and their worth.[12] For scholars like Tamir and Kymlicka, it is cultural heritage specifically that provides the mirror.

Kymlicka's focus is two sorts of cultural diversity. National minorities denote "previously self-governing, territorially concentrated cultures" now incorporated into a larger, multination state. These national minorities often demand some type of self-government to ensure the cultural survival of their distinct societies. Ethnic groups denote loose associations of individuals and families who immigrated into and now want to become full members of the larger society, now a polyethnic state. Although they may seek recognition of their identity, they desire mainstream accommodation of their cultural differences, not separation.[13] His argument for group-differentiated citizenship with group-differentiated rights is grounded on the distinction between the unchosen incorporation of minority nations and the voluntary status of immigrants. The former have legitimate claims to self-government that the latter do not (66), although members of ethnic groups may properly claim polyethnic rights to various measures and exemptions that facilitate the expression of cultural particularity within the institutions of the dominant culture (see chapter 4).

The purpose of self-government rights is to protect the cultural autonomy of the societal culture, one "which provides its members with meaningful ways of life across the full range of human activities, including social, educational, religious, recreational, and economic life, encompassing both public and private spheres," typically concentrated geographically and using one language (76). Because cultural membership provides a context of choice, including both "a range of meaningful options" (83) and "a secure sense of identity and belonging" (105), access to one's culture is an entitlement that we should expect people to desire (86). Although individuals may integrate themselves into cultures other than their original ones, the difficulty of this enterprise suggests that if undertaken, this should be a matter of choice, not necessity. However, Kymlicka attends not only to the autonomy of national minorities collectively but also to that of their individual members. That is, he endorses external protections for societal cultures that promote their integrity within the larger national community, but he rejects internal restrictions, "which limit the right of group members to question and revise traditional authorities and practices" (37). He believes that freedom of choice requires cultural preconditions like the right to cultural membership but that we should not structure preconditions in ways that hamper subsequent choices.

Specifically, although we are "dependent on a cultural community for our self-development and for our context of choice," we may rightly claim independence, "as self-directed beings, from any of the specific roles and relationships that exist in the community."[14] On the one hand, cultural membership should not disadvantage individuals as a result of unchosen constituents of their identities. Thus for some, "Special political rights are needed to remove inequalities in the context of choice which arise before people even make their choices" (190). On the other hand, recognition of a cultural structure should not be used for the preservation of any particular cultural character. Although some theorists defend cultural membership as a primary good in order "to protect their particular preferred vision" of communal character (168), on Kymlicka's view "the cultural community continues to exist even when its members are free to modify the character of the culture, should they find its traditional ways of life no longer worth while" (167). The enforced maintenance of a particular cultural character would limit rather than protect the future choices of the culture's members, and "liberals are committed to supporting the rights of individuals to decide for themselves which aspects of their cultural heritage are worth passing on."[15] Although outside interference causing the disappearance of a culture *despite* its members' choices violates their right to cultural membership, its alteration or disappearance *because* of its members' choices to incorporate, for instance, aspects of the outside world does not.

Moreover, the same liberal defense of autonomy that upholds the right to cultural membership against the larger society also justifies the claims of the individual against traditional authorities and practices within a minority culture.[16] In both cases, individuals have rights against the group, or groups have rights against the nation-state, that ensure both that they can lead lives from the inside, in accordance with their own beliefs about value, and that they can form those values by questioning, examining, and possibly revising their current beliefs about value. Cultural membership functions as a primary good for Kymlicka, we can infer, not simply intrinsically but because we expect it to expand rather than to limit freedom. Although we are partly constituted by prior attachments and experiences as we make judgments about the good life for us, "no particular cultural practice has authority that is beyond individual judgment and possible rejection. . . . Nothing is 'set for us,' nothing is authoritative before our judgment of its value."[17] In each case, either the individual or the cultural collectivity must endorse a particular authority or practice if the values it expresses are to be judged as contributing to a life that is good for the individuals involved.

The desire to avoid the imposition of seemingly reasonable values on those who cannot identify with them is the major impetus behind both self-government rights for members of national minorities and polyethnic rights for members of ethnic groups who wish to maintain a degree of cultural particularity in the face of the dominant culture. According to Amélie Rorty, the arguments of theorists like Taylor and, indirectly, Tamir suggest that "the claim to the right of cultural survival and of cultural self-determination . . . appears to derive from the right accorded to citizens of a liberal state actively to pursue their conceptions of a good life. If the state legitimately promotes the self-defining activities of individuals—centrally, for instance, assuring their basic education—it is also charged with promoting the self-defining activities of its constitutive cultural groups."[18] The issue is not one of choosing between a nonexistent cultural neutrality and an accommodation of cultural differences but one of how the inevitable cultural differences should be handled. I shall summarize three other accounts of cultural membership that differ from Kymlicka's in important particulars, and these four accounts will then function as a basis for a consideration of the ways in which recognition of cultural membership may provide both a variety of cultural options and background conditions for development of the capacity for autonomy.

Cultural membership is a central concern for Chandran Kukathas, but for him it is the right of association, not the right of a cultural community, that is fundamental. Although the right of association is an individual right, nevertheless "it gives considerable power to the group, denying others the right to intervene in its practices—whether in the name of liberalism or any other moral ideal."[19] By privileging individual autonomy over cultural integrity in cultural structures where autonomy and critical reflection are not valued, for instance, Kymlicka in Kukathas's view undermines the very cultural rights he purports to defend. Since those disenchanted with the cultural character of a community may leave, "what matters most when assessing whether a way of life is legitimate is whether the individuals taking part in it are prepared to acquiesce in it" (124). Although Kymlicka's liberalism is compatible with minority rights, it does not in Kymlicka's view justify the rights of a culture against its own members.[20] Kukathas suggests, by contrast, that if the social unions or groups that compose a liberal society are to maintain their integrity, they "must *to some extent* be impervious to the values of the wider liberal society."[21] Overall, where Kymlicka's liberal society champions the substantive values of equality and individual autonomy, Kukathas defends one in which different ways of life can coexist even if some of those ways of life do not value equality and autonomy.[22] Kymlicka defends cultural membership through the protection of cultural structure, rather than content or practice; but Kukathas defends it by protecting its members' right to adhere to practices without the formal recognition of cultural structure.

A key variable in this dispute lies in the fact that where Kukathas perceives cultural membership as chosen by its adherents, Kymlicka does not—or at least not initially. For Kymlicka, "A liberal needs to know whether a request for special rights or resources is grounded in differential choices or unequal circumstances." In the case of native cultures, cultural minorities "have to spend their resources on securing the cultural membership which makes sense of their lives, something which nonaboriginal people get for free."[23] If cultural membership is a background condition or context of choice that necessarily grounds subsequent choices, individuals whose cultural context is disrupted are disadvantaged in a morally arbitrary way on the basis of unchosen constituents of their identities.[24] Although rights attached to cultural membership can strengthen cultural ties and identities, this effort to respond to differences, however, "may turn into a process of reification, leading to a false imputation of essentialist qualities to the members of some group, ignoring important variations within groups."[25] Essentialist or totalizing claims, then, may be made not only at the expense of groups within the whole but also at the expense of individuals within a particular group.

We may avoid this sort of essentialism in an approach like Tamir's, according to which "respect is due to cultural preferences not by virtue of their intrinsic contents, but because they reflect autonomous choices." Each of us is born with a particularistic identity, but this does not preclude our moving beyond these identities. "We can reflect on them critically and exercise choices regarding our future commitments and affiliations. . . . Furthermore, not only should individuals have a right to choose the . . . group they wish to belong to, but they should also have the right to define the meanings attached to this membership, that is, they should be the ones to decide on the cultural practices they wish to adopt, and on the ways of expressing them."[26] Because affirming one's identity with one's native culture and choosing a different cultural identity are equally matters of choice, both options should be subsidized, as it were, by according special rights if identity with one's chosen culture results in unequal circumstances compared with membership in other cultures. "Membership in a cultural community is a matter of personal choice, but this does not imply that members have chosen to be a minority" (41–42).[27] Moreover, once cultural membership is recognized, Tamir holds that individuals should interpret for themselves the meanings of their cultural identities, whether they choose their cultural memberships or affirm their original ones.

Although Tamir and Kymlicka diverge in their views of the extent to which the affirmation of unchosen constituents of identity is a matter of choice, both avoid essentialist or totalizing claims through their belief that members of a cultural community should be free to modify its character or to define for themselves the meaning of their membership, to become, in the words of Jeff Spinner, "self-interpreting."[28] Yet Spinner, like Kukathas, disagrees with Kymlicka "that liberal rights transcend cultures." Because he supports the preservation of a meaningful context of individual choice, Kymlicka's focus on cultural structure over content or practice buttresses individual choice both in maintaining and in changing a culture. But the net effect for Spinner is that "Kymlicka allows his liberalism to run amuck, destroying the very cultures he wants to protect. . . . In other words, the liberal state should protect minority cultures in its midst—as long as they are liberal!" (96). If community members who would reinterpret the practices of the Old Order Amish may do so, for example, while remaining in the Amish community, the resulting dilution of cultural homogeneity may cause these communities to disappear, actually allowing for far less diversity among distinctive cultures. "This shows a paradox of liberal theory; liberalism allows people to reject liberal values. The liberal state cannot insist that its citizens embrace liberalism. Liberalism allows people to think for themselves, to make their own decisions—or even to decide not to think for themselves" (97).[29]

On the other hand, Spinner disagrees with Kukathas that a cultural community is purely a private association and that as such it must therefore possess a high degree of internal autonomy. First, cultures change over time; a particular interpretation of cultural identity should not be permanently entrenched. "Second, not all cultural practices should be protected simply because they are someone's cultural practices. Illiberal practices should not be protected" (135–136).[30] Finally, cultural diversity can coexist with the economic subordination of some groups to others; celebration of the former should not eclipse the presence of the latter. Spinner's model of what he calls pluralistic integration appears as a compromise between Kymlicka's willingness to dilute cultural content or practices, on the one hand, and Kukathas's willingness to equate cultural communities with private associations, on the other. We may infer not only that cultural identity is not merely a private affair but also that the degree to which it *is* private is publicly determined and is therefore a public concern. By discouraging or forbidding illiberal practices and by emphasizing specific practices rather than cultures, "pluralistic integration rejects the idea that cultures are somehow sacrosanct and need to be protected at all costs" (76).[31]

But if Spinner's distinction constitutes a compromise, how much room is there really for cultures that want to remain distinctive? If no society is truly culturally neutral, correspondingly no culture can celebrate or even tolerate all practices, not even the civic culture of liberalism. Although a focus on cultural practices rather than on structure may legitimate a greater number of practices, the larger community decides on the legitimacy of given practices, thus still controlling the content of cultural identity by extending or withdrawing its protection. Thus the right to a cultural context involves not only a cultural claim but also a political one, a facet of cultural identity not always recognized by its defenders.[32] Another way of putting this is that the liberal polity itself is the legal expression of a particular cultural structure. On this view, the liberal polity is a voluntary association with substantive purposes. It is "not merely . . . a gathering of individuals striving to improve their lot, but rather . . . a community struggling to preserve its distinctive character."[33] The question is how this distinctive character may be expressed in both its commonalities and its diversities. In my view, particularistic cultural membership has value when it expresses and enhances the critical reflection that is the hallmark of individual autonomy. It does not have value when it hinders this autonomy.

Minority Cultures

Let us now examine the case for group-differentiated rights for members of national cultures who are effectively national minorities within a liberal nation-state. For Kymlicka, our original cultural situation is an unchosen constituent of our identity. If it is the culture of a national minority, it should therefore be accorded the protection that only special legal status affords against the encroachment of the dominant culture. Kukathas and Tamir, however, both imply that membership is always chosen. But where Kukathas would support membership as acquiescence in a way of life simply by honoring freedom of association, Tamir would accord legal protections and exemptions to cultural minorities because they *are* minorities, however members came by that status. For Kukathas, because the affirmation of our birth culture and our choice of affiliation with a different culture are equally matters of choice, no reason exists to facilitate one choice over the other. For Tamir, on the other hand, either choice may afford us minority status, and it is this minority status in the face of the dominant culture that requires compensation, rather than the fact that we may adhere to an unchosen status. For Spinner, by contrast, culture may or may not be chosen by its adherents, but the *practices* of a culture are chosen, implicitly, by the individuals who are its members. Although he is unwilling to dilute cultural content or practices incompatible with liberalism to the extent that Kymlicka is, neither does he join Kukathas in equating cultural communities with strictly private associations. If the liberal polity is itself the legal expression of a particular cultural structure that it must often struggle to preserve, as I have suggested, the values of subcultures like national minorities and other ethnic groups will often diverge from the values instantiated by the national political community. This confluence of developments in turn increases the possibility that various individuals or groups will experience the impact of the larger society's values as a form of imposition.

If cultural membership provides a context of choice, providing both a range of options and a source of beliefs about value, as Kymlicka asserts, it implicitly functions as a precondition of the development of the capacity for autonomy, which in turn enables us to question, examine, and revise or reaffirm our current projects and goals. If this membership is a precondition rather than an object of autonomy, however, it is in some sense a given and not itself subject to critical reflection and possible revision. Because Kymlicka would grant greater protection to the cultural distinctiveness of individuals maintaining their allegiance to their culture of origin than to those who have exercised their autonomy to revise their cultural commitments, his position is ironic. As Geoffrey Brahm Levey writes, "Those groups whose cultural rights Kymlicka's theory was originally designed to defend—namely, indigenous groups—tend to be among the nonliberal groups whose self-government rights require some other defense than his autonomy-based theory."[34] That is, Kymlicka implicitly justifies cultural membership by its contribution to the capacity for autonomy but simultaneously suggests that the groups for whom a defense of cultural membership is most crucial are those least likely to emphasize the development of this capacity. Because nonliberal groups generally do not value autonomy, for such groups cultural membership cannot be its precondition.

Levey, however, would reverse the relationship between cultural membership and autonomy and interpret cultural membership as the *expression* of autonomy rather than as its precondition. I agree. On maturity, we affirm our original cultural membership or affiliate with a different culture as a matter of implicit choice, ideally grounded in critical reflection. Liberals should base the protection of cultures or of particular cultural practices directly on the value of individual autonomy, bypassing the intermediate value of cultural membership as a context of choice. If a disparity is thought unjust in the legal status accorded to some practices as compared with others, for example, "then it is not in virtue of mere disparity, nor because people are being denied some abstract access to a culture as a context of choice. It is that citizens are being denied . . . a particular and preferred option that is entirely consonant with liberal values" (237). Similarly, we may accord self-government rights to nonliberal groups, but for liberal reasons. In Levey's view, groups that steadfastly maintain their societal culture, territorial concentration, and institutional embodiment in social institutions display a degree of solidarity, sincerity, and "moral seriousness" such that they should be accorded at least a prima facie right to political autonomy. Yet the proper justification for such policies is not a right to respect for cultural membership as a context of choice but a right to autonomy (239–240).

If cultural membership is an expression of autonomy, however, we must be wary of equating with autonomy every expression of this membership. Levey on the one hand justifies the costs of special provisions for cultural minorities, such as the provision of court interpreters for persons who do not speak English, on grounds that without the ability to communicate, individuals cannot be "critically reflective and self-directive" or act as autonomous agents (234). In other cases, respect for autonomy requires that we *not* facilitate individual preferences that seem unauthentic, irrational, or threatening to the autonomy of oneself or others. Thus, "Viewing cultural practices as the exercise of individual autonomy need not imply that every personal choice, idiosyncratic whim, or experiment in individuality should be accommodated, if not supported, by government" (235). On the other hand, Levey believes that self-governing, nonliberal minorities can make at least an initial claim against the imposition of liberal values, regardless of whether their members are "critically reflective and self-directive" in the way they conduct their lives, individually and collectively. In other words, even if we interpret cultural membership as an expression of autonomy rather than as its precondition, this does not mean that autonomy itself has no preconditions, but only that cultural membership in one's culture of origin is not one of them. Membership in some culture is a precondition of any sort of human agency, but membership in any particular culture on maturity is an expression of autonomy. My focus, then, is on the nature of preconditions that maximize the likelihood that cultural membership will represent an expression of autonomy.

THE COMMON MORAL STANDPOINT

For Kukathas, the dilemma posed by conflict between the larger political community and its subcultures is a function of a particular conception of political community. Any community "is essentially *an association of individuals who share an understanding of what is public and what is private within that association*";[35] a political community simply shares this understanding with respect to matters within that polity. Because any community is also a partial association, or only one among several to which individuals have ties, liberals are mistaken when they assume the centrality of the political community, vesting in it the "ultimate authority [in] determining what practices or ways of life are permissible" (96). The question of the limits of cultural tolerance arises, then, only because liberals inadvisedly resemble communitarians in presupposing the existence of a common moral standpoint. "Toleration . . . arises as an issue . . . because of the possibility of dissent—whether by word or by practice—from the values implicit in that common standpoint."[36]

For Kukathas, the state differs from its subcultures or subcommunities in that it, and by implication only it, is an association of diverse associations, or "an area of convergence of different moral practices" (84). Thus, although it is acceptable for illiberal subgroups themselves to prevent the formation of liberal subgroups within their own midsts, it is morally illegitimate for liberals to prevent the formation of illiberal subgroups within the state (93–99). "The state is a political settlement which encompasses these diverse associations, but it is not their creator or shaper" (94). Having no legitimate claims in its own right, it lacks the authority to impose norms, liberal or not, on its members as subcommunities do on theirs. The efforts of theorists like Kymlicka to promote meaningful individual choice threaten the cultural integrity and identity of subcultures that do not affirm the value of individual autonomy and choice.[37]

Kymlicka responds, however, that identifying which sorts of minority claims are consistent with liberal principles differs from imposing those principles.[38] He perceives in fact an asymmetry between contemporary liberals' growing reluctance to impose liberalism outside the nation-state and their greater willingness to impose it on national minorities within the state. Negotiation and agreement should replace coercive interference, to the point that this might in specific circumstances exempt a national minority from the applications of federal bills of rights or judicial review. Although liberals should speak out against injustice and offer incentives for reform, "liberals in the majority group have to learn to live with this, just as they must live with illiberal laws in other countries."[39] Thus in practice, Kukathas and Kymlicka alike share a reluctance to allow the national political community to interfere with the practices of cultural minorities. Although Kymlicka suggests that intervention is justified by systematic violations of human rights in slavery or genocide (169), the actual point of intervention is a practical and empirical matter, dependent on the severity of these violations, the consensus within the relevant community, the ability of dissenters to leave, and the existence of historical agreements. Both men imply that any change should emanate from the minority culture itself. The difference is that whereas Kymlicka would empower individuals to influence cultural character from the bottom up, within a secure cultural structure, Kukathas wants cultural traditions or authorities to have primacy and to sanction any change from the top down, so that individual members who want change would leave rather than changing the culture from within. And even Kukathas suggests that "the acceptability of cultural norms and practices depends in part on the degree to which the cultural community is independent of the larger society."[40]

As the legal expression of a particular cultural structure, however, the liberal polity cannot and should not, I believe, avoid the instantiation of a common moral standpoint. Michael Walzer reminds us that "toleration is not absolute even in international society," noting the common albeit uneven practice of humanitarian intervention.[41] Moreover, the settlement governing the nature of political society to which Kukathas refers is not a finished product of a moment in time but instead emerges through ongoing negotiation that represents "the gradual shaping of a common . . . political life" (108). As new groups arrive or become visible, the settlement is renegotiated on new terms of inclusion or exclusion, depending on specific social practices.

Political society may be an association of diverse associations, but at any given point, we can still identify an established moral standpoint, even though this changes over time. If, as Kukathas argues, all communities, including the political one, are partial associations whose members share an understanding of what is public and what is private within their particular association, different political societies will draw the distinction in different places. And the *same* political society will mark the distinction differently at different points in its history. Domestic violence between spouses or that of parents against children, for example, was in Western countries once deemed a private matter; change in the status of marital rape provides another instance. Therefore, even a community by Kukathas's definition is open to the possibility and probability of displaying a common moral standpoint.

If all communities share some understanding that emerges and is negotiated and renegotiated over time, no external rule exists that dictates what this understanding should look like. Whether the public realm simply represents a convergence of different moral practices, as Kukathas advocates, or instead embodies a common moral standpoint that regulates some of the practices of subcultures makes no difference. Even a collective decision to treat the public realm as an area of convergence that allows the widest possible scope for varied cultural practices still emerges from a common moral standpoint at that time in that polity. It is not feasible, then, for a polity to reject the notion of a common standpoint altogether. It can only reject certain *kinds* of standpoints, those that conflict with the understanding currently shared. To put the matter differently, if we agree that the public realm shall operate as an area of convergence for different moral practices, we are affirming these practices, not directly, but by affirming a distinct conceptualization of what the public realm should look like, whatever the specific conceptions of morality that various groups bring to this convergence. We are thus affirming a metatheory of the public realm that is itself a moral standpoint. Although the polity may decide to practice laissez-faire, nevertheless it is neither culturally nor morally neutral.

AUTONOMY AND CULTURAL STRUCTURE

Given the ineluctability of nonneutrality, then, how do we maximize the likelihood that cultural membership will represent an expression of autonomy, resulting from critical reflection rather than from unthinking affirmation? Although Kymlicka wants to protect cultural structures as preconditions of autonomy, his accompanying desire for internal guarantees to protect individual dissenters, and implicitly to function as expressions of autonomy, seems incompatible with the group-differentiated rights that he advocates. My own commitment to promoting conditions for the development of the capacity for autonomy impels me to opt for individual expression over cultural protection when these values conflict, as I believe they often do. Here I shall explain why.

John Rawls's political conception of the person describes citizens as capable of taking responsibility for their ends, including tastes and preferences, and of adjusting them in the light of realistically formed expectations, whether or not these tastes and preferences have arisen from our actual choices. Thus, "Given their capacity to assume responsibility for their ends, we do not view citizens as passive carriers of desires. That capacity is part of the moral power to form, to revise, and rationally to pursue a conception of the good."[42] Yet Rawls also distinguishes between citizens' public or institutional identity, which remains the same even when they revise their determinate conceptions of the good, and their moral or noninstitutional identity, according to which "they may regard it as simply unthinkable to view themselves apart from certain religious, philosophical, and moral convictions, or from certain enduring attachments and loyalties" (31). This distinction parallels that between the political and ethical values of autonomy, whereby citizens may simultaneously realize autonomy as a political value, by affirming the principles of justice and the values these protect, but reject autonomy as a comprehensive and ethical value, or as a regulative ideal to which all other values are subordinate even in private life (77–78, 98–99, 199). Autonomy, then, describes our public but not our nonpublic identity.

As Kymlicka points out, however, Rawls implicitly assumes that our religious, philosophical, and moral convictions may constitute our identities to such a degree that we cannot stand back to question, examine, and revise projects and goals that are informed by these convictions. Although Rawls makes this assumption to avoid imposing a robust conception of autonomy on those who do not value the capacity to revise their conceptions of the good, argues Kymlicka, Rawls's description of nonpublic identity is actually a communitarian one, and "Rawls has not explained why people who are communitarians in private life should be liberals in political life."[43] Those who view their commitments as constitutive of the self may experience difficulty in divesting themselves of these commitments for purposes of exercising political judgment. And to the extent that they are successful, this habit may permeate their private identities and cause them to value autonomy more comprehensively than their expressed commitments allow. "Rawls is mistaken, therefore, to suppose that he can avoid appealing to the general value of individual autonomy without undermining his argument for the priority of civil rights. The mere fact of *social plurality,* disconnected from any assumption of *individual autonomy,* cannot by itself defend the full range of liberal freedoms" (163).

In short, Rawls cannot simultaneously defend both the nonrevisability of nonpublic commitments and also the political value of autonomy. Moreover, this contradiction bears on the issue of the extent to which we are responsible for our desires and preferences. If our religious, philosophical, and moral convictions are constitutive of our nonpublic identities to the extent that we cannot question, examine, and revise these convictions, how then can we take responsibility for them? Yet Rawls states not only that we are not passive carriers of desires but also that we are responsible for our tastes and preferences *whether or not* these emanate from choices we have actually made. If this is true, and I believe that it is true both ontologically and also as a requirement of successful social cooperation, then we must regard *all* our moral commitments as revisable.

Although Kymlicka faults Rawls for limiting the potential revisability of our moral commitments in order to limit the reach of autonomy and thereby to broaden the reach of his overlapping consensus, Kymlicka himself, however, implies that cultural membership is a nonrevisable commitment, albeit for different reasons. As we have seen, Kymlicka would grant unique protection to those who maintain their allegiance to their culture of origin, even when such cultures do not encourage or positively discourage their members from questioning, examining, and revising their projects and goals. On my own understanding of the capacity for autonomy, it is not mandatory that individuals actually revise these projects and goals. Although the exercise of autonomy involves questioning and examining them, this examination may lead one either to affirm them or to revise current commitments and to make new ones. What is crucial is the capacity for and the exercise of rational deliberation and criti-

cal reflection, whatever the outcome of this process. Therefore, it is not problematic in itself for me that Kymlicka favors groups that are typically cultures
of origin over groups that are chosen cultures. Large numbers of individuals
remaining in their cultures of origin, after all, may well have deliberated about
and reflected upon their allegiances. But because often we can only judge the
autonomy of preferences by the history of preference formation, the degree
to which a group or subculture encourages rational deliberation and critical
reflection is at least a necessary if not a sufficient indicator of the extent to
which its members are acting autonomously.

Other aspects of Kymlicka's account, however, are in fact problematic in my
view. First, cultures or groups that do not encourage or that actively discourage
critical reflection are more likely to be cultures of origin than cultures that comprise many new adherents or devotees, the point made by Levey. After all, the
latter type of culture is by definition constituted by those who did question,
examine, and actually revise their previous commitments. And the former sort
of culture is a candidate, on Kymlicka's interpretation, for rights that enable it
to maintain its distinctiveness, perhaps rendering even more difficult its members' efforts to engage in critical reflection. But Kymlicka supports these rights
because he views cultures of origin as contexts of choice that provide a range
of meaningful options and sources of beliefs about value, whereas cultures of
choice apparently either do not perform these functions or do not require this
protection. Defenders of cultural membership like Kukathas and Tamir avoid
this distinction and its attendant difficulties, Kukathas because he eschews cultural rights altogether, and Tamir because she would extend them to members
of any group with minority status. But by valorizing the protection of cultures
of origin over subsequently chosen ones, Kymlicka suggests that they play a
unique role. Although he never explicitly suggests that our cultural commitments are nonrevisable, there is something about our cultures of origin and
their effects on us that merit special protection. "Someone's upbringing isn't
something that can just be erased; it is, and will remain, a constitutive part of
who that person is. Cultural membership affects our very sense of personal
identity and capacity."[44]

Second, I believe that *any* given culture can function as a context of choice
for its members, providing both a range of meaningful options for choice and
a source of beliefs about value. Kymlicka is right to assert that upbringing is a
constitutive part of our identity; our experiences during our formative years
mark us in undeniable fashion. But if we opt to leave our original culture to
associate ourselves with a different culture, does not this new culture then
become for us our new context of choice, providing perhaps a different range

of options and a source of different beliefs about value? And together do these not provide a different, but still essential, sense of identity and belonging? I would answer both of these questions in the affirmative. If, as Kymlicka declares, "nothing is 'set for us,' nothing is authoritative before our judgment of its value" (51), cultures of origin and cultures of choice should be equally central to our identities.

Our alternatives are initially those offered to us within the context of our culture of origin, both the particular options among which we may choose, and also the amalgam of cultural values that we utilize to confirm the worth of our own choices. But in a different culture, one of our own choosing, the alternatives found there still function as a context for *future* examination, questioning, and revision of our current projects and goals, just as the alternatives within our culture of origin once served. Tamir suggests that the contextual individual can autonomously choose his or her ends and affiliations because he or she "is situated in a particular social and cultural environment that offers . . . evaluative criteria."[45] But the individual is *always* situated in some cultural environment, whether one of origin or one of subsequent choice, and either offers these evaluative criteria. Or, put differently, to the extent that cultural membership may be regarded as a precondition of autonomy, everyone is culturally situated, whether by origin or by choice, and therefore the claim that cultural membership requires protection is generalizable enough to appear trivial.

Third, despite his critique of the communitarianism he perceives in Rawls's account of the political value of autonomy, Kymlicka's own conception of cultural membership as a precondition of autonomy is itself grounded in some communitarian assumptions, suggests Don Lenihan. Kymlicka hypothetically asks, "Why not let minority cultural communities disintegrate, and assist those who suffer that misfortune to assimilate to another culture?"[46] But because of the ostensible uniqueness of one's culture of origin in identity formation, he concludes, "respecting people's own cultural membership and facilitating their transition to another culture are not equally legitimate options" (176). On this argument, notes Lenihan, "Then any cultural group which wants to make a claim to special protection (rights) against assimilation by another group must demonstrate that the move will better promote the well-being of its members than assimilation."[47] But this conclusion is welfare-based rather than autonomy-based and contradicts Kymlicka's general intuition that we must ourselves endorse the values that ground our lives, whatever others might believe, if we are to lead what are good lives for *us*.

Finally, Kymlicka's privileging of one's culture of origin blurs the distinction he wants to make between cultural structure, which he would protect as a context of choice, and cultural character, which he endorses not as defined by tradition or authority but only by its members who should be free to advocate change. If cultures of origin play a unique role, then in theory they should be maintained in their original character for paternalistic reasons against any impetus to change, even if this comes from inside the culture. "For his argument rests squarely on the claim that the *character* of cultural communities has a unique moral significance which political institutions and practices must respect. But this is precisely what the character/context distinction seemed to deny" (416).[48] Once again, his claim to special significance for cultures of origin emphasizes their constitutive role in individual identity formation, but without showing how they function as preconditions of autonomy in ways that chosen cultures cannot. As Allen Buchanan suggests, "An appreciation of the value of cultural membership cannot by itself . . . support a right to the continued existence of any particular culture. What is important is that an individual be able to belong to a culture, some culture or other, not that he be able to belong, indefinitely, to any particular culture."[49]

If cultural membership provides a context of choice, including both a range of options and a set of evaluative criteria, the choices offered within our specific cultural situation, however, are opportunities for the *expression* of autonomy. Buchanan suggests that a culture's function as a context of choice is both to limit the range of alternatives to a manageable set and to offer continuity and structure for otherwise fragmented goals (356). Thus, it provides a framework within which choices are made as a precondition of agency; and certain kinds of choices, those grounded in rational deliberation and critical reflection, will constitute an expression of autonomy. But the presence of a range of options and of a set of evaluative criteria, although necessary conditions of human agency, appear in all cultures, not only in our cultures of origin. Moreover, cultures are not necessarily separate, distinct, or internally homogenized. All traditions are defined and characterized by conflict; their development presents us with no conclusion "which is not open to further revision, elaboration, emendation, or refutation."[50] If cultural membership is to function as a precondition or as an expression of autonomy, this is partly because of the diversity that it presents, both within and among cultures.

DIVERSITY AND CULTURAL STRUCTURE

Both equality of access to one's original culture as a context of choice and historical agreements generate justifications for the protection of cultural rights, according to Kymlicka. The promotion of cultural diversity, however, is overrated as a justification in his view. Because he would protect cultures of origin as contexts of choice for their existing members, diversity is valuable for those within such a culture only insofar as public policy protects their own cultural membership. He implicitly views national minorities as instances of separate cultures within the national state rather than as cultural subdivisions, as it were, of the larger culture. Whereas diversity within a culture ostensibly creates more options and expands the range of possible choices, for Kymlicka, "Indeed, measures to protect national minorities may actually reduce diversity within the majority culture, compared with a situation where minorities, unable to maintain their own societal culture, are forced to integrate and add their distinctive contribution to the diversity of the mainstream culture."[51]

The cost to the majority culture of granting group-differentiated rights to national minorities may be high, admits Kymlicka, compared to that of more varied immigration or of protection for the specific cultural practices of ethnic groups. Moreover, if our goal is diversity within the larger culture, "Why then does the value of diversity not also justify imposing a duty on members of the minority to maintain their traditional culture? If the benefits of cultural diversity to the larger society can justify restricting individual liberties or opportunities, why does it matter whether those restrictions are imposed on people inside or outside the group?"[52] Although he does not say so explicitly, from his viewpoint the argument from diversity proves both too little and too much. It proves too little because it does not show us why group-differentiated rights are preferable to other forms of diversity. It proves too much because it cannot maintain his distinction between cultural structures, which should be preserved, and cultural character, which will persist if and only if the culture's members desire it. If the members of cultural minorities should decide for themselves what their membership means and what aspects of their cultures are worth preserving, which I believe is correct, this point counts both against internal cultural tradition and authority and also against majority attempts to dictate cultural character. The value of cultural membership as Kymlicka interprets it, however, appears to militate in favor of cultural preservation at all costs.

I have been arguing that membership in some culture is a precondition of agency and that the exercise of cultural membership in a particular culture, whether a culture of origin or one subsequently chosen, is an expression of autonomy. But this presents us with a dilemma. If as members of a culture we engage in rational deliberation and critical reflection, and choose to change our culture in ways that narrow the range of options among which future choices may be made, we are sacrificing the preservation of diversity in the future to the present value of autonomy. If, on the other hand, we opt for the preservation of the greatest possible range of options for their own sake, we are sacrificing the present value of the expression of autonomy to the future value of diversity. Kymlicka wants to prevent cultural disintegration and assimilation from without because of the uniquely constitutive function performed by cultures of origin, and he wants to allow changes in cultural character from within on grounds of self-determination. But he defends neither policy for the sake of diversity, in the sense of preserving the greatest possible range of choice. If a cultural context provides a range of options for choice and a set of evaluative criteria as a basis for making those choices, however, might a broader range of options not be preferable to a narrower one? And might a larger set of evaluative criteria not be more valuable than a smaller one? If traditions are characterized by debate and conflict, and if they inevitably influence each other, then cultural protection cannot rely on a defense from diversity as compartmentalization, but it cannot do so for reasons different from those Kymlicka gives.

There is a broader reason for protecting cultural structures that multiply distinct opportunities and choices. The absence of such protection may lead to the obliteration of an entire way of life for those in the future who may find value in it, regardless of the value placed on it at present. Allowing matters to proceed unimpeded is not, Ronald Dworkin suggests, "neutral amongst competing ideas of the good life, but in fact destructive of the very possibility of some of those."[53] But on this interpretation, allowing either cultural structure to disintegrate or cultural character to change will destroy some ways of life for individuals who might find them good. Moreover, even if cultural structures are insulated and seemingly closed to outside influences, the very fact that they continue thus reflects the larger society's willingness to leave them alone. Just as the individual is dependent on social and cultural structures for central components of identity, cultures and national communities are also dependent on wider political or international structures that indirectly support them.[54]

But if cultures are in fact interdependent, perhaps the *larger* culture is really our context of choice, containing a range of options and a set of evaluative criteria, including all the options and criteria of the particular subcultures it comprises, plus those that are generated by our combining options and criteria from *different* cultures as we attempt to live our lives from the inside, and to examine, question, and possibly revise our current projects and goals. If cultures persist as sources of future options and of evaluative criteria for future decision-making, this is not as self-contained entities, but as components of a larger, more cosmopolitan culture. Individuals have genuine choice and evaluative capacity, contends Jeremy Waldron, only when they are *not* insulated from different practices from those to which they are accustomed. "Either people learn about value from the dynamics of their culture and their interactions with others or their culture can operate for them at most as a museum display on which they pride themselves" (109).

Kymlicka responds directly that although options may be derived from varied sources, this fact does not obviate the value of our belonging to separate societal cultures. Indigenous cultures understand their identities as dynamic, not static; they "demand the right to decide for themselves what aspects of the outside world they will incorporate into their cultures."[55] But to what extent may we change the character or content of our culture without also altering its structure? Michael Walzer writes, for example, that the same goods have different meanings in different societies. Many governments understand that they are entrusted with their citizens' welfare, but they do not necessarily provide the same goods. In medieval Europe, the cure of bodies was private; the cure of souls was public. "Among medieval Christians," he writes, "eternity was a socially recognized need; and every effort was made to see that it was widely and equally distributed. . . . Among modern citizens, longevity is a socially recognized need; and increasingly every effort is made to see that it is widely and equally distributed."[56] Both of these sorts of "cures" have arisen in what we call Western culture. But is the shift in emphasis from soul to body merely one of content and character? Or, because the change was preceded by the disestablishment of many state churches and by the secularization of the culture, is the shift also one of structure? In the end, although I sympathize with the effort to distinguish between the structure and character of a culture, I do not think the distinction can bear the weight that Kymlicka desires. If members of cultures may instantiate change while remaining in their cultures of origin, this is likely to change the cultural structure as well as its character. If, on the other hand, the members of a culture wish to preserve its structure, they will have to accord weight to cultural tradition or authority that is likely to prevent not only structural change but also alterations in content and character.

FREEDOM OF ASSOCIATION

The most difficult question concerning the cultural membership of national minorities is that of who within a culture has the authority to determine the meaning of that culture as a context of choice. This is the major point of disagreement between Kymlicka, for whom the right to determine for oneself the meaning of cultural membership is an individual right, and Kukathas, for whom the culture as a voluntary association determines this meaning without infringing on individual rights as long as individual members acquiesce and are free to leave if they do not. Their specific disagreement centers on whether members of indigenous cultures like that of the Pueblo Indians should be able to practice Christianity while remaining in the culture, of which the ancestral religion is considered an integral part.

For Kymlicka, individual religious liberty is paramount and does not interfere with the lives of any other members of the Pueblo reservation.[57] Moreover, we could argue that allowing religious liberty offers a greater range of options and a larger set of evaluative criteria to those within the Pueblo culture. For Kukathas, however, introducing the guarantee of meaningful individual choice into a culture that does not prize this value undermines the culture itself, even if the guarantee occurs under the rubric of a change in character. "If the change in character takes place as a result of dissident members of the minority community invoking 'rights' granted them by the dominant culture, then the change constitutes not a response to the new circumstances confronting it but a change enforced by the wider society interfering in its internal practices."[58] More generally, whereas for Kymlicka autonomy has independent value that *may* be served by policies of toleration, for Kukathas it is toleration itself that has independent value. In fact, we could argue that toleration of the practices of cultures that do not value meaningful individual choice increases diversity among *types* of cultures, again offering a greater range of options and a larger set of evaluative criteria, if not to members, then to those in the larger or dominant culture who draw on the contributions of other cultures or who simply value diversity.

The crucial difference between these two interpretations appears to turn on the question of how we decide when freedom exists in a society. For Kukathas, the amount of freedom is not based on the sum of the freedoms in all associations, on the number of associations that value freedom, on the number of people in freedom-valuing associations, or on the individual freedom to enter associations of one's choice. Some associations are devoted to helping people manipulate their first-order preferences; as such, Christian organizations, for example, should be able to exclude militant atheists. Some communities into which people are born do not themselves prize freedom, but "it is the freedom to accept or reject the restriction on one's freedom that is important."[59] Kukathas therefore concludes that freedom is grounded on the liberty to leave associations, especially because freedom of exit implies freedom to form new associations. Despite exit costs, which may be high, these costs do not obviate the fact that one is still free to leave. Thus Kukathas does not advocate the group-differentiated rights supported by Kymlicka: members of cultures are free to bear the costs of remaining within them, just as they are free to leave, without special consideration.

Directly addressing the role of socialization in preference formation through the hypothetical Muslim wife of a Malay fisherman, Kukathas asserts that she is free neither because she is content with her lot nor because she has deliberately or reflectively chosen her life. Rather, "Fatima is free because she may live a life she has not rejected and is not forced to live a life she cannot accept. She is . . . free because she enjoys a certain 'inner freedom'; however, that inner freedom is not autonomy or self-direction. It is liberty of conscience" (15), which is "enjoyed when an individual can indeed live his life under the guidance of conscience (which identifies right and wrong conduct) and is not impeded by others from doing so" (16). Liberty of conscience requires freedom of association, but because some may choose not to associate with us, freedom of association must be the freedom to *dissociate* on the basis of conscience. Moreover, because this freedom requires both substantial freedom from intervention in a group's practices and an open external environment or wider society that is receptive to exit, freedom of association is therefore incompatible with a subsuming legal order that regulates associations according to centralized moral standards. Because this wider society must uphold freedom of association and therefore probably other liberal freedoms as well, "this suggests that it may be necessary that the wider society itself be one that could be described as embodying a liberal political culture."[60]

Kukathas, then, defends cultural membership by protecting members' rights to adhere to particular practices, thereby maintaining cultural character without the formal recognition of cultural structure. This formulation avoids some of the difficulties that Kymlicka faces, most notably with the claim that membership in one's culture of origin is always unchosen in ways that other memberships are not, and with his attempt to distinguish neatly between cultural structure and cultural character. Yet Kukathas's formulation faces difficulties of its own. First, as we have seen, he believes that the larger political society should be an association of diverse associations without its own common moral standpoint and thus one in which members of these associations can exercise freedom to exit. Given his belief, however, that different ways of life should be able to coexist even if some do not value equality and autonomy, it seems he is allowing the large society to provide the slack to individuals not provided by their particular cultures. And if the larger political society is, as he suggests, a liberal political culture, it cannot be an association without a common moral standpoint. It provides equality and the scope for autonomy not afforded by more particularistic cultures, even if this is by default. This logic exemplifies Waldron's point that particular cultures are dependent upon and are sustained by the wider community. In Kukathas's case, it is the existence of a wider community that makes meaningful the opportunity to exit.

Second, serious concerns attend Kukathas's admirably straightforward argument that freedom means the freedom to dissociate from those with whom one cannot in good conscience agree. Associations are self-policing because intolerable practices will cause their members to leave. Those who remain, therefore, have acquiesced and are free. A. John Simmons has suggested, however, that with respect to the principle of fair play, acceptance of "open" benefits that are not readily avoidable, like regular police patrols if one lives in a neighborhood, cannot generate the same obligation as benefits that are merely "readily available," such as special police protection I might receive with a restraining order.[61] We should not be required to alter our lifestyles to avoid benefits that generate obligations we do not want to honor. But if we cannot be thought to acquiesce in the receipt of *benefits* that are avoidable only through extraordinary effort, why must we be assumed to acquiesce in the assumption of *burdens* that may also be avoidable only with similar difficulty? Leslie Green notes that although John Stuart Mill tolerates polygamy, in the sense of refusing to endorse its extirpation because exit is possible, he is not therefore endorsing the practice itself. "But it is no part of a liberal theory that justice can be secured merely by providing an exit. If a certain social structure is unjust, it cannot become just merely by becoming avoidable."[62] Although Kukathas would respond that I am mistakenly assuming the existence of a common moral standpoint that is independent of those held by the individuals who acquiesce in the practices of particular cultures, I have explained why I believe that a larger political society without such a standpoint is neither possible nor desirable.

A third difficulty surfaces with respect to the rights of minority cultures, which, although appearing as an objection to Kymlicka's formulation, also counts against that of Kukathas. Kymlicka justifies formal rights for minority cultures because, lacking relative power and resources, they can less readily than the majority defend their unchosen but valued contexts of choice against outside incursions. But although cultural rights may protect minority cultures against the majority, they do not protect internal minorities, who may be as powerless against protected minorities as the latter are against the majority. Protected minorities may argue their own weakness in comparison to the majority but may still compel internal social conformity once they have the institutionalized power to maintain their distinctiveness. As Green concludes, a liberal regime is then allowing treatment of internal minorities that it would not countenance on the part of the larger community (263). On the other hand, if internal minorities are then entitled to rights against larger, protected minorities, not only may the character of the latter protected cultures disintegrate but also the cultural structure itself, the context of choice that is the initial impetus behind cultural rights. Kukathas would respond that this dilemma is a function of defending cultural membership through the protection of cultural structure, rather than by protecting members' rights to adhere to practices without formal recognition of cultural structure. The solution would lie in freedom of association as the right to exit from associations by which one feels oppressed.

But this solution simply re-creates on a larger scale my initial difficulties with the assumption that legitimacy is defined by acquiescence. Internal minorities may accept or acquiesce in the lives they lead, but they know neither their potential alternatives nor what they might desire if they did possess this knowledge. Their context of choice is limited because their range of options is narrow and their set of evaluative criteria is small, even assuming no conscious attempts to limit people's knowledge or to engage in any sort of psychological coercion. Kukathas states that if the liberty to exit is to have meaning, the society into which group members exit must have many of the characteristics of a liberal political culture. I suggest that if liberty to remain in one's culture of origin is to have meaning, it must afford an awareness to its members that there are other ways of life that emphasize other values. Neither Kymlicka nor Kukathas fully appreciates the position of internal minorities or dissenters, Kymlicka because he limits formal legal protection to certain minorities, and Kukathas because he would protect no minorities as a matter of public policy but would anticipate self-protection through the liberty to exit. As Green states, "Yet without respect for internal minorities, a liberal society risks becoming a mosaic of tyrannies; colourful, perhaps, but hardly free" (270).

AUTONOMY-BASED LIBERALISM

These considerations ultimately return us to the level of the individual, because it is the individual who expresses cultural membership by remaining in a culture of origin, by leaving it, and/or by joining with others in forming or maintaining other interpretations of their original cultures by choice. The capacity for autonomy requires that we experience second-order desires and volitions, or that we prefer to have certain desires over others and that we also care what these desires are. Only thus do we identify with desires in a way that gives continuity to our lives and allows us to live life from the inside, and only thus can we also draw back and imagine ourselves with different projects and goals, enabling ourselves to question, examine, and possibly to revise them. As a precondition of autonomy, the possession of a context of choice containing a greater range of options and a larger set of evaluative criteria is a necessary condition of participation in cultural membership that will then be an expression of autonomy. In my view, cultural membership as an expression of autonomy implies the presence of rational deliberation, critical reflection, and by implication the second-order desires and volitions that activate deliberation and reflection.

Does this mean, then, that liberals should not permit or facilitate ways of life that do not meet this demanding sort of standard and that such ways of life are *not* in fact expressions of autonomy? Those who do not engage in critical reflection still possess freedom, on Kukathas's terms; his hypothetical fisherman's wife has not autonomously chosen or endorsed her life but is free because she has not rejected her way of life and therefore must be viewed as accepting it. As Kymlicka notes, however, someone who lacks education and opportunities to interact with those of other cultures "does not have a substantial freedom to leave because she lacks the preconditions for making a meaningful choice."[63] Even if the lack of education and interaction is not a matter of policy, the end result is the same. Perhaps we can say that for some, cultural membership is an expression of autonomy in its full-blooded sense. For others, it expresses autonomy in a very thin sense, in that we assume either that people's first-order desires are congruent with what their second-order desires would be if they were conscious of them, or that perhaps they do experience second-order desires in spite of what appears to constitute an absence of preconditions.

Tamir makes a helpful distinction between *rights-based liberalism,* which focuses on individual rights "without conceiving of those rights as grounded in autonomy-entitlement and choice prerogatives," and *autonomy-based liberalism,* which "tolerates and respects only autonomy-supporting cultures—namely, liberal ones." Autonomy-based liberalism values communities only insofar as they may contribute to the development of their members' capacities for autonomy, it encourages the assimilation of illiberal cultures, and "it endorses toleration towards illiberal cultures only as a means for a slow, yet permanent, liberalisation of such cultures." Rights-based liberalism, however, "places at its core a commitment to equal concern and respect for individuals, their preferences and interests, regardless of the way these were formed." Thus it not only tolerates but also respects "decent illiberal cultures which do not foster the ideal of personal autonomy but which respect their members and allow them some means of participation and social influence."[64] Illiberal yet "reasonable" communities may not provide or may even prevent the development of the capacity for autonomous lives yet still may be valued by their members as communities worth inhabiting. Even rights-based liberals can arouse resentment in their inter-actions with illiberal cultures, because those who fear assimilation have more to lose than liberals do (170). Although she does not recommend a retreat to cul-tural relativism, Tamir concludes "that liberals should limit both their demands towards and their expectations of illiberal cultures. . . . The most that can be achieved is an untidy compromise which all parties resent to some extent. There is then no right solution, but a set of reasonable ones" (171).

Tamir's approach appears to be a compromise. She neither respects all cul-tures equally, nor does she respect only those that encourage their members to live autonomous lives. As long as a culture admits "a measure of liberty of conscience and freedom of thought," or allows its members "some means of participation and social influence" (167–168), it is a decent and reasonable community. Equal concern and respect dictate respect for individuals' efforts to live according to their own traditions and values when these do not harm others. But *how much* liberty of conscience, freedom of thought, participation, and social influence is enough for us to conclude that the community is decent or reasonable? Moreover, a liberal polity, unlike an illiberal one, has princi-pled reasons based on liberty and toleration to refrain from enforcing its own animating values on its subcultures. Thus, liberal states cannot be as thor-oughgoing in expressing their collective values in their national life as can illiberal ones. Finally, Tamir's compromise in an important way does not really split the difference, so to speak. Whatever meaning we assign, after debate, to "reasonable" and "decent" as descriptions of subcultures whose practices we will accept or respect, we are endorsing these practices as part of our common or established moral standpoint as a polity. This does not mean that compro-mise is never in order. It does mean that we must be clear about what we are doing, which is compromising the value of the development of the capacity for autonomy for the sake of other values.

The crux of the dilemma is that on the one hand, a liberal polity must be tol-erant of diversity, without which the larger culture will be homogeneous and without a range of options and evaluative criteria. On the other hand, in order to make full use of the available options and criteria, individuals must be able to reflect critically on the nature of the life that is good for them if they are to endorse the lives that they live, by imagining themselves with different proj-ects and goals and by either reaffirming their current lives or revising them so that they can endorse them anew. In other words, autonomy is worth more in a context of choice that offers diversity, but diversity is also worth more when individuals possess the capacity for autonomy. Perhaps we may think of autonomy as existing along a continuum, which obviates the necessity of classifying cultures and individuals as completely autonomous or nonautonomous. David Johnston distinguishes three kinds of autonomy in this context. First, autonomy may be understood simply as *agency*, or the capacity to act on projects and values independent of or unrelated to our own experiences. An agent might save another from drowning not merely from the instinctive sympathy of a sentient being but also from the abstract value put upon human life. Second, *moral autonomy* implies the capability of having both a conception of the good and also a sense of justice. Just as we have projects and values that we want to realize, we also recognize other individuals as agents with claims deserving of recognition and respect. This recognition requires self-limitation on one's own claims if others are also to succeed in their pursuits.[65]

Finally, *personal autonomy* implies self-authorship, in that the individual subjects projects and values to critical appraisal and fashions them into a way of life that functions as a coherent whole. One attends, that is, to second-order desires as well as first-order desires. Perfectionist liberal theories, unlike rights-based theories, require these three types of autonomy for a good society. Although the attribute of personal autonomy has great value, Johnston nevertheless concludes that unlike agency and moral autonomy, personal autonomy does not appear to be "an essential ingredient in a good human life in association with others" (91). For Johnston, individual attempts to create meaningful and worthwhile lives by pursuing projects and adhering to values are much more central to human dignity than is the process of critical appraisal in the choice of projects and values (87–99). "To dismiss the values of a person who does not wish to be personally autonomous would be to fail to take seriously the project for himself the person wishes to pursue" (94). Critical self-appraisal does not necessarily help us to discern some inherent value in things, to ensure improvement or human progress in general, or even to develop worthier projects and goals than otherwise. Personhood most plausibly "consists of the imaginative capacity to formulate projects and values," which may or may not require reflective self-evaluation (93). Social measures to promote personal autonomy can lead, if not to despotic paternalism, at least to disorientation and the disintegration of one's existing values, which in turn may undermine rather than support effective agency.

Yet simultaneously, Johnston suggests "on balance, that *some* degree of ability to appraise or reappraise one's projects and values critically is essential to a good life for human beings in association with others." Not only will critical self-appraisal help us to formulate the projects and values that are suitable for us, but also it will help us restrain our own claims and recognize others' projects and values, thereby contributing to our effective sense of justice. In fact, "In order to be morally autonomous, a person must possess and use, to some degree, the skills that are constitutive of personal autonomy" (97), and therefore a society should foster these insofar as they contribute to reflective agency (98). This process parallels that by which the effective integration and deployment of first-order desires is enhanced by our development of and reflection on second-order desires.

I endorse Johnston's intuition that some degree of critical self-appraisal is necessary for living a good life in association with others. But I experience the same difficulty with "some degree" that I do with Tamir's endorsement of illiberal cultures that admit "a measure of liberty of conscience and freedom of thought" and that allow its members "some degree of participation and social influence." How much? For Johnston, personal autonomy should be fostered insofar as these conditions contribute to effective agency. But how much is *that?* If effective agency means the imaginative capacity to formulate projects and values, then a greater degree of personal autonomy contributes more than a lesser degree, I should think, to the development of this imaginative capacity. A greater ability to engage in critical self-appraisal would produce a greater capability of conceiving and acting on projects and values unrelated to our own experiences. It should also aid us in formulating appropriate conceptions of the good and in recognizing and respecting others' projects and values, thus contributing to our sense of justice. Overall, the capacity for personal autonomy contributes both to effective agency and to the moral autonomy integral to a life in association with others.

Writers like Kymlicka, Tamir, Kukathas, and Johnston wish to allow some slack for groups and individuals who do not value personal autonomy and self-appraisal. The views that we have considered with respect to cultural membership, however, in one way or another imply that a life grounded in rational deliberation and critical reflection is indeed superior to one that is not so grounded. Although Kymlicka, unlike me, views cultural membership as a precondition of autonomy rather than as its expression, his desire to protect cultures of origin is still based on the desire to protect choice. The protection of a context of choice does not guarantee critical reflection, but it opens up a space within which this activity may take place. Tamir's formulation makes cultural membership both a precondition and an object of choice. Although her rights-based liberalism purports to ignore preference formation, she accords respect to illiberal cultures only if they meet certain conditions—conditions that just happen to foster personal autonomy, as in their allowing a modicum of freedom of thought. Moreover, she suggests a direct relationship, if not a guaranteed one, between the ability to lead a satisfying life and the ability to view one-self as an active member "of a worthy community."[66] But judging the worthi-ness of one's community implies at least the possibility of critical reflection as one determines this worthiness. It implies the individual ability to step back from the community to make this judgment, and the possibility that under the evaluative criteria used, we might conclude that some communal practices are *not* worthy of what one expects from one's community. It admits, that is, the desirability of rational deliberation and critical reflection. As Levey notes, Tamir's "rights-based liberalism draws on the force of individual autonomy more than she realizes."[67]

Even Kukathas, as we have seen, relies on the liberal culture of the larger society to influence nonliberal subcultures, both through typical interactions and through its provision of a place into which those exercising freedom of exit may enter. As Levey puts it, "Despite his account of liberal theory, Kukathas responds to the spectre of oppressive and unjust minority cultures by being only too prepared to let 'non-basic' liberal norms transform them" (8). In addi-tion, freedom of exit is itself arguably a liberal norm that, unlike others, should in his view be forced on groups that do not voluntarily embrace it as the price of toleration. "Put simply, why is the right to choose to leave any less a liberal good (or any more a neutral framework) than is respecting the autonomy of the person?"[68] Moreover, for aboriginal cultures the freedom to dissociate has historically been a function of the law imposed by European settlers, not of spontaneous generation.[69]

Finally, freedom of exit itself is not only a liberal norm in the abstract, but it is also an option best appreciated in a context of critical reflection. That is, individuals who know they may leave may also come to understand their orig-inal cultural membership as a matter of choice and personal commitment, whether or not they actually do leave. Although Kukathas might respond that freedom of exit is then indeed sufficient protection for individuals against the tyranny of their cultures, I would argue that this freedom is necessary but not sufficient. Those for whom leaving does not appear as a viable option, to be embraced or rejected, as in the case of some battered wives, are also those insufficiently protected by the mere existence of this option. On the other hand, those for whom leaving *is* a viable option psychologically may engage in crit-ical reflection and reflective self-evaluation as they consider their options, thus embracing characteristics of personal autonomy.

I believe, then, that cultural membership in some culture provides a context of choice, and as such it is a precondition of agency, in Johnston's sense, or of the imaginative capacity to formulate projects and values. Any culture provides a range of options for choice and a set of evaluative criteria. In my opinion, a larger range and a broader set provide a richer and fuller context of choice. As individuals use these options and evaluative criteria to live their lives, their practice of cultural membership involves formulating appropriate conceptions of the good and recognizing and respecting others' projects and values. As such, this practice is an expression of *moral* autonomy. Finally, if they engage in critical reflection and rational deliberation to examine, question, and revise or reaffirm their projects and values, their cultural allegiances constitute an expression of *personal* autonomy. Cultural protections for national minorities may be justified in terms of particular practices, but only if this protection does not threaten the development of the capacity for personal autonomy.

4. Ethnic and Gender Identity

Ethnic minorities and women typically wish to be full members of the larger society yet to retain and seek recognition of certain features of their identity that may diverge from what is considered characteristic of the majority or of what is viewed as the norm. Ethnic groups are not national minorities, but they still resist giving up their cultural allegiances to assimilate totally into a cosmopolitan culture. How much protection do they merit against the thrust of the dominant culture? To what extent should members of the dominant culture engage in some accommodation of their own? In the case of gender, are women who are treated like men being asked to assimilate into a "male" culture? Or is the dominant culture an androgynous one that until recently has been dominated by males? I believe that all individuals, whatever their ethnicity or gender, should decide for themselves the meaning of their unchosen identities in the context of their own lives. They cannot choose their ethnicity or gender at birth. But they do have a choice as to how they want ethnicity or gender and its purported attributes to function for *them*. In any specific instance, we should assess the relationship between cultural membership and the capacity for autonomy.

Ethnicity

Ethnic groups differ from national minorities. The latter seek to remain distinct societies and to do so often demand some type of self-government; ethnic groups are loose associations of individuals who typically wish to become full members of the larger society but who also may desire the accommodation of cultural differences in order to maintain valued cultural practices. On this distinction, individuals should define and interpret for themselves their particularistic identities. They should not face a forced choice between defining themselves solely or primarily by their communitarian or private identities, on the one hand, and embracing cultural conformity or public identity at the expense of their communitarian identities, on the other. Acknowledging this tension, however, requires that we distinguish between what is required by liberal democratic principles and what is not.[1] Moreover, although certain principles and practices must be part of the public culture, "this does not mean that every person must be a liberal democrat in her heart of hearts" (51). I have discussed national minorities or minority cultures at some length in order to argue that it is *individual* choice or affirmation that constitutes a true expression of autonomy. Attempts at formal protection of cultural structure or content, whether on a model like Will Kymlicka's or Chandran Kukathas's, are well-intentioned but may too often subordinate individual self-interpretation to imperatives of structure or content that are defined by others. Although members of ethnic groups generally do not seek the same kinds of formal recognition that often characterizes national minorities, I believe that they require the same opportunities to define their identities as individuals.

The existence of ethnic groups within a national community typically arises from immigration, which we normally regard as a matter of choice. Kymlicka's case for group-differentiated rights for indigenous cultures and minority nations is based on the assumption that these were existing groups involuntarily subsumed under a broader national authority. Therefore he distinguishes between "the coerced assimilation of minority nations and the voluntary assimilation of immigrants."[2] Although African Americans are in many ways atypical immigrants, Kymlicka's general claim is that whereas immigrant or ethnic groups may at times accuse the larger community of forced *exclusion,* they cannot charge the larger community with forced *inclusion.* Their relinquishment of their national culture is voluntary (62), as is their intent to join an existing society (96).

The plight of refugees fleeing persecution, however, blurs this distinction. Although Kymlicka would protect against the disadvantages of unequal circumstances that are unchosen, from a practical standpoint he suggests that few countries would accept refugees if they thereby incurred obligations like those toward national minorities. Moreover, because refugees' national rights are really claims against their own governments (98), their next best hope is to be treated like immigrants, for whom accommodation of diversity may ensure "access to a societal culture which provides them with meaningful options encompassing the range of human activities" (101). The example of refugees, however, illustrates to me that we cannot draw the firm line of demarcation between circumstance and choice that Kymlicka desires. Asks Sherene Razack about immigrants, "How much of a choice is it to flee poverty and starvation in lands ravaged by a global economy dominated by the first world? Who is ultimately responsible for such flight?"[3] Although fear of oppression or starvation does not obviate the existence of choice, I have argued that we must examine the history of preference formation to determine whether preferences are truly free or autonomous. The question, then, is not one of where to draw a firm distinction between choice and circumstance, but where to place groups on a continuum.

Yael Tamir, as we have seen, differs from Kymlicka in that where the latter would only subsidize differences resulting from unchosen constituents of our identities, the former would not only accommodate or subsidize disadvantaging differences resulting from choice but would do so precisely because they *are* matters of choice. For her, the only facet that is unchosen is the disadvantage of minority status. Observant Jews who wish to keep the Sabbath or to wear yarmulkes in the workplace have chosen to be observant, and their choices should be accommodated whether they were born Jews or converted to Judaism. When we resist the accommodation of personal preferences, it is often because of their eccentricity rather than because these preferences, because chosen, are therefore somehow inauthentic. In other words, cultural membership can be both chosen *and* constitutive of identity. "Cultural choices, like religious ones, belong in the category of constitutive choices, which due to their importance to individuals, should be granted special weight."[4] On the other hand, we cannot expect "that any culture individuals might be interested in should be protected. The right to culture is by no means ultimate, and other rights may override it in situations of conflict, an argument similarly used to justify restriction of other freedoms" (37).

Liberal political communities must therefore decide for themselves, in the cases of both national minorities and immigrants, which aspects of the public culture are required by liberal democratic principles, which are optional and therefore permissible, and which are completely alien to these principles and should therefore be forbidden. I have alluded to Jeff Spinner's claim that illiberal cultural practices should not be protected. In my view, illiberal practices are not only those that, in Kymlicka's words, constitute a "gross and systematic violation of human rights" like slavery, genocide, or torture[5] but also those that interfere with or impinge upon the development of the capacity for autonomy. I have argued that the larger community decides on the legitimacy of given cultural practices from its common moral standpoint, controlling the content of cultural identity by extending or withdrawing its protection. The liberal polity itself is the legal expression of a particular cultural structure. Yet insofar as it recognizes that particularistic ties are and ought to be central to and constitutive of human identity, the influence of public and private is reciprocal and works both ways.

Spinner's conception of pluralistic integration exemplifies this reciprocal effect. Liberalism is a prescription not only for public institutions but also for "the public square. In many different settings liberal citizens may see others whom they dislike, but liberalism calls on them to control their feelings."⁶ We must treat others equally or at least civilly, even when we do not think they really are equals. But our behavior affects our thoughts. "Habituated to treat others equally or at least civilly, liberal citizens may begin to look upon others equally or civilly" (48). These demands reveal that components of liberal citizenship exist that keep liberalism from moral agnosticism about the character of citizens and that render liberal citizenship more robust in content than critics often acknowledge.

Although Spinner does not require approval of others' practices, he does believe that liberal citizenship requires more than grudging toleration. When ethnic groups are accepted, their practices should not disappear but should become "diffuse" (173), or part of the mélange that characterizes the larger community (59). The liberal polity has not always reflected this hope. For example, we have often demanded cultural conformity of African Americans as the price of success in mainstream institutions (114). With respect to immigrants, "Too often citizens demand complete conformity from immigrants; at other times, citizens grant that they will merely tolerate others. Both of these attitudes enable citizens to escape the hard work that should be done by liberal society in accepting immigrants" (74, 167). That is, liberal citizens should constantly revise their image of citizenship with the arrival of new members or the development of new practices that are not illiberal, rather than exerting pressure to conform (75, 80).

Spinner's point is that cultures change and that true accommodation requires mutual and reciprocal change. Most current citizens and their families were once immigrants; at some point new immigrants and their families will no longer be immigrants. Meanwhile, as David Johnston argues, "Individuals need real recognition from the other members of their society as whole persons, and not merely in their role as citizens, in order to pursue their values effectively."⁷ In other words, public recognition of the legitimacy of particularistic identity broadens the ways in which individuals may understand and interpret themselves. For example, "Jews can now interpret their own identity; they can decide for themselves what it means to be Jewish. . . . Liberal citizenship does not mean the inevitable end of Jewish identity, but it does mean that Jews can drop, add, and combine cultural practices in ways that will transform Jewish identity."⁸ Similarly, "Denied the right to define themselves," the claim by some African Americans to nationhood "can be seen as an attempt for them to become self-interpreting" (30). Traditionally, culture was a private matter. "When one version (a white version) is the norm in society, however, the relegation of

Black identity to the private realm denies equal citizenship to Blacks by perpetuating an exclusive version of citizenship." Recognizing such culture and institutions as legitimate shows "that there is more than one way to be an American citizen and that there is more than one set of cultural institutions and practices worthy of American citizens" (125–126).

At least two conclusions follow, I believe, from Spinner's model of pluralistic integration. First, it both expands and contracts our context of choice. It expands our context because the diffusion of cultural practices broadens our range of options and our set of evaluative criteria, creating a more cosmopolitan culture for everyone than would be the case if ethnic groups simply assimilated by relinquishing all traces of cultural distinctiveness. Groups may maintain a range of their native practices, they may adopt various practices of the larger culture, and members of the latter may adopt or adapt certain practices from more particularistic cultures. On the other hand, this model also contracts our context of choice, or at least it demonstrates that this occurs through the diffusion of cultural practices. As Spinner recognizes, cultural permeability means that social interaction among members of various cultures will change and weaken the existence of robust ethnic and cultural identities, even in the absence of social pressures to conform. Thus potentially, in the long run, a narrower range of options and a smaller set of evaluative criteria will exist than formerly. The character of ethnic identity develops, evolves, and changes, however, because of the choices of individual human beings who carry this identity. I believe we should not want to freeze a particular manifestation of it as a museum display, in Jeremy Waldron's terms, even if this were possible.

Second, Spinner's account of the virtues of liberal citizenship suggests a behavioralistic interpretation of the relationship between particularistic and civic identities as this relationship evolves. As liberal citizens, we must treat people as equals in the public square whatever our private opinions, but over time, our behavior can influence our opinions. In Aristotle's moral philosophy, suggests L. A. Kosman, virtues are dispositions toward feelings as well as toward actions, despite the fact that action is regarded as a matter of choice where feeling is not. We may initially decide to act virtuously in a particular situation for prudential reasons, without the proper moral disposition, but over time this sort of action may become habitual. "On this view one becomes virtuous by impersonating a virtuous person, and in that impersonation, through the process of habituation, becomes the virtuous person one impersonates." We do not directly or deliberately choose our feelings. Nevertheless, "A person may act in certain ways that are characteristically and naturally associated with a certain range of feelings, and through those actions acquire the virtue that is the disposition for having the feelings directly. Acts are chosen, virtues and feelings follow in their wake, though in logically different ways."[9] Some of the "hard work of liberal citizenship" that Spinner commends may be accomplished by behaving as liberal citizens should behave, regardless of our current feelings.

This account may appear overly facile to some critics. Alan Wolfe, for example, suggests that self-interpretation of one's particularistic identity is in reality a rejection of this identity. The "claim that we can take the best in our ethnic traditions while leaving behind the worst reveals a complete lack of a tragic sense of life. Ethnicity is a package deal: when you are loyal to an inherited tradition, you take the good with the bad. The challenge of ethnic life lies precisely in the unstable combination of being tied to a clan and wanting to be free of the clan."[10] Wolfe concludes that to the extent that identity is socially constructed, what is constructed in the United States is American, not ethnic. I do not object to calling a reconstructed ethnicity American. I reject the idea, however, that we cannot lay claim to a redefined ethnicity and call it ethnic— as a way of *being* both ethnic and American.

The thrust of this book is to highlight the centrality of the individual capacity for autonomy amid the diversity of a liberal society. Surely this must include the moral right to credibility as to what we claim our identity to be. Although, as Charles Taylor suggests, human identity has a dialogical character, in that it is worked out in dialogue with others, we are each entitled to draw our own conclusions in the imputation of meaning to this dialogue. Recent debate over the addition of a "multiracial" option on census forms and the subsequent decision instead to allow individuals to identify themselves as members of more than one race speaks to this intuition. So do claims that some African Americans do not accept black Puerto Ricans as black, and some Latinos do not accept them as Latino, though many Puerto Ricans identify themselves with both heritages.[11] Two specific examples may also illustrate the point. In the first, a Mexican-born Texas resident of the Lakota spiritual tradition was arrested and sentenced to ten years in Mexico for the possession of peyote he was conveying to spiritual ceremonies, on grounds that peyote is authorized for ceremonial use only by Native Americans. While individuals who live in native communities and speak only a native tongue are classified as Indians, those who move to cities and learn other languages like Spanish are classified by many governments not as indigenous but as mestizo, a mixture of Indian and Spanish. Those sympathetic to the convicted man suggest "that governments can determine who is a citizen, but cannot determine people's identities."[12] Second, a newspaper columnist engendered criticism for suggesting that Victoria's

Secret catalogs should feature more minority women, with one caller declaring, "I am very disappointed that you favor equal opportunity degradation." The columnist responded that black women, like those of other races or ethnicities, are not "monolithic"[13] and should not be treated as such.

In these examples, we find a rejection of essentialism, of the idea that membership in a group is somehow self-defining, irrespective of what that membership means to the individual member. Where the recognition of particularistic or communitarian identity is a value, the question of how to accomplish this recognition without lapsing into essentialism provides a constant source of tension. Iris Young, for example, rejects both a liberal assimilationist ideal that rejects group difference and a separatist ideal that can oversimplify and freeze group identity in favor of a relational conception of difference, according to which groups participate in the same society but hold "a differentiated place," including "a special representation of oppressed or disadvantaged groups to ensure political influence for all perspectives."[14] Kymlicka observes, however, that "her list of 'oppressed groups' in the United States would seem to include 80 percent of the population. . . . In short, everyone but relatively well-off, relatively young, able-bodied, heterosexual white males."[15] And as Walzer notes, "groups cannot be assigned rights unless they are first assigned members,"[16] a necessity that conflicts with the imperative of self-interpretation or self-definition.

Although I cannot here discuss the intricacies of group representation, I want to highlight the fact that the hard work of liberal citizenship includes the difficult task of steering a course between homogeneity and essentialism. However this course may be steered, individuals must be able to decide for themselves as individuals the claims of their particularistic identities as they live their lives from the inside, examining and rejecting or reaffirming their current commitments, and working out over time the meaning of American citizenship for themselves. This process in my view closely approximates Michael Sandel's description of human agency as requiring the self not only to choose but also to reflect, "to turn its light inward upon itself, to inquire into its constituent nature, to survey its various attachments and acknowledge their respective claims . . . to arrive at a self-understanding" that is never fixed but is constituted and reconstituted over a lifetime.[17] Just as cultures change over time if they are not frozen as museum displays, individuals themselves may do so also. In the end, of course, the hard work of liberal citizenship is done within the context of specific issues. It is to several of these that I now turn.

LINGUISTIC POLICY

In the United States, those who wish to use a language other than English do not possess the territorial concentration and institutional embodiment that mark francophones in the Canadian province of Quebec. Instead, activity has centered on making English the "official" language of the United States, with the focus on prohibiting the use of other languages by employees in both public and private settings. For example, a 1988 constitutional amendment in Arizona that made English "the language 'of all government functions and actions' "[18] was struck down by federal district and appeals courts in 1990 and 1994; the Supreme Court in 1997 held the case moot, as the affected employee no longer worked for the state. Although twenty-two states have enacted a variety of official-English laws, in most cases these laws are basically symbolic.[19] Within the last decade, however, a growing number of businesses have promulgated formal or informal rules requiring that their employees speak only English on the job.

Although federal law allows language restrictions only in cases of business necessity, such as dealing with members of the non–English-speaking public, "the bulk of legal challenges to such restrictions involve conversations among employees." English-only laws in various governmental jurisdictions have encouraged the issuance of regulations to enforce these laws, particularly in communities infused by a large number of immigrants. In the Los Angeles area in 1990, a Filipino nurse was reprimanded, demoted, and reassigned for speaking Tagalog and for campaigning against an unwritten English-only rule in her department of a hospital.[20] In northern California in 1992, a nurse's aide in a nursing home with an English-only policy was fired after being caught a second time speaking Spanish with coworkers.[21] In 1997 in Brooklyn, New York, two fellow-employees were dismissed from a home-care agency when they objected to a prohibition against speaking Spanish that extended to lunchtime walks in front of the office building.[22] And in Amarillo, Texas, in the same year two women hired by an insurance agency because they spoke Spanish lost their jobs when they refused to sign a pledge that the office would be English-speaking except with non–English-speaking customers; they had been chatting together in Spanish. While the agency's co-owners experienced the latter as rude, like whispering behind one's back, the women felt they were being told to deny their heritage.[23]

Overall, though it might be critical for all employees to speak English in a hospital operating room or an air traffic control tower, casual conversation hardly qualifies as such. In these situations, the desire for uniformity at the expense of diversity often lacks a rational purpose; the minority should conform so that the majority can feel comfortable. A former Alabama legislator who sponsored an English-only measure passed on a statewide ballot in 1990 likened the situation to requiring dollars rather than rupees or pesos. "We have standardization, which serves to unify the country. . . . Otherwise things get bemuddled."[24] In my opinion, however, the conviction that the use of languages other than English in casual and private conversation promotes disunity is what is "bemuddled."

In the United States, English and the culture associated with its use will not weaken and disappear in the absence of public policies for its preservation. Knowledge of English is an economic necessity for anyone who wants to participate in the mainstream of American occupations. In the case of Quebec, by contrast, although its desire for recognition as a distinct society is rooted in "a deep commitment to liberal values,"[25] its definition of the good life centers on the survival and flourishing of French culture, unachievable through purely private activity. The goal of cultural survival is aimed not only at the present use and preservation of French but also at *creating* a community that ensures the identity of future generations as French-speakers.[26] In other words, public policy in Quebec addresses not only citizens' first-order desires, or the survival of their preferred language and culture, but also their second-order desires, or the way the preference for French language and culture is created and sustained.

The question that arises, however, is whether these second-order desires that shape future choices may crowd out the first-order desires of current citizens to live their lives from the inside, and to interpret themselves as anglophone Quebecers, if that is what they are. Yet such citizens have real choices, in my opinion. Because Quebec gives preference to French-speaking immigrants over others, and because the children of allophone immigrants, those not originally francophones or anglophones, must like francophones attend French-speaking schools in which they may also learn English if they attend public schools, French culture is undoubtedly perpetuated. Yet anglophone children may attend English-speaking schools, francophone immigrants who do not want a French cultural milieu need not apply for admittance to Quebec, and allophones who prefer English education can also apply for admission to other Canadian provinces. Thus, although immigration and education policy does create preferences, those affected either view the preservation of French culture as a good they themselves favor, or at least as an acceptable alternative because they do have other options.

It may appear arbitrary that French is the dominant language simply because francophones are a majority in Quebec, when anglophones constitute a majority in Canada as a whole. Yet as Spinner notes, "It is hardly fair that English is the dominant language in the United States, but it wouldn't be any fairer if the dominant language was Spanish or Yiddish or Hindu. Some language must dominate in an industrial state."[27] Moreover, an absence of state involvement "would also restrict choices, but it would restrict the choices of a different set of people" (159). Quebec's policies restrict the choices of those who are not francophones, but alternative policies—or the absence of policies—would have restricted the choices of francophones. Once again, given that cultural neutrality is logistically unachievable, instituting and upholding French as the language of public and civil interaction in Quebec is not an illiberal policy.

EXTERNAL MANIFESTATIONS OF CULTURAL DIVERSITY

The second issue I shall address is that of specific items of apparel that are manifestations of cultural diversity. In 1989 in France, three young women who were Muslim North African immigrants attracted attention when they insisted on wearing headscarves in class in a public secondary school. Although they were initially suspended for posing what appeared to be a religious challenge to the national policy of secularism in education, the principal then decided that a compromise prohibiting the headscarves only in class was acceptable. This compromise, however, was unacceptable to one of the families, the issue became a national one, and finally the minister of education instructed the principal to readmit the girls even if they wore headscarves to class.[28] The question posed by this issue is that of how the liberal polity maintains its own identity, in this case a militantly secular one, yet also accommodates expressions of both autonomy and diversity in its midst.

The typical liberal model of political toleration, suggests Anna Elisabetta Galeotti, prescribes not only noninterference with individual choices regarding conceptions of the good but also public indifference to differences, two stances that can at times conflict. Because of a headscarf's visibility, in the initial objection "the three students were making a *public* statement of what is a legitimate position only of the *private* conscience, and thus were trespassing illegitimately in the public domain where religious choice, beliefs, and affiliations do not belong and should not count."[29] Differences on this view should be reduced to individual claims to protection against provable harms like discrimination and harassment, rather than perceived as claims on public recognition, respect, esteem, or approval. But true equality of respect, Galeotti argues, requires "the public recognition of collective identities" (597), or public respect for people who assert their social differences rather than keep them hidden. After all, the liberal public sphere has always recognized the particular collective identity of the white Christian male. If *this* particularistic identity commands public respect, so also should others (600). Although some intellectuals on the French left have argued that Islamic cultural practices constitute religious oppression for which secularism is the antidote,[30] Norma Claire Moruzzi suggests that as both immigrants and women these students must learn to form workable identities that include elements of more than one culture. We should not use one cultural practice to counter another, and at worst, a prohibition on headscarves may radicalize individuals who view this practice as a legitimate private option (663).

This controversy is instructive because it reveals that even when we admit that a political entity neither can nor perhaps should achieve complete cultural neutrality, the existing nonneutrality is often more extensive than we realize. Moruzzi's point is that the left's defense of French national culture as secular is congruent and coincides with the right's defense of it as Christian. Public bareheadedness has become interpreted as a secular practice, but it is a religious marker to those whose religious traditions do carry specific markers, like yarmulkes or headscarves. The same is true of Sunday as the only full holiday of the French school week; a seemingly secular practice has a religious definition and identity to those whose holy days are other than Sunday. Secularists and Christians "can both energetically defend the cultural practices of that school system because those cultural practices are amenable to both traditions" (654). To put the matter differently, the nonneutrality represented by secularism is compounded by a second sort of nonneutrality, that favoring the religious practices of the dominant group in French culture.

French society need not accord the same weight to diversity as is accorded by a country of immigration like the United States. Nevertheless, the issues raised by the headscarf controversy bear out Spinner's contention that in the United States, at least, we have too often demanded cultural conformity before affording members of various groups complete inclusion in mainstream institutions. Because the unavoidable cultural nonneutrality of the larger society is compounded by a common moral standpoint that favors, even if unconsciously, some specific manifestations of culture over others, I agree with Spinner that liberal citizens must engage in the hard work of revamping their images of acceptable practices. The development of the capacity for autonomy requires that we afford members of all groups the opportunity to interpret their particularistic identities and to do so in ways they can endorse for themselves. To prohibit headscarves for Muslim women students in order to free them from the cultural tyranny of family and tradition would narrow their range of options and complicate their attempts to work out their own identities, or to shape lives, lived from the inside, that they can endorse. And by affording members of diverse groups the opportunity to work out their identities and to be self-interpreting, we also reexamine, reinterpret, and revise the ways in which we define our own identities as members of the larger society.

In a policy change under a more rightist government in 1993, however, France responded to the perceived failure to integrate Third World immigrants by backing a primary school principal who had suspended two Turkish and two Moroccan students for wearing headscarves. Fearing possible infiltration of France by Islamic fundamentalists, the government rejected multiculturalism in favor of cultural homogeneity, "using schools to turn . . . children into French men and women." Any emphasis on cultural or religious differences, like teaching Arabic or wearing headscarves, was thought to feed a xenophobia that causes many French to view even the French-born children of immigrants as foreigners, and in turn causes these individuals to perceive themselves as members of their cultures of origin rather than as French. Although alienated young men can be targets of recruitment by Islamic fundamentalists, young women are often motivated to succeed in order to avoid the cloistered lives dictated by their cultural traditions, leading the Social Affairs Minister in 1993 to suggest that immigrant women are "a secret weapon." One of her advisers suggested that time will resolve the problem of cultural integration. "The consumer society has de-Christianized France. Why won't it de-Islamicize the Muslims?"[31]

If accounts of the difficulties of cultural integration in France are accurate, we cannot dismiss threats to national unity. The ministerial adviser is suggesting, however, that interactions between Muslim and French culture have as much potential to transform the former as the latter. Most obviously, they could influence those in the larger society to cease to regard headscarves as religious markers, just as bareheadedness in public is not viewed as a religious marker. In this sense, Muslims can be de-Islamicized without abandoning Islam, or even without abandoning cultural practices that signify their allegiance. Rather, Muslims are de-Islamicized according to the perceptions of non-Muslims, who no longer invest items of apparel with the alien significance that now obtains. Though I do not wish to tell the French nation how it should define and accomplish national unity, I do want to emphasize that more than one form of integration exists. We can use a preexisting standard or definition of what it means to be French or American. Alternatively, however, we can embark on the more difficult course that recognizes the particularistic identities of individuals, and with these the fact that there is more than one way to be a Frenchman, Frenchwoman, or American and more than one set of practices worthy of citizens of these nations.

Controversies over items of apparel have also arisen in the United States, typically over turbans for Sikh males and headscarves for Muslim women employees. Two employees of U.S. Airways were told to remove their headscarves but eventually kept their jobs and headscarves after protesting. One was a utility worker cleaning planes on the midnight shift and therefore without public contact. The other, a flight attendant, was moved to a training job without public contact or a uniform requirement. U.S. Airways stated that "in the interest of presenting a neutral face to the public," it prohibits even religious symbols like crucifixes or Stars of David; moreover, an employee with a headscarf might not be recognized as one in an emergency situation.[32] Other companies such as Taco Bell, J. C. Penney, and Office Depot have objected to headscarves, but most have accommodated employees after further explanation or legal pressure. It is evident that such headwear functions here as a religious and cultural marker in ways that bareheadedness does not. Again, however, I believe that the public can become accustomed enough to diverse items of apparel with religious and cultural significance that they are not perceived as a "face" that is nonneutral. Their current unfamiliarity is the difficulty. It has been suggested that women wearing headscarves are particularly strong persons because of their willingness to withstand criticism (A14). The implication is that we need not fear their making choices they cannot themselves endorse.

ILLIBERAL PRACTICES

The third issue is that of cultural practices that many would perceive as illiberal. I agree with Spinner that although the liberal values of equality and nondiscrimination should be realized in the public sphere and in civil society, they should not be imposed at all costs in the private sphere.[33] Nevertheless, we need not accept all cultural values even there. A stark example of cultural clash is provided in Northern England by cases of British-born daughters of rural Pakistani immigrants who have left home and sought protection, often through new names and papers, from their own families rather than submit to arranged marriages to Pakistani partners. Because the families of defiant daughters are stigmatized, male family members have used bounty hunters, kidnappings, and sometimes beatings, scarrings with acid, and deaths by burning, often explained as suicide following depression. One woman, on calling home to ask if the family would remove its death threat to her and her English husband, was told by her brother that "he would make it his 'mission' to find them, kill them 'slowly,' and bring them home in body bags."[34]

In Lincoln, Nebraska, in 1996, an Iraqi refugee arranged and celebrated the marriages of his thirteen-year-old and fourteen-year-old daughters to two Iraqi men who were twenty-eight and thirty-four years old. The father's defenders cited ignorance of the law, cultural custom, and religious freedom; legal authorities maintained that we cannot have one law for native-born individuals and another for immigrants.[35] Other cultural differences involve styles of child-rearing and discipline. Some foreigners in the United States fear state intervention if they discipline their children "the right way," threatening to take children home to punish them and worrying that if parents cannot beat them, the police will shoot them for infractions outside the home.[36] Others encounter difficulty for being *more* permissive than Americans, as in cases involving a Danish tourist in 1996 and a Russian immigrant in 1997 who left children outside unsupervised while they ate or worked. Although some observers believe that child protection agencies react too rigidly to cultural differences that do not involve abuse, others again retort that laws must apply to Americans, immigrants, and tourists alike.[37]

The case of retaliation for defiance exemplifies the threat of physical harm as well as the curtailment of liberties normally guaranteed to all members of a liberal polity. The same would be true, in my opinion, of the nonwestern practice of female circumcision, infibulation, and other customs that critics classify as genital mutilation of young girls and that some immigrants have attempted to bring with them to their adopted countries. Like these examples, the underage marriages in Nebraska also fall into the realm of practices that curtail both the diversity of options available to individuals and also the development of the capacity for autonomy. Laws that prohibit certain practices with lasting effects carry the rational purpose of ensuring that individuals have a context or protected space within which to survey, question, examine, and revise their options—that is, to decide what their lives should be, even if this means reaffirming their current way of life. Particular styles of punishment, however, absent harms such as broken bones and obvious brutality, do not typically foreclose options in the same way as underage arranged marriages and female genital alteration. On child supervision, I agree that the law must be uniformly enforced; moreover, leaving children alone in public may threaten permanent harm that a spanking does not.

Some anthropologists like Richard Shweder advocate fundamental changes in the law to accord a broad tolerance to controversial cultural practices, accommodating "almost any practice accepted as valid in a radically different society if it can be demonstrated to have some social or cultural good," including female genital alteration, which defenders equate with male circumcision.

Meanwhile, "Asylum seekers . . . are turning up at American airports begging to escape from tribal rites in the name of human rights," a development that renders this sort of debate "less and less theoretical."[38] As we have seen, cultures are not monolithic, and intracultural diversity, I believe, deserves consideration along with intercultural diversity. Moreover, if morality changes along with geographic locale, as cultural relativists often imply, the liberal polity is entitled to declare some practices unacceptable in *its* geographic locale.

When a direct imposition of liberal values on individuals is inappropriate, on the other hand, we should remember that precisely because the public culture is not and cannot be neutral, it communicates by example. As Joseph Carens suggests, when a liberal democracy tolerates patriarchal religions, as it should, by simultaneously granting equal legal rights to women, "it communicates a message about the status of women that is subversive of traditional patriarchal values and creates a resource that makes it easier for women to leave a social context ordered by that patriarchal religion."[39] In other words, when individuals are exposed to a range of options, this sets the stage for critical self-reflection as they compare and contrast their own ways of life with those of others around them. It may impel them to question whether their current lives are the best lives for them, to wonder if they might more wholeheartedly be able to endorse another sort of life, and, in short, to reexamine their projects and goals. The existence of a range of options is not a sufficient condition for the development of the capacity for autonomy, but it is surely a necessary one.

Gender

The juxtaposition of gender and ethnicity may seem curious at the outset. Short of sex-change surgery, sex is a given. Short of a transsexual lifestyle, one's sex is apparent to the casual observer. If one dissociates oneself from one's ethnic origins, on the other hand, that identity can disappear, and except in the case of racial differences, which in some cases may also be hidden, no one else need know the nature of these origins. I perceive two similarities, however, between ethnicity and gender. First, although we can choose neither our birthright ethnicity nor our gender, we can nevertheless exercise choice about how we want these features to function in the contexts of our own lives. Second, members of the dominant culture too often make this self-definition or self-interpretation more difficult than it needs to be. Sometimes they emphasize difference in circumstances when ethnic minorities and women wish to emphasize the commonalities they share with others; at other times they ignore difference when individuals in these groups wish to claim their differences as essential to their own self-definitions or self-interpretations. In either case, members of ethnic minorities and women experience difficulty in living life from the inside, or in living out the self-interpretations they have chosen or affirmed on the basis of critical reflection. In other words, they may be hindered in their expressions of autonomy.

Liberals as well as communitarians like to think that the common moral standpoint is a legitimate basis for the aspirations of individuals who are members of all groups in society. Yet the historical practices and roles through which we pursue shared ends, though often defined as universal attributes of the human condition, have often been the particularities that characterize propertied white males.[40] Persons without these characteristics are often marginalized, their own particularities either denied legitimacy or else apotheosized in such a way that no *other* attributes of these individuals are accorded legitimacy. Both culture and gender, then, exert an impact on the development of our capacity for autonomy. The development of this capacity should not require the suppression of our cultural and gender identities but should build on them so that the expression of our particularistic identities is also an expression of autonomy.

This requires, however, that we interpret these particularistic identities for ourselves. The process of self-interpretation can be endangered from either of two directions. On the one hand, as Iris Young observes, detachment is too often obtained by abstracting from particular affiliations and commitments. "A person's particular sense of history, affinity, and separateness, even the person's mode of reasoning, evaluating, and expressing feeling, are constituted partly by her or his group affinities."[41] As individuals we may transcend or reject group identity, but we cannot pretend that it does not exist without risking co-optation by the values of the larger culture. On the other hand, we can allow the particularities of our experience to define us too completely, a danger especially relevant to sex difference, which most typically is a matter of being rather than a chosen affinity. In a critique of androgyny, Jean Elshtain suggests that liberal environmentalists "evade the possibility that human beings may have a 'nature' of some sort that is not exhausted with reference to the social forces that have impinged on it."[42] Because our bodies are not simply contingent facts, but are constitutive of the rational subject, even "our knowing is essentially tied to our experiences of ourselves as bodies" (149). But because we cannot leave our bodies as we can our cultures, I believe the danger is greater that we may allow this experience to become congruent with our identities.

The dilemma is this. Others' tendencies to view the experience of sex difference as constitutive of the self may construct the subject who wishes to stand beyond the reach of experience and choose its ends. Contrarily, others' attempts to abstract from these particularities in the search for a "universal" standpoint may act to deny a part of the self the subject wishes to affirm. This tension characterizes the "dilemma of difference" as described by Martha Minow. "When does treating people differently emphasize their differences and stigmatize or hinder them on that basis? and when does treating people the same become insensitive to their differences and likely to stigmatize or hinder them on *that* basis?"[43] Nancy Fraser asks similar questions. Too much feminist theory, on her view, vacillates between an antiessentialism that denigrates all differences as repressive and a multiculturalism that views all differences as features to be celebrated. But "*Which* politics of recognition best serves the victims of misrecognition? Revaluation of difference or deconstruction of identity?"[44] Each of these options can either enhance or detract from the development of the capacity for autonomy. Which identity claims provide both a range of possibilities and the capacity to engage in critical reflection on what these mean for our own lives? The objective reality of sex difference will persist, unlike cultural difference that may change or disappear, through reinterpretation or assimilation. The crucial issue, then, is what we do with the reality of sex difference, whether this means ignoring it, celebrating it, or doing something in between.

ESSENTIALISM

For some theorists of difference, much political thought that is apparently neutral in abstracting from the particularity of sex difference begins with a self-understanding that is historically male, and thus from a particularized understanding after all. This in turn implies a particularized or essentialist understanding of women. For Carole Pateman, although the social contract has operated as a paramount metaphor for conditions of autonomy, women are subordinate to men according to the terms of a hypothetical or imaginary sexual contract, the scope and terms of which are not freely chosen but are authorized by the state. Biology has been destiny for both men and women. Indeed, feminist constructions of an "ostensibly sex-neutral 'individual'" in reality force women to become replicas of men.[45] And even with the civil standing of men, women are often viewed and view themselves primarily as wives (135–142).

Because Pateman believes that the social construction of the self includes its sexual construction, in a patriarchal society the centrality of experience and contingency, both biological and social, constitutes the female self and its resulting ends. That is, we place women in a structural position that shapes and narrows subsequent understandings of women and, more important, women's self-understandings. From one perspective, Pateman's view is antiessentialist in that difference and identity do not emanate from a group's objective or unalterable character or essence. In another sense, however, for Pateman women apparently cannot will the transcendence of their biological constitution to challenge their social construction, whether in patriarchal society or elsewhere. "The body and the self are not identical, but selves are inseparable from bodies" (206), characterized by differences that cannot be chosen or rejected. Pateman desires a social framework that recognizes that both the social and biological construction of the female self has limited her self-understandings and her choices. But because women should not strive to be "individuals" or replicas of men, she wants to abandon the "masculine, unitary individual" (224) for two coequal types of individuals. Juridical freedom and equality provide the proper context, but "women's equal standing must be accepted as an expression of the freedom of women *as women,* and not treated as an indication that women can be just like men" (231).

In contrast, Zillah Eisenstein recognizes the social construction of the female self as society and culture convert biological sex into gender, but without suggesting, as Pateman does, that women who are "individuals" are replicas of men. Women can be individuals in their own right but may need different treatment to accomplish this. "To recognize the particularity and specificity of woman's body need not be to define her as 'different.' . . . Differences must be reformulated so that diversity between the sexes is not incongruous with equality between them."[46] The law has traditionally constructed legislative classifications involving pregnancy and veterans' preferences to ignore women but has treated them as nondiscriminatory, because significant numbers of nonpregnant persons and nonveterans exist of each sex (67). She concludes that "sex/gender-specific legislation is not inherently problematic or progressive. It is made so by its aim and its political content" (206).[47] Equality is the constitutive goal, she implies, whereas the alternatives of same or different treatment are derivative from this goal.

Overall, I am wary of Pateman's admonition that we should treat women "as women." All individuals, women as well as men, like members of national minorities or ethnic groups, should be enabled to interpret their identities for themselves, to embrace whatever attributes they take on critical reflection to be constitutive of selfhood. But they must also be able to detach themselves from attributes they do *not* wish to claim and to embrace others they may have chosen, or which, on reflection, they believe more constitutive of identity than those originally thought to define them by others or by themselves. Biology will of course structure both reflection and choice. If this particularity is ignored, the female subject who wishes to embrace its imperatives as she understands them will fall short as a "sex-neutral" individual premised on male assumptions. But if, on the contrary, this particularity is taken for granted as central in the social construction of the self, the female subject may lack opportunities to stand beyond the reach of experience to reflect on and choose her ends. In the first case, we resemble what Fraser views as deconstructive antiessentialists, who view any particularistic identity as a repressive fiction. In the second case, we resemble her multiculturalists, who celebrate any particularistic identity as worthy of recognition simply because it is distinguishable from others. In either case, the individual capacity for self-interpretation is potentially circumscribed, because the way others deconstruct or celebrate our identities is a context of choice affecting the way we ourselves interpret our identities.

A provocative approach to the dilemma of difference is offered by Minow. In contrast to the traditional-rights approach, she proposes a social-relations approach, according to which differences are grounded in relationships, not in immutable and fixed attributes of individuals.[48] Although the traditional rights approach may prescribe either equal or special treatment, depending on circumstances, it still presumes "that differences reside in the different person rather than in relation to norms embedded in prevailing institutions" (108). The social-relations approach challenges the tendency to define individuals on a group basis, instead locating "difference as a comparison drawn—by somebody—between groups" (119). Her treatment of *California Federal Savings and Loan Association et al. v. Mark Guerra et al.* may serve as an example of this approach.[49] In this case on the issue of pregnancy leave, Minow suggests that too often, men have been represented as the norm and women as deviant from that norm. But here, the Supreme Court upheld a California statute protecting women's jobs after pregnancy leave on the grounds that the law allows women *and* men to rear families without risking their jobs. Because women are uniquely burdened by their reproductive roles, "the Court used women's experiences as the benchmark and called for treating men equally in reference to women, thus reversing the usual practice."[50] Perceived difference dissolves in the face of an overarching similarity. Because this solution still locates differences in persons, however, Minow notes that a true social-relations approach would challenge the public and private power arrangements that have constructed the social meanings of reproductive traits and have thus maintained structures that exclude and discriminate (282). If power can construct, power, she implies, may also be used to deconstruct these social meanings and also by extension to broaden our self-understandings.

The idea that identity must be viewed as open-ended if we are to engage in real self-interpretation is also captured by Nancy Hirschmann. On her view, Isaiah Berlin's negative and positive conceptions of liberty describe the two impediments to human agency, external constraints and internal barriers, but the latter can shape the former. Customs and social rules emanating from male domination have "become constitutive not only of what women are allowed to do but of what they are allowed to *be* as well; . . . such rules are not simply external restrictions on women's otherwise natural desires; rather they create an entire cultural context that makes women seem to choose what they are in fact restricted to."[51] Instead of asking the typical liberal question of how free individuals become obligated, Hirschmann would reverse this to ask how initially limited individuals become free. She adapts the model of negative liberty by expanding it to "highlight the way in which things that are considered 'internal' barriers within positive liberty are externally generated, culturally mediated and created," so that inner barriers often are not individualized but result from social conditioning (53). The model of positive liberty remains valuable as a reminder that individuals' wills and desires can become implicated "in supporting the very structures that apparently restrict them. . . . What these barriers have already constructed as internal identity may remain. That identity may be 'genuine'; . . . but its 'genuineness' does not foreclose questions of liberty" (56). Feminist freedom requires, for Hirschmann, both the individuation central to negative liberty and the recognition of context central to positive liberty, if individuals are to become "capable of making choices for themselves and of understanding themselves in and through those relationships that give us our 'desires' and 'will' in the first place" (63).

Hirschmann's account supports the point that what appears to be in accordance with the identity of women may instead reflect the cultural context within which women define and interpret these identities. This sort of tension can be found in *E.E.O.C. v. Sears,* in which the Equal Employment Opportunity Commission represented women charging Sears with sex discrimination in hiring policies for commission sales jobs and in certain managerial pay scales.[52] Sears was acquitted on its argument that it had not in fact discriminated by refusing to hire women, but that instead women chose not to apply for such jobs, which accounted for the low numbers of women. Those supporting the plaintiffs argued that because women were already victims of implicit social norms discouraging them from some kinds of employment, Sears should have been more aggressive in its recruitment procedures. Sears's supporters responded, however, that because women have distinct familial needs and interests, high-pressure jobs are less likely to attract them. As Sondra Farganis describes this argument, "Women are . . . people who have internalized different interests from men and who have a different set of goals respecting work."[53] This case illustrates the overlap pinpointed by Hirschmann between negative and positive liberty. Members of historically subordinate groups may accept gendered patterns "out of an acceptance of their legitimacy and the legitimacy of the authorities who formulate them" (65). When this has been the case, "how women viewed the world of work was affected by how the world viewed women" (59). The larger issue is the significance of difference. If men and women have different interests, these are not necessarily ineluctable and unalterable, and a liberal polity should encourage critical reflection on this possibility.

STRUCTURALISM

If individuals are to be able to detach themselves from attributes or interests they do not wish to claim and to embrace others they may have chosen as more truly constitutive of their identity, structural change appears to be in order. But this approach is also problematic. For theorists like Susan Okin, we are collectively responsible for making changes that would induce the world, in Farganis's terms, to view women in ways that would broaden the manner in which women view the world of work. In Okin's view, the traditional "division of labor within most families raises psychological as well as practical barriers against women in all other spheres."[54] Women become vulnerable in anticipation of marriage as they seek traditional positions with flexible hours but also poor pay, working conditions, and mobility (144); vulnerable within marriage as they give priority to their husbands' careers, which in turn perpetuates the traditional domestic division of labor and lessens their commitment to outside work (146–159); and vulnerable through separation or divorce, due to husbands' greater earning power and to inequitable divisions of property that do not recognize earning power as the asset it is (160–169). Altogether these vulnerabilities are both socially created and asymmetric, influencing both the quantity and quality of available options even when we are unaware of the context of choice.

The *Sears* case resonates here because even though Sears might not have engaged in discriminatory hiring practices with regard to actual applicants, it is, like other institutions, implicated in a larger context that structures how individuals perceive their options. To the extent that women buy into identity claims that are congruent with the perception of narrowed options, they are affirming an identity that upholds relationships of inequality and domination. Okin advocates structural reforms that "encourage and facilitate the equal sharing by men and women of paid and unpaid work, of productive and reproductive labor. We must work toward a future in which all will be likely to choose this mode of life. A just future would be one without gender" (171). Public policy should not differentiate between the sexes, and the workplace and family law should be changed so that no such differentiation would be necessary (170–186). When families choose a traditional division of labor, household income should be considered jointly earned even when the labor of one partner is unpaid. Okin clearly prefers the genderless family, however, as more just to women, more conducive to equal opportunity, and more favorable to the rearing of just citizens (183).

Okin's account has the virtue of showing not only that our context of choice greatly affects the way we perceive our options but also that the socioeconomic structure also structures our context of choice. Fraser observes that too often, concerns of identity tend to promote the recognition of difference, whereas concerns of redistribution tend to undermine this recognition. Yet the cultural injustice of domination and nonrecognition interacts with the socioeconomic injustice of exploitation and deprivation in a way that is mutually reinforcing.[55] Although my own preferences, like Okin's, gravitate toward equal sharing in paid and unpaid labor, I have reservations about the adoption of a universal set of prescriptions. I have maintained that the capacity for autonomy is lived out not in the selection of particular options over others, but in the exercise of critical reflection as we construct the ongoing narrative that our lives represent. If we are indeed to define and interpret our identities for ourselves, it is important not only that we recognize how the larger context structures the way we perceive our options but also that, after taking this dynamic into account, we reaffirm or revise our current commitments based on our own desires, both first and second order, rather than living in accordance with what may *appear* to be autonomous to others. We need conditions that facilitate critical reflection, but beyond this, there is no litmus test that would demonstrate the exercise of autonomy by the outcomes of this reflection.

Okin suggests that if gender disappears, "one's sex would have no more relevance than one's eye color or the length of one's toes. No assumptions would be made about 'male' and 'female' roles. . . . It would be a future in which men and women participated in more or less equal numbers in every sphere of life."[56] To me, the numbers matter less than the reasons that guide our selections. Martha Nussbaum wonders whether the experience of sexuality can be accurately compared with the experience of eye color, or whether sexuality does not go deeper.[57] I think that generally, sex is constitutive of selfhood in ways that eye color is not. But each of us needs to determine that extent for

ourselves if we are truly to be self-interpreting. Whether we commit to projects now regarded as atypical of our particular sex or develop more conventional commitments, we should be able to engage in these pursuits without
assumptions by others that these projects must not be freely chosen or affirmed.
Okin's proposed reforms make an important contribution, but less to the disappearance of gender than to the structuring of a context of choice that presents
both a range of alternatives and alternatives that may be viewed as realistic options in practice.

Once this structure is in place, however, each of us should be able to engage
in critical reflection as we examine our possibilities and define our identities
through the choices we make. It is for individual women to decide the extent
to which they wish to live their lives espousing projects and goals traditionally
attributed to men, those typically attributed to women, or some of each. We
should be free either to embrace or to reject attributes that may initially be constitutive of our personhood. If, as Alasdair MacIntyre suggests, the unity of
the self is rooted in a narrative quest that links our experiences over time, these
experiences and the alternatives they present constitute the raw material, while
our self-conscious and critical reflection enables us to process this material
effectively and to build good lives on the basis of identities that we define for
ourselves.

When Okin, for example, suggests that in families choosing a traditional
division of labor, both partners should share legal entitlement to all household
earnings, this arrangement is by definition consciously chosen rather than
assumed. Yet a "traditional" division might encompass families in which the
wife earns the bulk of the income and families headed by gay or lesbian cou-
ples who divide the required labor "traditionally." One partner in each case is
likely to be vulnerable to the socioeconomic realities of traditional marriage,
without some of the reforms that Okin advocates. As we have seen with regard
to culture, commitments need not stem from unchosen constituents of our
identities to disadvantage us.

Yet Okin is correct, I believe, to reject assumptions about the roles people
will choose. For example, Iris Young supports group-specific or gender-con-
scious policy that "publicly acknowledges culturally based gender differences"
but is "directed at rendering femininely gendered cultural attributes costless for
women."[58] This approach is unconcerned with whether differences are natural
or not but aims to preclude either reward or punishment for following what
would traditionally be considered a male or female lifestyle. Yet although a gen-
der-conscious policy allows the individual to *affirm* specific experiences and particularities, we must take care that it does not *confirm* these particularities too

easily. The acceptance of structured social gender differences may relieve the tension that impels us to reexamine our affinities and attachments, to arrive at new self-understandings, and perhaps to make new choices. Some families, for example, may opt for traditional roles for a time, but the caregiving partner may at some point want to rethink his or her chosen role. If policies are in place that confirm traditional differences, individuals in these roles may be subtly discouraged from reflecting on the question of whether their current arrangement is the best life for them. I am not suggesting that we should not protect the vulnerable because they may then become too comfortable. I do think that institutions must be structured so that individuals always view themselves as possessing options.

In sum, individuals should be able to choose female, male, androgynous, working, or caregiving lifestyles without cost, but the recognition of difference should not structure categories so that those who inhabit them automatically affirm them without periodically engaging in critical reflection on their projects and goals. If we decide to subsidize ways of life that are matters of choice by making them "costless," we should ensure insofar as possible that they *are* in fact matters of choice instead of representing the line of least resistance. The point that cultural membership is the expression of autonomy rather than its precondition is applicable in this context. If the availability of male, female, and androgynous lifestyles is regarded as a precondition, this suggests nothing that ensures that the lifestyle that we follow results from critical reflection. It presents a menu of options but says nothing about the reasons that should count in the making of selections from this menu. If, however, the pursuit of various lifestyles is regarded as the expression of autonomy, the emphasis is first on the process through which we arrive at decisions, and only secondarily on the end state that results.

The affirmation of specific affinities and particularities need not negate our need to question, examine, and revise or reaffirm our current commitments, projects, and goals. We can admit the importance of difference without essentializing it, just as we can assert the importance of autonomy without denying its relational character. Individuals should not have to abstract from their specific affinities and particularities if they wish to affirm them or if they wish others to affirm their personhood. On the other hand, they should not be forced to define themselves by them, nor should others insist on viewing them as essential. We should be able to affirm particularity without being trapped by it. Only then can we define and interpret our identities for ourselves by choosing which affinities will matter.

5. Toleration and Religious Belief

Among the sorts of diversity that liberal societies have traditionally privileged is that of religious belief. On a standard account like that of John Rawls, the Protestant Reformation and subsequent controversies over religious toleration formed the historical origin of liberalism, as evidence accumulated that agreement on one comprehensive religious, philosophical, or moral doctrine was not in fact a necessary condition of social order and stability. More generally, the political and social conditions of modern democratic societies ensure not only that a diversity of reasonable comprehensive doctrines will persist as a permanent feature of the public culture but also that this diversity will develop if it does not already exist. Finally, the inevitability of diversity as a permanent feature ensures that frequently, shared agreement can be maintained only through coercion by the state.[1] It is for these reasons, of course, that Rawls seeks a political conception of justice grounded in an overlapping consensus that can be endorsed by those holding widely different, often opposing, but still reasonable comprehensive doctrines.

Religious affiliation is a type of cultural membership in which members of particular religions, denominations, and sects are generally expected to adhere to particular beliefs and practices as a condition of continued membership. Liberal societies and governments have traditionally privileged religious belief, according toleration to practices that might not be accommodated if they did not emanate from such belief. Yet disagreement exists about the status of religious belief as a component of personal identity as well as about the correct rationale for tolerating a diversity of beliefs within the liberal polity. These issues are intertwined, as our views of the role of religious belief in individual identity may influence our perceptions of what practices should be tolerated and for what reasons. The liberal polity as I have described it is committed both to the maintenance of background conditions for individual autonomy and self-development and to a culture of diversity containing a plurality of options. Yet just as every state must necessarily be based on some set of determinate principles and commitments that reflect a particular cultural mix precluding legal and cultural neutrality, so also every state takes a particular stance toward religious belief. This in turn precludes religious neutrality by structuring the context of choice within which we survey our options and revise or reaffirm our projects and goals.[2]

The circumstances of toleration exist, first, where diverse practices obtain that some persons disapprove or dislike, and second, where those who disapprove refrain from using power they possess to interfere with or extirpate these practices.[3] The objects of toleration occupy a narrow space between practices that are intolerable because they are impermissible, on the one hand, and practices that are "intolerable" because they do not or should not arouse opposition in the first place, on the other hand.[4] Although liberalism has been hospitable to diversity and has accordingly championed the merits of toleration, the relationship between liberalism and toleration is not devoid of controversy. Where some critics object that liberals tolerate only what does not conflict with liberal values and are therefore less permissive than they pretend, others contend that liberals are merely indifferent, refusing to make judgments, and are therefore more permissive than they ought to be.[5] But true toleration, then, is not rooted in indifference or skepticism; it is the initial commitment to our own beliefs and practices and our ability and desire to suppress our rivals, after all, that give rise to the need for restraint.[6] Toleration means recognizing the value of other persons who are committed to particular belief systems and who freely choose particular ways of life. It does not imply any lack of commitment to our own way of life.[7]

I shall first discuss variations in the meaning of toleration and the functions that toleration can perform in the liberal state. Next, I shall examine the nature of religious belief, focusing on ways in which its role as a particularistic feature of our identity can constitute an expression of autonomy. Belief may represent choice not only when we abandon our ancestral religion and embrace a different faith but also when we examine, question, and reaffirm our current faith, adhering to it for our own reasons rather than simply from custom and habit. If we can choose our faith by reaffirming it under conditions of critical reflection, the accommodation of particular religious sects can protect autonomy. I shall then discuss some of the functions served by this accommodation and how we might distinguish between practices that should and should not be so accommodated. Again, however these conflicts may be resolved, the settlement cannot be neutral.[8]

The Nature of Toleration

An attitude of tolerance and a practice of toleration toward a variety of beliefs and practices appear congruent with the values of both autonomy and diversity. If we recognize human diversity and value the existence and perpetuation of a plurality of options, we should understand the need to tolerate that which we dislike. If, in addition, we value the human capacity to question, examine, and revise or reaffirm our projects and goals, which is central to personal autonomy, we should understand that this capacity must be exercised from the inside, as we each discover for ourselves what is a good life for us. From the liberal perspective, as Susan Mendus suggests, "The belief in autonomy and the requirement of neutrality both imply that ways of life, commitments, moral ideals, are at root matters of individual choice. Political toleration is then a necessity if such choice is to be fostered."[9]

If one justification for toleration is rooted in the value of individual choice, a second is based on what might be termed the value of communal integrity. This justification requires a perceptual shift in understanding those we tolerate not merely as the agents of particular beliefs or practices, but as persons like ourselves, motivated by a cognitive system in which our actions and beliefs are rooted. This approach to toleration appeals to second-order reasons or a larger context in which we may value ways of life independently of particular "wrong" beliefs or actions that others espouse. Toleration then not only respects individuals but also promotes social cohesion.[10] To put this differently, the demand for toleration represents a desire to belong to a larger whole, but on one's own terms. Toleration is a way of promoting and sustaining a sense of common citizenship, although it alone is not a sufficient condition. A feeling of belonging requires from others not simply grudging toleration of beliefs and practices, but respect and esteem for the individual persons who hold or act on them.[11]

Policies of toleration and the grounding for these are often contingent matters, derivative from other goals rather than intrinsically constitutive of a particular political morality.[12] This point should not surprise us, even with respect to liberalism. The commitment of liberals like Locke to popular governance, religious toleration, the rule of law, and other liberties was a means to the specific ends of peace, prosperity through economic growth, and intellectual progress.[13] Locke himself exemplifies a transition from the view that mere outward conformity to imposed practice cannot adversely affect one's spiritual fate and nevertheless fulfills the moral duty of civil obedience, to the view that because belief cannot be compelled, individuals must within limits be allowed to act on their beliefs as to what practices are necessary for salvation. The reasons for his shift to policies of toleration bear interestingly on the role that religious belief plays in individual identity.

Because he recognizes both the permanence of diversity and also the centrality of particularistic beliefs to individual identity, Locke in his early writing tends to oppose policies of religious toleration. He views religious motivations and attachments as distinctive among beliefs that animate ethical sensibilities. Entailing ultimate concerns about the meaning of life, religious beliefs are characterized by an emotional commitment not subject to rational argumentation. The centrality of religious conviction to identity accordingly prevents the believer from envisioning alternative modes of thinking either for oneself or for others.[14] In Sandelian terms, the believing self is encumbered and its beliefs are constitutive attributes of identity, rather than contingent features chosen by a detached and unencumbered self. A denial of civil jurisdiction in religious matters in favor of individual judgment too easily eventuates in a similar denial in civil matters, leading to conflict and potential anarchy. Although sovereign authority is not unlimited, if we must choose between the authority of a myriad of consciences and that of a single center of judgment, for Locke the common good admits only one answer. Lest this viewpoint be thought overly alarmist from a contemporary perspective, recall the discussion of forced marriage and female genital alteration in chapter 3. Moreover, under the Religious Freedom Restoration Act of 1993, before its partial overturning in 1997, about 200 decisions were handed down by courts in cases brought by prison inmates claiming that regulations on drug use, dress, and grooming infringed on their free exercise of religion,[15] and there were periodic anecdotal reports of attempts by inmates to argue that their religious practice mandated the ceremonial use of weapons.

Eventually, however, Locke becomes convinced that the implementation of toleration will itself mitigate the dangers of religious identification, both by establishing boundaries between private and public and also by introducing psychological constraints on individuals. First, in the practice of what Ingrid Creppell terms "public privacy," Locke suggests that God should be publicly worshiped through the public presentation of one's private beliefs before the larger community, despite the fact that the community witnessing the presentation is not a unified one. This practice legitimates an individuation of belief by protecting public presentation from interference and by creating a buffer zone between the purely private and purely public that combines communal expression and recognition with juridical distance and protection.[16] Second, this sphere of public privacy facilitates and is complemented by the experience of psychological pluralism within individuals, who view themselves as loci of multiple experiences, allegiances, and points of view that can give meaning to their lives (230). If the earlier Locke is disturbed by the collapsing of distance between oneself and one's beliefs, the later Locke's solution is the creation of contingencies that *encourage* one to distance oneself from one's beliefs, to envision enough detachment to understand alternative ways of thinking. In a society open to diverse beliefs and identities, we may infer, constraints on unacceptable levels of conflict may be internalized by encouraging individuals to recognize that the commitments with which they identify are, in effect, but one possible mode of self-interpretation. Such a grounding for toleration promotes the values of both individual choice and communal integrity.

Nevertheless, religious toleration for Locke is circumscribed by civil authority. Although the correct test for public interference with religious rituals and practices, he believes, is that of actual bodily injury to the individual or the body politic rather than offense to others' sensibilities or beliefs (224), the definition of injury is itself problematic and dependent on one's beliefs and perspectives. Therefore, the civil authority must establish a civil criterion of worldly injury to life, liberty, and property that then determines the appropriate scope of religious belief and practice. The line between the civil and the religious is an object of civil determination, rather than one of conscientious belief, and may change along with the demands of the public interest, which is itself civilly determined.[17] The criterion of worldly injury is an attempt to make civil law neutral with respect to religion, but it does so by rendering irrelevant any consideration of or reference to the validity or appropriateness of religious practices on their own terms. Locke's stance resonates with Martha Minow's social-relations approach to difference, which presumes that differences do not necessarily reside in the person or object that is judged to be different but instead are a function of the norms embedded in prevailing institutions.[18] Because the norms of believers often differ from those of unbelievers, as sacred norms do from secular ones, no stance appears neutral to all.

Purported neutrality toward conceptions of the good itself constitutes a metatheory of the good, as it eliminates conceptions that can only be realized in communities that are not themselves neutral toward conflicting conceptions of the good.[19] In Locke, because civil authority determines the boundary of religious practice, civil law that is neutral with regard to the religious truth of particular practices is *not* neutral or politically indifferent toward the practical embodiments of some religious visions of the good society. As Kirstie McClure suggests, the difficulty is that "the civil discourse of facticity itself has become a site riddled with conflicting interpretations of which particular sets of social 'facts' are to be considered indicative of the sort of 'harm' appropriately subject to political jurisdiction."[20] Her examples include Marx on property and Catharine MacKinnon on pornography, who characterize seemingly isolated practices as embedded within systems "which operate to reconstitute as injurious, and hence political, 'facts' which were previously understood as civilly benign" (384).

Although Locke's concern is religious practices that may be questionable from the standpoint of civil interest, his interpretation also applies to "civilly benign" practices that partisans of particular religious and ethical beliefs may view as injurious. People who believe abortion is wrong because the fetus is a human being from the moment of conception hold different worldviews and accept different sets of social facts about the nature of social morality and the proper role of women and children than do those who believe that abortion is a matter of personal choice.[21] Pro-life proponents want to use *their* set of social facts to reconstitute as civilly injurious the legality of abortion that pro-choice advocates and civil law classify as benign. Similarly, those who believe that abortion is rightly a matter of personal choice argue that the severe limitation on reproductive choice represented by abortion's criminalization constitutes worldly injury to the civil interests of women, to their agency and their moral and personal autonomy. Because each side begins with a different set of social facts, they hold different views of what is injurious and what is civilly benign. Neither camp wants its viewpoint denied empirical validity and relegated "to the category of speculative truths without worldly effect."[22]

Although the tradition of the Protestant Reformation sanctions individual freedom of conscience, wherein individuals may choose to adhere to, change, or reject religious affiliation altogether, religious toleration need not be equated with freedom of conscience. Another version of religious toleration is a group-rights model, which grants official status and a degree of self-government to several religious communities. The latter may enforce internal religious orthodoxy, allowing little individual dissent or freedom to change one's affiliation.[23] Will Kymlicka's primary example is the Ottoman millet system between 1456 and the Ottoman collapse during World War I, during which time the Greek Orthodox, Armenian Orthodox, and Jewish non-Muslim minorities were officially recognized as self-governing communities or millets, which together were, "in effect, a federation of theocracies."[24] Modern variations on this legal arrangement include the self-government rights of Native American tribes, partial exemption from mandatory education laws granted to some religious groups in the United States and Canada, and requests from some British Muslim leaders for milletlike protections for culturally traditional educational and family practices that violate current law against coercive arranged marriages and sexual discrimination.

These two models of toleration together reflect the overall tension between toleration grounded in the value of individual choice, on the one hand, and toleration based on the protection of communal integrity, on the other. Liberals who value autonomy perceive autonomy and tolerance as mutually reinforcing. For Kymlicka, "What distinguishes *liberal* tolerance is precisely its commitment to autonomy—that is, the idea that individuals should be free to assess and potentially revise their existing ends."[25] Liberal toleration, then, is grounded in the value of individual choice. This in turn may require not only toleration but also a fostering of diversity as a context of choice and a precondition for autonomy.

Alternatively and "by contrast, toleration may simply involve accommodating those diverse forms of life which already exist."[26] Toleration grounded in the value of communal integrity concentrates on the accommodation of existing diversity, as in the millet system. Such a system "assumes that people's religious affiliation is so profoundly constitutive of who they are that . . . they have no interest in being able to stand back and assess that identity."[27] In fact, Moshe Halbertal questions whether the millet system even exemplifies toleration. Existing historically for the convenience of and on terms defined by the Muslim majority, it did not exhibit the political manifestation of "an attempt to shape a common political structure shared by radically diverse groups."[28] Yet the Lockean model, as we have seen, does not accord decisive authority to liberty of conscience. And the millet system's guarantee of collective freedom of worship rendered recognized minorities better off than they would otherwise have been, affording them membership in the wider community without requiring that they totally assimilate to its values. If the model grounded in freedom of conscience is more bounded than we sometimes think, the group-rights model also offers advantages. If toleration includes the accommodation of already-existing diversity as well as individual choices producing new manifestations of diversity, the group-rights model qualifies.

If the freedom-of-conscience model, grounded in the value of individual choice, is the "gold standard" of liberal toleration, however, it must be grounded in the capacity of individuals to examine, question, and possibly revise their current projects and goals. Rawls believes that citizens can espouse autonomy as a political value while rejecting it as a comprehensive and ethical value that shapes both public and private life.[29] If, however, we view our religious and other moral commitments as constitutive of our private identities, how, as Kymlicka asks, do we divest ourselves of these commitments for purposes of exercising political judgment?[30] Or if we are indeed successful in this endeavor, how, I would ask, do we prevent our public identities from permeating the private identities that may reject revisability as a core value? Because *liberal* toleration is grounded in the value of individual choice, its own value is derivative from a context of independent thought and critical reflectiveness.

In short, we cannot simultaneously defend both the nonrevisability of non-public commitments and also the political value of autonomy, which arguably is itself a necessary condition for the shaping of a common political structure under conditions of diversity. As we have seen, however, Locke believes that religious motivations and attachments are distinctive in their emotional appeal, in their imperviousness to rational argumentation, and in their tendency to block out alternative modes of thinking by believers. If religious beliefs are qualitatively different from other forms of diversity, as attachments so constitutive of the self that this precludes any interest other than that of protecting and advancing this form of identity, then religious factionalism and diversity cannot be considered in the same manner as the cultural membership discussed in chapter 3.

Choice and Religious Belief

One of the two justifications for toleration to which I have alluded is that grounded in the value of individual choice. If we value the human capacity to examine, question, and revise or reaffirm our current projects and goals, we must also value the existence of the range of options necessary to our exercise of this capacity from the inside, as we decide for ourselves individually what constitutes the good life for us. As we have seen, Rawls describes the capacity to take responsibility for our ends and to adjust these as necessary as "part of the moral power to form, to revise, and rationally to pursue a conception of the good; and it is public knowledge conveyed by the political conception [of justice] that citizens are to be held responsible," whether or not our tastes and preferences have arisen from our actual choices.[31] Rawls is implying that although we experience first-order desires that we have not chosen to experience, we also experience second-order desires that may mitigate, enhance, and otherwise order the former, thus enabling us to take responsibility for them. Liberal toleration in particular is grounded in the liberal commitment to autonomy, to the revisability of our projects and goals.[32]

Liberal toleration may, however, lay claim to an alternative ground. Yael Tamir makes a distinction between autonomy-based liberalism, which "tolerates and respects only autonomy-supporting cultures—namely, liberal ones," and rights-based liberalism, which focuses on individual rights regardless of whether these are grounded in autonomous choice. Whereas autonomy-based liberalism promotes the conditions of autonomy and the assimilation of illiberal cultures to liberal ones, rights-based liberalism "places at its core a commitment to equal concern and respect for individuals, their preferences and interests, regardless of the way these were formed."[33] With respect to religious belief, Tamir's formulation suggests that toleration may be grounded in individual rights and interests regardless of whether these include choice, just as in the millet system toleration is accorded regardless of the way beliefs and values are generated. Moreover, traditional liberalism "was committed to protecting a set of freedoms which were meant to allow individuals to pursue their preferences, desires and interests, regardless of whether these were formed autonomously or were forced upon individuals by their culture or tradition" (168). In the latter circumstance, I infer that Tamir includes interests grounded in unthinking habit, perpetuated neither by conscious reaffirmation nor by actual coercion in the face of resistance.

Alternatively, then, perhaps toleration of religious belief is most properly grounded not in choice but in its absence. For a characterization of religious belief with which many persons of faith would probably agree, I should like to quote in full the words of an Episcopal hymn.

> In your mercy, Lord, you called me
> Taught my sin-filled heart and mind,
> Else this world had still enthralled me,
> And to glory kept me blind.
>
> Lord, I did not freely choose you
> Till by grace you set me free;
> For my heart would still refuse you
> Had your love not chosen me.
>
> Now my heart sets none above you,
> For your grace alone I thirst,
> Knowing well, that if I love you,
> You, O Lord, have loved me first.[34]

These verses make clear that in the minds of many believers, they do not choose initially to have faith in God. Rather, he chooses them, inspires them, and in some manner invites them into relationship with him. Although this invitation may constitute a transformative experience, they still exercise agency in their responses. In the second verse, the writer did not freely choose God *until* grace freed him from worldly entanglements, enabling him to perceive a better way of life. Subsequently, however, he does choose to respond to God's invitation, always mindful of the fact that he could not have exercised this choice without the bestowal of grace. Although other religious faiths will not give the priority to grace that we find in Christianity, for any that ground faith on personal interaction between human beings and a deity, the role of choice in religious belief is not a simple one.

According to Andrew Murphy, early advocates of toleration argued that because conscience was a faculty of the understanding rather than the will, liberty to follow the dictates of conscience required religious voluntarism. But "Voluntarism is not the same thing, strictly speaking, as *choice:* in other words, tolerationists did not claim that one *chose* one's beliefs, but rather that the understanding was persuaded, inexorably so, of the truth of a given faith." Individuals were to follow God's will but "voluntarily and without threat of punishment for nonperformance, or else the obedience lacked merit."[35] In the twentieth century, conscience-based belief, whether sacred or secular, is viewed as "extravoluntary," and therefore "sacrosanct" (7).

Although I agree that beliefs and many of the practices that attach to them are appropriate objects of toleration in the face of others' disapproval, whatever the degree to which they are chosen, I disagree, however, that they are as unchosen as many suppose. I have argued that Kymlicka, by privileging cultural membership as a precondition of autonomy in one's culture of origin over membership in cultures of choice, implies that cultural membership is a nonrevisable commitment. Moreover, to protect this context of choice, his conception of cultural rights potentially accords the most protection to groups that do not value individual autonomy as the capacity to reexamine and possibly to revise one's projects and goals. I agreed instead with Geoffrey Brahm Levey that cultural membership is best conceived not as a precondition of autonomy but as an expression of autonomy. With respect to the realm of conscience, adherence to a religious faith may not be "chosen" in the same way that ordinary preferences are said to be chosen, but I believe that religious faith and practice, like cultural membership, can also constitute an expression of autonomy. Therefore, where toleration is appropriate to protect individuals' beliefs and values, these are "sacrosanct" not because they are "extravoluntary" but because they are a feature of identity to which individuals attach great importance and that may function as an expression of autonomy. Moreover, individuals must decide for themselves the claims of their particularistic identities *or* faiths, working out their meanings over time, because meaning is not self-defining or self-interpreting. Therefore, in the end religious faith, like cultural membership, functions as an expression of autonomy. Let us turn now to the issue of how belief and conscience may both be viewed as aspects of identity that are constitutive, yet also operate as expressions of autonomy.

CONSTITUTIVE CHOICE

Susan Mendus observes that in discussing religious beliefs, we correctly favor references to recognizing, seeing, and acknowledging them over descriptions of choosing, opting for, or deciding on them.[36] This point is paralleled by Michael Sandel's observation that liberal theorists overemphasize the voluntarist dimension of human agency, which stresses choice, at the expense of the cognitive dimension, which focuses on recognition or understanding of an already-existing situation.[37] We often fail, he suggests, to recognize the extent to which attributes we think we choose as detached selves are in fact constitutive features of our identities that encumber us from the start, although ones that we may not immediately recognize. Human agency, however, requires the self not only to choose but also to reflect, "to turn its light inward upon itself, to inquire into its constituent nature, to survey its various attachments and acknowledge their respective claims . . . to arrive at a self-understanding less opaque if never perfectly transparent," as over a lifetime the self participates in constituting its identity (153). We must examine this contrast between choice and understanding if we are to arrive at a true appreciation of the nature of freedom of conscience.

For Sandel, the liberal polity's insistence on governmental neutrality among moral beliefs and values is grounded on the assumption that individuals choose their projects and goals from a detached and unencumbered viewpoint. But this framework is not truly neutral. It overlooks the possibility that individuals are encumbered by beliefs and ties that are constitutive attributes of identity.[38] The reality that the perceived neutrality of a public stance depends on which set of social facts is used to measure the acceptability of a particular practice reveals itself in Supreme Court opinions. As Sandel argues, even dissents from opinions striking down religious practices have valorized neutrality by arguing that the majority has established a religion of secularism incompatible with "true" neutrality.[39] In other words, a purportedly neutral stance will appear neutral only on some interpretations of the factual circumstances, but not on other interpretations. Moreover, even if this stance did appear neutral to all concerned, it presumes a self that is detached from its professed beliefs rather than constituted by them, and it is thus nonneutral with regard to competing conceptions of the self.

To the framers of the Constitution, writes Sandel, freedom of conscience suggested freedom to act according to the dictates of one's beliefs without civil penalty (87). The modern form of freedom of conscience, however, suggests freedom to *choose* one's religious beliefs without interference and is rooted in respect for the individual capacity and right to make this choice (85–86). Most explicitly, Justice John Stevens's majority opinion when the Supreme Court struck down the moment of silence for voluntary prayer in public schools claims "support not only from the interest in respecting the individual's freedom of conscience, but also from the conviction that religious beliefs worthy of respect are the product of free and voluntary choice by the faithful."[40] For those of the founding generation, by contrast, "It is precisely because belief is not governed by will that freedom of conscience is unalienable." That is, "Where freedom of conscience is at stake, the relevant right is to exercise a duty, not make a choice" (88). Religious duties are not matters of choice but of conviction, serving constitutive ends inseparable from personal identity.

Sandel's example of the modern Court's view is the case of *Thornton v. Calder, Inc.*, in which a Supreme Court majority of eight to one struck down a Connecticut statute that guaranteed to Sabbath observers the right to take their weekly entitlement of one day off on their Sabbath. The Court believed that the law unfairly advantaged Sabbath observers over nonobservers, as only the former could select a coveted weekend day for their guaranteed day off. "But this objection confuses the right to exercise a duty with the right to make a choice. Sabbath observers, by definition, do not select the day of the week they rest; they rest on the day their religion requires."[41] Because the Court had earlier upheld Sunday closing laws on the grounds that these now serve a secular purpose and carry a recreational rather than a religious character, *Thornton* points to a perverse conclusion. "A state may require everyone to rest on Sunday, . . . so long as the aim is not to accommodate the observance of the Sabbath. But it may not give Sabbath observers the right to rest on the day of the week their religion requires. . . . It aptly reflects the constitutional consequences of seeing ourselves as unencumbered selves" (89–90).

More palatable from Sandel's perspective is the viewpoint expressed in *Sherbert v. Verner*, in which a Supreme Court majority overruled the denial of unemployment compensation to a Seventh-Day Adventist fired for refusing to work on her Sabbath of Saturday. A state attending to Sabbath observance on this view is not violating neutrality but is enforcing it in the light of religious differences. To force workers to choose between their religious convictions and their means of support would itself violate the imperatives of neutrality, advantaging those without religious duties over those with duties the exercise of which may conflict with secular expectations. "In this case at least, the Constitution was not blind to religion but alive to its imperatives."[42] It could be argued that *Sherbert* embodies neutrality by securing equal opportunities for Sabbath-observant and also Sabbath-nonobservant workers to live by or advance their conceptions of the good without penalty or civil disability. Even for Rawls, although the priority of the right over the good "allows that only permissible conceptions (those that respect the principles of justice) can be pursued," nevertheless, "the state is to secure equal opportunity to advance any permissible conception."[43] Under *Sherbert*, those for whom religious duties are constitutive of selfhood are not receiving special treatment but instead may secure accommodation for their conceptions of the good in the same way as those who do not understand themselves as thus obligated. Just as allowing women to resume prior jobs after unpaid pregnancy disability leave may be interpreted to suggest that women *and* men should be allowed to rear families without risking their jobs, Sandel's example suggests that the observant *and* the nonobservant should be allowed to live according to their convictions without risking their means of support. The Sabbath-observant are burdened in the workplace by their religious convictions in ways that the nonobservant are not.

The two cases exemplify the alternative meanings of freedom of conscience. In Kirstie McClure's terms, the set of social facts grounding *Thornton* classifies Sabbath observance as a choice; therefore, according more freedom to observant than to nonobservant workers in selecting a day off is not a civilly benign practice but is civilly injurious to people with less choice. The set of social facts grounding *Sherbert*, however, classifies Sabbath observance as a duty; thus according freedom to observant workers to refuse work on their Sabbath without forfeiting employment benefits is civilly benign across the board. Although applicants must accept available work to be eligible for benefits, Sabbath work is *not* "available" in the sense that observant workers may choose to perform it. In view of these social facts, it is civilly injurious to penalize Sabbath-observant workers, who have less choice than do the nonobservant, who can choose to accept available work at any time. The same conflict is reflected in *Wisconsin v. Yoder*, in which the Supreme Court exempted the Old Order Amish from state law requiring school attendance until a child is sixteen.[44] In sum, accommodation of practices stemming from religious belief is not neutral and is thus civilly injurious to the nonreligious when religious practices are viewed as matters of personal choice. On the other hand, this accommodation does seem neutral, and failure to accommodate would itself be nonneutral, when religious practices are perceived as matters of duty beyond the scope of personal choice. Because the appearance of neutrality is a function of one's interpretation of the factual circumstances, there can be no policy that all parties perceive as neutral.

I agree that religious belief can function as a core constituent of identity and that therefore we must be free to engage in a range of practices flowing from these beliefs in all the diversity to which these beliefs give rise. But freedom of conscience requires more than the liberty to exercise duties, a liberty emphasized by Sandel but also compatible with the Ottoman millet system. If we are not to view ourselves as passive carriers of beliefs, in Rawls's terms, we must be as open to the possibility of questioning, examining, and revising our beliefs as to affirming or reaffirming them. Both sorts of activity must be protected. I agree with the view of David A. J. Richards that the First Amendment's free exercise and antiestablishment clauses are grounded in different but complementary aspects of equal respect for human moral powers. The free exercise clause protects current conscientious belief against state coercion of the observance or expression of beliefs, whereas the antiestablishment clause focuses on "the formation and revision of conscience," protecting "the processes of forming and changing such conceptions."[45] Moreover, even individuals who share a faith often have different and conflicting interpretations of what duties and obligations flow from these shared convictions. And all who share an interpretation of what their convictions require do not place the same priority on these obligations in their individual hierarchy of values. In sum, unless we wish to relegate religious faith to a series of watertight compartments like the Ottoman millets, I am convinced that religious belief is not a precondition, in the sense of an encumbrance or an ineluctably constitutive feature, of our identity but is instead an expression of it, and more specifically, an expression of autonomy.

For example, consider the interpretation of religious belief suggested by Tamir, who does not accord protection to unchosen constituents of identity, like membership in a minority culture, because *membership* is unchosen, as Kymlicka does, but because *minority* status is unchosen. Whatever our original frameworks or contexts of choice, we can engage in critical reflection, exercise choice regarding future commitments, and define the meaning of membership regarding current commitments.[46] Cultural membership and religious affiliation then are matters of choice, as are the ways in which we interpret the meanings of our cultural and religious identities. From this perspective Tamir criticizes Sandel's lament that the Supreme Court in *Goldman v. Weinberger* upheld an Air Force prohibition that prevented an Orthodox Jewish captain from wearing a yarmulke while serving in a health clinic, regardless of whether the Air Force could show that the religious exception would impair military discipline. For Sandel, in *Goldman* as in *Thornton,* the tendency to conflate religious duty with personal choice "forgets the special concern of religious liberty with the claims of conscientiously encumbered selves."[47]

Tamir argues, however, that although Sandel is correct to want to defer to the free exercise of religious obligations, he is incorrect as to the grounds for doing so. First, if Goldman were to convert to a different faith or to become nonobservant while remaining a Jew, we would not force him to wear a yarmulke or to abstain from Sabbath work on the argument that he is perpetually encumbered by these duties. Second, if Goldman had converted to Judaism and had thereby assumed responsibility for these religious observances, would we accord less weight to his request because it does not stem from a birthright encumbrance? "If it cannot be proven that this ought to have made a difference, then the issue is not that Captain Goldman's Jewish feelings are so deeply embedded that he cannot but act in a particular way, but that he has chosen a certain course of action." Tamir identifies freedom of conscience with what she terms constitutive choice. Membership in a religion or culture is chosen, but we may subsequently view such membership as imposing particular duties on us. "It should be recognized that, by making a religious choice, people have expressed a readiness to follow the practices and traditions constitutive of a particular religion. Hence, proof that a certain practice plays a constitutive role in the history of a certain religion should count as an argument in favor of allowing individuals to adhere to it."[48] Membership is not a precondition of autonomy, because membership is itself neither a necessary nor a sufficient condition of autonomy. Membership and the fulfillment of obligations we see as flowing from that membership are, however, expressions of autonomy.

To return to the Episcopal hymn, we could say that the writer sees himself as encumbered before God's call, enthralled by the world and blind to divine glory, as the first verse describes. Thus encumbered, he cannot "choose" God until God has first "chosen" him through the bestowal of divine grace. Grace frees him from his former encumbrances, but it does not simply replace one sort of enthrallment with another. Grace, rather, opens the possibility of an alternative way of life. But this alternative must be chosen, or, if the notion of choice seems inappropriate, it must at least be affirmed. Duties will stem from this new way of life, and he will see these as welcome encumbrances that are constitutive of his identity. But his freedom of conscience is more than simply the liberty to perform duties with respect to which he now believes he has *no* choice. Instead, his freedom of conscience represents the liberty to make a *constitutive* choice, the choice of a way of life, and the duties and obligations that are incurred by this choice *then* become constitutive of his identity. He is an encumbered self, but he is encumbered because he has allowed himself to *become* encumbered. If, on the other hand, the writer had religious convictions from his earliest memories, we would expect that there were still points at which he became aware of different, perhaps more secular, alternatives. And at some level, he considered and reaffirmed his original encumbrance, thus allowing himself to *remain* encumbered.

To put this differently, constitutive choice can be equated with second-order desire. A life encumbered by duties grounded in religious conviction is not simply a life we desire to pursue, or a first-order desire, but it is also a life we *want* to desire to pursue. The capacity for reflective self-evaluation involves both second-order desires and second-order volitions. In the present context, religious convictions typically animate individuals both to want to prefer certain desires over others and to want those desires to constitute their wills, or to be the desires on which they act. Thus, although these desires possess the constitutive status of being inseparable from the way individuals interpret their identities, they emerge from constitutive choices about the set of desires with which individuals want to be encumbered. Additionally, these choices may represent a degree of reflective evaluation that is consistent with autonomy. Certainly there are believers who may never question or examine religious convictions with which they would say they have always identified. My point, however, is that encumbrance and choice are not mutually exclusive groundings for freedom of conscience and that the concept of constitutive choice helps us to understand how this can be the case.

APPLICATIONS

Belief and conscience, then, function much like other constituents of personal identity. Like cultural membership, religious conviction is in some sense chosen, defined, and interpreted by the individuals who possess such conviction. It is therefore subject to question, examination, and revision or reaffirmation like other projects and goals that are central to personal autonomy. Yet there are instances of individuals whose accounts of religious belief seem alien to any sort of engagement in rational deliberation and critical reflection and thus seem impossible to square with the exercise of personal autonomy. Moreover, to base religious toleration and individual freedom on respect for autonomous choice may exclude those who do not value autonomy. I shall argue, however, that individuals may engage in critical reflection even in unlikely circumstances and that therefore their revision or affirmation of belief may indeed still flow from the exercise of personal autonomy.

Halbertal argues that Paul's conversion on the road to Damascus is "a paradigm for a nonautonomous revision of the concept of the good." First, Paul did not simply revise his projects and goals but was completely transformed, becoming a different self through conversion. Second, this conversion was forced on him by God, and his own role was merely that of a passive receptacle for this inspiration. Third, the conversion did not stem from rational assessment or critical reflection on his options but represented a leap of faith. Finally, once converted, Paul did not view himself as open to continual questioning and reexamination of his projects and goals but saw his conversion as final. We should respect nonautonomous revisions like Paul's, argues Halbertal, neither because they are achieved through rational assessment, nor because such individuals might in future engage in critical reflection after all. Rather, Paul's right to Christianity "is rooted in the fact his present state is of enormous importance to him, because that state shapes his identity, and forcing him out of it means destroying his individuality and violating what for him is perhaps the most important and meaningful aspect of his being."[49]

By valuing toleration primarily for its capacity to enable the revision of our projects and goals, suggests Halbertal, theorists like Kymlicka and Rawls minimize its role in protecting our present lifestyles. To return to Richards's classification of the First Amendment, if the antiestablishment clause protects our ability to form and revise our beliefs, while the free exercise clause protects our current beliefs, Kymlicka's formulation amounts to a First Amendment without a free exercise clause. Many facets of our identities are worthy of respect regardless of whether they are products of rational choice or any choice. Education, suggests Halbertal, may be aimed either at "producing a chooser . . . who has the skills to make informed and rational judgments about different goals and forms of life," or, as in the approach of the Old Order Amish, at "transmitting a particular tradition and developing a strong commitment to that particular way of life" (111). Where the autonomy argument for toleration senses intolerance in threats to the ability to form and revise one's beliefs, the harm argument for toleration imputes harm to the violation of deeply held beliefs and therefore senses intolerance in threats to the maintenance of one's current beliefs. Although the community should not penalize the choice of alternative ways of life, "the value of toleration does not obligate a community to pose that alternative to students and present it as a legitimate option for choice" (112). In general, "The basic wrong that coercion produces is not failing to allow for revision of one's ends but forcing people away from what is important and central in their life, thus causing tremendous pain and harm" (110).

Halbertal is certainly correct to attribute harm to failure to respect people's current beliefs. Given my argument, however, that the capacity for autonomy encompasses affirmation of one's current beliefs as well as revision of one's projects and goals, I believe that Halbertal defines autonomy too narrowly. Geoffrey Levey suggests that although Paul's own conversion does not represent the rational revision typically associated with autonomy, he subsequently engages in argument with others and seeks to persuade them to change their ways of life also, even though their change will respond to persuasion rather than to a sudden revelation. "In a very clear sense, Paul remains an autonomous agent, fully capable of giving an intelligible account of his ends to himself and to others and of taking responsibility for his ends."[50] Moreover, whether or not Paul views himself as open to reexamination of his new way of life, "respect for persons is predicated on their capacity for self-reflection and self-direction as a matter of principle and they are to be treated *as if* one day they may want to change their mind." Finally, both the harm *and* the autonomy arguments for toleration protect individuals against penalties for their adherence to current deeply held beliefs, because they protect the will of those who have already converted from one set of beliefs to another (18).

Autonomy is a broad enough concept, then, to encompass critical reflection that is followed either by revision of one's projects and goals or by affirmation of them. We must of course take care that autonomy does not become such a protean concept that it covers any exertion of agency at all. In my view, however, the independent variable that identifies the exercise of autonomy is engagement in rational deliberation and critical reflection as a prelude to action, not necessarily the revision of one's current projects and goals as opposed to their affirmation. Persons who are impelled to revise their way of life from heedless impetuosity and whim are no more autonomous than are those who remain unthinkingly in a way of life they have never thought to question or examine. Correspondingly, those who upon reflection examine and reendorse their current projects and goals are as autonomous as those who make radical changes as a result of this examination. Although a change in one's way of life may be more likely to reflect critical reflection than is a simple continuation of one's present course, both revision and reaffirmation are compatible with critical reflection and self-direction.

In the example of Paul's conversion, then, we can look not only at the manner in which he was impelled to change his way of life in order to determine whether his freedom of conscience represents an exercise of autonomy. We can also look at his manner of life after his conversion. Here we find a continuous effort to persuade others of the truth of his experience and to make representations as to why others should follow him in changing their own lives as well. Each effort at persuasion represents a reaffirmation of his current beliefs and practices as a Christian. Because he must make sense of his experience to others if he is to have any hope of persuading them, he must give an intelligible and therefore rational account of this experience. Although any experience predicated on revelation probably requires a leap of faith at some level for one adopting the convictions associated with it, these individuals must first decide whether or not to make the leap.

Paul apparently did not "decide" in the conventional sense of engaging in a rational assessment of his options. For him, conversion would be more accurately described as the experience of recognizing, seeing, and acknowledging the truth of God's revelation in his experience on the road. But in recounting this experience to others, he must explain it in terms that impel others to choose, to opt for, or to decide on that leap of faith. And by so doing, he is also reinforcing his own convictions. By giving a rational account of his experience that he hopes will persuade others, he is simultaneously reaffirming his own faith in these terms. We might equate the leap of faith with a first-order desire or volition: as I make the leap, the desire to do so determines my will. But the *decision* to make the leap is a second-order desire or volition: I *want* the desire to make the leap to determine my will. Once I have indeed made the leap, I then become encumbered by duties that I view as constitutive of my identity. But my initial action was one of constitutive choice. Both Paul and those he later persuades exercise constitutive choice. The difference is that where others exercise this choice in the revision of their current projects and goals by becoming Christians, Paul does so by continually reaffirming over time *his* current project and goal, that of professing Jesus as the Messiah. His freedom of conscience, then, indeed represents an exercise of autonomy.

Another way in which the affirmation of one's projects and goals can function as an exercise of autonomy is found in Amy McCready's account of conscience in the writings of John Milton. Milton in writing his tracts was apparently torn between his desire to focus on poetry and his call to become involved in advocacy of church reform. For McCready, the conscientious or ethical individual differs from the liberal self because it feels impelled to act against its own inclination and for the common good. Yet this self also differs from the communitarian self, because conscience is a personal reference point and authority that prompts questions about the legitimacy of social institutions.[51] In one sense, Milton in his writing against the established church acts on promptings not entirely his choice. He must do so if he is to validate and affirm himself in his own eyes (193). Yet the new identity that follows on his actions he recognizes as his own. Conscience "freed him from external powers, civil and divine, by providing an alternative source of authority and identity. It enabled him to possess himself and to be conscious of himself as self-possessing" (94). Conscience integrates parts of the self, and in doing so it promotes self-knowledge (97–100).

McCready's account suggests that we need not choose, in Sandel's terms, between the role of willing subjects confronted by objects of choice and that of knowing subjects presented with objects of understanding. Our understandings may be shaped by contingencies beyond our direct control, like Paul's experience on the road to Damascus, like Milton's exposure to the controversy over church reform, or like any circumstances that disturb our complacency and call forth a perhaps reluctant response. But through this response we bring to bear our agency on the circumstances confronting us, thereby altering both the circumstances themselves and also our identities and self-understandings. If we continue on our course thus set, we are potentially not simply knowing subjects reflecting on objects of understanding but also willing subjects rationally deliberating on objects of choice. Reflexivity exists in the relationship between knowing and willing, understanding and choosing. Contingent circumstances may become essential constituents of self-definition, thereby affecting and defining the scope of future choices, just as chosen courses of action influence future self-understandings.

Moreover, although we are apt to connect revision of our projects and goals more readily than affirmation of them to the states of willing and choosing, as we have seen, we can deploy will and choice in affirming a course of action, however we came to pursue it at the start, if rational deliberation and critical reflection play a role in this affirmation. Additionally, we can deploy these qualities in the activity of knowing and understanding, as well as in that of willing and choosing. Insofar as we each possess many possible constituents of identity, we must survey these various attachments, as Sandel suggests, and "acknowledge their respective claims" if we are to enhance our self-understandings.[52] Finally, when freedom of conscience represents the exercise of autonomy, McCready's account suggests that the result is "an ethical self . . . cognizant of its dependence on its community and cognizant of its own morality."[53] Modern interpretations of conscience or the self often focus on an inevitable opposition between individual and community, or on an independent and choosing self opposing a self largely determined by its social identity. McCready's interpretation of conscience, however, both opens and closes distance between the individual and the social order (98). For Milton, obeying the conscience means obeying oneself, as denying it "would be denying one's identity." Yet conscience also reinforces social identity through a self-imposed duty to enter into social engagement and public action (99). Such a self "is neither radically situated nor radically free" (100).

This account recalls Creppell's discussion of "public privacy," according to which one is impelled to express, to present, and to witness the nature of one's faith before the community as a whole, even when belief is individuated and perhaps protected as such. Another example of the public role of conscience might appear in Martin Luther's defense of his beliefs at the Diet of Worms when he said, "Here I stand; I can do no other. God help me. Amen."[54] In all of these cases, the principals evidently feel that in one sense they have no choice in their courses of action but are compelled to embrace particular projects and goals. What is especially clear in McCready's account of conscience, however, is the extent to which this embrace is still a voluntary one, chosen because only affirmation and action in accordance with this way of life will express the self-understanding that each principal possesses. Paul in theory could have rejected the implications of his experience on the road, Milton could have opted to confine his writing to poetry rather than engaging in political and religious writing, and Luther could have avoided proclaiming his understanding of Scripture and also avoided endangering his personal safety. But each chooses a new way of life, or chooses to affirm a way of life now central to his self-understanding. Duties flow from these understandings and encumber each. But each choice or affirmation, complete with its encumbrances, is at the second-order level a constitutive *choice*. Those with religious convictions may experience a divine revelation that affects the trajectory of their lives. But their response to this revelation is neither automatic nor a given. Rather, they must interpret the meaning of this revelation as it applies to their own lives.

I have argued that although liberal societies have traditionally privileged a range of religious beliefs, they have not always agreed on the principles that might ground this sort of toleration. Some scholars suggest that because beliefs are unchosen constituents of our identities, concern and respect for the individual dictate policies of toleration. I am suggesting, instead, that we may take responsibility for our ends even in the area of conscience, which represents the expression of autonomy when the affirmation or revision of religious belief results from rational deliberation and critical reflection on one's beliefs. But toleration is best grounded not only on the idea that we originally chose our beliefs but also that we choose to *affirm* particular beliefs, to order our lives by them, and to treat them as constitutive choices that affect our self-understandings. Not all beliefs are expressions of autonomy, as they may be arrived at or sustained unthinkingly, and we do not always know which is the case. But when we tolerate beliefs and the practices that flow from them, we are honoring and respecting the possibility or potential they possess for the expression of autonomy.

If beliefs are in fact subject to constitutive choice, policies of religious toleration may appear less defensible than would be the case if beliefs are regarded as unchosen constituents of identity. We might expect less consideration from society toward individuals who, after all, can simply choose not to affirm beliefs the implications of which are inconvenient to the unity or stability of the social order. I think, however, that this would be a mistaken conclusion. As we have seen, in the *Letter* Locke asserts that although individuals should be allowed to act on the basis of their religious beliefs, the line between public and private, or between matters civil and religious, must still be civilly determined. Whether a practice is civilly benign or civilly injurious must be determined by public authority, and the set of social facts taken into account in making this determination will affect the outcome. Thus, even the conviction that belief is unchangeable need not sanction a broad liberty of conscience when belief becomes practice. In Rawlsian terms, even if as believers citizens are seen as passive carriers of desires, they must still adjust their ends to what they anticipate the civil authority will reasonably accommodate. Belief is not privileged by representing itself as unchangeable. Rather, beliefs are among the many components each of which may be partially constitutive of identity. But each of us must order and interpret these constituents for ourselves. If public authority recognizes our capacity to engage in this ordering and interpretation, it will exhibit not only toleration toward beliefs that are chosen but also respect for the expression of autonomy.

Belief, Toleration, and Autonomy

If regarding religious belief as in some sense chosen allows us to consider religious practices as an expression of autonomy, as I believe it does, in theory we should allow broad scope for the expression of this belief and for the practices that flow from it. As individuals we have chosen or affirmed obligations that we value highly, and these choices and affirmations should be respected. Guarantees of autonomy to some individuals or groups, however, appear to interfere with the autonomy of others. Moreover, just as the determination of whether the accommodation of a particular religious practice is civilly injurious or civilly benign, or whether it violates neutrality or instantiates it, may vary with the set of social facts considered, so also will the impact of particular practices on the individual development and/or expression of autonomy vary with these social facts. Therefore, arguments about the merits of toleration for particular practices must include discussion of the merits of emphasizing some sets of social facts over others. This point can be illustrated by two different approaches to the permanence of diversity in our comprehensive religious, philosophical, and moral doctrines.

Rawls, for example, attempts to broaden the appeal of political liberalism and to maximize the possibilities for an overlapping consensus by eliminating comprehensive doctrines as components of public reason. Because he wants to alienate as few individuals and groups as possible, public reason must be guided by values that all can endorse, and its independence of comprehensive doctrines renders the political conception of justice "freestanding."[55] Although Rawls acknowledges the potential comprehensiveness of private commitments, he believes that citizens will gain more than they lose in policy debates by eschewing the deployment of arguments that are comprehensively grounded.

Although Rawls intends to foster inclusivity, his concern for preserving the integrity of public reason often forces him to retreat from it. As Murphy notes, he expects individuals with attachments to comprehensive doctrines that are marginal or outside the mainstream either to abandon these doctrines, to be disingenuous about the true reasons that motivate them, to engage in divisive action to change the scope of public debate, or to deploy only the publicly acceptable elements of their comprehensive doctrines.[56] Because of the diversity of comprehensive doctrines that we espouse, Rawls holds "that politics in a democratic society can never be guided by what we see as the whole truth. . . . The only comprehensive doctrines that run afoul of public reason are those that cannot support a reasonable balance of political values."[57] Rawls is correct to suggest that we can never agree on "the whole truth." But what reasons we might "reasonably" be expected to endorse and what constitutes "a reasonable balance of political values" will often depend on what set of social facts is considered in determining what is reasonable. We may be hard-pressed to agree that his conception of public reason extends the ideal of liberty of conscience when individuals are apparently largely prohibited from bringing to bear their most deeply held values in the forum of public or political activity.

If one solution to the permanence of diversity is the creation or discovery of an overlapping consensus through the use of public reason, another alternative is to clarify or strengthen a seemingly existing consensus that is in danger of disappearing or of being lost. According to Charles Taylor, Americans enjoy a collective religious consciousness or civic theism that is independent of specific confessional allegiances. That is, religion as religious consciousness does not necessarily decline when its institutionalized expression in churches does.[58] Although Americans often seek to redefine foundational ideas in the light of contemporary understandings, "the original nonconfessional theism still resonates with many Americans" to the extent that "to excise God is to eviscerate the common purpose, as they understand it." Liberal or individual freedom may be endangered without civic freedom, or without the guarantees of "a political system that enshrines common purposes still held in reverence by the citizens" (108).

Where Rawls seeks an overlapping consensus through the use of public reason that will not admit argument based on comprehensive doctrines, Taylor moves in the opposite direction, suggesting that the elimination of certain seemingly foundational moral doctrines is a cause of dissension rather than consensus. He perceives widespread agreement on two of three major implications of the separation of church and state. Citizens should not be excluded from "the public process or opportunities" because of religious difference. They should not be forced to support "religious forms they do not adhere to, as often happens with an established church." And citizens should "define symbols and forms of expression that all can recognize themselves in" (110). But if Rawls's project prohibits the deployment of some of our most deeply held values in public debate, Taylor's framework assumes a consensus on values about which I believe he is overly sanguine. First, agreement on the implications of the separation of church and state is more elusive than he supposes. Second, the protection of liberal freedom carries positive obligations of a substantive nature that do enable it to serve as a worthy common purpose.

According to Taylor, first, citizens should not be excluded from the public process or from opportunities because of religious difference. "The public process" covers public life, including the political process and all elected and appointed offices. Taylor is probably correct to assert this principle, unsupported even by Locke, as uncontroversial in Western democracies today. But "opportunities" also suggests a broad range of activity in civil society, encompassing membership in private organizations as well as more common implications such as employment in the private sector. For example, participation in the Boy Scouts is thought by many people to provide training that may lead to enhanced career opportunities for these young men. But the traditional requirement that Boy Scouts affirm a belief in God, however conceived, excludes those who cannot affirm this belief from opportunities they could otherwise enjoy.

Second, citizens should not have to support "religious forms they do not adhere to." Certainly there is implicit agreement that taxes should not support particular communities of faith or their rituals. But disputes often center on which set of social facts should be heeded in deciding whether a specific policy constitutes establishment within the meaning of the First Amendment. With respect to *Sherbert v. Verner*, for example, one can argue that religious believers may secure unemployment compensation under circumstances in which nonbelievers cannot: they may refuse to work on the Sabbath they observe and still receive benefits if they lose their jobs. Because unemployment compensation is funded by tax revenues, taxpayers who are not Seventh-Day Adventists, as in this case, are being forced to support a religious form to which they do not adhere. Although this exemption is open to any employees who might otherwise be forced to choose between their religious convictions and their means of support, in the United States a minority of communities of faith observe their Sabbaths on a day other than Sunday. Therefore, the exemption is more likely to apply to minority faiths, which means in turn that a greater percentage of taxpayers is being forced indirectly to support alien religious forms. Although this does not constitute establishment in the conventional sense, it does illustrate the point that avoiding the support of religious forms to which one does not adhere is more problematic than Taylor indicates.

Moreover, if we entertain the suggestion that religion need not be defined by the substantive criterion of theistic content but may encompass any comprehensive belief system or conception of moral order, this interpretation raises doubts as to whether nonconfessional theism is as central to our common purposes as Taylor suggests. If humanism is a nonconfessional *non*theism that functions like a religion, this suggests that the jurisprudence Taylor would see as burdensome to theistic belief is now civilly benign, whereas jurisprudence now considered benign or neutral would appear to burden nontheistic belief systems like humanism.

For example, for Taylor the right to observe the Sabbath according to the dictates of one's conscience would be civilly benign as congruent with the national religious consciousness of nonconfessional theism and would in fact be essential to this consciousness as part of our common purpose. Therefore, *Thornton v. Calder*, by overruling the state law that allowed Sabbath observers to choose their day off, unfairly burdens theistic belief over nontheistic beliefs that do not require any particular day of observance. Adherents of humanism, however, would agree with the Court, arguing that practices that flow from *their* belief systems were burdened under the law because these could not command the same support that theists could command for theirs. *Thornton* thus places humanists and theists on an equal footing because neither can enjoy exemptions on the basis of belief. For humanists, the result in *Sherbert* is *not* civilly benign but instead allows theists who claim Sabbath observance to refuse work without forfeiting unemployment compensation where humanists cannot. Why should theistic beliefs be privileged through exemptions granted for practices flowing from them, when other types of deeply held beliefs are not? In this case, it is theists who agree with the Court. In sum, if humanism is not deemed a religion, policies that in effect support it over theism appear to be neutral. But if humanism is regarded as a nontheistic belief system that functions as a religion, policies that potentially privilege humanists over theists appear to constitute an establishment—in this case, of humanism.

The question of the status of humanism as a religion exemplifies a dispute over what set of social facts shall be accepted as the basis for judging whether a particular policy is neutral or whether it favors one manifestation of belief over another. Any stance toward religious belief will appear nonneutral from some viewpoint, and the prevailing stance structures the context of choice within which we survey our options and revise or reaffirm our projects and goals. Therefore, it is not surprising that Taylor himself admits lack of consensus on the third implication of the separation of church and state that he discusses, that citizens "should define symbols and forms of expression that all can recognize themselves in" (110). Although he cites the issue of support for sectarian schools as an area of particular controversy, we have just seen that the seemingly simpler issue of Sabbath observance defies efforts to define symbols with which all can identify. Taylor suggests that widespread agreement on nonexclusion from opportunities on the basis of faith and on noncompulsion of support for religious forms to which citizens do not adhere perhaps lessens need for agreement on forms and symbols (111). But the lack of consensus we have seen on the first two principles both renders controversy on the third difficult to avoid and raises the stakes therein. Citizens who think they are compelled indirectly to support questionable religious forms, for instance, may invest symbols with greater importance than otherwise. It is no wonder, then, that Taylor concludes that perhaps the best we can hope for is that each side of the debate recognize the legitimacy and good faith of the other and that this in turn "could lead to the recognition that it is part of the public philosophy of America that this very philosophy should be a matter of continuing discussion and debate" (113).

If this is his conclusion, however, is it nonconfessional theism itself that is central to our common purpose? Or is it continuing discussion and debate in an atmosphere of mutual respect that is central to our common purpose? I suggest that it is the latter question that resonates. Taylor notes that we often seek to redefine foundational ideas in the light of contemporary understandings. This sort of debate is part of that redefinition. This brings me to my second area of disagreement with Taylor, which is that the protection of liberal freedom is itself a positive obligation of a substantive nature and that this enables it to serve as a worthy common purpose. Even a liberal political society cannot avoid espousing some common moral standpoint, despite the thin conception of community of theorists like Chandran Kukathas. I suggest that this common moral standpoint serves as an adequate common purpose, despite Taylor's thick definition of common purposes. Michael Walzer argues that the nature of political society is not fixed at one moment in time but instead emerges as the product of ongoing negotiation, which represents "the gradual shaping of a common . . . political life," renegotiated over time as new groups make their presence felt.[59] When we debate and redefine foundational ideas in the light of contemporary understandings, as Taylor suggests that we often do, this activity constitutes the continuing negotiation or renegotiation of our common political life.

Even when a society attempts to be neutral toward religious belief, the varying sets of social facts that may be the basis for a purported neutrality renders this term susceptible to differing definitions and points toward different strategies. The common moral standpoint represented by *Thornton* views theistic religious belief as private; Sabbath observance should not receive public exemption, and any resulting individual disadvantage relative to particular observances is not a public concern. The standpoint represented by *Sherbert*, however, views theistic belief as an allegiance that, if not public, at least should not incur penalties for those who engage in observances that may flow from it. This viewpoint need not derive from an argument like Sandel's that observance is a duty beyond the realm of choice, but it may derive from the conviction that religious belief, however originated, is a central constituent of identity that individuals may choose to emphasize and affirm. Our understandings of the appropriate role of religious belief shift and change over time. But what continues is discussion and debate. In other words, our common purpose is served by determining *some* role for religious belief, but this purpose does not require that we settle on any *particular* role.

Moreover, although Taylor implies that the prospect of continuing debate in an atmosphere of mutual respect is second best, as it were, to the definition of symbols and forms of expression with which all can identify, I believe that this mutual respect and acknowledgment of good faith that he correctly desires is more difficult to attain than he implies. What Jeff Spinner calls the "hard work" of liberal citizenship[60] comprises enough substance to constitute a common purpose. According to Spinner, liberal citizens must often treat others as equals even when they dislike the practices of these others, but this does not mean that all cultural practices automatically merit protection. As a matter of constitutive choice, religious belief raises the same issues as cultural identity in a liberal polity. Membership in a community of faith, like membership in a culture, must be interpreted by the members themselves. And overall, both cultural and religious membership afford opportunities for the expression of autonomy.

But which practices are protected and which are not is subject to civil determination. And whether particular practices are considered as civilly benign or civilly injurious will depend upon the set of social facts used as the basis for making that determination. The relevant set of social facts is best decided, when there is disagreement, through discussion and debate, not by default to an existing consensus. But this is hard work, both in Spinner's sense and in and of itself. It requires that citizens listen to one another and that they consider carefully the question of whether the protection of particular practices enhances or diminishes both the value of diversity, as the existence and perpetuation of a plurality of options, and the value of autonomy, as the development of the capacity to question, examine, and revise or reaffirm our projects and goals.

In general, I believe that the protection of the broadest possible scope for the expression and practice of religious belief enhances both diversity and autonomy. Because religious belief, at least of the theistic type, typically involves membership in a community of faith, both freedom of conscience and freedom of association point toward liberty from interference by the larger community. Noninterference enhances diversity by encouraging a wide variety of options for choice, and it enhances autonomy in religious practice both by the group as a corporate body and by its individual members who ostensibly subscribe to its practices. Because no one is compelled to remain, freedom of conscience implies the right to choose a different affiliation if one can no longer affirm the beliefs and practices of one's original attachment. It also implies that current members subscribe to the beliefs and practices of the corporate body, or at least that they interpret their memberships in ways that do not threaten their compatibility with this body. Cultural and religious membership differ in this respect, because one may view cultural membership as a part of one's identity without the sorts of obligations or duties typically attached to religious affiliation. However, I want to discuss the harder sort of case in which liberal values are at stake because they appear to conflict with one another.

FREEDOM OF ASSOCIATION

Situations exist in which the protection of diverse communities of faith seemingly conflicts with the autonomy of individuals who do *not* subscribe to these communities' beliefs and practices but who for various reasons believe that their worldly or secular interests are compromised by their exclusion from these groups. In his *Letter Concerning Toleration,* Locke argues with respect to corporate belief that "no church is bound, by the duty of toleration, to retain any such person in her bosom as, after admonition, continues obstinately to offend against the laws of the society." Without the freedom to expel recalcitrant members, faith communities could not maintain a forum within which they may express and practice their shared values. Locke cautions, however, that this separation may not be accompanied by any action that would constitute civil injury, as "civil goods . . . are under the magistrate's protection." With respect to individual belief, "no private person has any right in any manner to prejudice another person in his civil enjoyments because he is of another church or religion. All the rights and franchises that belong to him as a man or as a denizen are inviolably to be preserved to him. These are not the business of religion."[61] Under permanent conditions of diversity, however, the religious convictions of some individuals lead them to engage in practices that do appear to prejudice others in their civil enjoyments. We want to protect a diversity of beliefs and also the practices of those for whom the expression of religious belief is an expression of autonomy. Yet we also want to protect the autonomy of those whose own beliefs do not accord with these.

To put this differently, a liberal society and polity favor two kinds of diversity. They favor inclusiveness or admission to the social mainstream of previously excluded individuals and groups who desire inclusion. But they also favor groups who wish to form or maintain a forum in which they may express and practice shared values that are *not* common to the larger society. As Spinner states, "When diversity [in the first sense] is taken too far, it flattens the rich associational life that ought to characterize a healthy liberal society. But the idea that a rich associational life means that discrimination is always acceptable will destroy the idea of equal opportunity and citizenship."[62] Spinner favors a classification of society into public, market, voluntary, and private sectors, allowing less discrimination for those closer to the public realm, but more for those closer to the private sector. If every group or institution must exhibit diversity within itself, reflecting "a mirror image of society" at large, "eventually it makes society more homogeneous rather than heterogeneous."[63] Ironically, "A society that has only diverse institutions will be more homogeneous than a society with some diverse institutions and some homogeneous ones. Respecting religious faith and allowing religious communities to exist means allowing for discriminating religions" (18).

Here I want to consider the often murky line between the market and voluntary associations through an examination of the Boy Scouts of America, classified by Spinner as a voluntary association. The Boy Scouts believes that its mission is one of building character and fostering good citizenship, and it views belief in God as a necessary condition of this enterprise. It is also exclusively male and is intended for males whose sexual orientation is heterosexual.

Spinner suggests that church youth groups are rightly allowed to discriminate as a part of the building of their own communities of faith and that the Boy Scouts should be able to do so also. Liberal citizens do not have the right to join any voluntary organization they choose; these organizations are entitled to regulate their membership in line with their grounding principles. But because the Boy Scouts discriminate against atheists and gays, Spinner believes that public institutions should not support the Scouts by allowing them free use of public school facilities for meetings. A liberal society should be inclusive not only of a diversity of individuals but also of a diversity of groups, some of which may not themselves practice inclusivity. "Like many people I think the scouts are simply wrong to argue that gay people cannot be good scout leaders, but it is one [thing] to think that their rules are mistaken, another to think they should be illegal" (30).

Chandran Kukathas argues that because individuals should be able to form associations that reflect their liberty of conscience, their freedom is determined not by their liberty to *enter* associations but by their liberty to *leave* associations whose restrictions they reject, which also implies freedom to form new associations whose principles are more congenial. I have argued that by providing equality and the scope for autonomy not afforded by membership in particularistic groups, the liberal polity also provides a broader forum or context of choice that makes meaningful the opportunity to exit. As long as we believe that a liberal polity should include not only a diversity of individuals but also a diversity of groups, not all of which may themselves practice inclusivity, I think we must agree with Kukathas that freedom to relinquish one's current attachments and to form new ones is a mainstay of liberal freedom with respect to freedom of association.

On the other hand, it is imperative that the larger society provide the potential for other opportunities, or the slack, as it were, that makes this freedom meaningful. When Locke argues that no religious organization need retain individuals whose practices offend its principles, he is defending the freedom of the like-minded to associate without threat from those who might alter these principles through their membership, either new or continuing. When he argues that no individuals, however, should be denied ordinary civil enjoyments because of their religious beliefs, he is indirectly addressing the importance of maintaining a forum that provides alternative opportunities. If the first point addresses the free exercise of conscientious beliefs and practices, the second point takes up the danger that establishment of an orthodoxy can pose to the exercise of alternatives. In this second point, Locke refers to private persons, not to corporate bodies like communities of faith or organizations founded on particular moral commitments. Yet if enough individuals *or* corporate bodies hold similar beliefs the adherence to which curtails the very existence of alternatives, then the context of choice or the slack that is crucial is lacking. In other words, diversity can be flattened in more than one way. If every organization *must* reflect the wider society, diversity is compromised. But if the larger political society is an association of associations most of which closely parallel one another spontaneously in their religious, ethical, and moral stances, diversity is equally compromised. And either circumstance in turn compromises individuals' capacities to question, examine, and revise or reaffirm their projects and goals.

THE BOY SCOUTS

The Boy Scouts of America is an organization that is internally diverse, as Spinner notes. Moreover, the nontheists and gays who have challenged Scout policy seek only to join the organization, not to change its focus. Scout statistics indicate that although the public schools sponsor more individual Scout members than any single sponsor, the largest single sponsor is the Church of Jesus Christ of Latter-day Saints, or Mormons. Others sponsoring large numbers of Scouts include Methodist, Roman Catholic, Presbyterian, Lutheran, and Baptist churches. Smaller numbers are sponsored by parent-teacher groups, service organizations, citizens' organizations, fire departments, and law enforcement groups. "Officials say the organization was founded for boys who believe in God and should remain true to those principles. But while the organization accepts Buddhists, who do not believe in a Supreme Being, and Unitarians, who seek insight from many traditions but pointedly avoid setting a creed, it does not tolerate people who are openly atheist, agnostic, or unwilling to say in the Scout oath they will serve God."[64]

In Illinois in 1992 and 1993, a federal district court ruled and an appeals court affirmed that because the Scouts is a private organization, not a public accommodation, the organization was within its rights to refuse admission to an agnostic boy who would not acknowledge a duty to God. The appeals court ruled that regulation that "scuttles" the Scouts' founding principles would risk "undermining one of the seedbeds of virtue that cultivate the sorts of citizens our nation so desperately needs."[65] Although the boy's attorney argued that discrimination on the basis of belief was akin to racial discrimination, an editorial on the subject notes that "religious beliefs are chosen, not passed along to you at birth in your genetic code."[66] Its support for the Scouts is implicitly grounded in the assumption that an aspiring Scout might alter his beliefs if scouting were a priority.

Meanwhile, twin boys in Orange County, California, were in 1991 expelled from their Cub Scout den when, as agnostics, they would not affirm God in the Cub Scout Promise. The American Civil Liberties Union Foundation of Southern California successfully sued in state court for their reinstatement on grounds of religious discrimination, and this decision was upheld by a state appellate court in 1994.[67] At that time, however, even a longtime atheist criticized the attack on the religious liberty of a private and voluntary organization, noting that an atheist organization would rightly protest against a claimed Christian "right" to membership. "Decent people should resolve disputes through reason and persuasion, not force, including the force of government. . . . Abandoning reason and persuasion, they have allied themselves with government power. For shame."[68] During this period, the Girl Scouts voted to alter their Promise, amid protests, to allow individual girls to substitute words with which they feel more comfortable for "God" if they wish.[69]

A second trajectory of protest against Scout policies has come from individuals favoring the inclusion of gays as Scouts and Scout leaders. National Scout policy "defines homosexuals as poor role models." In California in 1991, a superior court judge upheld the rejection of a gay applicant for the post of volunteer assistant scoutmaster as congruent with a group's right to exclude unwanted members, an inherent function of freedom of association.[70] In the same state in 1992, the Boy Scouts threatened to withdraw the charter of a troop that passed a resolution that it would not reject homosexuals as members. It eventually renewed the charter because the troop had accepted no homosexuals and had agreed not to seek any.[71] Meanwhile, in 1992 the United Way of the Bay Area withdrew its support for six Boy Scout councils in five counties because of the policy barring membership to homosexuals.[72] Also in 1992, two San Francisco–based companies whose corporate charters prohibit donations to organizations discriminating on the basis of religious belief and sexual orientation ceased donations to the Boy Scouts but were targeted for protest by Christian and family groups, and a third such company that had ceased donations but later resumed them was then targeted by the gay community.[73]

In 1996, however, with the approval of the national Boy Scouts, the San Francisco Bay Area Council of Boy Scouts, representing 33,000 Scouts in two counties, approved a policy akin to the armed forces' policy of "don't ask, don't tell": gays can participate in Scout activities if they do not openly advocate homosexuality. "The Boy Scouts of America does not ask prospective members about their sexual preference, nor do we check on the sexual orientation of boys who are already in scouting." Though local spokespersons explained that the new policy redefines scouting as "asexual and apolitical," national leaders asserted that this represented no change, as "we don't allow registration of avowed homosexuals."[74]

More recently, a New Jersey state appeals court in 1998 ruled that because the Boy Scouts publicly recruits nationwide and troops often meet in public places, it is a public accommodation and violated the state antidiscrimination law by excluding a gay Eagle Scout and former assistant scoutmaster who wanted to participate in adult scouting. The majority went beyond narrow points of law to state, "There is absolutely no evidence . . . supporting a conclusion that a gay Scoutmaster, solely because he is homosexual, does not possess the strength of character necessary to care for or to impart B.S.A. humanitarian ideals to the young boys in his charge. . . . Plaintiff's exemplary journey through the B.S.A. ranks is testament enough that these stereotypical notions about homosexuals must be rejected."[75] The plaintiff, James Dale, realized in college that he was gay, became an activist, and was featured in a news article that led to the revocation of his Scout membership. He argued that scouting involves no explicit message about sexual orientation and that the scoutmaster handbook refers sex and sexuality issues "to the child's parents or pastor. It isn't something that's discussed."[76]

Reactions to the ruling were mixed. Syndicated columnist Dennis Byrne argues that as a returning Scout leader, Dale would have to choose between teaching "the complete Scouting agenda," despite public knowledge of his own status, and violating Scout principles by saying that homosexuality is legitimate. If he takes the second option and is terminated, will he assert free speech rights and will the courts then force the Scouts to reinstate him? If parents then establish a parallel organization that does exclude homosexual leaders, will the courts in turn invalidate the exclusivity of the new organization? By ruling not only on the membership but also on the leadership of a private organization, the court "assaults more than the right of parents to decide how their children will be reared. It also assaults every American's right of association and conscience."[77] Other commentators assert, however, that most fights for civil rights center on winning the right to participate in typical or ordinary activities when the individuals wishing to participate differ from the norm. Individuals who have become "so visibly gay" desire assimilation, not segregation. "They have come out so that they can stay out, if they choose, or go back in—on their own terms, as themselves. If they succeed, they may surprise their critics by becoming largely invisible again."[78]

Final dispositions of such cases at the state level have thus far conflicted. The California Supreme Court in 1998 ruled in two cases argued together that because the Boy Scouts is a private and selective group, it is not governed by state civil rights laws and can therefore exclude agnostics, theists, and gays. "Scouts regularly meet in small groups . . . that are intended to foster close friendship, trust, and loyalty. . . . The Boy Scouts is an expressive organization whose primary function is the inculcation of values in its youth members."[79] The New Jersey Supreme Court in 1999, however, "based on little more than prejudice," unanimously ruled in the Dale case that the Boy Scouts is a public accommodation and that Dale's expulsion violated state antidiscrimination laws. The Boy Scouts, states the court opinion, is not selective in its membership, is neither an intimate nor an expressive association, and does not "associate for the purpose of disseminating the belief that homosexuality is immoral." Therefore, retaining gay Scouts does not violate the organization's expressive rights.[80] Reactions to these opinions have been both mixed and predictable. The president of Gays and Lesbians for Individual Liberty has stated, most interestingly, that the New Jersey ruling is harmful to the rights of all associations, including homosexual ones, who seek to provide "safe" spaces for persons who are different. Moreover, public discrimination that regulates intimate associations through state antisodomy laws and prohibitions on same-sex marriage is best combated through broad definitions of the private sphere and narrow definitions of the public sphere.[81]

The common thread running through these controversies involving the Boy Scouts is the question of whether the organization is a public accommodation that must therefore be inclusive or a private association that can unilaterally establish its criteria for membership. Two relevant tests may be applied to determine an organization's status. First, in *Roberts v. United States Jaycees*, the Supreme Court ruled not only that Minnesota's interest in eradicating sex discrimination was a compelling one but also that offering the Jaycees' advantages to women would neither "impede the organization's ability to engage in these protected activities or to disseminate its preferred views," nor would it "change the content or impact of the organization's speech" in more than minimal ways necessary to accomplish the state's legitimate purposes.[82] In her concurring opinion Justice Sandra Day O'Connor argued, however, that the constitutional protection of membership selection should depend not on the content or rationale of its message but on a second distinction. In an expressive association, its very formation "is the creation of a voice, and the selection of members is the definition of that voice" (633). In a commercial association, however, activities enjoy only minimal protection, and such an association is defined by default "when, and only when, the association's activities are not predominantly of the type protected by the First Amendment" (635). O'Connor argued that although the Jaycees did engage in political and public advocacy, it was primarily engaged in recruiting and selling memberships (639) and was therefore a commercial association. She implied, then, that even if the public regulation of membership does alter the group's message, this regulation is legitimate for a predominantly commercial association. A predominantly expressive association, however, should enjoy full autonomy in its membership selection, even if absence of this autonomy would *not* change the message.

An association, then, may comprise both expressive and commercial elements. At one extreme, a church or other community of faith would be an expressive association, as its formation and maintenance are grounded in a shared viewpoint or set of principles. At the other extreme, a hotel or restaurant would be a commercial association; the patrons of a place of public accommodation do not converge on the basis of shared principles. The Boy Scout Oath and the Scout Law do set forth principles that are affirmed at every troop meeting. One who affirms the Oath promises on his honor "To do my duty to God and my country and to obey the Scout law; . . . To keep myself physically strong, mentally awake, and morally straight." According to the Scout Law, "A Scout is trustworthy, loyal, helpful, friendly, courteous, kind, obedient, cheerful, thrifty, brave, clean, and reverent."[83] The *Boy Scout Handbook* explains that one's family and religious leaders teach one how God is served and that "as a Scout, you do your duty to God by following the wisdom of those teachings in your daily life, and by respecting the rights of others to have their own religious beliefs" (550). The explanation of reverence in the law is similar: "A Scout is reverent toward God. He is faithful in his religious duties. He respects the beliefs of others" (8). Boys generally join the Scouts for the fun and camaraderie, and perhaps for the training in skills and leadership, not because they want to focus on religious expression and practice. Nevertheless, the theistic orientation is clear and public.

Although nothing prevents Scouts from taking the Oath with mental reservations, the *Handbook*'s explanation of trustworthiness in the law is that "a Scout tells the truth. . . . Honesty is a part of his code of conduct" (7). Moreover, the Oath's "on my honor" means that one is giving one's word; the *Handbook* instructs that "you must hold your honor sacred" (550). The conflict posed by intellectual dishonesty means that those whose nontheistic convictions are strongest will experience the greatest difficulty; those who are unconcerned may go along with the Oath without experiencing a conscious sense of conflict. One cannot simply choose a religious belief that is convenient for other purposes without being persuaded of its truth. Yet as I have argued, we do decide on the priority and importance of religious belief and of the practices that flow from it in our lives, and in that sense we do "choose." Those for whom nontheistic belief is a central constituent of identity but who also want to be Scouts may raise the issue publicly, as in the preceding cases; by implication they are choosing their religious beliefs over the lure of scouting, as they will have to abide by the outcome of the challenges they pose. Like Spinner, although I believe that the Boy Scouts is mistaken in its insistence on a public affirmation of theism, because many nontheists could contribute to and benefit from other focuses of scouting, I also believe that with respect to religious belief, the Boy Scouts is an expressive association within the meaning here discussed. It is ironic, however, that those in scouting who view secular humanism as a religion do not include this belief system among religious beliefs to be respected in other Scouts.

Its status is murkier, I believe, on the issue of sexual orientation. Scouts promise in the Oath to keep themselves "morally straight," which in the *Handbook* means "to be a person of strong character; guide your life with honesty, purity, and justice. Respect and defend the rights of all people. Your relationships with others should be honest and open. Be clean in your speech and actions, and faithful in your religious beliefs. The values you follow as a Scout will help you become virtuous and self-reliant" (551). The values here expressed are quite general in nature. Those who believe that nontheists and gays have at least a moral right to join an organization in which they seek only to participate, not to change fundamentally, will see irony in the admonition to respect and defend the rights of all. No heterosexual affirmation parallels the theistic affirmation in the Oath, and therefore there is not the same possibility of hypocrisy. The California troop that resolved not to reject homosexuals as members, and whose charter was renewed because it had not accepted homosexuals and had agreed not to seek any, had simply not accepted any *known* homosexuals and would not seek anyone simply on the basis of sexual orientation. That is, the troop might already contain homosexuals and might unknowingly admit some in future. And the San Francisco Bay Area Council policy of "don't ask, don't tell," adopted with the approval of the national organization, admits as much.

Further evidence of the lack of any clear and public affirmation of heterosexuality, apart from national leadership statements against allowing the registration of "avowed homosexuals," is found in the 1998 statement of James Dale, the Eagle Scout and assistant scoutmaster in New Jersey. If sexual orientation and related issues are referred to parents and pastors and are not discussed at Scout meetings, it is difficult to conclude that with respect to sexual orientation, the Scouts is an expressive organization in the sense that its formation created a voice and membership selection defines that voice. That is, its formation and maintenance does not seem grounded in a readily accessible, publicly stated, shared viewpoint and set of principles. In Creppell's terms, the Boy Scouts' beliefs about sexual orientation do not have the status of public privacy. They are not expressed, recognized, or presented in public before a community in the same way that theism is in the Oath.

From this perspective it is not surprising, I believe, that the New Jersey appeals court majority here suggested that there is no evidence that a gay scoutmaster is unqualified to lead or will undermine the Scouts' fundamental beliefs. If it is not explained in the *Handbook*, how fundamental can the emphasis on heterosexual orientation be? And if it is not explicit, how can it be undermined? Anecdotal evidence appears in a letter to the editor from an Eagle Scout, who remembers an emphasis on civic responsibility "but not being taught to adopt any particular political philosophies. . . . I learned that true civic responsibility doesn't mean thinking what someone tells you to think, and that it certainly doesn't mean silencing minority perspectives. Rather, it means being able to think critically about social issues by considering all viewpoints."[84] Similarly, when Dennis Byrne objects that Dale must either teach "the complete Scouting agenda" in violation of his own identity or must stand by his convictions in violation of Scout principles, if matters concerning sexuality are not specifically discussed, there is no "agenda" to teach in this area. Discussions of sexual orientation and practice are not a part of the duties and obligations of leadership. Therefore, no conflict of interest exists between Dale's convictions and the agenda he is to teach. Byrne also objects to the court's dictating the leadership of a private organization. But there is a difference between such "dictation" when it may affect the publicly stated, shared viewpoint that an organization teaches, as if a church were forced to accept a candidate for the priesthood who espoused agnostic beliefs, and dictation when a leader's beliefs and practices need not impinge on the performance of official duties. Moreover, when the national office of the Boy Scouts accepted the "don't ask, don't tell" compromise, this change did more than publicly acknowledge that gays might be admitted, even if unknowingly. It also implied that one's sexual orientation alone need have no bearing on one's qualifications to participate in scouting.

Although the Scouts do not now put forward a clear and public statement, regularly affirmed, on the centrality of heterosexuality as they do on the importance of theism, they could in theory develop such a statement in the future. If so, I would then reluctantly have to support the Boy Scouts' right as an expressive association to set the qualifications of its own members. This would not prevent homosexuals from becoming members if they were willing disingenuously to affirm the value of heterosexuality, just as nontheists may now join if they are willing to affirm a belief in God. I should prefer that the Scouts change its stance on sexual orientation. But Byrne displays a legitimate concern when he wonders whether the courts insisting that the Scouts admit gays might also invalidate the policies of any parallel organization established exclusively for heterosexuals. In the two state decisions, exclusivity is supported in California and inclusivity is buttressed in New Jersey. But whichever side of the controversy may receive support nationally, in a liberal polity like-minded individuals should be able to associate to express and practice their beliefs in private organizations without fear of being coerced to accept those who disagree. This is especially true for those who need a refuge, whose belief may be "out of favor" in mainstream organizations. In fact, Nancy Rosenblum suggests that an association is expressive and that its membership selection should be protected regardless of "whether public expression is regular and consistent or spontaneous and sporadic." In the case of the Scouts, the messages of theism or heterosexuality merit protection not because either or both define the association but because the members have created them. "Expression has to do with who we are and are perceived to be, not just what we say."[85]

The importance of freedom of association as a refuge for individuals outside the mainstream may be illustrated by the examples of the current status of Christianity in the People's Republic of China and in Russia. The Chinese government allows religious worship and the existence of official religious organizations. But these official churches "are rigidly managed by the state. Preachers must be registered with the government's Religious Affairs Bureau. They are not allowed to preach outside their own province. They are not allowed to speak about the second coming of Christ. They are not allowed to baptize anyone under eighteen years of age." Underground churches also exist. But their leaders' homes have sometimes been raided, religious texts have been confiscated, unofficial meeting places have been closed, and members have been sent to reeducation camps where starving, beating, and torture are not unknown practices. On occasion, "priests from government-run churches have even testified against members of the underground church and been present during police interrogations." Although leaders in the National Council of Churches have reported that these incidents stem only from overzealous local officials, evangelistic interference by outsiders, or "the wish to preserve authentic religious and cultural traditions,"[86] they still provide a cautionary tale.

In Russia in 1997, the Parliament passed a bill granting favorable treatment to religious associations recognized fifteen years previously when Russia was part of the Soviet Union, including the traditional Orthodox Church, plus Jewish, Islamic, and Buddhist organizations. But it restricts Roman Catholics, unofficial Baptist groups, Pentecostals, Seventh-Day Adventists, dissident Russian Orthodox groups, and newer Islamic and Buddhist sects. Where established organizations can own property, control radio and television stations, receive tax exemptions, distribute religious literature, run schools, and conduct services in hospitals and cemeteries, other organizations must register annually, and this only entitles them to engage in financial transactions and charitable activities, rendering them less influential.[87] In a liberal polity, however, all expressive associations should enjoy the same legal status. This at least means that they should exercise internal autonomy in determining whom they will admit as members.

In accordance with the inevitable common moral standpoint of the larger society, however, public aid to or sponsorship of organizations that discriminate in a manner contrary to public policy should cease. For example, in 1998 the city of Chicago declined to continue its sponsorship of Boy Scout programs until or unless the group changes its stance toward nontheists and gays; formerly it simply paid the salaries of city employees involved in career-focused Explorer Scout programs.[88] The withdrawal of financial support, either directly or in kind, as in the participation of public employees or in allowing Scout troops to meet in public schools, does not interfere with the membership or the actual practices of private organizations. They may secure the participation of employees in the private sector or of public employees on their own time, and they may be sponsored by churches or other voluntary organizations, meeting on the premises of these associations. Individuals must possess the freedom to form associations on the basis of their convictions and to exclude those who do not share these, as Locke asserts. But if individuals are to be accorded the ordinary civil enjoyments that Locke also states must not be denied on the basis of belief, the larger society as represented through the liberal polity must be able to assert *its* beliefs in the form of a common moral standpoint that prohibits discrimination in the public sector and does not render aid to organizations that discriminate in ways prohibited in the public sector.

EXCLUSIVITY, INCLUSIVITY, AND THE COMMON MORAL STANDPOINT

Expressive associations grounded in convictions that accord with the common moral standpoint of the larger society may do better than those whose convictions conflict with it. But because such a standpoint is unavoidable and inevitable, as I have argued, this will always be the case. Although the liberal commitment to diversity requires freedom for associations that are not themselves inclusive internally, it also allows for greater encouragement of those that *are* inclusive. Although the diversity that is a permanent feature of liberal society renders this eventuality unlikely, if enough voluntary organizations or associations held parallel beliefs, this would curtail the very existence of alternatives. If, hypothetically, most organizations were internally inclusive, I would not be overly concerned even though this would flatten, in Spinner's terms, the diversity of "the rich associational life" of a liberal society. Individuals would still enjoy access to a broad array of alternatives, which would provide a broad context of choice or forum within which individuals may exercise their autonomy by questioning, examining, and revising or reaffirming their projects and goals. Those who desired more exclusive alternatives could still form them in association with others of similar viewpoint.

If, however, most organizations were internally exclusive, and exclusive in the *same way,* I believe we would have greater cause for concern. If very few organizations of any kind wanted to admit agnostics, atheists, or homosexuals, the combined effect would be to curtail drastically the breadth of the forum or context of choice within which individuals exercise their autonomy. As we have seen, Taylor perceives widespread agreement on the proposition that citizens should not be excluded from the public process or from opportunities because of religious difference. I have noted that these opportunities suggest a broad range of activity encompassing civil society, or in Spinner's terms both the voluntary and the market sectors. Because participation in organizations like the Boy Scouts provides training in skills, leadership, and character, which translate into enhanced career opportunities for members, and if the vast majority of such organizations excluded agnostics, atheists, or homosexuals who were honest about their status, I would be gravely concerned about the prejudice toward these individuals, in Locke's terms, in their civil enjoyments, or in their career opportunities as compared to those of others not excluded on the basis of important constituents of their identities.

We might then want to revisit the *Roberts* case. When Justice O'Connor argued that the correct distinction is between commercial and expressive associations, the implication was that it is legitimate to regulate a commercial association, even if this alters its message, but not to regulate the membership of an expressive association, even if this would not change the message disseminated. One strategy would be to argue that because religious belief does not touch the actual activities of the Boy Scouts but is confined to the regular declamation of the Oath, activities are then untouched by the admission of nontheists, and there is no cogent rationale for protecting the message. This strategy is on stronger ground with respect to the exclusion of homosexuals, however, as there is no clear public statement on that subject as there is on religious belief. But in both instances, expression is severely curtailed.

Alternatively, a less drastic strategy would be to argue that given the critical mass of exclusive organizations with parallel criteria of exclusivity, the resulting curtailment of opportunities for individuals renders many of these organizations more commercial than expressive in nature. That is, with less diversity, the formation and maintenance of these organizations is less than otherwise the creation and definition of a distinctive voice. And the access that these organizations function to provide or deny to individuals is such that they become more like public accommodations. I would not welcome such developments. But if a critical mass of organizations truly did share parallel criteria of exclusivity, we might have to admit that we no longer possess the context of choice or the forum that should be characteristic of a liberal political culture.

I have argued that neither nonconfessional theism nor any other particular formulation of religious, philosophical, or moral belief is permanently central to our common purposes as a nation. Instead, it is continuing discussion and debate, deliberation and reflection that is central as over time we negotiate and renegotiate the terms of our common life. This requires, however, that we be allowed to be straightforward about our religious identities in the same way that we are increasingly straightforward about our cultural identities and the imperatives that these present. As an example, the Clinton administration in 1997 issued guidelines requiring that civilian executive branch agencies respect religious as well as nonreligious speech by employees. Muslim women can wear headscarves, Christian employees may keep Bibles on desks and read them during breaks, workers can discuss their faiths as long as coworkers do not object, and agencies must accommodate the observance of holy days as much as possible.[89] This directive was partly a reaction to earlier attempts by the Equal Employment Opportunity Commission to define religious harassment so broadly that it seemed to ban any religious discussion and symbols from the workplace altogether.

On the other hand, because I have argued that religious identity, like cultural identity, is not a given but is instead a matter of constitutive choice, I may appear to have weakened the case for accommodation of individual religious beliefs. This tension appears in actual disputes. In 1997, the application for employment as a manager by a Sikh, religiously prohibited from cutting his hair, was rejected by Domino's Pizza because the enterprise wanted clean-shaven employees. Although the man claimed religious discrimination, Domino's argued that the issue was not one of civil rights because, while "race . . . is not a choice, . . . [but] something we're born with . . . religion is a choice." A representative of an Orthodox Jewish group, however, countered that "when it comes to people's religions, we don't view that as a 'choice.' Religion is part of what people are, who they are."[90] I have argued, nevertheless, that religious identity, like cultural identity, should be accommodated not because it is an unchosen or unalterable constituent of identity, but because it is an expression of autonomy. Whatever our religious beliefs or lack of them, we must define and interpret for ourselves individually what they mean to us and their place in our lives. In this sense, then, religious identity is a constitutive choice. It requires not only the same concern and respect as unchosen constituents of our identities but perhaps more, precisely because it is an expression of autonomy.

It is true that regarding religion as a matter of constitutive choice means that the protection of religious beliefs and practices may evoke less sympathy than otherwise. What is to prevent any of us at any time from asserting that some seemingly bizarre practice should be accommodated and respected simply because we choose to engage in it? On the other hand, the hard work of liberal citizenship, as Spinner reminds us, is a two-way street. We need to learn about and in many cases to accommodate expressions of both religious and cultural identity. Simultaneously, those expressing this identity need to take responsibility for their ends, in Rawls's sense, including responsibility for the tastes and preferences that they view as means to these ends. That is, some kinds of tastes and preferences may be accommodated with relatively minimal inconvenience, whereas others are incompatible with the common moral standpoint of a liberal polity. It is impossible to determine categorically which tastes and preferences characterize each category. As we have seen, the existence of competing sets of social facts means that the status of particular practices is often determined by which set of facts is taken into account.

I have argued that religious beliefs and practices may constitute an expression of autonomy when their adherents engage in critical reflection on their spiritual projects and goals. Because we cannot know when adherents have actually engaged in this reflection, we should err on the side of accommodation. At the same time, however, the liberal polity is entitled to regulate, limit, or even ban practices that interfere with the capacity for autonomy. Viewing religious belief as a matter of constitutive choice means that neither individuals nor communities of faith can assert that particular practices are religious imperatives that no one should deny to those who believe in them. Practices incompatible with liberal citizenship must be rethought. I do not believe that this approach trivializes religious belief and practice. Instead, it potentially deepens the deliberation and reflection that affect both the definition of our individual identities and the negotiation of our common purposes.

6. Sexuality, Neutrality, and Autonomy in the Liberal Polity

The subject of sexual orientation and practice differs in several ways from other issues in this book. First, sexuality is typically viewed as a private matter. Like cultural or religious affiliation, it may be deemed of no concern to public authority; even more than culture or religion, it falls within the sphere of the intimate life of the individual. Thus, it is doubly private. Second, this attribution of privacy to sexuality admirably suits people who would preserve the traditionally dominant consensus that nonconformists can comfortably exist on the fringes of the polity and need not and should not be the subjects of legislation that appears to constitute approval of their practices. It is sometimes forgotten, however, that public authority does take notice of sexuality not only by confining civil marriage to contracts between men and women but also through legislation that in many states makes consensual oral and anal sex a crime even behind closed doors.[1] Finally, my focus on the capacity for autonomy may seem to accord poorly with the topic of sexuality. People who champion the right of homosexuals to equal recognition typically ground these claims on the unchosen nature of sexual orientation, arguing that individuals should not suffer disadvantages because of unchosen constituents of their identities. I shall maintain, however, that although sexual orientation, like one's initial cultural or religious identity, is unchosen, how one handles or responds to that orientation is chosen or affirmed. Like cultural membership and religious affiliation, sexual orientation should be respected in a liberal polity not because it is unchosen but because it is a central constituent of personal identity.

"It is only a slight exaggeration to say that the two main opinions in *Bowers v. Hardwick* make the case look like a battle between Yahoos and perverts."[2] In the case to which Mary Ann Glendon refers, the Supreme Court upheld the constitutionality of a Georgia statute criminalizing sodomy in the home of the man convicted. The conflicts that develop about how to frame the debate about a community's shared conceptions of the good are well exemplified in this case. Glendon's comment exemplifies a widely held view that "Yahoos" and "perverts" share equal moral status in their efforts to influence the stance of the liberal polity on matters of sexuality in general. This conviction is shared by William Galston, who with regard to *Bowers* suggests that "public recognition of private conduct is no less a part of American history than is the quest to cast off public restraints." Therefore, the recognition of cultural differences among the states by upholding antisodomy laws suggests the value "of honoring and accommodating the claims of both juridical liberalism and moral traditionalism."[3] Whatever its intrinsic value, he concludes that the function of moral traditionalism is that of promoting the stability of the liberal political order as a community with its own set of defining beliefs and values. The subtext of views like Glendon's and Galston's is that a compromise exists that, if not strictly neutral, gives equal consideration and respect to strongly held convictions on each side of a disagreement that arouses strong emotions.

I have maintained that political arrangements are not strictly neutral. To the extent that they are aimed at neutrality, they do so within a context that weighs a particular set of social facts in deciding whether specific policies embody civil harm or benefit. As we saw in the case of Sabbath observance, whether one considers this a choice or a duty determines one's conclusions as to what policy serves neutrality. To the extent that a degree of neutrality can be achieved, this extent must be measured or judged by a standard independent of neutrality itself. In my view, this standard should be that of the promotion of the capacity for autonomy, and the goal should be that of autonomy-based neutrality. Theorists who value diversity over autonomy, however, suggest that the principle of equal respect does not allow a privileged position for personal autonomy, which is simply one of many conceptions of the good. Therefore, they argue, if neutrality is to be measured by a standard independent of neutrality, diversity-based neutrality, rather than autonomy-based neutrality, best exhibits equal respect for individuals with divergent conceptions of the good. But for theorists like Will Kymlicka, David McCabe, and me, "The central thing worth respecting in human beings is their capacity for rational self-government and for shaping their lives as they see fit."[4] The norm of equal respect, like that of neutrality, then, does not conflict with the centrality of autonomy but is in fact grounded in the capacity for autonomy.

On this interpretation, it is not individuals' conceptions of the good that merit equal respect but the individuals themselves who hold these conceptions. Liberals respect individual conceptions of the good because they are central to these individuals' self-understandings. "The state's obligation to respect conceptions of the good *derives from* its obligation to respect individuals" (73). The norm of equal respect then does not privilege a specific conception of the good but allows the liberal polity to promote or endorse virtues that enhance individuals' abilities to pursue self-chosen activities and ideals and to identify or determine the values that most merit their allegiance (77).

This account of autonomy-based neutrality reinforces the argument that culture, religion, and sexuality, because of their centrality to individual identity, belong in the realm of constitutive choice.[5] If these affiliations are undertaken or maintained in a context of critical reflection on one's projects and goals, they are expressions of autonomy. On this interpretation, I cannot agree with scholars like Glendon and Galston that policies respecting moral traditionalism offer an acceptable compromise. Although they recognize a diversity of opinion between traditionalists and nontraditionalists, where such compromises hold sway they sacrifice the autonomy of nontraditionalists to the comfort of traditionalists.

I have maintained that the liberal polity's hospitality to diversity does not mean that it must accept all cultural and religious practices, including those that are illiberal. For me, illiberal practices are those that interfere with the development of the capacity for and the exercise of personal autonomy. In the area of sexuality, unacceptable practices would include but might not be limited to pederasty, incest, rape, and female genital alteration. In my view, however, most sexual practices among consenting adults—whether homosexual, bisexual, or, for that matter, heterosexual—do not interfere with the development of the capacity for autonomy or with the exercise of it; instead, they may be expressions of autonomy. Many states have not legislated against homosexual practices, some have removed prohibitions, and still others do not enforce such laws as do appear on the statute books. This indicates that on some level, homosexual conduct is considered acceptable, at least in the sense that it is tolerated.

Individuals who engage in or defend an acceptable practice, I believe, should receive the same public consideration and respect as those who espouse other acceptable practices if we are to accord equal respect to varying expressions of personal autonomy. Otherwise, we are according greater consideration to those who would judge others' ways of life than to those who simply wish to form and pursue their own conceptions of the good without interference. I believe that a liberal community in particular should be open to consideration of diverse beliefs and practices, some of which over time contribute to the shared values of the community. Public distinctions between "better" and "worse" among acceptable practices impoverish the community both by foreclosing debate and possible revision of its shared understandings and by foreclosing to individuals sources of self-criticism that may enlarge their own understandings.

The subject of sexual orientation provides an interesting contrast with that of religious belief. Most people would accord equal consideration and respect to all individuals who engage in religious practices considered acceptable in a liberal polity. They would agree that religious practice is a matter of personal obligation or choice. They would not argue that respect for diversity requires that public policy treat the convictions of those who dislike certain manifestations of religious belief as worthy of equal consideration with the convictions of those who simply wish to engage in the practices dictated by their beliefs without loss of respect or civic standing. Yet on issues of sexuality, many people move in the opposite direction. They suggest that although individuals with distasteful sexual practices should be accorded grudging toleration, they should adopt a low profile and need not receive respect equal to that accorded to other practices. They argue that although sexuality is a personal matter, it is also a fitting subject of public regulation even when its manifestations affect only consenting adults. Finally, they argue that liberal hospitality to diversity means that persons who find sexual practices distasteful or think them wrong possess an equal entitlement to shape public policy that governs them as do those individuals whose practices they are.

Because sexual orientation, like cultural membership and religious faith, is critically important to personal identity, I believe that individuals who engage in acceptable practices in all these areas should be accorded the same measure of consideration and respect. Moreover, because of its centrality, the degree to which homosexuality is a choice does not really matter in the end. Religious conservatives may accept my argument that manifestations of identity can exemplify constitutive choice with regard to faith but may reject its applicability to sexuality. Progressive secularists, on the contrary, may accept this point with regard to sexuality but may resist its application to matters of faith. That is, conservatives may be more tolerant toward sexual orientation they understand as unchosen, whereas progressives may be more sympathetic toward religious faith that does appear to be chosen, as in some conversion experiences. I hope, however, that the parallel may help those of each viewpoint to better understand the other. If religious faith is the area in which the liberal polity is often most willing to accord equal consideration and respect to divergent practices, homosexuality is currently an area in which according this same consideration and respect is particularly controversial. If we respect religious identity as potential expressions of autonomy, we should respect sexual identity similarly. Toleration requires respect, not simply bare permission, for ways of life frowned on by the majority.

Toleration and Respect

The idea that the liberal polity should accord equal respect to homosexuality may be grounded either on a substantive argument from personal autonomy, or on a more strategic argument that grudging toleration does not promote the stability that proponents of this stance desire. The opposing positions in the substantive argument once again demonstrate the point that conflicting interpretations of civil harm and benefit stem from conflicting views as to which set of social facts is the correct measure of these effects. One moral view of sexuality embeds it in doctrines that valorize procreation and the perpetuation of traditional gender roles; a second view accords to sexual expression an intrinsic value in the context of intimate associations. Legitimating the latter view, whether by the repeal of antisodomy laws or by the recognition of homosexual marriage, threatens not only the conventional understanding of the good of sexuality but also the traditional assumption that this conventional understanding is a shared one. Nevertheless, on an argument from personal autonomy, individuals must be able to scrutinize and to reflect critically upon the meaning of sexuality and intimate association in the context of their projects and goals, as they do in other areas.

Karen Struening expresses this view by suggesting that freedom in intimate association is analogous to freedom of religion and expression; the process of forming our own judgments in these areas is a central constituent of self-definition. For her, "The regulation and repression of non-coercive and consensual sexual practices between adults is a direct assault on moral pluralism."[6] The dominance of social convention sacrifices our ability to determine both what we do and who we are or who we become. In Kymlicka's terms, we sacrifice not only our capacity to pursue self-endorsed lives but also our capacity to examine, question, and revise—or reaffirm—our current projects and goals. Although admitting the legitimacy of competing understandings of the good can complicate the efforts of the cultural or religious traditionalist to perpetuate his own mode of life, "we do not take from him what he needs to live *his life*" (512), as we would be taking from the dissident by censoring *his* practices concerning his own life. I concur in Struening's avowal that one's sexuality belongs to oneself and that sexual expression toward consenting adults should not be regulated by others, regardless of majority opinion (513). "Sexuality, like religious and moral beliefs, is our own in the sense that without it our ability to be self-determining and self-defining is seriously compromised" (522).

Many people will disagree with this sort of argument. Some who agree with it, on the other hand, suggest that for strategic reasons, liberals should not insist

on equal respect for dissenters, and that in doing so, they too often conflate toleration with approval. Steven Kautz, for example, asserts that liberals tend to
request not only permission but also esteem, and to bestow not only toleration
but also respect and praise, on unpopular ways of life. But for Kautz, this tendency in effect denies that private choices and pursuits are indeed private. The
vindication of the right to equal concern and respect requires "that the community undertake to teach each citizen what to think: 'sensitivity' is the new
liberal cousin to republican 'virtue.' "[7] Although Kautz does not explicitly
address the issue of sexual orientation and practice, his argument fits it well.
For him, one of liberal politics' "most splendid achievements" is its protection
of liberal individualists who are "moral strangers" to the community, even
when these strangers are neither understood nor admired. These individuals
should reciprocate by refraining from demanding more than grudging tolerance, thus honoring ordinary citizens "by refusing to repay this respectable
generosity with contempt."[8] Some ways of life may be privately tolerated or
even admired, without being openly praised.[9]

On the surface, Kautz may appear simply to be arguing against extremities
of political correctness, wherein some people advocate not only acceptance of
but also enthusiasm toward most manifestations of diversity. He criticizes a
communitarian emphasis on constitutive attachments in defining the individual (621), suggesting that liberal individualists or "moral strangers" do not need
praise but only permission. A community that offers only grudging tolerance
"is consistent with self-respect though not a right to equal respect" (628). The
individualist seemingly has recourse to an extracommunal standard of judgment outside the dominant consensus, which standard underpins self-esteem
and obviates the need for self-definition by a community standard. This stance
initially appears compatible with my conviction that individuals should live
their lives from the inside and engage in critical reflection on their projects and
goals, revising or reaffirming these so that they are self-endorsed. If the circumstances of toleration combine the existence of disliked practices with voluntary noninterference in these practices, grudging toleration would seem to
meet this test.

I believe that a stance of grudging toleration, however, implies that individuals who choose or affirm unpopular ways of life and their supporters
should simply be grateful for this modicum of toleration and should withhold
potential demands for measures that would end public discrimination and prevent private discrimination. The hard work of liberal citizenship requires the
equal and civil treatment of others in the public square, whatever our private

sentiments. Those who are different should not be pressured to conform by their silence any more than by their behavior. Individuals should be recognized or respected as whole persons, even when their practices are disliked, not encouraged or pressured to sacrifice the conditions of their own autonomy to the comfort of the majority.

Kautz, on the other hand, relies on a consensus wherein individuals measure their beliefs and practices by the standards of choiceworthiness espoused by the community, being accorded full social acceptance for some but only grudging permission for others. From a strategic standpoint, Kautz argues, many liberal interests are best defended not through direct arguments for liberal equality or autonomy, but indirectly, by persuading advocates for both democratic equality and republican virtue to leave liberals—dissenters from the dominant consensus and their supporters—alone. It is both dangerous and futile, he argues, to attempt to instantiate a liberal orthodoxy grounded in moral autonomy or equal respect. "Acrimonious fights, now called culture wars, will be evaded only if liberals do the evading."[10] That is, because dissenters and their supporters will lose, they had best avoid the fight altogether. More specifically, "The law at issue in *Bowers v. Hardwick* is surely illiberal; but it does not follow that every failure of respect . . . would be illiberal, even if these failures were to find their way into some of the laws of the community" (74). To Kautz, it seems that to protect unpopular practices is to legitimate them, and publicly to legitimate them is to praise them. In sum, Kautz believes that civil peace requires a degree of hypocrisy. Ordinary citizens and nonconformists should collude in a settlement in which dissenters exchange silence for toleration, with the unspoken acquiescence of both parties.

Although every political community, as we have seen, ranks some values above others, the essential question is how this hierarchy is to be determined. Alasdair MacIntyre emphasizes that one cannot seek the good only as an individual. Notions of worth and merit vary from one community to another, along with the practices, institutions, and traditions of these communities. These notions become determinate for an individual only within the context of that individual's social identity,[11] functioning, in Kymlicka's terms, as the social context or context of choice that grounds the individual's subsequent affirmations and choices. The difficulty is that communally determined notions of worth and merit too easily allow individual worth to be judged primarily in terms of how well one upholds these apparently constant norms, which in turn are grounded "within the dominant understanding of a particular community's traditions." On this view, argues William Lund, "citizens need to discuss and decide on a substantive conception of the common good and then use it to measure the legitimacy of their private beliefs and desires."[12]

Reliance on current norms does not suggest neutrality on a basis of autonomy or diversity toward individual definitions of the good but suggests that "we treat people as equals when we hold their beliefs and conduct up to currently accepted understandings of our traditions and shared purposes." This latter practice, first, raises, "perhaps to prohibitive levels, the costs of citizens revising their conceptions of the good away from a recognized consensus." And second, it also makes it "difficult for the community as a whole to have enough experience with, or to hear arguments about, alternatives that might cause it to revise or even reject its current understandings" (588). Rights claims by unpopular groups and their supporters, for instance, pose a threat for those who would enshrine current norms. "Rights talk . . . may lead them away from publicly recognized modes of flourishing" (591). In other words, enshrining the current context of choice not only does not encourage but positively discourages critical reflection on individual or collective projects and goals.

These observations introduce a contradiction in views like Kautz's. His worry about a political entitlement to equal concern and respect is based on the fear that this entitlement calls on the community to teach citizens what to think. That is, if public policies mandate equal treatment for those who adhere to unpopular beliefs and practices, the community is inculcating values that promote equal respect. Yet is not the purpose of exchanging toleration for silence to inculcate and reinforce dominant understandings of our traditions? The distinction certainly functions to teach citizens what to think, even though this teaching is indirect. It inculcates values that can be used to measure the legitimacy of our private beliefs and desires against the communal consensus, eliciting and rewarding some beliefs and practices but discouraging and stigmatizing others. Thus, the distinction between grudging tolerance and equal respect, if not praise, conveys a message with consequences for both individual and collective understandings of the good.

Moreover, as we have seen, Kautz believes that self-esteem springs most properly from sources beyond the community. But in that case, how can either approbation or its absence influence beliefs and practices in the ways that he desires? He cannot have it both ways. Either communal attitudes shape behavior, in which case he should admit that citizens are properly being taught what to think, or else individuals look to transcendent sources of affirmation beyond communal efforts, in which case the distinction between grudging permission and affirmation will mean little. As it is, he conveys the impression that teaching citizens what to think is abhorrent when it inculcates equal respect for beliefs and practices repugnant to the majority. But teaching citizens what to think is apparently acceptable or desirable when it promotes beliefs and practices that reinforce the current consensus on these matters.

Accounts of toleration that would defer to the dominant understanding like Kautz's appear to result from an overlapping consensus but constitute in reality a modus vivendi: we praise worth and merit as defined by the current consensus, whatever its content, and accord grudging permission to others, in order to preserve civil tranquility. The community's shared general conception of the good is based on the dominance of some reasonable comprehensive doctrines and the self-censorship of others, rather than on a truly overlapping consensus to which all participants are equally welcome to contribute. A modus vivendi model of the political order is not intrinsically illegitimate. Patrick Neal, for example, proposes a resurrection of "vulgar" Hobbesian liberalism, noting that neutrality theorists tend to overestimate both the instability of the modus vivendi model and the stability of their own models. In the face of pluralistic conflict, those attempting neutrality toward comprehensive conceptions of the good ignore the importance of a rough equality of power among competing groups to check both each other and the state. "Is it really the case that the continued stability of existing liberal regimes is in any way whatsoever dependent on a professor of philosophy's ability to define the terms of an overlapping consensus among alternative conceptions of the good life?"[13]

Rawls, however, suggests that an overlapping consensus is characterized by greater stability than is a modus vivendi, as people's moral commitments to the consensus itself will outweigh any tendency for their support to vary in proportion to the strength of their own views in society.[14] Yet if respect, even civic respect, consisting in equal and civil treatment of those whose practices are unpopular, is a reward only distributed in accordance with the individual's conformity to the dominant consensus, one of two conclusions follows. First, individuals unable to secure a commitment to equal respect for their own identities will demand this if and when the strength of their own view or the balance of power—that is, what appears to be the dominant understanding—makes this practicable. Second, if the balance moves to weaken unpopular groups still further, the ostensibly overlapping consensus may be interpreted to require even less respect for them than before. And because the consensus is interpreted in terms of the current understanding, the likelihood is great that the dominant view will gain support over time. Thus, what appears to be an overlapping consensus turns out to operate as a modus vivendi, rooted in the actual convergence of interests at given points in time. To put this differently, the stability of an overlapping consensus may be secured by a modus vivendi at the metatheoretical level, whereby certain conceptualizations of concepts of the good command insufficient support to become part of the dominant consensus and therefore remain hidden behind a veil of ignorance where prudence dictates that they remain.

Moreover, even if citizens do arrive at a consensus that they will continue to support, regardless of the relative strengths of differing viewpoints, in a liberal polity this consensus is better developed by forthright debate among individuals who are accorded equal respect than by the covert shaping of beliefs and practices by communal attitudes that both emanate from and reinforce the already dominant consensus. We maintain the right and the desire to influence the terms of the way of life to which we subscribe. For some, our history and tradition point in the direction not only of liberty of association but also of equal respect. In the case of sexual orientation, liberty may be exemplified by protecting intimate relationships from unwarranted state interference, and equal respect may be interpreted to require protection against discrimination on the basis of the sort of intimate relationships in which one engages. But these interpretations must be reflected on and discussed. In sum, there will always be a dominant consensus, but its construction should be both an ongoing and an interactive process. As Brian Walker writes, "Fighting for toleration is not a matter of attempting to align other groups with a preexisting order, but a form of dialogue in the course of which the picture of what toleration is and requires becomes clear. By attempting to build my ideal of toleration on the terrain of the other, I am myself affected by new and alien ideas, and perhaps my own view is changed."[15]

Autonomy, Affirmation, and Choice

If we practice toleration by refraining from using the power we possess to interfere with practices we dislike or of which we disapprove, most minimally, suggests Andrew Murphy, toleration "denotes forbearance from imposing punitive sanctions for dissent from prevailing norms."[16] Although we often associate punitive sanctions with actual legal prosecution and punishment, even engagement in legal practices that are unpopular may threaten social, economic, or political disadvantage to their practitioners. And critics of unpopular practices, both religious and sexual, sometimes have implied or do imply that practitioners willfully choose their ways of life and may perhaps be reeducated through social pressure. Public affirmation of one's religious or sexual identity may have serious implications for one's civic status. Although one strategy would be to resist social pressure by arguing that sexual orientation or religious belief is unchosen and therefore not to be penalized, a more promising strategy, I think, is to assert that these manifestations of identity are constitutive choices and should not be penalized because they are expressions of autonomy.

PROHIBITIONISTS AND LIBERATIONISTS: THE PROCRUSTEAN BED

For some commentators and social critics, the question of whether homosexuality is an innate or a chosen condition has no meaning. To people who would discourage, penalize, or prohibit it, observes Andrew Sullivan, homosexuality is simply a deviation that perverts the essentially complementary natures of male and female. Human identity is basically heterosexual, and homosexual behavior is an aberration in which some are trapped, out of conformity with their true natures. On this view, homosexual orientation is a contingent quality or a behavior, like lying, wasting money, or smoking, from which individuals may and should properly be diverted.[17]

The reverse image is that of the liberationists, for whom also homosexuality is not a naturally defining condition. It is instead a social construct of relatively recent vintage that should be cast off if individuals are "to be liberated from the condition of homosexuality into a fully chosen form of identity, which is a repository of individual acts of freedom" (57). Persons understand themselves as homosexuals only because of the social construct into which they are born and come of age (62). In other words, where prohibitionists would address deviant acts by proscribing them, liberationists would remove the label of deviance, which is itself a social construct. Where prohibitionists view these acts of aberrations from the normality of heterosexuality, liberationists see the labels themselves as aberrations in terms of a range of bodily pleasures that defy stringent classification.

Both the prohibitionist and liberationist interpretations of homosexuality involve contradictions. Sullivan himself recognizes the objective existence of a homosexual orientation independent of whether or how it is expressed, composed of sexual desire and emotional longing, central to individual identity, and as involuntary in most cases for homosexuals as a heterosexual orientation is for heterosexuals (17). The Roman Catholic Church in 1986 acknowledged that because homosexuality is an innate predisposition or unchosen condition in some people that is not itself a sin, the dignity of these individuals should be protected. Human beings in the likeness of God cannot be reduced to their sexual orientation (38). Yet the Church maintains that a tendency toward a morally evil practice is itself an objective disorder, although apparently not of the sort, like Down syndrome or epilepsy, that renders actions following from the condition blameless. Analogies to other disordered conditions do not help prohibitionists, Sullivan argues. Although the renunciation of "alcoholic acts" liberates the individual's true nature and potential for self-giving as in marriage, the renunciation of homosexual acts only liberates the homosexual "into sacrifice and pain, barred from the act of union with another that the Church holds to be intrinsic to the notion of human flourishing in the vast majority of human lives. Homosexuality is a structural condition which, even if allied to a renunciation of homosexual acts, disbars the human being from such a fully realized life" (44). The prohibitionist weakness is that homosexuality is an unexpungeable trait that recurs in each generation. A liberal culture that endorses moral autonomy can view homosexuality as a pathology that merits compassion. But if "sickness" is permitted, homosexuality can be neither prohibited nor stigmatized (49–50).

The liberationist weakness involves a different contradiction. Although sexual orientation may be viewed as an oppressive social construct, human beings always possess some separation from their cultures and some control over their identities, including a space within which they can operate as they will. Thus, suggests Sullivan, they "are not social constructions all the way down" (75). Individuals properly resist the established heterosexual order, but they should also resist the contemporary orthodoxy of liberationist outers who would reveal the sexual practices of others to destroy the tyranny of the closet, and for whom the aim of subverting the structure obliterates personal rights (75–83). The contradiction is that outers are enforcing their ideology with the same zeal that many prohibitionists use in enforcing their own. Sullivan is implying, then, that individuals should be self-defining in their sexuality as well as in other facets of their lives. It is as asphyxiating to be defined by others in the cause of sexual liberation as in the name of preserving traditional categories of sexuality.

Both prohibitionists and liberationists, I believe, teach us something about contexts of choice. Although the prohibitionists ricochet between viewing homosexuality as a blameless natural condition that nonetheless bars individuals from true self-fulfillment, and as an immoral activity that therefore should be proscribed, neither perspective allows for the exercise of autonomy. As a blameless condition, homosexuality is outside the individual's control. As an immoral activity, it is presumably a matter of choice. But because its immorality leads to its discouragement or prohibition, it is then not among the range of options the existence of which is a precondition of autonomy. Although the liberationists, on the other hand, ostensibly promote autonomous choice through their rejection of confining strictures and categories, they end up subordinating the value of individual self-interpretation to the goal of subverting oppression as they define it. Liberationists want to destroy the closet by emptying it. But, suggests Sullivan, "Most homosexuals are not, of course, in or out of the closet; they hover tentatively somewhere in between." Because untimely self-revelation can "actually limit freedom . . . this merely intensifies the desire to control the moment when that identity is revealed" (80–81). Patricia Boling explains that "coming out is a recurrent, never-finished process since all of us are constantly meeting new people, encountering new social and work situations, and thus having to confront over and over again how much of ourselves we wish to reveal."[18]

Homosexuals, then, face essentializing pressures similar to those confronting women. If women are to be self-interpreting, they must possess the ability to reject traditional roles and self-definitions, choosing other projects and goals. But they must also be able to affirm traditional roles, after questioning and examining them in a context of choice that presents them with genuine alternatives. Homosexuals likewise should be afforded the opportunity to step out of the closet without penalty but also to remain there if this course appears consonant with individual projects and goals. The actual choice is less fundamental than is the necessity of engaging in critical reflection while one is making it. We can admit the importance of difference without essentializing it. As Boling suggests, "Assuming an essentialized identity based on intimate affiliations or decisions likewise renders the diversity of people's experiences invisible and places normalizing pressures on different or dissenting group members" (79). Pressure to conform to the prevailing orthodoxy exists, whether we are discussing the heterosexual community that would prohibit, discourage, or ignore homosexuality or the liberationist community that would publicize and celebrate homosexuality, even against the wishes of those who, living their lives from the inside, would endorse a different course of action. Self-interpretation means deciding for oneself how to be a homosexual, and it is in making and living out this decision that one exercises autonomy.

CONSERVATIVES: PRIVATE TOLERANCE, PUBLIC DISAPPROVAL

Although they support individual liberties and pluralism, conservatives approve of public attempts to inculcate desired forms of behavior, thus, as Sullivan puts it, "protecting the fabric of society that makes such liberties possible in the first place."[19] Unlike prohibitionists and liberationists, they recognize homosexuality as a constitutive condition. But like Kautz, they combine private tolerance or even respect with public disapproval. The public affirmation of homosexual behavior is not "a neutral event." Rather, "It creates a social norm that says that sex is about personal gratification and not about marital procreation." Because "it devalues the social meaning of sex," it "*in itself is an assault on heterosexual union*" (99–100). Thus, conservatives would preserve social and familial stability and discourage waverers by refusing to acquiesce in the idea that homosexual and heterosexual lives are morally equivalent. "They mean by 'a homosexual life' one in which emotional commitments are fleeting, promiscuous sex is common, disease is rampant, social ostracism is common, and standards of public decency, propriety, and self-restraint are flouted" (106).

Sullivan responds, however, that the absence of social incentives, institutions, and guidelines with respect to homosexual behavior renders this description of homosexual life a self-fulfilling prophecy. The simultaneous celebration of both the traditional family and the stable homosexual relationship might in fact valorize heterosexual marriage as a model for commitment, a co-optation that conservatives should welcome as much as liberationists would abhor (112). Because the denigration of homosexuals is often expressed by people who also denigrate women and femininity in general, greater public respect for homosexuals might accompany greater respect for women, resulting both in more stable heterosexual marriages and in a more stable pluralist society that instantiates equal respect. To disapprove of homosexuality because of the ostracism and loneliness that often accompany this way of life is to ignore the fact that these consequences flow from the very disapproval that conservatives recommend (107–116).

Sustaining the distinction between private tolerance and public disapproval, argues Sullivan, rests on a sharper demarcation between private and public than is currently feasible. Maintaining a hidden identity is as difficult for a homosexual as it would be for a heterosexual to avoid public mention of a spouse or children, or of any activity that might reveal a heterosexual involvement (125). The quintessential example of this hypocrisy, of course, occurs in the current "don't ask, don't tell" policy of the armed forces, which requires discretion from homosexuals and self-restraint from heterosexuals (127–128). Many homosexuals now want to claim a public identity of homosexuality as a constitutive condition or orientation, without an inference by others of any particular practices, just as one cannot infer about a heterosexual either that she is promiscuous or a virgin. In this newly emerging distinction between public and private, "homosexuals claim publicly that they are gay, but seek privacy for whatever they may actually do in private" (130). Conservatives must then approve this public identity, on this argument, if they are to avoid discrimination for what they see as an unchosen constituent of identity. But they may express their private dismay at practices of which they disapprove, in a reversal of the traditional stance of private tolerance and public disapproval.

On Sullivan's account, I believe that the conservative politics of homosexuality allows for the development of the capacity for and the exercise of autonomy. Although homosexuality may be an objective experience, orientation, or structurally constitutive condition, the response to this experience is within the control of the individual homosexual. In the context of this book, we do not choose our culture or belief system of origin. These background conditions, however, provide a context of choice on the basis of which we may question, examine, and revise or reaffirm our projects and goals. We do not choose the conditions that ground us. But we may subsequently define the scope of their influence on us. We may affirm or reject this influence or revise its imperatives, arranging our projects and goals within the path of our original trajectory, or initiating new trajectories that encompass alternative projects and goals. With respect to sexuality as with other facets of our existence, then, we are or can be self-interpreting, thereby engaging in the exercise of autonomy. This suggestion may appear risky, playing into the arguments of those who declare that homosexuality is a willful choice of a perverse form of sexuality and that therefore we can legitimately encourage its rejection. Evidence that sexual orientation is innate, however, is unlikely in itself to engender equal respect for homosexuals. Although race and sex are biologically determined characteristics, this knowledge has not prevented historical judgments that African Americans or women are inferior to Caucasians or to men.

Advocates of conversion therapy or reparative therapy that would turn homosexuals to heterosexual relationships do not necessarily argue that homosexuality is voluntary. Whether genetically or environmentally determined, sexual orientation constitutes for them as for prohibitionists both a core feature of personal identity, yet also a psychological disorder or pathology.[20] Because homosexual behavior reveals the presence of a pathological compulsion, such behavior for prohibitionists cannot result from a true choice or the exercise of autonomy. The only way in which a psychologically homosexual individual can act autonomously, apparently, is to refuse to remain in thrall to this condition and to embrace heterosexuality through an act of will. Those who refuse to resist or reject this compulsion cannot be regarded as engaging in the critical self-reflection that is the hallmark of autonomy. They are instead either in the grip of a compulsion that prevents critical reflection or are willfully rejecting the opportunity to embrace health over disease, freedom over enthrallment.

I accept the judgment that sexual orientation is an objective condition, but reject the conservative distinction between private tolerance and public approval. I also accept the argument made by advocates of conversion therapy that sexual *behavior* or practices involve a choice, but reject their argument that only the pursuit of heterosexuality represents a true or legitimate choice. One's sexual orientation suggests a predisposition to engage in certain sorts of behaviors. A heterosexual experiences emotional and physical attraction to those of the opposite sex, a homosexual experiences attraction to those of the same sex, and a bisexual is attracted to those of both sexes. One may choose, however, either to act upon or not to act upon these attractions. Whether one chooses to affirm one's basic sexual orientation or repudiate it, the choice, when it results from an engagement in rational deliberation and critical reflection, represents an exercise of autonomy. As with choices involving culture and faith, choices involving sexuality do not change the historical fact of our original affiliation or orientation.

Moreover, whether our cultural, religious, or sexual allegiance is original or acquired, I believe that the liberal polity should protect us in our allegiances and in the practices that flow from them, as long as these practices are not unacceptable in a liberal polity. As I have maintained, observant Jews who wish to keep the Sabbath or to wear yarmulkes in the workplace have chosen to be observant, and their choices should be protected and accommodated whether they were born as Jews or converted to Judaism. Cultural and religious membership can either be affirmed or chosen anew, but in either case it may become constitutive of identity. As Yael Tamir states, "Cultural choices, like religious ones, belong in the category of constitutive choices, which due to their importance to individuals, should be granted special weight."[21] I would extend this same protection to sexual choices.

The relationship between sexual orientation and sexual behavior may be elucidated by considering individuals who choose a celibate life. Celibacy may be a function of chance or circumstance, as in the loss of a spouse or partner. It may also result from choice, as in decisions to join religious orders that require celibacy, or to foreswear intimate relationships for any number of personal reasons. But the decision to live a celibate life does not indicate that these individuals possess *no* basic sexual orientation. It may be that they possess weaker emotional or physical longings than do those who are not celibate, or they may experience typical longings but hold other values in higher regard than they do the value of intimate relationships. In fact, either of these contingencies itself facilitates both the choice and the living out of a celibate life. But the strength of their desires for intimacy is a quantitative matter, not a qualitative one. That is, overwhelmingly, the orientation of these individuals will be heterosexual, homosexual, or bisexual. But they have decided not to engage in the behaviors or practices of which their orientation is a precondition. Again, although their sexual orientation is an innate and objective condition, their deployment of this orientation in practice is a matter of choice.

If we are willing to protect practices that flow from religious belief as long as these practices are not illiberal, we ought also, I believe, to respect and protect practices that flow from sexual orientation as expressions of autonomy, as long as these practices involve only consenting adults. If we respect celibates, who choose not to act upon their sexual orientations, whatever these may be, we should also respect both those who affirm their orientations, heterosexual or homosexual, and those who decide to repudiate or disclaim their orientations, like homosexuals who seek conversion therapy. As Sullivan asks, "If someone genuinely feels he cannot live with himself as a gay man and decides to submit to grueling therapy and join a particular sect of American Protestantism to be able to live a heterosexual life, then who am I to stand in his way?"[22] The corollary, however, is that individuals who affirm their sexual orientations deserve the same respect as those who attempt to choose behaviors and practices counter to their orientations. Autonomy-based neutrality requires that we respect seekers of conversion therapy, rather than accusing them of pathological fear of homosexuality. But we should also respect homosexuals who act on their orientations, rather than classifying them as victims of pathology or psychological compulsion and as therefore incapable of autonomy. Although we cannot guarantee that critical reflection grounds these decisions rather than impulse, equal respect for individuals in their diverse identities requires that we make the prima facie assumption that their choices are autonomous ones. Moreover, the choice of how one is to live out one's sexual orientation is more likely to be one's own in the absence of social pressure and its consequences, thus increasing the likelihood that critical reflection is present.

Proponents of conversion therapy would undoubtedly respond that if celibates can foreswear their sexual orientations to pursue a life of celibacy, so then can homosexuals foreswear homosexuality to pursue a heterosexual life—or even a celibate one, which such proponents would prefer to homosexuality. Certainly homosexuals may do this; otherwise, conversion therapists would have no clients. The difficulty is in the implication that conversion to heterosexuality should constitute a second-order desire, that homosexuals ought to want the desire to convert, if they are not to be considered victims of pathology. Moreover, even if it could be demonstrated that celibates are in fact asexual and experience no sexual longings whatsoever, this would not prove that engaging in practices toward which one's sexual orientation is a predisposition is *not* an exercise of autonomy. The existence of seemingly asexual individuals no more suggests an absence of moral or personal autonomy in those who do experience particular longings than the existence of agnostics or atheists suggests an absence of autonomy in those who do experience spiritual longings and a desire for religious commitment. Just as we would not say that "cradle Episcopalians" exercise personal autonomy only if they seek instruction as Presbyterians, neither should we suggest that those of homosexual orientation exercise personal autonomy only when they seek conversion to heterosexuality. The affirmation of sexuality, like its rejection, is a constitutive choice, regardless of the "denomination," heterosexual or homosexual, that is the object of this choice. The affirmation of one's deepest emotional commitments, like the affirmation of one's deepest beliefs, is capable of reflecting both the capacity for and the expression of autonomy.

The equation of sexuality with culture and faith easily gives rise to objections. James Button, Barbara Rienzo, and Kenneth Wald note that sexual orientation may be hidden in ways that race, for example, cannot be concealed. Moreover, "Race is not normally viewed as a behavioral characteristic."[23] African Americans often fear that the limited resources available for pursuing discrimination complaints will be further diluted as more groups become objects of protection. "The claim that gays 'choose' a lifestyle often resonates with black critics, who pointedly emphasize that they had no choice about their race or the way they were treated by the white majority."[24] Critics of my argument may suggest that if specific behaviors and practices may be chosen for oneself, homosexuals need only change their behavior if they wish to avoid potential discrimination, or, as Kautz advocates, behave as they wish but with discretion and circumspection.

Alternatively, writes Sullivan, though homosexuality is a mixture of innate identity and behavior, it "does not fall, either, into the category of protected religious faith, since few people . . . regard it as simply and only a matter of choice. . . . Protecting it is not so easy when it isn't even clear what 'it' is."[25] I have maintained that conscience contains a larger element of voluntarism than some imagine, although it cannot be equated with the entirely contingent choice represented by a selection of wearing apparel. Under the English Test Act of 1673, repealed only in the nineteenth century, individuals were barred from holding public office who "would not renounce Catholicism or affirm the Trinity."[26] If matters of conscience were subject to completely unfettered choice, those dissatisfied with the legal disability could, once again, simply alter their beliefs to meet such tests. But because we must be able to endorse our projects and goals as we live our lives from the inside, we must scrutinize and reflect critically on them, making honest judgments about what we can or cannot sincerely endorse. Once we have made this decision, protection or accommodation may be justified not because these are unchosen constituents of identity but because of their centrality or critical importance to the nature of this identity. In other words, the degree to which homosexuality is a choice does not really matter in the end. What does matter is its centrality as a feature of personal identity. And this centrality characterizes heterosexual orientations as well as homosexual ones.

If we maintain the distinction between innate condition or orientation, on the one hand, and outward practices or behaviors, on the other, why do many homosexuals want to claim their orientation as a public identity? Ingrid Creppell's conception of "public privacy" in Locke is relevant to issues of sexuality, I believe. When beliefs and practices are private, they are hidden from public view, whereas that which is public displays or presents what is affirmed for public recognition. The public expression of religious identity tends to legitimize belief, to protect it from interference, and to create a buffer zone that is neither purely private nor public in which the particular manifestation of conscience can exist, thus promoting the toleration of seemingly alien beliefs. Moreover, institutionalizing spheres of public privacy creates contingencies that encourage the distancing of oneself from one's beliefs and the development of enough detachment to understand alternative ways of thinking.[27] This exposure promotes the recognition of the legitimacy of other ways of life in particular and fosters the expectation that multiple allegiances are not incompatible with communal integrity in general.

To apply this useful framework to sexuality, behavior and practice are private, but orientation is public. One's specific practices as a Roman Catholic, like one's specific behaviors as a homosexual, are hidden from public view. But one's claimed identity as a Roman Catholic or a homosexual is deployed in explicit self-presentation as a Roman Catholic or a homosexual before the political community as a whole. The openness of a communal forum provides general recognition and respect even for ways of life with which many may disagree. As Boling suggests, "Our privacy is not always empowering or protective. Keeping something private—our preference for same-sex partners, for example—may keep others from finding out about something we do not want them to know. But it may also make it more difficult for us to claim that the ability to choose sexual partners freely is a matter of legitimate public and political concern. Privacy is protective, but it can also *deprive* issues of public significance."[28] The ability to be public about one's private identity confers legitimacy on that identity. One may decide that what formerly seemed merely a personal dilemma is arguably an appropriate candidate for collective action (100, 104). This trajectory is presumably recognized and therefore discouraged both by prohibitionists, who want to deny that compulsive or pathological behavior could be legitimate, and also by conservatives, who want to maintain the distinction between private tolerance and public disapproval. That is, neither group wants to accord publicity to homosexuality because this publicity in turn lends it legitimacy.

LIBERALS AND LIBERTARIANS: TWO CONCEPTS OF ACCOMMODATION

Liberals tend to reject the conservative stance of private tolerance combined with public disapproval, but they often disagree on the proper strategy for promoting full acceptance for homosexuals. Some liberals favor antidiscrimination measures such as the inclusion of homosexuals in civil rights legislation; others, whom I shall call libertarian, would simply eradicate all vestiges of public discrimination against homosexuals, maintaining that the simplest measures often have the most profound effects. As an exemplar of the libertarian camp, Sullivan objects that antidiscrimination legislation may render society more inclusive, but it also attempts in paternalistic fashion to inculcate in citizens more virtuous attitudes and behavior.[29] Yet liberals by this stance not only abandon the distinctiveness of their traditional neutrality toward different ways of life, but they also embark on a culture war that prohibitionists will too often win (159). If conservatives resemble Kautz by advocating bare toleration without full acceptance, on this interpretation many liberals resemble Kautz in his warning that according a right to equal respect requires teaching citizens what to think and that serious social conflict can be avoided only if it is liberals who practice avoidance.

The civil rights revolution, on this view, flowed from the idea that state neutrality constituted acquiescence in some groups' oppression by others. But by augmenting the goal of public equality through close involvement in private life or civil society, liberals have subordinated free association and speech to the mitigation of adverse effects on others that these activities may cause, Sullivan suggests, thereby "undermining liberalism in order to strengthen it" (145). Prohibitionists portray antidiscrimination laws as the granting of special rights, and debate deteriorates into a contest between "perverts" and "bigots" (160). But liberty is for everyone, including bigots, and we all lose when liberty is curtailed for anyone (162). When liberals abandon state neutrality in order to identify the liberal tradition with a particular way of life, they surrender the unique appeal of liberal politics as a bridge that can transcend otherwise irresolvable conflicts.

Sullivan himself would combine a libertarian emphasis on liberty of action in civil society with persuasion that may indirectly change public opinion. He recommends simply the end of *public* discrimination against homosexuals and the according of rights and responsibilities to homosexuals that heterosexuals routinely enjoy (171, 163). We should replace political attempts to teach tolerance or respect for different ways of life, he maintains, by ending sodomy laws that single out homosexuals and through equalization of the legal age of consent, the teaching of objective information about homosexuality in government-funded schools, enforcement of antidiscrimination policies in public bodies, equal opportunity in the military, and legal marriage and divorce. An end to the military ban would facilitate acceptance of equality for homosexuals more surely than any antidiscrimination laws that regulate individual actions, in the eyes of both others and themselves (171–178). Equal access to civil marriage represents public recognition of the integrity of a private commitment (179), and conservatives should welcome the emotional security and economic stability that marriage affords (184).[30] Moreover, because many homosexuals are biological or adoptive parents, the government should acknowledge a compelling interest in stable homes by allowing same-sex marriage, as many states permit adoption regardless of parental sexual orientation.[31] Although these changes would be politically difficult, a properly liberal neutrality neither compels particular behaviors by heterosexuals nor seeks to infuse compassion and tolerance.[32] But it does set an example that may exert an indirect influence.

If the end of public discrimination influences individuals and groups in civil society to alter their own attitudes, this is indeed commendable. But is the state not still teaching citizens what to think, even by indirection? If the state perpetuates public discrimination against homosexuals, it implies that they are second-class citizens, indirectly sanctioning private discrimination against them also. If, however, it ends public discrimination, it also sends a message, this time one in which I entirely concur with Sullivan, that homosexuals are entitled to the same privileges and responsibilities that apply to heterosexuals. But either way, a message is sent. Moreover, if the state does this by ending public discrimination, it should also be able to legislate against discrimination in civil society.

The state, once again, cannot be neutral in the abstract. It may be nonneutral, as it is now, by implying that a way of life affirming homosexuality is less worthy than one that endorses heterosexuality exclusively, a stance to which

Sullivan objects. Alternatively, the state may be nonneutral in the eyes of prohibitionists and conservatives by a stance that places homosexuality on an equal footing with heterosexuality. That is, those who believe that homosexuality is wrong are no more likely to view an end of the military or marriage prohibitions as an instantiation of neutrality than those who believe abortion is wrong are likely to see the broad availability of abortion to those who want it as a manifestation of neutrality.

Libertarians like Chandran Kukathas believe that liberalism should promote no particular interests, attachments, character, identity, projects, preferences, or interests but should only uphold the framework within which individual and group interests are determined and pursued.[33] But the framework itself cannot be neutral, because any given legal structure is by definition nonneutral in its effects on the various interests within it. The dilemma is parallel to that regarding exemptions for Sabbath-observant workers, which policy on one interpretation embodies neutrality by securing equal opportunities for both the observant and the nonobservant, but on an alternative interpretation is nonneutral because it takes notice of an interest in Sabbath observance at the expense of those with other interests. Moreover and by extension, if political arrangements cannot even be neutral regarding the public sphere, they cannot be neutral regarding civil society or the private sphere of associations and individuals. By refusing to pursue any explicit goal, the state is nevertheless determining which set of social facts counts for purposes of deciding whether particular policies constitute civil injury or benefit. That is, by refusing to intervene in the "free market" of associations, the state is exercising power by withholding its influence, thus playing a role by default.

If the legal framework of the liberal state cannot itself exhibit neutrality toward all conceptions of the good, then it can only be neutral within the limits of some vision of the good at the level of metatheory, or according to a standard independent of neutrality itself. Because diversity-based neutralists accord equal respect to all conceptions of the good, they would have to accord equal respect both to those who favor and those who do not favor policies that place homosexuality on an equal footing with heterosexuality. Depending on one's viewpoint, either stance may be regarded as nonneutral. Thus, diversity-based neutralists possess no traction allowing them to break the tie, as it were. Autonomy-based neutralists, however, favor both the pursuit of our own projects and goals in ways consistent with values that are self-endorsed and the formation of our own conceptions of the good, regardless of others' opinions. An autonomy-based model of neutrality, then, requires that homosexuals receive treatment equal to that of heterosexuals. Homosexuals, like heterosexuals, are self-interpreting. They must decide what is entailed in the living out of this orientation. If they are to live their lives from the inside in ways they themselves can endorse, they must be accorded the same liberty as heterosexuals to pursue the projects and goals that critical reflection has impelled them to choose or affirm.

To put this point differently, liberals who are autonomy-based neutralists do indeed view the state as endorsing a conception of human well-being. Yet they also exhibit suspicion of circumstances in which some individuals judge the lives of other individuals. Their concern is the context of choice that structures both the availability of options and also the process by which these choices are made. Where diversity-based neutralists perceive a threat when government structures the choices of individuals, autonomy-based neutralists view choices as already structured externally by existing institutions and entrenched attitudes.[34] Thus, the context of choice can impede critical reflection. The breadth of the range of options and the likelihood that individuals will engage in critical reflection may either be enhanced or threatened by government action, and specific instances must be decided by debate. But if government action can broaden the range of options and promote the capacity for autonomy in particular instances, I believe that measures to combat private discrimination on the basis of sexual orientation, like those applicable to race, are as legitimate as those that may be used to end public discrimination.

Homosexual Intimacy: *Bowers v. Hardwick*

Bowers v. Hardwick, in which the Supreme Court upheld the Georgia statute criminalizing sodomy, exemplifies divergent ways of framing the debate about a community's shared conceptions of the good. Writing for the majority and relying on the shared goods of family relationships and of acquiescence in long-standing majority beliefs, Justice Byron White frames the issue as that of whether the Constitution confers "a fundamental right to engage in homosexual sodomy."[35] Because this case involved none of the fundamental rights recognized in previous cases concerning family relationships, marriage, or procreation, White concludes that the defense of sodomy is not warranted under the rubric of a fundamental right.

In his dissent, Justice Harry Blackmun suggests that we need to look not only at the types of rights that have been classified as fundamental but also at the reasons why these practices have been so designated. When we protect rights to family relationships, we do so neither because of their direct contribution to the public welfare nor because we prefer traditional households but because these rights are so central to individual life and happiness. "The fact that individuals define themselves in a significant way through their intimate sexual relationships with others suggests, in a Nation as diverse as ours, that there may be many 'right' ways of conducting these relationships, and that much of the richness of a relationship will come from the freedom an individual has to *choose* the form and nature of these intensely personal bonds" (204–205). Courts can distinguish private and consensual sexual conduct that injures no other parties from other sorts of sexual conduct (209). Moreover, historical and traditional condemnations of sodomy do not justify using the law to endorse private biases (210–212). Overall, "Depriving individuals of the right to choose for themselves how to conduct their intimate relationships poses a far greater threat to the values most deeply rooted in our Nation's history than tolerance of nonconformity could ever do" (214).

Not only do majority and minority diverge in *Bowers* on the basis of what values are to be defended, but also interpreters diverge on the proper grounds for defending them. Blackmun's argument focuses on individual autonomy as the justification for freedom in intimate relationships, a focus emblematic of a general historical shift. Although the Supreme Court first invalidated laws against contraceptives because interference in their use violated the privacy of the marital relationship, subsequent decisions, explains Boling, protected such privacy not to secure a valued social practice like marriage but to secure individual choice free of governmental intrusion. She suggests that where the earlier arguments portrayed procreative choice as fundamentally important because it is private, or central to an intrinsically valuable and private relationship, the later argument views procreative choice as private because it is fundamentally important. But this does not explain *why* some values concerning sexuality are of such fundamental importance as to deserve constitutional protection, when others, like those expressed in incest or spouse battering, are not. In *Bowers*, White applies privacy arguments to traditional obligations such as marriage and family relations, but Blackmun extends them to intimacies that contribute to an individual sense of self. "Is privacy," Boling asks, "an essentially conservative idea or value, used in the service of powerful interests to reinforce traditionally condoned relationships and forms of intimacy, which we have long recognized as 'private' and deserving of protection? Or is privacy a liberatory value, crucial to allowing people the freedom to develop manifold relationships, forms of intimacy, and notions of happiness?"[36]

Michael Sandel would answer these questions by suggesting that an autonomy-based defense of privacy is itself problematic. He argues that specific practices are better defended for their "intrinsic value or social importance" than as instances of autonomy and individual choice.[37] One might argue with respect to homosexual unions not only that intimate associations should be matters of individual choice but also "that much that is valuable in conventional marriage is also present in homosexual unions. On this view, the connection between heterosexual and homosexual relations is not that both are the products of individual choice but that both realize important human goods" (104). Both provide opportunities for mutual support and self-expression in ways that other relationships do not. Sandel concludes that the neutral or procedural case for toleration, what McCabe calls autonomy-based neutrality, is inadequate. First, the voluntarist or choice-based justification of autonomy rights "is parasitic—politically as well as philosophically—on some measure of agreement that the practices protected are morally permissible." Second, precisely because they are not based on substance, voluntarist justifications of autonomy rights may secure merely "a thin and fragile toleration. A fuller respect would require, if not admiration, at least some appreciation of the lives homosexuals live" (107).

Sandel's claim that basing rights on the value of autonomy alone may restrict the range of reasons for protecting them, however, does not always hold true. First, although the range of possible defenses may expand if we can demonstrate the intrinsic value or social importance of tolerating a practice, we might correspondingly withdraw toleration from a practice with no perceived value or importance, which would then restrict the scope of toleration. If the definition of the common good—Sandel's intrinsic value or social importance—is rooted in the dominant understanding of a particular community's traditions, it will be used, as we have seen, to measure the legitimacy of individuals' private beliefs and desires. Thus, although privacy is currently a human good in the context of the dominant understanding of the goods of intimate association, if this changed we might find little protection for privacy on the grounds of autonomy or anything else.

Second, a community whose notions of the common good are circumscribed by the dominant understanding will have little incentive to rethink this understanding and possibly to interpret accepted human goods in new ways. And those who lose out in the search for approval on substantive grounds will lose their claim to equal respect. As Lund argues, "Grounding coercive or even merely hortatory legislation on contested accounts of what is 'intrinsically good' inevitably puts into play a publicly backed appraisal of citizens and their conceptions of the good. In the absence of various liberal constraints, those will be used to justify unequal distributions of the opportunities and costs of various lives, and they will be so used whether or not those who are penalized actually accept the worth of the 'good' in question."[38] With a constitutive conception of community, we cannot be completely constituted by today's community without losing the possibility of critical purchase, the ability to distance ourselves somewhat from today in order to contemplate what notions of right or intrinsic goodness we want the community to embody tomorrow. Moreover, if we are each constrained by our membership in terms of the current consensus on values, then this constitutes us with our differences as well as our similarities. How can the community make a distinction between what merits full social acceptance and what merits only grudging toleration if the beliefs and practices considered are all alike products of our membership and constitutive of our personhood?

My wariness about requiring substantive justification for specific practices does not mean, however, that we must retreat to a procedural case for toleration, as Sandel implies. Referring to practices such as incest, prostitution, and polygamy, Philip Selznick observes that "to say that there are many 'right' ways [of conducting intimate relationships] is not to say that *any* way is right . . . Not every intimate association is defensible, nor is every one so fundamental as to merit constitutional protection."[39] I believe that in a liberal polity, the question is one of deciding which ways are "right" without our becoming completely submerged in, and therefore constituted by, the current consensus. Perhaps the fact that the toleration of certain practices protects autonomy itself functions to impute intrinsic value or social importance to the ways of life so justified. I hope, therefore, that debate about the validity of beliefs or practices where this influences public policy or social attitudes would center on the implications for individual autonomy of either their toleration or curtailment, and that participants in this debate would recognize both the intrinsic value and the social importance of this autonomy.

Sandel's justification of homosexual intimacy, deriving as it does from the human goods achieved by all intimate relationships, suggests that the toleration of sexual relationships and expressions varies directly with the extent that these resemble heterosexual marriage. A defense grounded in privacy or individualism for him equates homosexual relationships with the enjoyment of obscene materials, in which "the only intimate relationship at stake . . . was between a man and his pornography."[40] But on this interpretation, Bonnie Honig argues, Sandel upholds intimacy rather than marriage or reproduction as the new test of acceptable sexual behavior, still relegating the consumer of pornography to the status of other and therefore outside the communitarian ideal.[41] We may be defining deviancy down, as it were, in that behavior formerly regarded as deviant is no longer regarded thus. But the category still exists, and it functions to exclude some individuals as alien or other, because their attempted participation in the community is on terms that the latter will not accept.

Although Honig may be thought to imply that any sort of intimate association or erotic activity is defensible, I infer a warning instead. Because any political community must be grounded in certain determinate principles and commitments, as I have maintained, the community can be too quick to make judgments as to which desires should be repressed. The only preventive is a commitment, both individual and collective, to question, examine, and possibly to revise our beliefs about what gives value to our lives, both individually and collectively. As Honig states, "It turns on a commitment to live life without the assurance that ours is the right, good, holy, or rational way to live" (194). Living out this commitment requires the capacity for narrative imagination, as described by Thomas Bridges, which recognizes the possibility of commitment to different ideals from those to which one is committed, or of giving different narrative readings to the same series of life events.[42] It requires, as described by Eamonn Callan, an emotional generosity and imagination that recognizes that "our inescapable rootedness in history shapes but does not undermine our critical scrutiny of that history"[43] and that "the relevant consensus cannot be complacently identified with the one we happen to have at this moment in history."[44]

These formulations suggest the importance of sympathetic and imaginative engagement with other ways of life. Although Sandel is using the test of the intrinsic value and social importance of relationships to move the line of demarcation between acceptable and deviant behavior to a different place from where it has traditionally been drawn, he is actually suggesting an argument from autonomy in spite of himself. That is, he is deploying narrative imagination, with Bridges, to give a narrative reading to homosexual relationships that accords them the intrinsic value of heterosexual unions. He is recognizing, with Callan, that the relevant consensus is not necessarily the current or dominant consensus. But the sympathetic and imaginative engagement with another way of life that Sandel embraces is grounded in his own implicit recognition that homosexuals as well as heterosexuals must be able to live their lives from the inside, in accordance with self-endorsed conceptions of the good, and that those who participate in the dominant consensus should be persuaded to question, examine, deliberate, and possibly revise their own conceptions of the good. This imaginative engagement requires the sort of critical scrutiny that is the developed capacity for autonomy. Although arguments like Sandel's maintain a particular distinction between intrinsically valuable and deviant behavior about which for present purposes I shall remain agnostic, they nevertheless imagine life events within the framework of an alternative narrative structure, both broadening our sympathy for diversity and enhancing our capacity for autonomy.

From a different perspective, perhaps intimacy between homosexuals and heterosexuals may be defended *both* for its intrinsic value and social importance and for its instantiation of autonomy and individual choice. Ferdinand Schoeman writes that the value of privacy connotes both privacy from intrusion or control and privacy for participation in various associations and relationships. "Privacy is meant not to secure isolation from social pressure but to facilitate social involvement and intimacy."[45] Conceptualizing privacy as a positive good, not simply as a negative right, may appear vulnerable, like Sandel's defense, to the vagaries of the community's dominant understanding of the values of self-expression and intimate association. But if, like Struening, we interpret these values as a process through which individuals wrestle with and develop their own moral judgments in an ongoing attempt at self-determination and self-definition, this outcome is less likely. Even if privacy is viewed as a positive good, we must still determine what it means to us as individuals in terms of social involvement and intimacy. Once again, we must be self-interpreting if we are to live our lives from the inside, and this in turn requires that we engage in critical reflection on our current projects and goals. Intimate association carries intrinsic value and social importance in general, but the determinate nature of this value and importance must be defined by each of us, not by the dominant consensus.

Returning then to *Bowers*, we should note that like White's majority opinion, Blackmun's dissent also singles out certain aspects of family relationships and of values deeply rooted in our history and traditions. Yet on Blackmun's view, when we look to history and tradition, we need to look not simply at what specific rights or practices have been protected but at the broader purposes that family relationships and traditional values might serve. From this perspective, he finds them essential to and instrumental in individual self-development, which in turn requires reflection and choice. "A necessary corollary of giving individuals freedom to choose how to conduct their lives is acceptance of the fact that different individuals will make different choices."[46]

In sketching the value of interpersonal relationships, Blackmun cites without comment *Roberts v. United States Jaycees*. For present purposes, we should take note of two points. First, the Court in *Roberts* stated that unlike the Jaycees, an intimate association deserves special protection for its members' freedom of association, which "reflects the realization that individuals draw much of their emotional enrichment from close ties with others. Protecting these relationships from unwarranted state interference therefore safeguards the ability independently to define one's identity that is central to any concept of liberty."[47] Second, in her concurring opinion, Justice Sandra Day O'Connor stated that both intimate associations and others that are instrumental in the effective exercise of First Amendment freedoms fall under the rubric of expressive associations, the formation of which "is the creation of a voice and the selection of members is the definition of that voice" (633), and which merit greater constitutional shelter than other types of association that are commercial in nature (635).

Although in *Bowers* Blackmun relied on Fourth Amendment guarantees of domestic privacy rather than on the First Amendment (207–208), the language of *Roberts* nevertheless illuminates issues discussed in *Bowers*. An intimate association is an expressive association. The sexual component that inheres in certain intimate associations, including but not limited to that of marriage, is a species of free expression that might be interpreted to fall under First Amendment protection. As a type of expressive association central to individual development, a consensual intimate association between adults that includes sexual expression would not be subject to state regulation of its membership or of its other associational activities—that is, of the form that sexual expression might take. Engagement in homosexual sodomy is not itself a fundamental right. But engagement in an intimate association that may or may not include that practice *is* such a right, carrying both intrinsic value and social importance, and as such it and its components are constitutionally protected.

Both the majority and the minority in *Bowers,* then, are adducing arguments that take into consideration the intrinsic value and social importance of particular practices. It is not that the majority is defending shared goods of a determinate sort and that the minority is making a merely procedural case for toleration. Rather, each is adducing a different conception of what these shared goods are or what an overlapping consensus should embody. The majority defends a traditional definition of the good or of intimate relationships and a historically sanctioned interpretation of traditional values; the minority adopts a broader definition of the goods served by intimate relationships and by our history and tradition. Practices may be defended by looking at their intrinsic value and social importance, as Sandel suggests, but we are often confronted with conflicting interpretations of what meets these tests. It is for this reason that I have suggested that we look to the relationship between the toleration of particular practices and the promotion of autonomy as engagement in critical reflection on one's projects and goals, concluding that the protection or promotion of autonomy is itself a source of intrinsic value or social importance. Autonomy-based neutrality provides a context within which neutrality may be measured without abandoning the value of substantive goods, and on this basis the privileging of one particular sexual orientation over others violates both neutrality and the promotion of equal respect.

I am not suggesting, however, that autonomy-based neutrality is then independent of competing conceptions of the good. Although metatheoretical neutrality is unachievable on a second-order level or at the level of metatheory, we can still strive for neutrality at the first-order level when this is defined within the framework of a particular second-order conception of the good, whether this is autonomy, diversity, or some other value. Autonomy-based neutrality represents for me an accurate approximation of liberal values as I understand them, and I therefore feel entitled to advocate it for the reasons I have discussed. In this sense I am in agreement with Neal that neutrality theorists are in error to suggest that further refinements can render their models truly neutral or impartial. What is needed, rather, is a frank assertion that although comprehensive neutrality on all levels is unattainable, neutrality within the boundaries of some particular context is a goal worth pursuing. The context for some individuals may be diversity or some other value. For me, the proper context is that of autonomy, even as I recognize the importance of diversity as a broad range of options for choice.

Civil Rights: *Romer v. Evans*

Because I support autonomy-based neutrality, I support the creation of a context of choice that promotes individuals' capacities to live self-endorsed lives on the basis of critical reflection on their projects and goals. Therefore, I must also support antidiscrimination laws that encompass sexual orientation. The absence of such laws in a context of discrimination conveys a message as surely as does the presence of them. Autonomy-based neutrality in my view requires not only the termination of policies that function as encumbrances on some individuals' pursuits of their projects and goals but also the initiation of positive actions when individuals are disadvantaged solely because of their sexual orientation. From my perspective, so-called "special rights" are special only in the sense that their beneficiaries need them if they are to enjoy the opportunities that others do without these rights.

In *Romer v. Evans,* the Supreme Court upheld the action of the Colorado Supreme Court in striking down a 1992 constitutional amendment known as Amendment 2, passed by referendum in reaction to antidiscrimination ordinances addressing sexual orientation passed by Aspen, Boulder, and the city and county of Denver. Amendment 2 not only repealed these ordinances but also prohibited the enactment, adoption, or enforcement by any state entity or political subdivision of any legislation granting protected status on the basis of sexual orientation. The Colorado Supreme Court ruled that the trial court must subject the amendment to strict scrutiny, because only a compelling state interest would justify depriving homosexuals of the fundamental right to participate in the political process, requiring them and their supporters to amend the state constitution to enact future antidiscrimination legislation instead of arguing for it directly. The trial court on remand found no compelling state interest at stake, and the Colorado Supreme Court then affirmed its earlier ruling.[48] Supporters of measures like Amendment 2 asserted that antidiscrimination laws represent a governmental seal of approval on homosexuality, and opponents responded that these laws do not compel people to hold any particular opinions about homosexuality.[49]

In his opinion for the six-justice majority, Justice Arthur Kennedy of the U.S. Supreme Court adopts a broad interpretation of the implications of Amendment 2, reasoning that homosexuals under it could become a solitary class denied legal protection from both private and public discrimination. Because Colorado law prohibits discrimination in state employment on the basis of specified traits or "nonmerit" factors, for example, even a hiring decision implying that homosexuality is irrelevant would itself appear invalid under Amendment 2. More generally, the rights withheld under Amendment 2 are not special rights but "are protections taken for granted by most people either because they already have them or do not need them; these are protections against exclusion from an almost limitless number of transactions and endeavors that constitute ordinary civic life in a free society."[50] Amendment 2 imposes a broad disability on one particular group, the reasons for which seem "inexplicable by anything but animus toward the class it affects," therefore failing to meet even the test of a rational relationship to legitimate state interests (632) and constituting "a denial of equal protection of the laws in the most literal sense" (633). Despite Colorado's argument that without Amendment 2, the freedom of association of employers or landlords with objections to homosexuality is threatened, in reality "Amendment 2 classifies homosexuals not to further a proper legislative end but to make them unequal to everyone else. This Colorado cannot do. A State cannot so deem a class of persons a stranger to its laws" (634–635).

Justice Antonin Scalia's dissenting opinion argues that Amendment 2 should be narrowly interpreted, as the Colorado Supreme Court stated that it should not affect Colorado laws against arbitrary discrimination; it only attempts to preserve traditional moral values (636–639). First, if a state may criminalize homosexual conduct as in *Bowers*, "surely it is constitutionally permissible for a State to enact other laws merely *disfavoring* homosexual conduct," especially in view of the fact that Amendment 2 disfavors no conduct but simply prohibits the bestowal of special protections. "If it is rational to criminalize the conduct, surely it is rational to deny special favor and protection to those with a self-avowed tendency or desire to engage in the conduct. Indeed, where criminal sanctions are not involved, homosexual 'orientation' is an acceptable stand-in for homosexual conduct" (641–642).

Second, certain communities contain disproportionate numbers of homosexuals. With relatively high disposable incomes and greater interest in homosexual rights issues than the general public, "quite understandably, they devote this political power to achieving not merely a grudging social toleration, but full social acceptance, of homosexuality" (646). They are entitled to do this, but others are also entitled to use the democratic process to counteract these efforts. The Eighteenth Amendment illustrates this sort of activity through constitutional amendment at the national level. Moreover, the constitutions of five states singled out a sexual practice by prohibiting polygamy, four of them because Congress required this as a condition of statehood, and the fifth as a territory, when the Supreme Court upheld a statutory provision depriving polygamists of the franchise (647–651).[51] Overall, the Court should not take sides in this culture war, in which "Amendment 2 is designed to prevent piecemeal deterioration of the sexual morality favored by a majority of Coloradans. . . . Striking it down is an act, not of judicial judgment, but of political will" (653).

Kennedy's key conclusion, in my opinion, lies in his statement that antidiscrimination laws afford "protections against exclusion from an almost limitless number of transactions and endeavors that constitute ordinary civic life in a free society" (631). I have argued that although individuals must possess the freedom to form associations on the basis of their convictions and to exclude those who do not share them, other individuals must be accorded ordinary civil enjoyments despite *their* beliefs and practices, which may be offensive to some. Because public policy even in a liberal polity is always expressive of a common moral standpoint, whether directly or by default, the liberal commitment to diversity not only requires some freedom for associations that are not themselves inclusive internally but also allows for greater encouragement of those that *are* inclusive. The greater the number of opportunities, the broader the context of choice or the forum within which individuals may exercise their autonomy through critical scrutiny of their projects and goals.

With Amendment 2, if *enough* potential employers or landlords, for example, held parallel beliefs objecting to homosexuality, this would curtail the existence of job opportunities or living situations, or the number and variety of alternatives that constitute the context of choice within which individuals exercise their autonomy. If citizens should not be excluded from the public process or from opportunities because of religious differences, neither should they be excluded because their sexual orientations are different from that of the majority. Both religious conviction and sexual orientation are in a sense objective conditions, in that one cannot arbitrarily choose them as one might a suit of clothes. But they each involve choice in another sense, in that they may be affirmed or denied, acted on or not, through specific practice.

The decision to live one's life in accordance with one's religious convictions or sexual orientation is central, in Struening's terms, to the "positive goods of self-expression, self-determination, self-definition, and intimate association."[52] One should not be forced to conceal one's religious beliefs or sexual orientation in order to be accorded ordinary civil enjoyments that are open to others, either in the public sphere or in the private realm of civil society. Although homosexuals excluded from employment opportunities or living situations could start their own businesses that employ only homosexuals, or cooperate in buying properties that rent only to homosexuals, for example, these opportunities directed towards homosexuals would still constitute a minority of opportunities. Moreover, I cannot in principle condone the exclusion of heterosexuals from these opportunities any more than I agree with the exclusion of homosexuals from more conventional civil enjoyments. A nightclub in Port Richey, Florida, that fired two bartenders and two cocktail waitresses, all of whom were straight women, when it became a gay bar caused a loss of opportunities and resulting economic hardship as surely as if it had been a straight bar firing gay employees.[53]

To put the matter differently and in the language of *Roberts*, if *Bowers* was wrongly decided, in my view, because intimate relationships are expressive associations and therefore are protected by the First Amendment, *Romer* was rightly decided because individuals with personal or religious objections to homosexuality are not such associations. If the formation of an expressive association "is the creation of a voice, and the selection of members is the definition of that voice,"[54] persons who provide employment or housing to others rarely conduct business for the specific purpose of creating a voice that expresses a point of view. Although certain businesses may become known for expressing a particular business philosophy, this is incidental to the primary purpose of providing goods or services in exchange for remuneration. Open housing laws designed to prevent racial discrimination often exempt properties below a minimum number of units, as in the case of a family home. But even here, landlords do not rent space in order to create a voice or express a viewpoint; their doing so is incidental. And according to *Roberts*, any association not predominantly of these types is a commercial association, "and therefore subject to rationally related state regulation of its membership and other associational activities" (635), enjoying only minimal constitutional protection even if regulation does alter the message conveyed by the group. Although the expressive function or business philosophy may be important to each individual employer or landlord and deserving of respect, in the aggregate, the commercial element becomes predominant in the cascade of cumulative effects on potential employees or tenants who may be excluded, according to Kennedy in *Romer*, "from an almost limitless number of transactions and endeavors that constitute ordinary civic life in a free society."

With respect to Scalia's dissent in *Romer*, I cannot agree, first, with his argument that the criminalization of homosexual sodomy logically legitimizes the disfavoring of homosexual conduct. The majority in *Romer* seeks not to protect homosexual conduct but the civil rights of those who disclose homosexual identity. As Didi Herman argues, "Amendment 2 cannot derive its (un)constitutionality from *Bowers* any more than an initiative to prevent prostitutes or gun lobbyists from seeking civil rights protections can derive its authority from laws that criminalize selling sex or firing guns."[55] More centrally, because I have argued that although sexual orientation is unchosen, one's response to one's orientation is a matter of constitutive choice, I cannot agree with Scalia that orientation is properly classified as a stand-in for conduct. Some individuals with a homosexual or bisexual orientation may, as prohibitionists wish, refrain from acting on the basis of this orientation.

More specifically, however, when Scalia declares that it is rational to deny protection to those with a "self-avowed" homosexual tendency, policies such as that embodied in Amendment 2 reinforce the power of the closet. One cannot be denied an employment opportunity or housing situation if one conceals one's nonheterosexual orientation, but simultaneously, one should not have to conceal a matter like sexual orientation that is central to identity any more than one should have to conceal one's religious convictions. Jeffrey Rosen suggests that "in some ways, Amendment 2 is a civil, statewide version of 'Don't Ask, Don't Tell.' It recognizes that homosexuals exist, even tolerates their private lives, but refuses to grant them any public recognition as equal citizens." Equal rights are fine, "as long as the rights aren't demanded too obviously. It's the anti-discrimination law that dare not speak its name."[56] This interpretation fits Kautz's formulation that "individualists" in the liberal community should refrain from demanding more than tolerance from the majority, out of gratitude for the generosity betokened by that tolerance.

Commentators such as Jonathan Rauch, on the other hand, believe that homosexuals should "junk the oppression model," which portrays them as pitiable, and work against ostracism through public criticism and moral example rather than by seeking antidiscrimination measures.[57] But without such legislation, the price of self-exposure may be too high for many. A case in point is that of Robin Shahar, from whom the offer of a staff job was withdrawn by Georgia Attorney General Michael Bowers when he learned that she planned a religious marriage ceremony to another woman. When Shahar sued, the federal court of appeals ruled that although she had a protected First Amendment interest in her intimate relationship, this was outweighed by Bowers's contention that her staff position "might lead the public to question his office's credibility and its commitment to enforce the law against homosexual sodomy." He did not express concern, however, about staff members' possible fornication or heterosexual sodomy, although he admitted the hypocrisy revealed by the disclosure that he himself had carried on a decade-long adulterous affair when adultery is also against Georgia law.[58] Because homosexuality can be hidden, and in the views of theorists like Kautz should be hidden, many homosexuals may be tempted to remain hidden if the price of becoming moral exemplars appears too high.

Scalia's second point in dissent focuses on the disproportionate political influence of homosexuals, due to their relatively higher incomes, interest in civil rights issues, and geographic concentration in particular communities. In a survey of five criteria that measure the extent to which homosexuals are victims of oppression, Rauch concludes that only that of direct legal or governmental discrimination is met. Homosexuals are denied neither the political franchise nor education. With respect to human rights violations, gay bashings may have increased, but so has crime in general. Finally, homosexuals not only do not suffer relative impoverishment, but surveys have shown a higher level of both education and income for homosexuals than for heterosexuals.[59] Sullivan notes that because homosexuals, like heterosexuals, are born into every generation, race, and class, they do not suffer from cumulative economic disadvantage, unlike members of some other groups.[60]

Moreover, a number of observers differentiate the situation of homosexuals from that of other beneficiaries of civil rights. Writes columnist Vernon Jarrett in comparing homosexuals with African Americans, "I consider it offensively disrespectful of the recorded and unchronicled sufferings of millions of my people who were kidnapped, chained, shipped and sold like livestock, brutalized, branded and castrated when caught seeking freedom, and then publicly lynched for trying to enjoy the simple justice won on many a battlefield. . . . Gays were never declared 'three-fifths' human by the U. S. Constitution. . . . Never did the Supreme Court tell gays that they 'have no rights' that others are bound to respect."[61] Some observers fear a dilution of resources for combating discrimination if more groups are added to the roster of those claiming a right to such aid,[62] and some conservative African Americans have seen "gays as practicing a sinful lifestyle by choice and believed that gays had therefore forfeited any claim for legal redress" (89).

Herman, however, perceives "a fundamental instability" between the conviction that the immensity of gay economic and political power makes rights unnecessary, on the one hand, and that sexual behavior is mostly willful choice and therefore undeserving of protection, on the other. "To overstate the case, why not choose 'the gay lifestyle' and get rich quick?"[63] Concerning economic and political influence, Kenneth Sherrill notes, exit polls and other demographic surveys indicate that homosexuals "are as likely to be earning incomes under $15,000 as to be earning incomes over $50,000, and that . . . respondents are overrepresented in income categories below $30,000 and underrepresented at incomes over $50,000. This hardly is the picture of affluence."[64]

Furthermore, homosexuals are "born into a diaspora" and thus do not enjoy cumulative advantages. That is, they are not born into geographically concentrated communities, and homosexual identity is not transmitted within families (469). American National Election Study quadrennial surveys show that feelings of coldness and distance toward homosexuals come close to being rivaled only by cold feelings toward illegal aliens (470). A 1994 study by the Los Angeles County Commission on Human Relations found that in 1993, gay men were both the largest victim group and also the one most violently victimized, typically by physical assaults. Fear affects the openness of both homosexuals and heterosexual support, and the absence of these elements functions in turn as "both a source and a consequence of gay people's powerlessness" (471). Finally, 1992 exit polls indicated that except for an above-average concern with health care, self-identifying gay, lesbian, and bisexual respondents are similar to the rest of the electorate in the priority they accorded to a variety of issues affecting their presidential votes in that year's election. To Sherrill this indicates an absence both of a collective political identity and a "distinct gay agenda" (472). Overall, these findings seem to refute Scalia's contention that homosexuals command an inordinate level of political power that necessitates countermeasures like Amendment 2.

Third, although Scalia cites the prohibition of polygamy as the singling out of a particular sexual practice, Sullivan argues that even those who object to homosexuality view it as occupying "a deeper level of human consciousness than a polygamous impulse. . . . Polygamy is an *activity*, whereas both homosexuality and heterosexuality are *states*."[65] In his view, monogamy is central to all marriage. Allowing homosexuals access to this institution would not open the door to polygamy, as some fear, but would set before them, as before heterosexuals, the ideal of monogamy. Analogously, we could say that the state or *condition* of the human body is such that the health of most individuals requires the consumption of vegetables but that the consumption of artichokes in particular is an *activity* the pursuit of which is *not* necessary to health. Offering vegetables to those currently deprived of them will improve individual health, but we might still have legitimate public policy reasons for prohibiting the consumption of artichokes. Overall, the longing for emotional and physical intimacy is widespread if not universal. Where the unavailability of polygamy deprives no one of the long-term emotional commitment that marriage represents, the unavailability of marriage to homosexuals does deprive them of the possibility of a commitment that is routine for heterosexuals.

Scalia's final point is that the Court is taking sides against the majority of Coloradans, who want to prevent the "piecemeal deterioration" of the sexual morality that they favor. Initially, I would note that in matters of faith and sexuality that are central to individual self-definition, regulation or prohibition exerts greater impact on those principally concerned than the lack of it exerts on those offended by particular manifestations of faith or sexuality. According to John Stuart Mill, "There is no parity between the feelings of a person for his own opinion, and the feelings of another who is offended at his holding it; no more than the desire of a thief to take a purse, and the desire of the right owner to keep it."[66] As is well known, Mill criticizes the theory of collective or social rights, according to which it is one's right that every other person "act in every respect exactly as he ought" (89), and scorns the "belief that God not only abominates the act of the misbeliever, but will not hold us guiltless if we leave him unmolested" (91). To those who suggest that because sexual orientation is indubitably a private matter, it should be *kept* private, Mill would reiterate that the doctrine of social rights "acknowledges no right to any freedom whatever, except perhaps to that of holding opinions in secret, without ever disclosing them" (89). This returns us to the tyranny of the dominant consensus and to "don't ask, don't tell."

Scalia's final point nevertheless raises a significant issue. As put by T. M. Scanlon, this is the extent to which "all members of society are equally entitled to be taken into account in defining what our society is and equally entitled to participate in determining what it will become in the future." A public policy of toleration not only requires an institutional equality of legal and political rights but also extends to "the informal politics of social life," which involves the right to participate in defining the social ethos.[67] Scanlon himself desires that others appreciate the literature and music he does, for example, and will be distressed if religion becomes central to public discourse. But although such concerns are legitimate, he objects to "the attempt to restrict individuals' personal lives as a way of controlling the evolution of mores. Legal moralism is an example of intolerance, for example, when it uses the criminal law to deny that homosexuals are legitimate participants in the informal politics of society" (230).

Although measures like Amendment 2 do not criminalize homosexuality, singling out one group and its advocates on the basis of sexual orientation and assigning to it the necessity of extraordinary procedures for the passage of antidiscrimination laws in my view denies that homosexuals are equal participants in both the formal politics of institutions and the informal politics of society. Although in many private associations the actual meaning of particular goods, like religious sacraments or party labels, is dependent on the acceptance of certain beliefs, the goods of the larger, political society "do not lose their meaning if they are extended to people with whom we disagree about the kind of society we would like to have, or even to those who reject its most basic tenets" (233). That is, although it is a risky practice with high stakes, true toleration requires not only that we accord to other ways of life the grudging toleration of benign neglect but also that we respect their proponents as fellow citizens enough to allow them to participate in defining the contours of our society. Everyone should have access to the same *sorts* of opportunities in this regard. *Romer* does not mandate the passage of antidiscrimination laws; it does prohibit efforts to make more difficult for some groups than for others the attempt to pass such laws.

The Importance of Context: Religion, Sexuality, and Moral Slavery

I have argued that because both religious belief and sexual orientation are forms of conscience central to self-expression and self-definition, discrimination grounded in sexual orientation is as illegitimate as that based on religious beliefs. It does not comfort traditionalists, however, to suggest that if they disapprove of homosexuality, they simply should not themselves engage in homosexual practices any more than it comforts opponents of abortion to be told that they simply ought not to have abortions or directly enable others to have them. While advocates of antidiscrimination laws may claim a right against discrimination on the basis of sexual orientation that is central to identity, opponents of these laws may argue that their right to discriminate is sanctioned by their religious beliefs and therefore must not be infringed. I argue that a right against discrimination and a right to discriminate are not morally equivalent.

According to Samuel Marcosson, just as liberal rights can admit no "generalized liberty-based right to discriminate," neither may they admit "a specific *religious* liberty-based right to discriminate."[68] That is, the killing of others would be no more permissible because it stemmed from a religious conviction concerning the imperatives of human sacrifice than it is permissible because one might have a taste for human flesh. The right not to be killed is not a "special right," despite the fact that its enforcement infringes on the liberty of those who want to kill. And the right of individuals to be accorded ordinary civil enjoyments outweighs the right of others to deprive them of such.

Moreover, suggests Marcosson, we must consider the social context of a measure if we are properly to assess its legitimacy. First, if homosexuals do wield a disproportionate amount of political power in some locales, as Scalia maintains, this suggests that just as whites fled to the suburbs to escape the perceived threat of central cities, homosexuals have fled to the cities in pursuit of safer existences. Scalia's opposition to homosexual efforts towards self-protection declares that "the very majoritarian animus directed at you—from which you fled in the first place—may reach across geographic lines and strike at you and remove even the localized protections you have managed to carve out. You are not safe; we will come and get you."[69] Second, although Scalia argues that the criminalization of sodomy endorsed by *Bowers* legitimates the "mere" disfavoring of homosexuality instantiated in Amendment 2, for Marcosson, *Romer* provides a context that clarifies the illegitimacy of *Bowers*. *Bowers*, like Amendment 2, has denied homosexuals the "equal protection of the laws across a wide range of transactions" (233), a result now repudiated in its effects by *Romer*.

Finally, the denial of legal recognition to same-sex marriages must also be placed in context. Marcosson views exclusively heterosexual marriage as "an enclave that preserves the separateness and presumptive superiority of the group that has shut the door behind it" (244), in this case that of heterosexuals, in the same way that the exclusivity of white suburbs and the until recently single-sex character of Virginia Military Institute have symbolized white and male identity and privilege (243–250). If we place these issues in context, we encounter once again an effort to preserve the dominant consensus and to avoid the critical reflection that necessarily accompanies the exercise of autonomy, both individually and collectively.

The context within which we find discrimination grounded in race, sex, and sexual orientation is described by David A. J. Richards as that of moral slavery, which abridges human rights of conscience, speech, association, and work that constitute individual and cultural resources in a class of persons. Moral slavery is sufficient to ground suspect classification, thereby triggering strict scrutiny, he maintains, apart from traditional tests of the immutability or salience of particular traits, or the political powerlessness of groups characterized by such traits. The evil of prejudice and discrimination is its irrationalist marking not of a feature that cannot be changed or hidden but of features that are central to moral personality. "Moral slavery, thus understood, reflects the illegitimate degradation of classes of persons to a servile status based on the unjust deprivation of culture-creating rights. Its essential evil is an unjust moral paternalism that dehumanizes one class of persons from their status as bearers of rights to servile dependents of another class of persons."[70] The moral harm of disowning traits that could be concealed entails the loss of familial and communal ties and "an unreasonable sacrifice of basic resources of personal and ethical identity" (270). The silence of those subject to moral slavery that is often mistaken for consent or complicity has been "itself the product of moral slavery. Deprivation of such culture-creating rights enforced social death, a vacuum of the cultural resources through which persons express in public and private culture their reasonable moral powers as free and equal persons and shape public and private culture accordingly" (274).

On Richards's interpretation, it is clear why members of unconventional groups should not be satisfied with grudging tolerance from the more conventional majority. Although Kautz suggests that exchanging silence for toleration means "refusing to repay this respectable generosity with contempt,"[71] there is nothing generous about an exchange that requires abrogation of honesty about one's personal identity as the price of toleration. By acquiescing in this bargain, individuals are giving up both their present integrity and their ability to participate in defining the contours of society in the future. As David Johnston suggests, "Individuals need real recognition from the other members of their society as whole persons, not merely in their role as citizens, in order to pursue their values effectively."[72] Where antisodomy laws and the *Bowers* majority threaten expressive association in private culture, in Richards's terms, Amendment 2 and the *Romer* minority threaten expressive association in public culture.

Rather than relying on race and sex as bases for comparison to sexual orientation, however, Richards, like Struening and me, regards "political homophobia" as "a constitutionally illegitimate expression of religious intolerance," arguing that laws embodying this prejudice are suspect as a violation of religious toleration.[73] The selective enforcement of traditional moral values against claims by homosexuals to equal respect suggests an equation of gay and lesbian identity with traditionally despised religions, accompanied by the same implication that adherents should either convert or remain silent.[74] A measure like Amendment 2 directed against the specific protection of Jews would be condemned "as an unconstitutional expression of religious intolerance because such laws serve precisely the forms of majoritarian religious intolerance that constitutional guarantees of religious toleration condemn as a basis for law" (389). Yet demands for recognition of the legitimacy of devalued conscientious convictions when these concern sexual orientation are interpreted as claims on special rights.

In a liberal culture, however, whether with regard to religion or to sexuality, all persons must possess "the cultural resources that enable them critically to explore, define, express, and revise the identifications central to free moral personality" (366). I have maintained that sexual identity, like religious belief, results from conscientious conviction about who one is and what is centrally defining in the context of thought and experience. Both are matters of constitutive choice. Because this process requires conscientious scrutiny and critical reflection, it perhaps describes the experience of homosexuals even better than it does that of heterosexuals. Because heterosexuality is typical, young people mature under the initial assumption that they are heterosexual. Those who turn out to be homosexual or bisexual experience emotional attachments that cause them to engage in internal deliberation and critical reflection about who they really are and on how to apply this new knowledge to their own lives. In essence, they are questioning, examining, and revising what they had initially thought to be their projects and goals.

The difficulty with the equation of sexuality with faith is that this interpretation will itself be considered a sectarian one by adherents of traditional moral values. From one perspective, humanistic views, particularly what detractors call secular humanism, themselves function as a religion when this is broadly defined as a belief system or worldview concerning ultimate values, although secular humanism is popularly defined as nontheistic. I say "popularly defined" because there are persons with theistic religious convictions who also believe that the faculty of human reason is God-given and that human beings are endowed with the responsibility of developing it, honing it, and engaging in critical reflection about alternatives in arriving at one's convictions, projects, and goals.

Nevertheless, I have maintained that there can be no assurance that on every question subject to public decision, a neutral resolution can be found that will offend the interests and conscientious convictions of no one. As we have seen in the case of Sabbath observance, whether one considers this a choice or a duty determines one's conclusions as to what policy serves neutrality. Because there is no neutral criterion in the light of which to define neutrality, I have argued that a liberal polity must espouse a criterion that is admittedly *nonneutral* as a basis for judging neutrality. I have argued that in my view, this criterion is that of autonomy-based neutrality. We can make judgments regarding neutrality on a first-order level only if we select a criterion on the second-order level that gives us a reference point for making these judgments. I have suggested throughout that with autonomy as a criterion, individuals should engage in critical reflection as they select, question, examine, and revise or reaffirm their projects and goals. The liberal polity should uphold and support its citizens in this endeavor, and it should do so not because these projects and goals are unchosen constituents of their identities but because they are centrally important to these identities. I have favored the expression of cultural membership and religious belief as central to individual identity, and I have now extended this interpretation to sexuality.

Autonomy-based neutrality toward homosexuals means not only that public policy should not favor heterosexuals at homosexuals' expense, as in anti-sodomy laws, the military ban, and the marriage exclusion. It also means that beyond the fact that homosexuals are a numerical minority, it should not be harder to be a homosexual than to be a heterosexual, just as it should not be more difficult to be Sabbath-observant than to be Sabbath-nonobservant. We may circumscribe the available range of options and opportunities not only by eliminating alternatives but by raising the costs of unconventional and unpopular choices to heights that are unacceptable in a liberal polity. Collective deliberation will always be necessary to decide which among many practices are inimical to liberalism. But this goal is best achieved by forthright debate, not by subscription to the current orthodoxy. Moreover, when we do allow practices that we could forbid, we should accord full respect to individuals who engage in these practices, even if we continue to disagree with their views. We should not make a group pay reparations for our "generosity" through the back door, through a toleration that is only a grudging one, for costs that we did not extract through the front door.

Liberals, as opposed to communitarians, tend to defend moral norms like that of fundamental human equality as right in a universalizable sense, rather than as local customs in accord with the dominant consensus.[75] This means that liberals often defend toleration not simply because of its potential contribution to political stability but because there is something about toleration that inherently conforms to the demands of liberal principles. People will differ about what does so conform. But in a liberal polity, toleration should be less a matter of acceding to a given or current consensus than a commitment to deliberation among equals about the meaning of liberal principles when these are applied to specific issues.[76] Such deliberation requires that each of us has the opportunity to engage in critical reflection as we examine, question, and revise our projects and goals and to be forthright without legal or social penalty about where this critical reflection is leading us.

7. Education for Citizenship

I have argued throughout this book that a liberal polity should encourage individuals to live their lives from the inside and to engage in the rational scrutiny of their projects and goals as they examine, question, and revise or reaffirm them. The liberal polity, then, is committed both to the maintenance of background conditions for individual autonomy and self-development and to a culture of diversity that contains a plurality of options. But these values themselves are often incommensurable, and the tension between them emerges with particular clarity in conflicts over the proper education of future citizens. This conflict appears, for example, in John Rawls's description of the political virtues required in a stable liberal democracy, which include toleration, mutual respect, and a sense of fairness and civility.[1] He rejects the values of autonomy and individuality as too comprehensive and therefore too exclusive to be publicly fostered in citizens, arguing that political liberalism requires "far less." Education should inculcate knowledge of citizens' basic constitutional and civic rights; it should "prepare them to be fully cooperating members of society and enable them to be self-supporting; it should also encourage the political virtues so that they want to honor the fair terms of social cooperation" (199). In other words, citizens may embody these virtues, Rawls suggests, without engaging in critical reflection on their projects and goals. Therefore, his political liberalism is unlikely, he concludes, to exclude those who do not value personal autonomy.

Personal autonomy, I have maintained, is marked by the process of rational scrutiny and critical reflection through which we decide on our projects and goals, not by the intrinsic nature of these goals themselves. Precisely because of its hospitality to diversity, the liberal polity must avoid easy conclusions that ways of life that we may dislike or disapprove cannot represent autonomous choice and that therefore we are entitled to exert pressure on citizens to make different choices. This does not mean, however, that the liberal polity need do nothing to influence choice. First, as we have seen, the liberal polity, like other polities, is the legal expression of a particular cultural structure. Ontologically, it cannot be neutral with regard to law, culture, religion, or sexuality but always represents some common moral standpoint. That is, even a liberal polity never "does nothing." Thus, it must pay attention to what it does do, even by default.

Second, if the individual capacity for autonomy is central to liberalism, as I believe, the liberal polity must encourage and foster the development of this capacity. It cannot legitimately instruct citizens in *what* to choose, but it can and should provide instruction in *how* to choose. This should be the focus of civic education. Because a liberal polity should not, I believe, exert pressure at the first-order level of actual choice, its role at the second-order level of how choices are made becomes crucial. Therefore, in spite of Rawls's attempt to avoid education for autonomy, I do not believe that eschewing this kind of civic education is compatible with liberalism as I interpret it.

This conclusion of course leaves untouched the very dilemma that Rawls attempts to solve, that of offering a civic education that does not force the value of personal autonomy on those who are indifferent to it or who reject it altogether. We are then confronted with three options. The first is to accept the conflation of comprehensive and political liberalism, make a virtue of necessity, and conclude that a stable liberal democracy requires education for autonomy. This option is exemplified by Amy Gutmann and Eamonn Callan. The second alternative is to backpedal, to decide that if political liberalism requires education for autonomy, political liberalism in itself, at least in its Rawlsian incarnation, should be rejected. This option is exemplified by William Galston. The third alternative is to redefine the requirements of political liberalism in such a way that they do not constitute the constraint on the development of our privately held comprehensive ethical convictions that some observers believe that these requirements are. This option is exemplified by Stephen Macedo.

I argue that the civic respect necessary for liberal democratic citizenship requires a sympathetic and imaginative engagement with other ways of life. I shall outline the controversy between adherents of autonomy and of diversity as competing core values of education for citizenship in the liberal polity, agreeing with Gutmann and Callan that true respect for diversity requires the development of the capacity for autonomy. Then I examine two court cases in which parents have sought to withdraw their children from the threat they perceived public education to pose for freedom of conscience. The decision in one champions the claims of diversity; the other can be interpreted to support the claims of autonomy. Even if we accurately deduce both the nature of the virtues required of liberal democratic citizens and the moral constraints the state should respect in trying to engender these virtues, I agree with Callan that we must still strike the correct balance between "a self-defeating cultural aggressiveness" and "an equally destructive cultural complacency."[2] In the first case, we must be careful that in our zeal to inculcate the virtues of toleration and mutual respect, we do not violate their spirit. In the second case, we must take care that honoring these virtues does not cause us to abdicate attention to the framework or context of choice that perpetrates them. Overall, I believe that the practice of critical reflection is incumbent not only on those who to liberals appear to live unexamined lives but on all of us.

Autonomy versus Diversity

I have maintained that autonomy requires that we develop the capacity for critical reflection on our projects and goals and that diversity requires both a range of possibilities and the ability to envision what those possibilities entail. If we attempt to maximize pure diversity, the range of choice is increased, but so is the possibility that some individuals and groups will discount or even denigrate the development of the capacities and imagination required for envisioning other choices. Yet if we impose conditions that mandate efforts to develop these capacities, we risk foreclosing some options or types of options, thereby impoverishing the existing supply of possibilities overall. Either way, one of the core values of liberalism is the loser.

Amy Gutmann argues that all citizens should be taught to engage in rational deliberation and critical reflection so that they can evaluate competing ways of life, including modes different from those of their parents. The pluralism fostered by diversity among citizens or families who may each represent an uncritical or unreflective consciousness "serves as little more than an ornament for onlookers."[3] The goal of civic education both authorizes and obligates professional educators "to cultivate in future citizens the capacity for critical reflection on their culture."[4] For example, a liberal democratic society must cultivate the capacity "to choose rationally (some would say 'autonomously') among different ways of life" (77), and it "must aid children in developing the capacity to understand and to evaluate competing conceptions of the good life and the good society."[5] Moreover, Gutmann's conception of civic education incorporates a specific goal, that of preparation for citizenship in a society that advantages those who can participate in collective deliberation on public policy (34, 42).

Gutmann implicitly agrees with Rawls's specification of toleration and mutual respect as political virtues required in a stable liberal democracy. But she is more definite about what these seemingly uncontroversial virtues entail. Mutual respect requires not simply toleration, she argues, but also "requires a favorable attitude toward, and constructive interaction with, the persons with whom one disagrees." More specifically, mutual respect characterizes "individuals who are morally committed, self-reflective about their commitments, discerning of the difference between respectable and merely tolerable differences of opinion, and open to the possibility of changing their minds or modifying their positions at some time in the future if they confront unanswerable objections to their present point of view."[6] Although she maintains that political liberalism intends only to educate for citizenship, not for autonomy, Gutmann admits the near impossibility of teaching the virtues of democratic citizenship without also teaching the skills of personal autonomy.[7] Children should learn to think for themselves, she argues, even about issues with little explicit political content, because only thus will they learn to make judgments about what issues are or are not political. Advocacy of this position may appear partisan, but it is no more so, she contends, than the competing position that parents can use their own religious freedom as a basis for preventing their children from learning to think for themselves (575). For Gutmann, the civic virtue of mutual respect does not deny the value of diversity but instead promotes it by exposing children to the potential value inherent in different ways of life.

Along similar lines, Callan notes that the sense of fairness or capacity for a sense of justice in Rawls requires both a commitment to moral reciprocity and a willingness to recognize the burdens of judgment, or the sources of permanent and irreconcilable disagreement among reasonable persons. Recognition of the latter conditions citizens' willingness to employ public reasons in public deliberation that are independent of privately held comprehensive doctrines. But from an epistemological standpoint, imaginative engagement with other viewpoints will not only develop a sense of justice but will also "profoundly affect" our comprehensive views or conceptions of the good. Attempting to understand the reasonableness of convictions alien to our upbringing "cannot be carried through without inviting the disturbing question that these convictions might be the basis of a better way of life, or at least one that is just as good. That question is unavoidable because to understand the reasonableness of beliefs that initially seem wrong or even repellant I must imaginatively entertain the ethical perspective the beliefs furnish, and from that perspective my own way of life will look worse, or at least no better, than what that perspective affirms."[8]

When we are examining or questioning the projects and goals that constitute a way of life, then, the same mental capacity is at work whether we are evaluating our own current conceptions of the good, on the one hand, or endeavoring to understand our fellow citizens, on the other. "What is required in each case is the ability to envisage a life alien to one's own from the inside so that the goods it makes possible can be understood to some degree in their vivid particularity."[9] This quality of imaginative engagement and sympathy requires a high level of self-reflection and openness. In sum, the educational requirements of political liberalism, like those of comprehensive liberalism, seem to require that we develop the capacity both to live life or imagine other lives from the inside and to question, examine, and understand the value of various sorts of projects and goals, whether these are our own or those of others. Argues Callan, "The political virtues that implement the fair terms of cooperation impose educational requirements that bring autonomy through the back door of political liberalism . . . [which then] is really a kind of closet ethical liberalism. . . . The partition Rawls labors to erect between ethical and political liberalism has collapsed."[10] Why not exit the closet and admit the centrality of autonomy?

Galston, on the other hand, charges that a public commitment to the development of the capacity for autonomy excludes and threatens individuals and groups that do not place a high priority on rational deliberation and personal autonomy. "Liberal freedom entails the right to live unexamined as well as examined lives."[11] Liberalism should protect diversity rather than valorize choice. To champion the latter "is in fact to narrow the range of possibilities available within liberal societies. It is a drive toward a kind of uniformity, disguised in the language of liberal diversity."[12] Galston believes that rational deliberation must on the practical level take second place to rhetoric in the formation of future citizens. Philosophic education focuses on the pursuit of truth and the conduct of rational inquiry and thus may have "corrosive consequences" for "structures of unexamined but socially central belief." The focus of civic education, however, is on individual effectiveness within the context of a specific political community, or "education within, and on behalf of, a particular political order."[13] This calls for instruction in "a core of habits and beliefs supportive of the liberal polity"[14] rather than through training in the exercise of rational deliberation.

Although the capacity for rationality and reasonable public judgment requires an appreciation of the need for social rules, an ability to respond to rational persuasion, and a disposition to employ public reasons in public deliberation about matters requiring collective action,[15] writes Galston, a Socratic emphasis on the capacity for critical reflection on different ways of life is a controversial notion of the good. It cannot and need not claim the allegiance of all liberal democratic citizens. For example, adherents of religious doctrines that require close control over individuals' formative social and political environments view the traditional liberal insistence that they forswear this demand as a restriction on free exercise of religion. Most individuals and groups in a liberal society will find expression for "their distinctive conceptions of the good.

But for those who are left out, it is hard to see how liberalism can be experienced as anything other than an assault."[16]

For Galston, then, a liberal society or government that values and tries to inculcate the capacity for autonomy in all citizens does not promote diversity but undermines it. At the heart of liberal tolerance is not critical reflection on various ways of life but "the refusal to use state power to impose one's own way of life on others. Such refusal need not be incompatible with an unreflective commitment to one's way of life."[17] To refrain from inculcating in all citizens the idea that toleration requires mutual respect among those who practice different ways of life does not contradict the ideal of tolerance but instead exemplifies and instantiates it. Galston doubts, however, "that tolerance, so understood, can be cultivated without at least minimal awareness of the existence and nature of those ways of life." Therefore, the state may pursue "this compelling interest" in tolerance, but without explicitly requiring or inviting students to criticize their own ways of life.[18] But first, *how* minimal can our awareness be? Apparently it must be minimal enough that we are not encouraged to become skeptical or critical of our own practices, yet comprehensive enough that we find reasons to tolerate other practices. This is a fine line to tread, and it is not apparent that this balance can be achieved easily if at all.

David Johnston distinguishes between *moral* autonomy, which implies the capability of having both a conception of the good and also a sense of justice, and *personal* autonomy, which suggests the capability of subjecting projects and values to critical appraisal and fashioning them into a life that functions as a coherent whole. Personal autonomy is not "an essential ingredient in a good human life in association with others,"[19] and the subjection of one's projects and values to critical appraisal is less important than the simple pursuit of these projects with accompanying adherence to their values. The projects of individuals who discount personal autonomy should nonetheless be taken seriously; social measures to promote personal autonomy may range from despotic paternalism, at worst, to a disorientation from one's original values, at best, which may undermine effective agency.

Yet just as Galston suggests that liberal tolerance requires a minimal awareness of the nature of other ways of life, Johnston suggests that "*some* degree of ability to appraise or reappraise one's projects and values critically is essential to a good life for human beings in association with others" (97). If, as Johnston argues, moral autonomy involves both the recognition of other agents whose claims deserve respect and also an according self-limitation on our own claims, the critical self-appraisal required for personal autonomy should help us to restrain our own claims and recognize others' projects and values, thereby contributing to our effective sense of justice. Although Johnston concedes that moral autonomy requires to some degree the skills constitutive of personal autonomy, he still suggests that a society should foster personal autonomy "only insofar as . . . those conditions can be expected to contribute to individuals' capacities to be effective agents" (97–98). But if effective agency means the imaginative capacity to formulate projects and values independent of our own experiences, as Johnston suggests (22–24), then a greater degree of personal autonomy would contribute more to the development of this imaginative capacity than would a lesser degree. Thus, the ability to engage in critical self-appraisal that is characteristic of personal autonomy contributes both to effective agency and to the moral autonomy through which we recognize and respect others' projects and values, facilitating our sense of justice and the cooperation required for a life in association with others.

To place this point in the present context, liberal democracy requires the inculcation of the virtues of tolerance and mutual respect. But in my view, this requires the imaginative capacity to view circumstances as others might, to recognize and respect their claims, and to restrain our own. And these dispositions in turn require the capacity to understand and evaluate different ways of life. That is, they require the development of the capacity for personal autonomy. This conclusion casts doubt on Rawls's contention that the political virtues of toleration, mutual respect, and the sense of fairness necessary for social cooperation require "far less" substantive civic education than would the inculcation of the comprehensive values of autonomy and individuality. It also impels one to question whether the ability to respond to rational persuasion and the disposition to employ public reasons in public deliberation, crucial elements in Galston's conception of the capacity for rationality, can be fully developed without the corresponding capability of subjecting one's projects and values to critical reflection and appraisal. This process conditions our ability to perceive the value in others' projects and goals as well as to commit to our own. Moreover, the ability to respond to rational persuasion and the disposition to employ public reasons suggest one of the components of mutual respect for Gutmann: openness to the possibility of modifying or changing one's position in the face of unanswerable objections to the current one.

Galston's first point to which I have responded is that tolerance requires only minimal awareness of other ways of life. Second, he maintains that his "Diversity State" need not imply moral indifference but is also compatible "with engaged moral criticism of those with whom one differs. Toleration means . . . the commitment to competition through recruitment and persuasion alone."[20] Despite his commitment to diversity and pluralism, then, Galston's

Diversity State does not practice toleration simply by refraining from inter-ference with objectionable practices. We may criticize constructively the ideas of others whom we believe to be in error, and we may attempt to persuade them that our own beliefs or practices are preferable. But not only does this activity require a greater understanding of other ways of life than Galston admits; it also implies the practice of mutual respect as Gutmann describes it. It would seem to involve constructive interaction, a reciprocal positive regard, and an openness to the possibility of changing our minds—unless, of course, we expect self-reflection and openness to characterize only those whom we crit-icize but not us ourselves! This suggests that the requisite awareness of other ways of life and the inculcation of the competencies and virtues of liberal cit-izenship (529) demand the sort of sympathetic and imaginative engagement with other beliefs and practices that Callan describes. Galston may want to backpedal from what he sees as the rigid structure of a seemingly perfection-istic Rawlsian political liberalism,[21] but his own, purportedly more inclusive, alternative requires similar political virtues that lead ineluctably to the devel-opment of a capacity for autonomy.

Third, Galston advocates decentralized political decision-making on many contested issues, pairing a strong freedom of association with an emphasis on a meaningful right of exit. This latter requires an awareness of alternatives, a capacity to assess these alternatives, freedom from brainwashing, and the indi-vidual ability to participate effectively in other ways of life besides that being abandoned.[22] Yet these conditions point not simply to a bare awareness of alter-natives but toward, in Callan's words, "the ability to envisage a life alien to one's own from the inside so that the goods it makes possible can be under-stood to some degree in their vivid particularity."[23] The capacity to assess alter-natives requires the developed capacity to engage in critical reflection on these goods if we are to make the best choice for *us*. And the ability to participate effectively in other ways of life means that not only our specific skills but also our ways of thinking must be flexible enough to allow us to make successful transitions. If, as both Gutmann and Galston believe, individuals should be educated to function effectively within and to support their political commu-nity, they should be able to do this in more than one role. Therefore, even if we leave aside the question of whether tolerance in the liberal democratic polity requires the teaching of mutual respect, our freedom and ability to live a good life for *us* requires the development of the capacity to engage in rational delib-eration and critical reflection.

Fourth and finally, Galston's concrete policy recommendations do not al-ways protect across the board the diversity that he valorizes, and in some cases they reconstruct practices that seem coercive to some citizens. I cannot here engage in detailed analysis, but among the policies stemming from his advocacy of a functional traditionalism aimed at bolstering beliefs and habits that he associates with the security of liberal rights are measures that privilege intact two-parent families and discourage divorce,[24] support for state law embodying morally traditional attitudes toward homosexuals,[25] and similar support for state law requiring a moment of silence at the start of the school day.[26] I am less concerned here about the intrinsic validity of his particular stands than I am about the combination of his moral traditionalism with his conviction that rational deliberation must take second place to rhetoric in the formation of future citizens. Because disputes about the human good cannot be definitively settled philosophically, Galston maintains, "On the practical level, few individuals will come to embrace the core commitments of liberal society through a process of rational inquiry. If children are to be brought to accept these commitments as valid and binding, the method must be a pedagogy that is far more rhetorical than rational" (243).

I am extremely wary of what seems to be a recommendation that we paper over moral complexity and ambiguity. I agree with Callan, first, that although Galston cites courage, law-abidingness, and loyalty as fundamental virtues of the liberal state (221), "law may be enacted or administered in ways that betray the fundamental values of liberal democracy" that Galston is anxious to uphold.[27] Because the historical and political tradition in which we are embedded is subject to varying interpretations, "the pressing question is, What is the best of this tradition? Rather than, What are the dominant or most powerful elements in this tradition?"[28] Second, I agree with Callan in rejecting the consensual conception of common education, according to which "the proper content of common education is given by whatever corpus of substantive educational values can be supported by a highly extensive agreement in our society."[29] Consensus itself is not negative, but "the relevant consensus cannot be complacently identified with the one we happen to have at this moment in history" (260). Galston's rhetorical approach is far too likely simply to endorse the current consensus rather than requiring "a serious intellectual and imaginative engagement with the plurality of values to which my fellow citizens adhere . . . where the plurality of values is really embodied in the lives of different participants" in this engagement (264). True openness to cultural diversity, in my view, is grounded not in a consensual conception of common education but in equal respect, which in turn requires civic education grounded in more than rhetoric.

Macedo's liberalism is a muscular version that is unapologetic about the fact that communities or families with totalistic belief systems may be undermined by public policy that advances critical thinking and public argument as appropriate means of political justification.[30] Although freedom is central to liberal politics, "successful constitutional institutions must do more than help order the freedom of individuals . . . they must shape the way that people use their freedom and shape *people* to help ensure that freedom is what they want."[31] Accomplishing these goals "requires liberalism with a spine"[32] and a recognition of "the supreme importance of constituting diversity for liberal ends."[33] On the other hand, unlike Callan, who holds that liberal citizens should develop the ability to enter into sympathetic and imaginative engagement with different ways of life, Macedo argues that "it would go too far to suggest that good citizens must have positive regard for each others' extra-political beliefs and practices." The promotion of sympathetic and imaginative engagement with rival views, particularly with religious ones, "comes too close to espousing a 'comprehensive' ideal of life as a whole, such as autonomy, and would seem to infringe on individuals' freedom to disagree deeply and vigorously about religious and moral matters. Political liberalism stands for the importance of critical self-examination in politics. Citizens decide on their own what attitude to take toward their religious beliefs."[34] Children should learn that diversity is both typical and persistent and that respect for diversity is a part of citizenship. But although this might be hard to learn "without being 'open to the possibility' that the religious convictions of one's parents are unreasonable, public school educators should not seek directly to sow religious doubt" (311).

Macedo admits that teaching equal respect for fellow citizens but not positive regard for their beliefs may seem a specious distinction. "Teaching children the importance of thinking critically about public affairs may have the effect of encouraging them to think critically about religious matters as well" (312). As with Rawls, Gutmann, and Callan, education for citizenship may actually constitute education for autonomy. Yet Macedo still desires a balance between neutrality and perfectionism. "Explicitly or not, liberal regimes endorse and promote autonomy. But we still respect the non-autonomous: people have the right to lead lazy, narrow-minded lives, and we minimize and soften interference with their choices."[35] Like Gutmann and Callan, then, Macedo advocates a comprehensive civic education that develops the capacity for rational deliberation and critical reflection about public affairs; but like Galston, he rejects the explicit use of this capacity with respect to citizens' private and more comprehensive religious, philosophical, and moral convictions. "Public schools may seek to inculcate the civic importance of religious toleration" but "have no business speaking to the religious dimensions of toleration, equal respect, or other political questions."[36] Yet to maintain this distinction, Macedo relies on a "transformative constitutionalism" in which emphasis on the segmentation of religion and politics tends indirectly to diminish the centrality of religious convictions in tension with liberal democratic values.[37] In fact, he argues that the defenders of individuals who feel censored or marginalized because they will *not* compartmentalize their political and religious beliefs should realize that the true difficulty is these believers' hypersensitivity. And their defenders' "real problem is in thinking there is something necessarily wrong with practices that in effect marginalize those who reject liberalism" (79, n. 53).

As we saw in Callan's critique of Rawls and as Macedo himself admits, however, critical thinking about civic concerns readily spills over into critical self-examination about more comprehensive matters as well. First, Macedo asserts that "the stability of a liberal regime requires that the personal moral and religious views of many people will (when illiberal) be mended to support the liberal settlement. Ideally, this transition will take place via candid, open public arguments."[38] And marginalized groups whose beliefs are under threat from the wider liberal culture and whose practices are imperiled by the public policies of the liberal state may need to make adjustments themselves rather than to petition for exemptions from these policies.[39] But these statements do not comport with Macedo's assertion that citizens should determine their own attitudes toward the imperatives of their religious beliefs, even if they cannot always carry through these imperatives in a liberal polity. If marginalized groups must make adjustments, his formulation suggests that dialogue between those who support the dominant consensus and the members of dissenting groups is a one-way street. The latter must simply adjust when the former declare that atypical practices are illiberal. Those who think I need to alter my supposedly illiberal views *are* in fact challenging my personal moral and religious views when they point to the need for change. And by implication, they are inviting the critical self-evaluation of my comprehensive views the insistence on which Macedo thinks an infringement on religious and moral diversity.

Second, even if Macedo were consistent when he advocates critical reflection about public affairs but withdraws his insistence with respect to private, comprehensive convictions, there is no inherently clear distinction between the political and the nonpolitical. Practices that stem from my comprehensive beliefs may seem to me to carry political implications that make them fit subjects for political discussion and critical examination. If I may decide what attitude to take toward my beliefs, this includes my deciding to what extent they are political or not, especially if my ability to adhere to them is affected by political decisions on public policy. Rawls's overlapping consensus is abstracted from religious, philosophical, and moral doctrines that citizens support; even it is not exclusively nonpolitical in the sense of having no nonpolitical origins.

Third, although Macedo contends that it is only illiberal views that must be adjusted or mended, once again, there is no inherently clear distinction between the liberal and the illiberal. Competing sets of social facts may be adduced, each of which points to a different conclusion about the liberality or illiberality of particular beliefs and practices.[40] It is through rational deliberation and critical reflection that we decide what is benign or injurious in its effects on the liberal settlement as we understand it. Although Macedo says that the mending of intolerant views should occur through open public argument, those on *both* sides of the argument ought to display reciprocal positive regard, self-reflection, and openness to unfamiliar arguments. After all, if I am to mend my views or to make adjustments in them, I must be able to enter into sympathetic and imaginative engagement with conceptions of the good other than my own. And you who want me to make these adjustments should do the same if you want to determine accurately how radical these adjustments should be. Once again, all citizens of the liberal polity should develop the capacity to engage in rational deliberation and critical reflection. Liberalism makes demands on all its citizens, not only on those who liberals think are illiberal. Although Macedo focuses on the importance of the capacity for autonomy, his manner of doing so impels me to prefer Gutmann's and Callan's formulation.

For Diversity

The theorists whose views we have examined hold specific views on education for citizenship. Although none believes that the instantiation of cultural neutrality is compatible with the maintenance of liberal values, all evidence strong support for the virtue of tolerance and for policies of toleration. But while Gutmann and Callan argue that tolerance requires the inculcation of mutual respect, Galston maintains that such a program threatens liberal hospitality to diversity, specifically to individuals who reject the critical self-reflection that the development of mutual respect seems to require. And although Macedo endorses a robust sense of civic or political respect, he implicitly rejects the necessity of respect for nonpolitical beliefs and practices. Although on a theoretical level I support Gutmann and Callan more than Galston or Macedo, I believe that the disposition of this issue must take place with reference to the particulars of specific cases.

This issue is not merely a theoretical one. The transformative constitutionalism of Macedo is reflected in a 1994 resolution of the Lake County School

Board in Florida, which required teachers to "instill in our students an appreciation of our American heritage and culture such as our republican form of government, capitalism, a free enterprise system, patriotism, strong family values, freedom of religion and other basic values that are superior to other foreign or historic cultures." The local teachers' union charged that the resolution violated both the right to free expression and a state multicultural education law requiring education that fosters "appreciation and respect for people of other ethnic, gender, socioeconomic, language and cultural background."[41] Supporters of the resolution, however, argued that opposition was animated mainly by the fact that right-wing Christians on the school board supported it, which was an illegitimate basis for opposition. "That's the way they do it in other, inferior cultures." On this view, the "burgeoning multicultural industry" has intimidated us into public reticence about this country's superiority and its attractiveness to others who have sought refuge and a good life here.[42]

This controversy serves to highlight some of the issues under discussion. First, one can teach about our socioeconomic and political system in many different ways, some of which are compatible with an attitude of thoughtfulness and self-criticism. A unit on freedom of religion could emphasize primarily the ban on establishment, the enabling of free exercise, or both equally. The teaching of "strong family values" is not necessarily incompatible on its face with the strengthening of nontraditional family units. Second, although the mandate that the culture of the United States be portrayed as superior might appear congruent with Macedo's argument that the health of modern liberal democracy must not be taken for granted, even he confines these injunctions to the political level, where he also recommends the inculcation of civic or political respect for the diversity of views that will influence public judgment. All who desire the continued flourishing of the liberal polity seem to agree that the conditions for this flourishing require attention, but they disagree about what sort of attention is required. That is, the liberal polity is worthy of this effort and is thus superior in some sense to cultural and political manifestations that might replace it if care is not taken. But controversy centers on how heavy-handed this effort must be.

In *Wisconsin v. Yoder*, the Supreme Court in a six-to-one majority upheld Old Order Amish communities in Wisconsin in their desire to terminate their children's formal schooling after eighth grade, in accordance with their "fundamental belief that salvation requires life in a church community separate and apart from the world and worldly influence,"[43] which was thus deserving of protection under the free exercise clause. Beyond eighth grade, formal education is supplemented in Amish communities by the learning of manual work and self-reliance and by experience that promotes values favoring community welfare and spiritual growth. The record "abundantly supports the claim that the traditional way of life of the Amish is not merely a matter of personal preference, but one of deep religious conviction, shared by an organized group, and intimately related to daily living" (216). If education is compulsory until age sixteen, in accordance with state law, pressure to conform to the larger society poses a real danger that the Amish community and its religious practices will be undermined. The fact that the dispute involves conduct typically required of all does not absolve the state from the free exercise limitation on its power or from the possibility that it unduly burdens this exercise (219–221).

Although Wisconsin argued that the standard educational requirement was necessary both for effective and intelligent political participation and also for self-reliant and self-sufficient social participation, the Court ruled that further compulsory education that may be necessary preparation for life in modern society may be optional "if the goal of education be viewed as the preparation for life in the separated agrarian community that is the keystone of the Amish faith." Moreover, Amish practices historically foster productive and law-abiding membership in "a highly successful social unit within our society," as recognized by Congress in exempting such groups from the payment of social security taxes (222). Children who may choose to leave the community before traditional adult baptism carry with them a readily marketable vocational education through their training in reliability and self-reliance. Finally, the case centered on the free exercise rights of the parents, not on any conflict between parents and children. Therefore, despite fears that parents might foreclose their children's opportunities "to make an intelligent choice between the Amish way of life and that of the outside world" (232), the fundamental interests of parents in guiding their children's religious education combined with their free exercise rights outweigh any demonstrated state interest in compulsory education (230–236).

Justice William Douglas concurred in the result because the child who testified in this case asserted that it was *her* religious beliefs that kept her from attending high school. But he dissented from the idea that the religious interest of children had no bearing. Parental notions of religious duty should not be imposed upon their children, and if a mature Amish child does wish to attend high school, the state might want to override parental objections. "It is the future of the student, not the future of the parents that is imperiled by today's decision. If a parent keeps his child out of school beyond grade school, then the child will be forever barred from entry into the new and amazing world of diversity that we have today" (245). If the child rebels against this course of action, the child's judgment must be preferred to that of the parents (241–249).

The majority's ruling fits the interpretation in which freedom of conscience means to theorists like Sandel the right of an encumbered self to exercise a duty, not the right of an independent self to make a choice. The Court emphasized the extent to which the Amish claim stemmed not from personal preference but from deep religious conviction constitutive both of the members of the Amish community and of their way of life itself. Although the long, historic tradition of Amish practice demonstrates the sincerity of the Amish claims, I argue that it should not matter whether one's religious affiliation is regarded as stemming from the affirmation of a duty, from the making of a choice, or in fact from the affirmation of a first-order duty that results from the making of a second-order choice. That is, whether I am born into an Amish community or "convert" upon learning the virtues of that way of life, an admittedly unlikely prospect given the nature of that community, I should be accorded the same freedom of conscience and right to engage in the free exercise of my faith. Either way, my doing so is an expression of autonomy as I live my life from the inside and perhaps question, examine, and revise or reaffirm my projects and goals.

I see at least two important issues in *Yoder* with respect to education for citizenship. The first concerns the adequacy of preparation of children for effective political participation and for self-sufficient social participation. For Jeff Spinner, liberal virtues need not be encouraged among the Amish because they do not want full membership in the mainstream of the liberal polity but, instead, partial citizenship. As we saw in Galston, "This shows a paradox of liberal theory: liberalism allows people to reject liberal values. The liberal state cannot insist that its citizens embrace liberalism. Liberalism allows people to think for themselves, to make their own decisions—or even to decide not to think for themselves."[44] Although the liberal virtues of "self-reflectiveness, equality, and autonomy" should typically characterize both the public sphere and the nonpublic institutions of civil society that serve the public, Amish involvement in both these areas is minimal. "When they do become politically active, it is almost always to protect their way of life," as in *Yoder* (98). In other words, schooling need not inculcate or develop the capacity to engage in rational deliberation and critical reflection, because the Amish consistently reject the facets of life in the liberal polity that would call upon these capacities. On this interpretation, some citizens of the liberal polity can opt out of certain liberal virtues.

The second issue centers on the context of choice for Amish youth. Although the Court suggested that the training provided within the Amish community constitutes a marketable vocational education for young people who wish to leave it, the context of choice is limited by children's lack of exposure to a range of options within their own community. The intent of the *Yoder* parents was precisely that of shielding their children from influences that might induce them to leave the community. Cultural membership is a context of choice that provides both a range of meaningful options for choice and also a source of beliefs about value. Together these offer "a secure sense of identity and belonging."[45] I have argued, however, that although one's culture of origin functions as a ground, context, or framework for choice, it is not itself a choice unless the individuals within such a framework engage in critical self-reflection by examining, questioning, and either affirming or revising their commitments. And as we have seen, Galston's conditions for a meaningful right of exit include not only an awareness of alternatives but also the capacity to assess these alternatives and the ability to participate effectively in other ways of life. This capacity and ability, then, bear both upon the question of education for citizenship and on the conditions for agency, moral autonomy, and personal autonomy.

Should education constitute preparation for life only in one's community of birth, or should it enable one consciously to weigh alternatives and to make those alternatives realistic options? Both Gutmann and Galston suggest that civic education is situated and particularistic in nature. Despite their differences, both involve civic education in the virtues necessary for the perpetuation of effective citizenship in a liberal democracy. Similarly, the Amish parents in *Yoder* focused on the perpetuation of the Amish community. Although one could argue that a greater proportion of Amish will leave their communities than the proportion of U.S. citizens who will become expatriates, and that we properly show greater concern for the acculturation of those within our borders than for the acculturation to the cosmopolitan community of those who choose to leave, the point remains. If we are concerned about civic education, either we are concerned about the practical aspects of Amish social and political participation, or we believe on some level that regardless of practicalities, the values of the larger culture are morally preferable to those of the Amish community. If the former, evidence suggests that Amish children learn in their community what they need after eighth grade to function effectively. If the latter, those who disagree with *Yoder* or who disagree contingently, like Douglas, must justify their desire to impose more civic education than the Amish parents desire.

Douglas suggested that he would take a child's part who rebelled against her Amish parents by wanting to attend high school, because not to do so would foreclose to her a range of choices that he believed should be available to her. But how broad must this range be? Noting that many Amish communities run their own elementary schools, Spinner asks, "How can the state know that people actually choose to join the Amish when their children live their entire lives in the Amish community and do not attend public schools?"[46] No one enjoys a context of choice that includes every conceivable option; people who are not Amish are neither encouraged nor required to spend time in Amish communities in order to render meaningful the right of exit from the larger culture. Spinner concludes that we may safely assume that the Amish choose to be Amish. As members of a minority culture, Spinner argues, they are aware of alternatives, and some Amish teenagers experiment with some of these before the time comes for baptism. They therefore fulfill three of the conditions Galston outlines for the meaningful right of exit: awareness of alternatives fulfills the awareness condition, and the existence of experimentation could be taken to fulfill both the capacity condition and the psychological condition. They possess the capacity to assess alternatives, and they are not brainwashed into remaining in the Amish community.

The sticking point is what Galston calls the fitness condition, or "the ability of exit-desiring individuals to participate effectively in at least some ways of life other than the ones they wish to leave."[47] Spinner notes that although few Amish leave to become nuclear engineers, many join more liberal Anabaptist communities where they may use many of the same skills in farming and manual labor that they learned in the Amish community. The fact that a number do leave evidences their ability to survive outside; the fact that large percentages do *not* leave, or that if they do they join similar communities, evidences the fact that their communities are indeed preparing them for the lives most will lead. But "if the number of young adults leaving the community for mainstream society increased from a trickle to a stream—then the *Yoder* decision would have to be revisited," perhaps by dictating mandatory attendance at public schools, the better to prepare children for their adult lives.[48] Although economically, it appears that the context of choice allows the Amish to fulfill Galston's fitness condition, I suggest, however, that individuals should be able to function effectively in more than one sort of role. That is, we may be aware of alternatives, possess the capacity to assess them, and be able to participate effectively in other ways of life, but the range of alternatives about which we possess this knowledge may be exceedingly narrow. This casts doubt on the proposition that the Amish choose to be Amish, at least with respect to engaging in a critical examination of a broad range of alternatives.

To put this differently, when Spinner notes that no one enjoys a context of choice with unlimited breadth, he is suggesting that individuals choose to be Amish on a first-order level. That is, they are presented with several actual options and choose among them, most deciding to remain in the Amish community. My concern is the second-order level, that of preference formation. Exposure or access to different *kinds* of options provides the raw material that enables us to live our lives from the inside, to examine, question, and revise or reaffirm our current projects and goals. This distinction is hinted at in Spinner's point that because only small numbers of individuals leave the Amish community, their education is adequate. If larger numbers were to leave, the state might require more education. In other words, their education is adequate for the actual choices that they confront. From the viewpoint of preference formation, on the other hand, it could be argued that the current education of Amish children might better be shown as adequate if larger numbers did leave. These individuals would be demonstrating a meaningful right of exit, including an awareness of alternatives, a capacity to assess them, and a confidence in being able effectively to participate in other ways of life, especially, in theory, if they engaged in occupations other than farming or manual labor. Although they are assuredly not brainwashed into staying, they also assuredly do not enter into anything resembling a sympathetic and imaginative engagement with other ways of life. The question here is that of how broad the context of choice must be.

First, I do not reject Spinner's paradox that liberalism allows people to reject liberal values. The notion of constitutive choice encompasses my ability to make a second-order choice, through which I may then become encumbered by duties that I view as constitutive of my identity on a first-order level. But first I must examine a range of values, including liberal ones, and decide that I *want* a way of life that thus encumbers me, whether this is a reaffirmation of my traditional way of life, or another that I recently discovered. I am more troubled, however, by Galston's assertion that "liberal freedom entails the right to live unexamined as well as examined lives." Does this mean lives that are *never* examined? Or can this mean that once an initial critical examination has taken place, we might make a constitutive choice that limits further self-reflective choices? In a likely scenario, I may make a constitutive choice that entails subsequent constitutive duties. But when I encounter other opportunities to choose as my life unfolds, I engage in self-reflection that results in my reaffirmation of the constitutive choice I made originally. Here, although my life may be unexamined and therefore rejects liberal values on the first-order level, it is continually reexamined on the second-order level. But in any scenario, self-examination should occur at *some* point.

Second, the ability to understand and to interact with a broad range of alternatives not only promotes our capacity to live what are good lives for ourselves but also allows us a greater understanding of the limitations of our choices, even when we continue to adhere to them. As Walter Feinberg suggests, learning about other cultures enables us to understand them and "also involves using that learning in a reflexive way to understand one's own behaviour and practices as a culturally constructed product."[49] For example, Macedo, in discussing public justification, asserts that "being a self-critical reason-giver is the best way of being a liberal and a good way (liberals must suppose) of living a life."[50] But even the situated autonomy that he advocates (213–227) requires not only that we possess the capacity to be self-critical reason-givers, but also, I believe, that we understand that this is what we are.

With respect to minority cultures, the liberal concern is both that children unexposed to other ways of life will have fewer opportunities and "that the children will not develop the capacity to choose whether or not they want to take advantage of those opportunities. It is not that the child will therefore end up repeating the life practices of the parent, but rather that the child will have no other choice but to do this."[51] At the second-order level, I need not only alternatives, and a broad range of types of alternatives, but also the qualitative and developed capacity to assess these alternatives and what they might mean for my own life. Even if I reaffirm my current way of life, engagement with these alternatives may help me to understand facets of my own life that have hitherto been unexamined.

What stands out is the importance of culture as a context of choice and the extent to which culture shapes the existence of alternatives, the nature of these alternatives, and the capacity of its members to assess and to utilize those alternatives of which they are aware. Although I have argued that cultural membership in any particular culture functions as an expression of autonomy rather than as a precondition of autonomy, I focused on mature membership as a product of rational deliberation and critical reflection. For children or youth, however, membership may function as a precondition in a different sense. Like membership in a family, cultural or religious membership in one's culture or faith of origin situates the individual in a particular context and grounds him or her in a specific constellation of options for choice and beliefs about value. But the mere fact of familial, cultural, or religious membership itself, however secure the sense of identity and belonging that it imparts, is not a sufficient condition for the development of the capacity for autonomy. Whether it functions as a precondition of autonomy depends upon its nature, its values, and the ways in which it seeks to inculcate these values. Precisely because liberal autonomy as I perceive it does allow us to eschew the practice of autonomy in our adult lives, it can be argued that we should initially in some forum develop and exercise the capacity to engage in critical self-reflection about our future course. Therefore, it behooves us to consider carefully when we examine the merits of dispensations from educational requirements.

The Amish and their supporters fear that the very education that may develop the capacity for autonomy will also increase the dilution of cultural homogeneity and cause the Amish way of life to disappear. The possibility of assimilation to the larger culture signifies a larger range of options for these individual members, but a narrower range overall, with the possible disappearance of that particular option for everyone. As Spinner puts the dilemma, it is easy to say with theorists like Kymlicka that members of the Amish community should interpret their identities as they wish, but we should then also allow the Amish community to reject some self-interpretations. In this regard Spinner resembles Chandran Kukathas in the latter's point that outside interference violates the associational freedom at the core of liberalism and that the right of exit is the ultimate liberal safeguard against coercion. The dilution or disappearance of the Amish way of life "will mean that the reinterpreters will live in a non-Amish community anyway but that those who wanted to live in an Amish community will not be able to do so," thus allowing less overall choice.[52] Spinner implies that cultural structure devoid of the ability to maintain cultural character renders the structure a hollow shell and that eventually the structure will disintegrate without continuity of content to maintain its form.

We could respond that because Spinner himself notes that no context of choice includes every conceivable option, the disappearance of some options simply exemplifies the inevitability of change. Moreover, despite efforts to preserve cultural character, cultures are never self-contained. Jeremy Waldron contrasts one model of cultural membership, in which individual identity is constructed within one culture, with a second model, in which identity in a multicultural society "will comprise a multiplicity of cultural fragments, bits and pieces of various cultures from here and there."[53] Individuals in a multicultural situation are never members of only one culture; cultures are always "implicated" with one another, even internationally through war and trade (107). Respecting or preserving a cultural framework as a basis for identity "means that one has to pin down a favored version of the cultural framework to be understood in this regard. But cultures and communities are developing things—their boundaries blur and their identities shift" (113). Waldron thus wants to avoid essentialism, or the notion that certain facets or characteristics of a culture constitute its essence, as any given constellation of facets is only one interpretation of that culture. Similarly, individual identity is itself multicultural, in that "individuals can no longer be regarded . . . as mere artifacts of the culture of the one community to which we think they ought to belong" (114).

We could apply Waldron's point to the Amish in two different ways. First, if every individual is indeed multicultural because of the blurring of boundaries, we need to do nothing to protect Amish youth against the limitations of their own communities. All Amish cannot but be conscious of the influence of the larger culture, with all the particularistic cultural influences that constitute it. Their belief that it is their religious duty to set themselves apart is a response to the larger culture, and their doing so is an affirmation of the project that being Amish represents. The Amish are defining for themselves the meaning of their overall membership in the *larger* culture and becoming self-interpreting. On the other hand, we could argue that because individuals are never purely members of one culture but are always to some degree implicated in other cultures, Amish youth need the sort of civic education that will develop their capacities for rational deliberation and critical reflection, even if they remain in their communities their entire lives thereafter.

In the Amish case, in the end I must reluctantly agree with the Court in *Yoder*. I do so because I believe that the Amish way of life is a matter of self-interpretation by Amish individuals over time, and the Amish community comprises individuals who agree on the meaning of their at least nominal membership in the larger community. Separation is not instrumental to being Amish but is intrinsic to and constitutive of what being Amish means. As we have seen, even Macedo holds that although critical self-examination is required by liberal politics, citizens should decide on their own attitudes toward their religious beliefs.[54] And here, the religious beliefs that the Amish affirm require separation from the larger society.

I am still troubled by the fact that Amish youth will not be exposed to the diversity they would otherwise encounter; the free exercise of religion by Amish parents in effect constitutes an establishment of religion for Amish youth. Therefore, I believe that Douglas's dissent makes an important point. Although children do not carry the full legal status of adult agents, their more limited agency deserves respect, and they should be canvassed in such cases for their own viewpoints. If they themselves desire further education, I agree with Douglas that they should be accorded this right against their parents' desires. Absent disagreement, however, the parents' free exercise rights should be honored, even as we uncomfortably recognize that the children's assent is not only not a mature one but also one not likely to be informed by critical self-reflection.

Beliefs are not automatically matters of faith and therefore removed from civil jurisdiction simply because an individual or group thinks they are or should be. The state could have decided, of course, that the deprivation of exposure to a diversity of beliefs and values constitutes worldly injury sufficient to render the dispensation from educational requirements an inappropriate expression of religious belief and practice. The criterion of worldly injury renders irrelevant any consideration of or reference to the validity or appropriateness of religious practices on their own terms. Recognizing the line between the civil and the religious as a matter of civil determination, however, does not mean that the state is necessarily correct in these determinations. When individuals with differing conscientious beliefs desire exemptions from civil requirements, some entity must possess the authority to arbitrate if we are not to face a situation in which any individual or group, for better reasons or for worse, can claim exemptions simply because this claim flows from these conscientious beliefs. In the modern world, that entity is the nation-state.

If we as citizens of the liberal polity, through the civil authority, do agree that the sincerity, logic, or worth of a belief is such that we allow a practice we could have forbidden, we should accord the same respect to this belief and practice that we do to others. Spinner suggests that we may allow a practice without approving of it in the sense of endorsing it. "Toleration of the Amish . . . does not mean celebration; liberal democrats . . . should not glorify the Amish. . . . A grudging tolerance of the Amish is different from a celebration of their culture and the pronouncement that it is equal to liberal cultures."[55] Although I am reluctant to grant the educational dispensation in *Yoder,* I would shrink from labeling my tolerance a "grudging" one. We may as a polity decide to accord what Galston terms "some intermediate status . . . for groups that are willing to abide by the basic laws of the community without making full claims upon it, in return for which they might be exempted from some of the requirements of full citizenship."[56] But if we do this, it is with full knowledge of what we may see as the lacunae in the Amish conception of liberal citizenship. Therefore, although we may never agree with them about the proper constituents of the latter, acceptance of their practices with appropriate qualifications means, in my view, *full* acceptance under the terms of the agreement.

This is why I am wary of Macedo's assertion that illiberal moral and religious views may require mending, or that marginalized groups may need to make their own adjustments rather than petitioning for exemptions. He argues that we should each determine our own attitudes toward our religious beliefs. Along these lines, we did not require that the Amish take a different attitude toward their own beliefs to secure a decision like that in *Yoder.* Even if *Yoder* had been differently decided, we still would not have required an alteration in Amish attitudes toward their own beliefs. We would simply have been saying, quite properly in my view, that the distinction between the civil and the religious is a matter of civil determination and that here is where the line is. Even Gutmann says that the democratic state is not *required* to recognize an educational exemption *if* this would shorten the exposure of Amish youth to essential components of democratic deliberation.[57] In other words, the matter is very much a contingent one.

Galston suggests that "it seems possible for liberal societies to manage the inevitable conflict with marginal groups in a spirit of maximum feasible accommodation" in a "particularized, but neither uncharacteristic nor unprincipled, practice of liberal generosity."[58] If the exceptionalism of the Amish community dictates that we in turn ought to make exceptions, generosity requires that once the agreement is made, we should accord full respect to the Amish, even if we continue to disagree with their views. To do otherwise is to make them "pay" for our generosity. I believe that on some level, a sympathetic and imaginative engagement with their views is what persuaded the *Yoder* Court to grant the educational dispensation. The dialogue between this marginalized group and those representing the dominant consensus was not a one-way street, and the larger society was the entity that made the "adjustments." Although we might wish that the views of the Amish were other than what they are, we ourselves cannot meet the requirements of liberal citizenship if we deny the possibility of constructive interaction and reciprocal positive regard. We may decide future confrontations of this nature differently. But we should not make a group pay reparations through the back door, in effect, for costs that we did not extract through the front door.

For Autonomy

In the second case to be discussed, *Mozert v. Hawkins County Board of Education*, seven families of fundamentalist Christians sued a Tennessee school board on the grounds that their religious beliefs were violated by the content of a series of textbooks that taught or inculcated values contrary to their beliefs. This case was litigated at the district level with decisions favoring the defendants, was appealed but returned to the district court for further development of the evidence, and was decided a second time at the district level in favor of the plaintiffs. On a second appeal, the appellate court agreed with the trial court's initial decision in favor of the school district.[59] Although originally one of the parents had secured agreement from the school principal for an alternative reading program, subsequently the school board eliminated all alternatives and required all students to attend classes using the one basic reading series.

In his opinion for the appellate court, Chief Judge Lively addressed three issues. First, although the plaintiffs objected to repeated exposure to objectionable material, Lively argued that exposure to ideas objectionable on religious grounds does not constitute a burden on the free exercise of religion. Moreover, structuring a public school curriculum to satisfy religious principles or prohibitions violates the establishment clause (1063–1064). Second, in successful free exercise cases like *Sherbert v. Verner,* free exercise was burdened by requiring the plaintiffs to perform specific *actions* that violated their religious convictions or else to forego benefits such as unemployment compensation, a job, or public education. But reading and discussing assigned materials is not compulsion as exists in cases "where the objector was required to affirm or deny a religious belief or refrain from engaging in a practice contrary to sincerely held religious beliefs" (1066). Third, although the plaintiffs maintained that they could not be tolerant in the sense of accepting other religious views as equal to theirs, only "a civil tolerance, not a religious one," was required. No one was required to believe or affirm that all religions are equally valuable, and although the school system encouraged the exercise of critical judgment and choice, these also were nowhere required (1069). In sum, the reading requirement did not unconstitutionally burden the plaintiffs' free exercise. It did not require religiously forbidden conduct but only elicited apprehensiveness that this reading might lead students to conclusions contrary to their families' beliefs (1070).

The other two appellate judges, Kennedy and Boggs, concurred with Lively but for different reasons. Kennedy suggested that a compelling state interest in teaching "students how to think critically about complex and controversial subjects and to develop their own ideas and make judgments about these subjects" would outweigh the plaintiffs' free exercise rights even if these were found to be burdened (1070–1071). Moreover, the readers' introduction of subjects and themes discussed across the curriculum would lead to students' dismissals from other classes in which objectionable themes arose, to the requirement that teachers determine in detail what materials were objectionable, and to the creation of a precedent for those of other religions who might request religious exemptions from core subjects (1071–1073). The more sympathetic Boggs argued that reading means engaging in acts or conduct as surely as reading books on the Roman Catholic Church's prohibited *Index* would have meant before 1962 (1073–1076). More important, if the plaintiffs were pressured to believe "that values come from within oneself, rather than from an external religious source . . . I think it clear that such teaching would violate the Establishment Clause," which would outweigh any compelling state interest prohibiting accommodation (1076–1077). Nevertheless, because the Court typically does not interfere with the setting of school curricula on free exercise grounds, schools need not justify *refusals* of individual requests for exemptions (1079). Moreover, civil toleration may indeed be taught without religious toleration. "Thus, the state may teach that all religions have the same civil and political rights, and must be dealt with civilly in civil society. . . . It may not teach as truth that the religions of others are just as correct *as religions* as plaintiffs' own" (1080). And even materials that appear unbalanced by seeming to preach religious toleration need not constitute an establishment.

Mozert differs from *Yoder* most obviously because the *Mozert* parents did not seek to sequester their children from public education as preparation for life in a separatist community but instead desired the benefits of public education minus the features they found offensive to their religious beliefs. Because these children will presumably function as citizens in the mainstream of the liberal polity, we can argue that they need to develop the capacity for rational deliberation and critical reflection. This in turn requires exposure to varying viewpoints and ways of life through a sympathetic and imaginative engagement with them. The deprivation of exposure to a diversity of beliefs and values constitutes worldly injury sufficient to make dispensation from these educational requirements an inappropriate expression of religious belief and practice. As Joseph Raz argues, "The autonomous life depends not on the availability of one option of freedom of choice. It depends on the general character of one's environment and culture. For those who live in an autonomy-supporting environment there is no choice but to be autonomous: there is no other way to prosper in such a society."[60]

The admission that educational requirements are necessary to generate or develop the capacity for critical self-reflection potentially betrays a fault line, however, in the traditional liberal effort to maximize both liberty and tolerance. Although a liberal society will value all ways of life grounded in autonomy, it may be unable both to promote autonomy and a policy of tolerance or inclusiveness toward ways of life that do not espouse this value. According to Susan Mendus, liberals who assume that autonomy itself is chosen optimistically wager, like John Stuart Mill, that it will always be chosen and never be voluntarily discarded. Therefore, the liberty of those who would renounce it can seemingly be restricted, as they obviously have not achieved autonomy. Other liberals, of whom Raz is one, believe that "the state of autonomy is surely the state from which I choose, not itself an object of choice . . . that autonomous life is not itself a matter of choice, but the basis on which choices are made."[61] Therefore, again, the liberty of those who do not value it should be restricted until they *learn* to act autonomously. In either case, "liberalism's claim to pluralism and tolerance are [*sic*] undermined or radically transformed. Tolerance becomes not a virtue, but merely a temporary expedient against the day when all are autonomous" (108).

On my own interpretation of constitutive choice, however, personal autonomy may indeed be discarded at the first-order level if I choose or affirm a way of life that encumbers me with duties that I view as constitutive of my identity. Moreover, I may choose or affirm a life that emphasizes critical reflection, coming to see *this* activity as a constitutive and unquestioned duty even when it might appear easier to follow some courses of action unthinkingly. I believe that we may "autonomously" renounce autonomy if our process of preference formation engages us in critical reflection before doing so. Thus, the commitment to an autonomous or nonautonomous life is in my view an object of choice. Autonomy at the second-order level, however, is the state from which we choose, or the basis on which choices are made. But precisely because here it cannot be an object of choice, education must address the inculcation at the second-order level of the *capacity* for autonomy. If we do not possess this capacity at the second-order level, we do not have the choice of using it or not at the first-order level. Because I allow for the renunciation of the practice of autonomy at the first-order level, I do not view toleration as a temporary expedient; rather, there is permanent need for it under ongoing conditions of cultural, religious, philosophical, and moral diversity. But because I do prefer that all develop the capacity for autonomy at the second-order level, my tolerance here appears more provisional, and I am therefore more exposed to Mendus's criticism that liberals often promote autonomy at the expense of inclusiveness.

In *Yoder,* the Amish parents' concern was that the education that shaped preference formation would influence not only the process through which ways of life are chosen or affirmed but also the outcome of this process. That is, inculcation of the *capacity* for autonomy at the second-order level predisposes us to opt for the *practice* of autonomy at the first-order level. Once the capacity for autonomy becomes the basis on which choices are made, a nonautonomous life is less likely to be a realistic object of choice. In *Mozert,* the fundamentalist parents shared a related concern that the manner in which we hold our religious, philosophical, and moral beliefs is not confined to the realm of form or procedure but also exerts an influence on the substance of these beliefs. If we ourselves are to enter into a sympathetic and imaginative engagement with ways of life that resist even exposure to competing viewpoints, we must understand these concerns about such exposure.

THE FUNDAMENTALIST VIEWPOINT

In *Mozert*, the plaintiffs felt that their free exercise of religion was not violated so much by exposure to particular hostile values that they did reject, like evolution, as by exposure to a diversity of values. "In other words, the plaintiffs objected to the very principles—tolerance and evenhandedness—traditionally used to justify liberal education."[62] Although the school district argued that mere exposure did not inculcate alien values, to the parents this exposure itself constituted interference with their free exercise. Invoking *Sherbert* and its recognition of the compulsion to breach religious duty as a burden on religious rights, they implicitly defined the *condition* of being exposed through reading objectional material, some of it aloud, as the participatory *act* of reading this material (600–604). The fear of the *Mozert* parents was not state influence on belief-formation, as might occur in a ritualized profession of belief like a flag salute, but the possibility of "state-inflicted injuries to already-formed beliefs" (607), as in requirements that one violate religious obligations addressed by *Sherbert*. That is, their claim viewed mere exposure as value inculcation and the program's encouragement of critical thought as a type of indoctrination (611).

Instead of accepting the conventional wisdom that critical reflection functions as a safeguard against indoctrination, the *Mozert* parents viewed seemingly neutral exposure to hostile beliefs as a mechanism for undermining religious absolutes in favor of personal opinion, aimed at reproducing pluralism (612–613). Mere exposure to other viewpoints itself implies that beliefs are simply subjective opinions and that fundamentalism, in the words of Nomi Maya Stolzenberg, is "just one among many possible belief-systems from which an individual might choose" (627). Where liberals believe that the development of the capacity for critical reflection is accomplished through education *about* different viewpoints or ways of life, fundamentalists believe that this process constitutes education *into* a particular normative and cultural tradition, that of secular humanism or liberalism. The *Sherbert* doctrine honors the claims of sincere belief over those of purportedly objective truth (630–631); appeals to individual reason are themselves coercive influences on individual beliefs. "In this conception, interference with the processes of belief-formation is defined not by coercion, but rather by the disruption of one culture's processes of socialization by another's" (634).

In my view, the core issue raised by *Mozert* is whether the diversity sanctioned by liberalism extends to the right to hold one's beliefs in a particular *manner*, in this case one which we do not typically regard as congruent with liberal values. As Stolzenberg notes, the parents fear both their children's rejection of their values and "the case in which their children remain attached to their parents' views, but only after coming to see those views *as such*—as subjective, contestable matters of opinion. There is a subtle difference between the faith that is innocent of alternatives and that which is not" (587, n. 26). One might, for example, be subject to a process of indoctrination yet through self-reflection become conscious of a desire to retain one's original beliefs. "But at this point, a degree of self-consciousness about beliefs has been introduced, which may well alter the experience of belief itself" (609, n. 162).

These parents would agree with Callan that political liberalism is a "closet ethical liberalism."[63] As we have seen, on the latter view exposure to a variety of viewpoints not only facilitates a sense of justice toward others but also influences our conceptions of the good. Attempting to understand the reasonableness of other ways of life means that I must imagine myself in another context, in which my own way of life will appear no better than the one I am imaginatively entertaining. We would expect these fundamentalists to object to attempts to understand a variety of viewpoints "from the inside." But even without attempts to involve children in sympathetic and imaginative engagement with other ways of life, simply the consciousness that competing viewpoints represent contestable matters of opinion to many people, rather than a conflict between right and wrong, will exert a pervasive influence on our ethical convictions and cause us to hold our beliefs in a different manner than otherwise. My original beliefs become just one possible narrative among others instead of the one that transcends all others.[64]

From a fundamentalist standpoint, then, this knowledge of consciousness of alternatives is a harm that, once introduced, can never be mended. Fundamentalist parents would take little comfort from Rawls's assertion that the acceptance of reasonable disagreement need not promote skepticism about the validity of one's own beliefs,[65] even if these beliefs were never seriously threatened. This is because the *manner* in which these beliefs are held is not only threatened but actually damaged, and the *way* in which beliefs are held becomes an intrinsic part of their content. Secular liberals and fundamentalists, then, not only espouse different beliefs with regard to the proper role of reason and critical reflection but also differ in their metatheories of the way in which beliefs ought properly to be held. Callan notes that sophisticated believers self-consciously adhere to faith beyond reason yet also eschew the use of arguments from faith in political argument. "This is a high-wire act" or unstable equilibrium, requiring a difficult and finely tuned balance between the demands of one's comprehensive doctrine and the imperatives of public reason.[66] Though Callan concludes that the educational requirements for political and ethical liberalism are more alike than Rawls wants to recognize, his argument also demonstrates why fundamentalist parents could experience "mere exposure" as a threat to their children's faith. In other words, it confirms the fundamentalist suspicion that an innocent-looking political liberalism in reality contains the tenets of ethical liberalism and that it is therefore the proverbial wolf in sheep's clothing.

INADEQUATE COMPROMISE

A possible compromise would encourage a weakened variety of autonomy, thereby avoiding a full-blooded commitment to autonomy at the expense of inclusiveness. I do not believe that this will work, but the suggestion is an attractive one. Kenneth Strike suggests that because any doctrine that accommodates reciprocity and tolerance should be regarded as reasonable, it need neither assume the inevitability of diversity nor promote character traits required by an assumption of irreconcilable disagreement. A discourse ethic suitable for reciprocal public dialogue will nevertheless emerge, because most Western religions and philosophies "have, after all, both conditioned and been conditioned by liberalism."[67] Will this strategy not still require the sort of reasoned argumentation that both requires and develops the capacity for autonomy?

For Strike, a view that affirms autonomy as instrumental to public dialogue and the construction of an overlapping consensus differs from one that affirms autonomy as an intrinsically central part of a good life. The instrumental view would encourage the capacity for tradition-constrained reasoning without allowing critical reflection to dominate, as in the teaching of biblical exegesis at a religious school. "In one theory [the instrumental one] autonomy is a requirement of reasoning within and between traditions. In the other it is the core commitment of a tradition" (45–46). Moreover, because all faiths implicitly admit the need for reflection, reason, and dialogue, a modest version of autonomy may be a commitment of most moral traditions anyway (46). This sort of discourse approach is hospitable to education within a particular tradition and to the idea that one can both view other traditions with hostility and respect others' rights, a stance reminiscent of Yael Tamir's rights-based liberalism. Where theorists like Gutmann and Callan in effect confirm the suspicion that liberalism is a comprehensive religion of secular humanism, Strike "would prefer to persuade people of faith that they can continue to be people of faith and liberals as well" (47).

I agree with Strike that we may be simultaneously both people of faith and liberals. The issue is what kinds of people of faith, or what kinds of liberals. Callan believes that Strike, like Rawls, accepts the justificatory ideal embedded in the recognized necessity of public discourse but nevertheless will not acknowledge its subversive implications. Because on Callan's view the capacity for autonomy is a necessary feature of any sort of liberalism that rests on the public justification of authority, both ethical and political liberalism, relying on public justification, require the development of the capacity for autonomy in liberal citizens. Strike's reliance on the congruence of our traditions with the imperatives of liberal democratic politics ignores illiberal cultural currents, eschewing "liberal aggressiveness by embracing liberal complacency."[68]

Strike's attempt at compromise is grounded on good intentions, but it also reveals the pitfalls of such an effort. I have argued, using Johnston's terms, that under conditions of permanent and irreconcilable disagreement, moral reciprocity requires the capacity for *personal* autonomy, or the capability of subjecting one's projects and values to critical appraisal and self-consciously constructing from them a life that functions as a coherent whole, as a precondition for the effective deployment of *moral* autonomy, or the capability of having a conception of the good and a sense of justice. Thus defined, personal and moral autonomy collapse in my view in the same way that ethical and political liberalism collapse for Callan. The sort of equivalency that Strike advances, however, will unduly limit the scope of public discourse if his goal is an overlapping consensus formulated by individuals capable of moral autonomy.

First, the tradition-constrained reasoning that he recommends may call upon reflection, reason, and dialogue. But if, on the one hand, it is constrained enough not to threaten people of faith like the *Mozert* parents, it is less likely to promote the understanding necessary to the formation of a conception of the good and a sense of justice under permanent conditions of diversity. Disagreement exists as to what beliefs and practices are intrinsic to a given tradition and which are extrinsic to it. As Alasdair MacIntyre suggests, the common life of any institution bearing a tradition of practice is "partly, but in a centrally important way, constituted by a continuous argument as to what a university is and ought to be or what good farming is or what good medicine is. Traditions, when vital, embody continuities of conflict."[69] The tension between the maintenance of cultural structure and the perpetuation of cultural character applies equally to traditions. Parents should of course be able to opt out of public education for their children, but public education itself should not be confined to the narrowest possible definitions of reason and reflection in deciding what pedagogical techniques to deploy, in order to define the liberal tradition as inoffensively as possible.

If, on the other hand, tradition-constrained reasoning is more broadly defined and includes critical reflection, along with attempts at sympathetic and imaginative engagement with practices and ways of life that liberal hospitality to diversity might suggest, it will not satisfy people like the *Mozert* parents. Exposure to different ways of life at issue in this case could be described as simply instrumental to the construction of a consensus, not as an intrinsic part of a good life. But because this dialogue implicitly introduces the idea that competing viewpoints might have value and that this value is a contestable matter of opinion, it teeters on the verge of suggesting that the capacity for autonomy *is* central to a good life if one is to make discerning judgments about these values. Although the development of this capacity may not be promoted as the core commitment of the liberal tradition, developing and using it to the degree required for reasoning within and between traditions may result in its spilling over into the areas of personal belief-retention and belief-formation. As Callan recognizes, the same mental capacities are in play whether we are evaluating our own conceptions of the good or attempting to understand our fellow citizens. Moreover, the development of the capacity for autonomy is not an end in itself even for those who cherish it as a core value. Rather, it is instrumental to deciding what constitutes a good life for each individual. Therefore, the distinction that Strike implies between autonomy as a constitutive feature of a good life and autonomy's value as derivative from the goal of forming an overlapping consensus tends to collapse.

Second, Strike's suggestion that a modest version of autonomy may contribute to or derive from most extant moral traditions renders the meaning of autonomy so broad as to render the concept vacuous in the context of the current discussion. Where Callan assimilates political liberalism to ethical liberalism because of their common dependence, in his view, on the need for critical reflection, Strike assimilates liberalism to Western moral traditions in general, because this move allows for a less demanding liberalism, one that need not insist upon a full-bodied interpretation of autonomy. Strike's notion of autonomy is perhaps akin to the concept of agency, or in Johnston's terms the imaginative capacity to formulate projects and values independent of our own experiences. Agency is indeed crucial to consensus, but the sufficiently reciprocal public dialogue that Strike suggests is also required calls for more, for moral autonomy and in my view also for personal autonomy. But these qualities are not part of a majority of moral traditions to the extent that he proposes.

Even within the Western tradition, as we have seen, vigorous disagreement exists between theorists who, like Rawls, conceive of citizens "as self-authenticating sources of valid claims," which carry weight apart from duties and obligations owed to society under a political conception of justice,[70] and those who interpret claims as deriving from a higher source of transcendent value. The liberal emphasis on the liberty and welfare of the individual is unique. To equate liberalism with other traditions in this regard blurs the significance not only of autonomy but also of liberalism itself.

Finally, Strike suggests that public dialogue will be sufficiently reciprocal absent the capacity for critical reflection because the religious and philosophical traditions of the West "have conditioned and been conditioned by liberalism." In other words, the rough edges of most comprehensive doctrines have been smoothed by the liberal tradition, rendering them—and their adherents—tractable without the necessity of any particular cognitive effort at understanding. But this claim is a circular one. If the workability of comprehensive doctrines bootstraps on the culture of liberal societies, but liberal culture also seems to bootstrap on the tradition of dialogue among comprehensive doctrines, where is the fulcrum that perpetuates this reciprocity? We are back to Callan's warning against liberal complacency. Developed nations in particular encompass increasing ranges of diversity, and the types of diversity that manifest themselves are often new to the liberal tradition, as the liberal tradition is new to them.

I must conclude, then, that Strike's attempt at compromise fails and that both Callan and the *Mozert* parents are correct to perceive "subversive" implications in educational preparation for critical reflection and participation in public discourse. We are back to the question of what accommodation liberals owe to those whose belief systems, religious or otherwise, extend to claiming a right to hold their beliefs in a particular manner, a manner that is innocent of the understanding of alternatives. I believe that we can be simultaneously people of faith and also liberals. We cannot, however, be people of faith who perceive competing viewpoints simply as conflicts between right and wrong and also be liberals or constructive citizens of a liberal polity. As liberals, we may hold to the conviction that our own viewpoints are correct, but we must also recognize that this correctness is a matter of opinion that is contestable. It is appropriate, therefore, for public education to expose students to ways of life and points of view in such a way that they are "threatened" with the prospect of developing the capacity for rational deliberation and critical reflection if they are to be prepared for the option of active citizenship.

Liberals nevertheless sustain a dilemma. Because the *Mozert* decision forced the fundamentalists to forego a free public education as the cost of sustaining their own interpretation of their way of life, it exposes the limitations of liberal tolerance.[71] To put this differently, a decision *against* the parents appears to be a decision against toleration, while a decision *for* the parents would appear to be one against *teaching* the values of toleration. Liberalism is historically inclusive of diversity, but the application of liberal principles can be inexorably assimilationist in its impact.

INADEQUATE ACCOMMODATION

A possible accommodation would defer to parents' wishes for their children's educations under specific circumstances but would override these wishes under others. Although such accommodations should be judged on a contingent basis, Shelley Burtt's modified principle of parental deference provides an interesting example that I believe is still inadequate for the needs of the liberal polity. Burtt argues that although a decision for the *Mozert* parents would have appeared to militate against teaching the value of toleration, excusing religious children from objectionable requirements teaches respect for differences as surely as requiring their exposure to discussions of toleration.[72] Deeply religious parents should not be regarded as opposing rational inquiry per se, but as simply desiring to preserve "a sense of the transcendent" as "the touchstone of moral reflection" or the true guide needed in the face of a materialistic culture (63–64). Moreover, because much theological work addresses questions of value formation, the rejection of secular standards of reasoning simply represents a choice of "civic responsibility grounded in religious faith against one grounded in secular certainties."[73] Finally, from a pragmatic standpoint, liberal democracy benefits from the ethos contributed by religiously committed citizens, argues Burtt, and children should not be presented with opposing ways of life that in effect do not offer a choice but instead make a secular choice for them. Moreover, because religious parents can opt out entirely through private schools, the liberal polity should accommodate their partial objections in order to preserve students' exposure to the remainder of the curriculum.[74]

Overall, Burtt supports a modified principle of parental deference that recognizes children's moral and spiritual developmental needs as well as their membership in distinct cultural communities.[75] Like Douglas in his *Yoder* dissent, she would uphold children's rights of free exercise if they desire ordinarily mandated education to which their parents object, like a state-required biology course. She would not, however, support children in objections to their parents' request for an alternative biology textbook in a course to which these

parents had in principle assented, as parental authority over the manner of presentation is acceptable (432–433). More generally, she would support the state
over parents if their religious beliefs or practices forbade the acquisition of fundamental skills like basic literacy or dictated "the active subversion of constitutional principles," like advocacy of racial segregation as a tenet public
education should inculcate. But educators should defer to parents in the absence
of constitutional affirmations. Parents whose religion affirms the legitimacy
of sex roles, for example, should be able to excuse their children from classes
that teach otherwise. "Girls raised in this way will make decent, law-abiding
citizens, even if, from the standpoint of liberal democratic ideals, they have not
been treated entirely justly."[76] Finally, Burtt would make a clear exception to
parental deference when the principal objection to a curriculum is its antipathy
to the "triumphalist" perspective, which advocates political activity that would
lessen the distance between church and society at large, a viewpoint opposed
by many religious as well as secular critics (68).

Burtt's is a reasoned and in many ways attractive account of a modified principle of parental deference. She is correct to suggest that the universal availability of condoms at school or a disciplinary policy that includes paddling
cannot be completely counterbalanced at home by thoughtful discussion of the
virtues of sexual abstinence or by completely nonviolent discipline.[77] Yet difficulties remain. First, failure to mention God as "the touchstone of moral reflection" is not the direct contradiction to familial upbringing that condoms or
paddling represents toward the values of abstinence or nonviolence. This failure
should be viewed, rather, as a lacuna in moral or spiritual training that can be
filled by families who see it as such. Although I agree with theorists like Stolzenberg that the way in which beliefs are held exerts an impact on the substance of
beliefs themselves, many different forces will contribute to this impact in a modern society. If we value the capacity for autonomy and civic competency, as
Burtt says she does also, I believe that educational programs that promote this
capacity on a secular basis have a legitimate claim to be part of this mélange.

Second, Burtt notes that theological works assuredly engage in rational
deliberation about the good life and that education for both autonomy and civic
competency can be grounded in religious faith rather than in secular values. I
hasten to agree. But theological works, like secular ones, that engage in rational
deliberation and critical reflection are certainly written by individuals who have
been exposed to and have grappled at least intellectually with alternative beliefs,
practices, and ways of life. Whether they consider alternative interpretations
of their own religious traditions or alternative traditions, religious or secular,
altogether, they are engaging in intellectual practices that prompt them to

examine, question, and revise or affirm their current beliefs, practices, projects, and goals.[78] Any sort of education for autonomy and civic competency, whether grounded in religious faith or in secular values, must in my view inculcate the capacity for rational deliberation and critical reflection. This education requires that the manner in which we hold our religious, philosophical, or moral beliefs be such as to admit that alternative viewpoints and ways of life, including our own, are matters of opinion the correctness of which is contestable, even though we may ourselves be thoroughly committed to our own. If we can develop and maintain this stance, we may be people of faith or not, but either way, we will nevertheless be liberals.

Third, Burtt argues pragmatically that because citizens of faith contribute a beneficial ethos to the liberal polity, we should not threaten religious faith and the beneficial ethos it promotes before it has fully developed. I believe, however, that we should also want citizens who embrace faith and the duties that flow from it as self-constitutive to do so self-consciously, as the result of critical reflection. Because we cannot have it both ways—faith is either self-conscious or not—I fear that we must take the chance that some who would have affirmed and maintained their faith if they had not been required to reflect on it will indeed lose it if they must reflect on it self-consciously. But if we welcome citizens of faith as beneficial to the liberal polity, as liberals we should want them to live their lives from the inside, to embrace faith because of its centrality to them as individuals, rather than because this embrace helps to sustain the polity. Burtt's point that accommodation may keep students in public education who might otherwise depart for totally sectarian educational settings is an incisive one. I still believe, however, that even at this risk, public educational programs must commit to development of the capacity for critical reflection if they are not to risk "selling out." Although parents should have wide latitude in transmitting their values, Richard Arneson and Ian Shapiro suggest that "to deny the moral appropriateness of requiring all guardians to promote in their charges the disposition to critical reasoning and the skills needed to practice it, it would seem that one must deny that an individual of normal potential competence is likely to benefit from such exercise of critical reasoning skills."[79]

Fourth, Burtt's modified principle of parental deference does have the virtue of focusing on children's needs over parents' conceptions of the good life. But if the principle measures the legitimacy of adult authority by the "ability and willingness to meet children's developmental needs, broadly conceived,"[80] this yardstick still allows for a good deal of disagreement over the definition of these needs. Arneson and Shapiro, as we have just seen, classify training in the capacity to engage in critical reasoning as a developmental need; Burtt of course does not. Specifically, I believe that the state should support students against their parents not only in their desire to participate in required courses but also in their desire to use the standard textbooks over alternatives. I would support the state in most instances, even when parents and students are in agreement, if I believed, on a case-by-case basis, that not only basic literacy or the instantiation of constitutional principles was at stake but also the capacity to engage in critical reflection. Burtt's distinction between the presence and absence of constitutional affirmations is a questionable one, in my estimation, because of the existence of differing interpretations of what is called for by the Constitution. Many would argue that the Fourteenth Amendment's equal protection clause, for example, applies to sex discrimination on the basis of legislation and its judicial interpretations. In my view, the modified principle of parental deference is not modified *enough* if it allows parents to shield their daughters from the questioning of sex roles. Such segregation does not meet girls' developmental needs as I conceive them, even if they as women "will make decent, law-abiding citizens."

In sum, I would not defer to requests for accommodation that may foreclose the possibility of critical reflection on one's projects and goals. The difference between *Mozert* and *Sherbert*, in my opinion, is that in *Sherbert* the contested burden on the performance of religious obligation, foregoing unemployment compensation if one rejected a job offer that interfered with Sabbath observance, fell on an activity that carried only religious significance. That is, the decision accommodated an activity, Sabbath observance, that had no intrinsic civil consequences. In *Mozert*, however, the burden was on an activity, shielding children from exposure to other ways of life, that did have repercussions of civil injury and benefit, in Locke's terms. That is, the accommodation requested by the *Mozert* parents does have a bearing on children's capacities for personal autonomy and civic competence. In cases like *Yoder* and *Mozert*, it is admittedly difficult to distinguish the religious and political dimensions from one another. But I am convinced by this very difficulty that the development of the capacity for rational deliberation and critical reflection is crucial, as it is through the use of these capacities that we decide questions of civil injury and benefit, separating out to the extent possible the political dimensions of an issue from the religious.

By championing the development of the capacity for autonomy, especially in a way that requires sympathetic and imaginative engagement with other ways of life, I realize that I am foreclosing the possibility of some kinds of good lives, those that rely on uncritical acceptance of values one has been taught. I may appear to be doing so, additionally, for one of the same reasons I criticize in Burtt: because this sustains the health of the liberal democratic polity. I have consistently maintained, however, that even the liberal polity cannot remain legally, culturally, religiously, sexually, and now educationally neutral, devoid of determinate principles and commitments. Where it appears neutral, this apparent neutrality serves to maximize particular values, even when this result is unintentional. The liberal polity appears to me to hold particularly strong claims to the legitimacy of autonomy-based neutrality, a nonneutrality that values the development of the capacity to engage in rational deliberation and critical reflection. And if, as Strike and Burtt maintain, most traditions do include a degree of critical reasoning, then they should not fear a fuller development of this capacity.

Moreover, as I have explained, inculcation of the capacity for autonomy at the second-order level increases the chances that citizens will want to engage in the practice of autonomy at the first-order level, but it does not compel them to do so. They may in fact utilize the capacity to examine their assumptions and then reaffirm their original religious, philosophical, or moral beliefs. I grant that they will now engage in this reaffirmation on a conscious rather than on an unconscious level, but I do not see any way around this problem without relinquishing altogether the value of the capacity for autonomy at the second-order level.

Finally, although I believe that a developed capacity to engage in rational deliberation and critical reflection will indeed promote a civic competence that contributes to the health of the liberal polity, my primary concern is neither political stability nor the predominance of "decent, law-abiding citizens." Critical reflection promotes criticism and questioning of the status quo, because we may be prompted to examine and question our current projects and goals, collectively as well as individually. My primary concern is that of enabling the individual citizen of the liberal polity to flourish *as an individual* in this context. The critical reflection that contributes to collective self-rule also contributes to individual self-rule;[81] the capacity for collective choice is also the capacity for individual choice.

The Uses of Critical Reflection

I have argued that in a liberal polity, the manner in which we hold our religious, philosophical, and moral beliefs should be such as to admit that alternative viewpoints and ways of life are matters of opinion, the correctness of which is contestable. Although I have applied this argument primarily to adherents of belief systems outside the mainstream, I believe that this injunction also applies to us who willingly embrace the beliefs and practices of liberals. As we have seen, Macedo suggests that our "transformative constitutionalism" tends to extend our critical thinking about public affairs to religious matters as well, diminishes the centrality of religious convictions in tension with liberal democratic values, and rightly marginalizes those who refuse to compartmentalize their comprehensive beliefs.[82] Although heavy religious burdens should be accommodated, he suggests, when they are "imposed on people for the sake of trivial public purposes . . . we should do so from a perspective that recognizes the supreme political importance of constituting diversity for liberal ends."[83] And although we should properly regret a transformation that swept away all communities that function as critical alternatives, "we should, however, assess worries such as these at retail, not wholesale. The extinction of many, if not all, of the communities that pose truly radical alternatives to liberal democratic political principles is to be welcomed."[84]

I obviously agree with Macedo's emphasis on the centrality of the developed capacity for rational deliberation and critical reflection. I agree that collectively "*we* must decide which communities are accommodated, and there is nothing wrong with deciding—so far as we can—on the basis of the best reasons that are available, with due confidence in the worth of preserving and protecting liberal institutions" (73). I am uncomfortable, however, with the adversarial tone of Macedo's arguments and conclusions. When he states that our concern with preserving a range of alternatives should be "at retail, not wholesale," he seems to imply that we should save our worries for the first-order level of people's actual choices, rather than fearing that our efforts to structure preference formation at the second-order level will unduly circumscribe the range of options. But this suggestion seems slightly disingenuous. If "successful constitutional institutions must . . . shape the way that people use their freedom and shape *people* to help ensure that freedom is what they want" (58), the structuring of preference formation at the second-order level will already have taken place "at wholesale," and concern about the narrowed range of options at the first-order level, or "at retail," will be too late. In other words, if we dislike the range of merchandise in the retail store, we may wish we had asked the merchant to pressure the wholesaler, who might then have stocked the warehouse differently.

To put this another way, from the second-order perspective I want people to want freedom at the first-order level as much as Macedo does. I welcome the likelihood that the development of the capacity for autonomy at the second-order level will predispose them to the practice of autonomy at the first-order level. Simultaneously, however, I think this same capacity for critical reflection enables us not only to distance ourselves from commitments that might otherwise be constitutive of our identities but also to distance ourselves from this very ability to maintain distance. One result of critical reflection may be a life that draws regularly on this capacity for reflection, yet another may be a way of life that renounces the exercise of this capacity in favor of the performance of duties in obedience to the tenets of a religious, philosophical, or moral belief system. We can autonomously turn our backs on the practice of autonomy, and I respect this choice, whether it represents the selection of new projects and goals or the reaffirmation of prior ones.

Moreover, although I agree with Macedo that the "we" who are citizens of the liberal polity must decide collectively which communities should be accommodated, we who decide are not and must not think of ourselves as a monolithic entity or fortification, the ramparts of which must be guarded against "them." Liberalism demands hard work of citizens in a liberal polity. But it makes demands on all of us, not simply on those who liberals think are illiberal. This means that we must recognize the particularity of our own moral stance, even when we believe that this stance is superior. Education that inculcates the capacity for critical reflection not only enables us to identify, choose, or affirm particular projects and goals as our own. By encouraging us in imaginative engagement with other ways of life, it should also enable us to understand ourselves as *"autonomy valuers"* and to recognize the strengths and weaknesses of that commitment. Otherwise, we are in danger of being unreflective about the process of critical reflection itself.[85]

Although humility, for instance, is a virtue within Western society that betokens an accurate assessment of oneself and one's talents and is not inconsistent with personal achievement or ambition, for the Amish, on the contrary, concern about accurate self-assessment itself belies the ideal of humility. Emphasis on accurate self-assessment betokens, on this view, an inappropriate self-centeredness. From learning about the Amish, then, we learn that although we are people for whom accurate self-assessment is a morally legitimate aim, this is only a partial image of humility, or of what humility might mean. Because the humility of the Amish need not stem from oppression, we can come to appreciate the limitations of the moral categories within which we think. Even if we disagree with their views on education, rather than clinging to a position of grudging toleration, we may come to perceive ourselves as people who overemphasize self-assessment and self-understanding (198–200).

To put this differently, we think of ourselves as individuals whose particular experiences constitute a narrative, which told from one perspective possesses a certain unity. But we must also recognize the contingent character of any particular narrative and the fact that its unity results from the way we have constructed it. Narrative imagination requires the possibility of commitment to different ideals from those to which one is committed, or of giving different narrative readings to the same series of life events. In the context of narrative imagination, rationality can be defined by the capacity to engage in critical reflection on our projects and goals and on the way we pursue them. Because we may affirm both particularistic ideals and also their revocability, in a liberal polity we must examine our particular desires critically.[86]

Instead of maintaining the adversarial position implied by Macedo's stance, then, narrative imagination impels us to understand how others may be constituted by sorts of values and ideals other than those that animate us. We may even understand how we ourselves might hold different values and ideals if we interpreted our own life events within an alternative narrative structure. This stance, by promoting sympathetic and imaginative engagement with other ways of life, broadens our openness to diversity. Yet it also enhances our capacities for autonomy by allowing us to imagine different ways of living life from the inside and promoting our ability to question, examine, deliberate, and possibly to revise our conceptions of the good, both individually and collectively. An understanding of the contingent character of any particular narrative should be sought not only by those whose liberal credentials seem questionable but also by the liberals doing the questioning.

Notes

I: NEUTRALITY, AUTONOMY, AND DIVERSITY

1. John Kekes, *The Morality of Pluralism* (Princeton, NJ: Princeton University Press, 1993), 27–28.

2. Jennifer Nedelsky, "Reconceiving Autonomy: Sources, Thoughts and Possibilities," *Yale Journal of Law and Feminism* 1 (1989): 21.

3. Rogers M. Smith, *Liberalism and American Constitutional Law* (Cambridge, MA: Harvard University Press, 1985), 29; see 14–17 and 44.

4. William A. Galston, *Liberal Purposes: Goods, Virtues, and Diversity in the Liberal State* (New York: Cambridge University Press, 1991), 251; see also 248.

5. Smith, *Liberalism and American Constitutional Law*, 93.

6. Ronald Dworkin, *A Matter of Principle* (Cambridge, MA: Harvard University Press, 1985), 191. Another exponent of this sort of view would be John Rawls, *A Theory of Justice* (Cambridge, MA: Belknap Press of Harvard University Press, 1971).

7. Ronald Dworkin, *Taking Rights Seriously* (Cambridge, MA: Harvard University Press, 1978), 272.

8. Galston, *Liberal Purposes*, 93; see 82–97, 116, and 180.

9. John Rawls, *Political Liberalism* (New York: Columbia University Press, 1993), 13; see 11–15. In the earlier *A Theory of Justice*, Rawls espouses a similar morality with less attention to consensus beyond the principles of justice.

10. Galston, *Liberal Purposes*, 82.

11. Susan Mendus, *Toleration and the Limits of Liberalism* (Atlantic Highlands, NJ: Humanities Press International, 1989), 53.

12. Michael Sandel, "The Procedural Republic and the Unencumbered Self," *Political Theory* 12 (February 1984): 82; see also 86, and Michael Sandel, *Liberalism and the Limits of Justice* (New York: Cambridge University Press, 1982), 10–11 and 62.

13. John Christman, ed., *The Inner Citadel: Essays on Individual Autonomy* (New York: Oxford University Press, 1989), 9.

14. Joel Feinberg, *Harm to Self* (New York: Oxford University Press, 1986), 33; see also 28 and 32.

15. Jon Elster, "Sour Grapes—Utilitarianism and the Genesis of Wants," in *The Inner Citadel: Essays on Individual Autonomy*, ed. John Christman (New York: Oxford University Press, 1989), 170–188.

16. Gerald Dworkin, "The Concept of Autonomy," in *The Inner Citadel: Essays on*

Individual Autonomy, ed. John Christman (New York: Oxford University Press, 1989), 60; see 60–61, and Robert Young, *Personal Autonomy* (London: Croom Helm, 1986), 72–73 and 78.

17. Thomas E. Hill Jr., "The Kantian Conception of Autonomy," in *The Inner Citadel: Essays on Individual Autonomy*, ed. John Christman (New York: Oxford University Press, 1989), 101.

18. Feinberg, *Harm to Self*, 33.

19. Sandel, *Liberalism and the Limits of Justice*, 58; see 57–58.

20. Feinberg, *Harm to Self*, 33.

21. Harry G. Frankfurt, *The Importance of What We Care About: Philosophical Essays* (New York: Cambridge University Press, 1988), 5. See 3–5, 24–25, 56–57, 75, and 95.

22. Smith, *Liberalism and American Constitutional Law*, 28.

23. Will Kymlicka, *Liberalism, Community and Culture* (Oxford: Clarendon Press, 1991), 10.

24. Frankfurt, *The Importance of What We Care About*, 16; see 12, 16–22, 41, and 82–88.

25. Alasdair MacIntyre, *After Virtue* (Notre Dame, IN: University of Notre Dame Press, 1981), 204; see 190–209.

26. Mendus, *Toleration and the Limits of Liberalism*, 63. See 59–68, 97–108, 11, 144, and 156.

27. Galston, *Liberal Purposes*, 153; see also 273–278.

28. Rawls, *Political Liberalism*, 74; see also 19.

29. Galston, *Liberal Purposes*, 129.

30. Kymlicka, *Liberalism, Community and Culture*, 33.

31. Brian Barry, *Justice as Impartiality* (Oxford: Clarendon Press, 1995), 133.

32. Galston, *Liberal Purposes*, 216; see also 153–154, 231–237, and 296–301.

33. Joseph Raz, *The Morality of Freedom* (Oxford: Clarendon Press, 1986), 391; see 390–395. Although my emphasis on the development of the capacity for autonomy in some ways resembles Raz's liberal perfectionism, in other ways it differs. Like Raz, I believe that the liberal polity can and should promote the availability of a wide range of options and the development of the mental abilities requisite for an autonomous life (425). On the other hand, just as Kymlicka sees freedom not as an end in itself but as a precondition for pursuing what one values, I do not view autonomy as an end in itself but as a framework within which one may select projects and goals that may not always themselves embody the practice of autonomy. Moreover, whereas Raz calls for the creation of conditions for autonomy through perfectionistic policies (426), I question the idea that the pursuit of conditions for the development of the capacity for autonomy is any more perfectionistic than is pursuit of conditions for the flourishing of diversity. That is, if establishing a range of desirable outcomes is by definition perfectionistic, then almost any political entity is perfectionistic, and the perfectionistic label lacks meaning.

34. David McCabe, "Outline for a Defense of an Unreconstructed Liberalism," *Journal of Social Philosophy* 29 (spring 1998): 66–67. Thomas Hurka criticizes this type of

view in his critique of Kymlicka's ideal of state neutrality, where neutrality is grounded on the value of self-endorsement. The motivation for an activity, asserts Hurka, does not determine its value. But Hurka mistakenly believes that Kymlicka thinks "each person's ultimate interest . . . is in living a life that meets objective standards of goodness," when Kymlicka holds that individuals must decide for *themselves* what gives value to life, apart from any objective definition (Thomas Hurka, "Indirect Perfectionism: Kymlicka on Liberal Neutrality," *Journal of Political Philosophy* 3 [March 1995]: 38; see entirety, 36–57).

35. Galston, *Liberal Purposes*, 329, n. 12.

36. J. Donald Moon, *Constructing Community: Moral Pluralism and Tragic Conflict* (Princeton, NJ: Princeton University Press, 1993), 219.

37. Charles Larmore, *Patterns of Moral Complexity* (New York: Cambridge University Press, 1987), 60.

38. Rawls, *Political Liberalism*, 64, n. 19; see also xvi–xvii and 185.

39. Patrick Neal, *Liberalism and Its Discontents* (New York: New York University Press, 1997), 37–38; see 34–47.

40. Michael Sandel, *Liberalism and the Limits of Justice*. See also Charles Taylor, "Cross-Purposes: The Liberal-Communitarian Debate," in *Liberalism and the Moral Life*, ed. Nancy L. Rosenblum (Cambridge, MA: Harvard University Press, 1989), 159–182.

41. Neal, *Liberalism and Its Discontents*, 40–41.

42. Pratap Bhanu Mehta, review of *Isaiah Berlin*, by John Gray (Princeton, NJ: Princeton University Press, 1996), in *American Political Science Review* 91 (September 1997): 723. See also William Lund, "Egalitarian Liberalism and the Fact of Pluralism," *Journal of Social Philosophy* 27 (winter 1996): 61–80.

43. Rawls, *Political Liberalism*, 186; see 186–187 and 33–34.

44. Bonnie Honig, *Political Theory and the Displacement of Politics* (Ithaca, NY: Cornell University Press, 1993), 135; see 131–156. See also Neal, *Liberalism and Its Discontents*, 122–125; Sheldon S. Wolin, "The Liberal/Democratic Divide: On Rawls's *Political Liberalism*," *Political Theory* 24 (February 1996): 97–119; and Ed Wingenbach, "Unjust Context: The Priority of Stability in Rawls's Contextualized Theory of Justice," *American Journal of Political Science* 43 (January 1999): 213–232.

45. Rawls, *Political Liberalism*, 161.

46. Michael Sandel, *Democracy's Discontent: America in Search of a Public Philosophy* (Cambridge, MA: Belknap Press of Harvard University Press, 1996), 20; see 17–24, and Michael Sandel, "Political Liberalism," review of Rawls, *Political Liberalism*, in *Harvard Law Review* 107 (1994): 1777–1782.

47. Galston, *Liberal Purposes*, 274; see 273–274.

48. Sandel, "Political Liberalism," 1786; see 1782–1789.

49. Sandel, *Liberalism and the Limits of Justice*, 57–64, 22, and 121–122.

50. Honig, *Political Theory and the Displacement of Politics*, 171. See 163–174 and 176–186.

51. Sandel, *Liberalism and the Limits of Justice*, 63.

52. Diana T. Meyers, *Self, Society, and Personal Choice* (New York: Columbia University Press, 1989), 94; see 92–97.

53. Honig, *Political Theory and Displacement of Politics*, 194.

54. Neal, *Liberalism and Its Discontents*, 46; see 43–47.

55. Mark E. Warren, "What Should We Expect from More Democracy?" *Political Theory* 24 (May 1996): 263.

56. Charles Taylor, *Multiculturalism and the "Politics of Recognition"* (Princeton, NJ: Princeton University Press, 1992), 32.

57. William E. Connolly, *Identity/Difference: Democratic Negotiations of Political Paradox* (Ithaca, NJ: Cornell University Press, 1991), 64; see 65–66 and 87–94.

58. Thomas Bridges, *The Culture of Citizenship: Inventing Postmodern Civic Culture* (Albany: State University of New York Press, 1994), 39. See 10, 35, 86, and 120 on the conflict between particularistic and civic identities, and 157, 165, 215, 234, and 264 on the grounding of civic freedom and equality in particularistic traditions.

59. Brian Walker, "John Rawls, Mikhail Bakhtin, and the Praxis of Toleration," *Political Theory* 23 (February 1995): 120; see also 109, 116–118, and James Bohman, "Public Reason and Cultural Pluralism," *Political Theory* 23 (May 1995): 269–270.

60. Melissa Williams, "Justice Toward Groups: Political Not Juridical," *Political Theory* 23 (February 1995): 69.

61. Neal, *Liberalism and Its Discontents*, 124.

62. Smith, *Liberalism and American Constitutional Law*, 200. See also 198–225, especially 223–225.

63. Warren, "What Should We Expect from More Democracy?" 257.

64. Bridges, *The Culture of Citizenship*, 173; see 168–189.

65. Connolly, *Identity/Difference*, 179.

2: NATIONAL CITIZENSHIP

1. Alexander M. Bickel, *The Morality of Consent* (New Haven: Yale University Press, 1975), 54.

2. Michael Walzer, *Spheres of Justice: A Defense of Pluralism and Equality* (New York: Basic Books, 1983), 62.

3. Yael Tamir, *Liberal Nationalism* (Princeton, NJ: Princeton University Press, 1993), 66; see 63–69.

4. Ibid., 94; see 63, 83–86, and 96–102.

5. Joseph H. Carens, "Aliens and Citizens: The Case for Open Borders," *Review of Politics* 49 (spring 1987): 253; see 252–254 and 255–264.

6. Frederick G. Whelan, "Citizenship and Freedom of Movement: An Open Admission Policy," in *Open Borders? Closed Societies? The Ethical and Political Issues*, ed. Mark Gibney (Westport, CT: Greenwood Press, 1988), 17; see also 26.

7. Charles Taylor, "Cross-Purposes: The Liberal-Communitarian Debate," in *Liberalism and the Moral Life,* ed. Nancy L. Rosenblum (Cambridge, MA: Harvard University Press, 1989), 166; see 166–170.

8. Michael Sandel, *Liberalism and the Limits of Justice* (New York: Cambridge University Press, 1982), 150.

9. Taylor, "Cross-Purposes," 159–163.

10. Amy Gutmann, *Liberal Equality* (New York: Cambridge University Press, 1980), 192.

11. Walzer, *Spheres of Justice,* 8.

12. Will Kymlicka, *Liberalism, Community and Culture* (Oxford: Clarendon Press, 1991), 50–51.

13. Alasdair MacIntyre, *After Virtue* (Notre Dame, IN: University of Notre Dame Press, 1981), 205.

14. Sandel, *Liberalism and the Limits of Justice,* 146.

15. Sanford Levinson, *Constitutional Faith* (Princeton, NJ: Princeton University Press, 1988), 185; see 180–194.

16. Whelan, "Citizenship and Freedom of Movement," 28–29.

17. J. Donald Moon, *Constructing Community: Moral Pluralism and Tragic Conflict* (Princeton, NJ: Princeton University Press, 1993), 46; see 8–9, 35, and 45–46.

18. Elizabeth Hull, *Without Justice for All: The Constitutional Rights of Aliens* (Westport, CT: Greenwood Press, 1985), 59.

19. Michael J. Perry, "Modern Equal Protection: A Conceptualization and Appraisal," *Columbia Law Review* 79 (October 1979): 1061; see 1061–1062.

20. *Graham v. Richardson,* 403 U.S. 365 (1971), at 372.

21. Peter H. Schuck and Rogers M. Smith, *Citizenship Without Consent: Illegal Aliens in the American Polity* (New Haven: Yale University Press, 1985), 107.

22. *Sugarman v. Dougall,* 413 U.S. 634 (1973), at 643.

23. *In re Griffiths,* 413 U.S. 717 (1973), at 720, citing *Truax v. Raich,* 239 U.S. 33 (1915), at 41.

24. *Foley v. Connelie,* 435 U.S. 291 (1978), at 296.

25. *Ambach v. Norwick,* 441 U.S. 68 (1979), at 70.

26. *Cabell v. Chavez-Salido,* 454 U.S. 432 (1982), at 438.

27. Rogers M. Smith, *Liberalism and American Constitutional Law* (Cambridge, MA: Harvard University Press, 1985), 81, citing *United States v. Carolene Products Co.,* 304 U.S. 144 (1938), at 152–153, n. 4.

28. *Ambach v. Norwick,* at 73–74.

29. *Cabell v. Chavez-Salido,* at 442.

30. *Hampton v. Mow Sung Wong,* 426 U.S. 88 (1976), at 102.

31. *Engineering Board of Engineers, Architects and Surveyors et al. v. Flores de Otero,* 426 U.S. 572 (1976), at 605.

32. *Bernal v. Fainter,* 467 U.S. 216 (1984), at 225; see 219–221 and 225–226.

33. *Nyquist v. Mauclet,* 432 U.S. 1 (1977), at 11; see 10–11.

34. *Plyler v. Doe,* 457 U.S. 202 (1982), at 221; see also 226, 230, and 234.

35. *Mathews v. Diaz,* 426 U.S. 67 (1976), 80; see 78.

36. See dissents in *Sugarman, Griffiths, Foley, Ambach, Cabell,* and *Bernal.*

37. Hull, *Without Justice for All,* 92.

38. Peter H. Schuck, *Citizens, Strangers, and In-Betweens: Essays on Immigration and Citizenship* (Boulder, CO: Westview Press, 1998), 55–56. In an earlier case, the Court had upheld a California statute barring the employment of undocumented aliens, and although the harm to children stemming from their parents' unemployment might be less direct than a denial of educational benefits, "both harms are eminently foreseeable" (379, n. 307, citing *De Canas v. Bica,* 424 U.S. 351 [1976]). On *Plyler* generally, see 54–57, 68, 72, and 150–154.

39. *Ambach v. Norwick,* 75; see 71–72.

40. Gerald M. Rosberg, "Aliens and Equal Protection: Why Not the Right to Vote?" *Michigan Law Review* 75 (1977): 1128–1129.

41. Celia M. Dugger, "U.S. Says Mental Impairments Might Be a Bar to Citizenship," *New York Times* (March 19, 1997), A1, A12.

42. Schuck and Smith, *Citizenship Without Consent,* 40; see also 4, 36–41, and 116–140.

43. Joseph S. Carens, "Who Belongs? Theoretical and Legal Questions about Birthright Citizenship," review of Schuck and Smith, *Citizenship Without Consent,* in *University of Toronto Law Review* 37 (1987): 423; see 423–426.

44. Schuck and Smith, *Citizenship Without Consent,* 99.

45. T. H. Marshall, *Class, Citizenship, and Social Development* (Garden City, NY: Doubleday, 1964), 84. See also Robert E. Goodin, *Reasons for Welfare: The Political Theory of the Welfare State* (Princeton, NJ: Princeton University Press, 1988), 84.

46. J. Donald Moon, "The Moral Basis of the Democratic Welfare State," in *Democracy and the Welfare State,* ed. Amy Gutmann (Princeton, NJ: Princeton University Press, 1988), 43.

47. *Roberts v. United States Jaycees,* 468 U.S. 609 (1984), 627–628; see also 623 and 626.

48. *Cabell v. Chavez-Salido,* 447.

49. *Foley v. Connelie,* 296.

50. Nancy L. Rosenblum, *Another Liberalism: Romanticism and the Reconstruction of Liberal Thought* (Cambridge, MA: Harvard University Press, 1987), 157. See also Michael Walzer, *Obligations: Essays on Disobedience, War, and Citizenship* (Cambridge, MA: Harvard University Press, 1970), 218–225.

51. Walzer, *Spheres of Justice,* 313.

52. Rosenblum, *Another Liberalism,* 166; see also 168–172.

53. Walzer, *Spheres of Justice,* 83.

54. Rosenblum, *Another Liberalism,* 172; see 172–173.

55. John A. Scanlan and O. T. Kent, "The Force of Moral Arguments for a Just Immigration Policy in a Hobbesian Universe: The Contemporary American Exam-

ple," in *Open Borders? Closed Societies? The Ethical and Political Issues,* ed. Mark Gibney (Westport, CT: Greenwood Press, 1988), 86; see also 78.

56. Rosenblum, *Another Liberalism,* 178.

57. Walzer, *Spheres of Justice,* 55.

58. Michael Walzer, *Interpretation and Social Criticism* (Cambridge, MA: Harvard University Press, 1987), 23.

59. Michael Lind, "Liberals Duck Immigration Debate," *New York Times* (September 7, 1995), A15. See also Michael Lind, *The Next American Nation: The New Nationalism and the Fourth American Revolution* (New York: Free Press of Simon and Schuster, 1995), 319–326.

60. Robert Wright, "Star Search," *New Republic* 214 (January 22, 1996): 6.

61. Roger Waldinger, "The Jobs Immigrants Take," *New York Times* (March 11, 1996), A11.

62. Robert Pear, "Academy Report Says Immigration Benefits the U.S.," *New York Times* (May 18, 1997), A1 and A12.

63. Deborah Sontag, "Illegal Aliens Put Uneven Load on States Study Says," *New York Times* (September 15, 1994), A8.

64. Jorge Oclander, "Immigrants in State Pay Their Ways Study Says," *Chicago Sun-Times* (May 16, 1996), 57; George Ramos, "Immigrants Aid California," *Chicago Sun-Times* (January 16, 1996), 34.

65. Richard Reeves, "What a Difference," *Peoria Journal-Star* (January 24, 1997), A4.

66. The Urban Institute, "Special Section on Immigration," *Policy and Research Report* 21 (winter–spring 1991): 11–13.

67. Dan Carney, "Law Restricts Illegal Immigration," *Congressional Quarterly Weekly Report* 54 (November 16, 1996): 3287–3289.

68. Jeffrey L. Katz, "Welfare Overhaul Law," *Congressional Quarterly Weekly Report* 54 (September 21, 1996): 2701–2702. See also Schuck, *Citizens, Strangers, and In-Betweens,* 193–202.

69. Schuck, *Citizens, Strangers, and In-Betweens,* 200.

70. Sam Howe Verhovek, "Legal Immigrants Seek Citizenship in Record Numbers," *New York Times* (April 2, 1995), A1 and A13.

71. Schuck, *Citizens, Strangers, and In-Betweens,* 149–160.

72. Gregory Rodriguez, "The Browning of California," *New Republic* 215 (September 2, 1996): 18.

73. Sam Howe Verhovek, "Immigrants' Anxieties Spur a Surge in Naturalizations," *New York Times* (September 13, 1996), A1 and A18.

74. Thurston Clarke, "Cultural Capital," review of Thomas Sowell, *Migrations and Cultures: A World View* (New York: Basic Books, 1996), in *New York Times Book Review* (June 2, 1996), 9.

75. "Becoming American, Bad Habits and All," *New York Times* (February 23, 1994), B12.

76. Peter Schuck, "On the Border," letter, *New Republic* 214 (May 6, 1996): 5. See also Peter H. Schuck and Rogers M. Smith, "G.O.P. Plank Errs on Immigrant Citizenship," letter, *New York Times* (August 12, 1996), A14. But see also Schuck, *Citizens, Strangers, and In-Betweens,* 170–171, 193, and 212–216, for an argument against the moral weight of a consideration of immigrant children's diminished life prospects.

77. Stephen Chapman, "Birth Control: Another Assault on Immigration," *New Republic* 214 (April 8, 1996): 14; see 11–12, 14. In 1999, Germany finally adopted a policy granting birthright citizenship to the children of guest workers born on German soil, reversing the long-standing policy that immigrants and their descendents, even if born in Germany, could never acquire citizenship ("Germany's Immigration Debate," *New York Times* [Aug. 12, 2000], A26).

78. Walzer, *Spheres of Justice,* 62.

3: CULTURAL PARTICULARISM

1. Yael Tamir, *Liberal Nationalism* (Princeton, NJ: Princeton University Press, 1993), 163.

2. Deborah Fitzmaurice, "Autonomy as a Good: Liberalism, Autonomy, and Toleration," *Journal of Political Philosophy* 1 (March 1993): 6.

3. Maeve Cooke, "Authenticity and Autonomy: Taylor, Habermas, and the Politics of Recognition," *Political Theory* 25 (April 1997): 269.

4. Charles Taylor, *Multiculturalism and "The Politics of Recognition"* (Princeton, NJ: Princeton University Press, 1992), 25.

5. Tamir, *Liberal Nationalism,* 33.

6. Thomas Bridges, *The Culture of Citizenship: Inventing Postmodern Civic Culture* (Albany: State University of New York Press, 1994), 157; see 35, 39, 53–57, 156–157, and 202.

7. Will Kymlicka, *Liberalism, Community and Culture* (Oxford: Clarendon Press, 1991), 192; see also 169–172.

8. Tamir, *Liberal Nationalism,* 7; see also 20–32.

9. Kymlicka, *Liberalism, Community and Culture,* 165; see 164–165.

10. James W. Nickel, "The Value of Cultural Belonging: Expanding Kymlicka's Theory," *Dialogue* 33 (1994): 635.

11. John Tomasi, "Kymlicka, Liberalism, and Respect for Cultural Minorities," *Ethics* 105 (April 1995): 584.

12. Adam Smith, *The Theory of Moral Sentiments,* ed. D. D. Raphael and A. L. Macfie (Oxford: Clarendon Press, 1976), 110.

13. Will Kymlicka, *Multicultural Citizenship: A Liberal Theory of Minority Rights* (Oxford: Clarendon Press, 1995), 10–11; see 14–15, 26–33, 45–48, and 58–59.

14. Kymlicka, *Liberalism, Community and Culture,* 127; see also 59–61, 87–89, 165–172, 185–193, and 237–242.

15. Will Kymlicka, "The Rights of Minority Cultures: Reply to Kukathas," *Political*

Theory 20 (February 1992): 142. See also Kymlicka, *Multicultural Citizenship,* 104 and 113.

16. Kymlicka, *Liberalism, Community and Culture,* 197; see also Kymlicka, *Multicultural Citizenship,* 152–155 and 125.

17. Kymlicka, *Liberalism, Community and Culture,* 50–51; see 47–53.

18. Amélie Oksenberg Rorty, "The Hidden Politics of Cultural Identification," *Political Theory* 22 (February 1994): 153; see 152–159.

19. Chandran Kukathas, "Are There Any Cultural Rights?" *Political Theory* 20 (February 1992): 117–118.

20. Kymlicka, "The Rights of Minority Cultures," 142.

21. Kukathas, "Are There Any Cultural Rights?" 127.

22. Chandran Kukathas, "Cultural Rights Again: A Rejoinder to Kymlicka," *Political Theory* 20 (November 1992): 680.

23. Kymlicka, *Liberalism, Community and Culture,* 186–187.

24. Kymlicka, *Multicultural Citizenship,* 126.

25. J. Donald Moon, *Constructing Community: Moral Pluralism and Tragic Conflict* (Princeton, NJ: Princeton University Press, 1993), 188; see 178–189, 8–9, 35, 42–43, 45–46, and 100. See also Jeff Spinner, *The Boundaries of Citizenship: Race, Ethnicity, and Nationality in the Liberal State* (Baltimore: Johns Hopkins University Press, 1994), 135–136.

26. Tamir, *Liberal Nationalism,* 37; see also 7–8.

27. Compare Kymlicka, *Liberalism, Community and Culture,* 189–190 and 237–242.

28. Spinner, *The Boundaries of Citizenship,* 30.

29. See ibid., 96–99 and 103–104.

30. See also ibid., 62, 66–73, 149, and Tamir, *Liberal Nationalism,* 37 and 48–53.

31. See also Spinner, *The Boundaries of Citizenship,* 183–188, especially 186.

32. Bernard Yack, "Reconciling Liberalism and Nationalism," *Political Theory* 23 (February 1995): 171–172.

33. Tamir, *Liberal Nationalism,* 127; see 124–130 and 160–162.

34. Geoffrey Brahm Levey, "Equality, Autonomy, and Cultural Rights," *Political Theory* 25 (April 1997): 227; see also 232–238, especially 233.

35. Chandran Kukathas, "Liberalism, Communitarianism, and Political Community," *Social Philosophy and Policy* 13 (1996): 84–85; see also 86–90 and 92–98.

36. Chandran Kukathas, "Cultural Toleration," in *Ethnicity and Group Rights: Nomos XXXIX,* ed. Ian Shapiro and Will Kymlicka (New York: New York University Press, 1997), 78; see 72–83.

37. Kukathas, "Are There Any Cultural Rights?" 120–124.

38. Kymlicka, "The Rights of Minority Cultures," 144–145, and Kymlicka, *Multicultural Citizenship,* 163–170; but compare with the latter, 94.

39. Kymlicka, *Multicultural Citizenship,* 168.

40. Kukathas, "Are There Any Cultural Rights?" 133.

41. Michael Walzer, "Response to Kukathas," in *Ethnicity and Group Rights: Nomos*

XXXIX, ed. Ian Shapiro and Will Kymlicka (New York: New York University Press, 1997), 106; see 105–111.

42. John Rawls, *Political Liberalism* (New York: Columbia University Press, 1993), 186; see 185–187, 33–34, and Kymlicka, *Liberalism, Community and Culture*, 36–40.

43. Kymlicka, *Multicultural Citizenship*, 162; see 158–163. Also see Fitzmaurice, "Autonomy as a Good," 11. Fitzmaurice also believes that the principles of autonomy and equal respect are interdependent, as autonomy promotes dialogue that minimizes, even if it cannot eliminate, relationships of domination and subordination (14–16).

44. Kymlicka, *Liberalism, Community and Culture*, 175.

45. Tamir, *Liberal Nationalism*, 33.

46. Kymlicka, *Liberalism, Community and Culture*, 173.

47. Don Lenihan, "Liberalism and the Problem of Cultural Membership: A Critical Study of Kymlicka," *Canadian Journal of Law and Jurisprudence* 4 (July 1991): 415; see 415–419 and 402–406.

48. See also ibid., 419, and Tomasi, "Kymlicka, Liberalism, and Respect of Cultural Minorities," 586–595.

49. Allen Buchanan, "The Morality of Secession," in *The Rights of Minority Cultures*, ed. Will Kymlicka (New York: Oxford University Press, 1995), 357.

50. Alasdair MacIntyre, *Whose Justice? Which Rationality?* (Notre Dame, IN: University of Notre Dame Press, 1988), 100; see 12, 122, 125, and 143–145.

51. Kymlicka, *Multicultural Citizenship*, 121–122; see 116–123. Compare Tamir, *Liberal Nationalism*, 30–32.

52. Kymlicka, *Multicultural Citizenship*, 122–123. See also Lenihan, "Liberalism and the Problem of Cultural Membership," 415.

53. Ronald Dworkin, *A Matter of Principle* (Cambridge, MA: Harvard University Press, 1985), 202; see 229.

54. Jeremy Waldron, "Minority Cultures and the Cosmopolitan Alternative," in *The Rights of Minority Cultures*, ed. Will Kymlicka (New York: Oxford University Press, 1995), 103; see 99–105, and Joseph Raz, "Multiculturalism: A Liberal Perspective," *Dissent* (winter 1994): 77–79.

55. Kymlicka, *Multicultural Citizenship*, 104.

56. Michael Walzer, *Spheres of Justice: A Defense of Pluralism and Equality* (New York: Basic Books, 1983), 87; see also 8 and 314.

57. Kymlicka, *Liberalism, Community and Culture*, 195–200; Kymlicka, "The Rights of Minority Cultures," 140–146; and Kymlicka, *Multicultural Citizenship*, 152–155.

58. Kukathas, "Are There Any Cultural Rights?" 122; see 118–129.

59. Chandran Kukathas, "Freedom of Association and Liberty of Conscience" (paper presented at the annual meeting of the American Political Science Association, Chicago, August 1995), 10–11.

60. Kukathas, "Are There Any Cultural Rights?" 134; see 124–134.

61. A. John Simmons, "The Principle of Fair Play," *Readings in Social and Political Philosophy*, ed. Robert M. Stewart (New York: Oxford University Press, 1986), 76–77.

62. Leslie Green, "Internal Minorities and Their Rights," in *The Rights of Minority Cultures,* ed. Will Kymlicka (New York: Oxford University Press, 1995), 266; see 262–267.

63. Kymlicka, "The Rights of Minority Cultures," 143.

64. Yael Tamir, "Two Concepts of Multiculturalism," *Journal of Philosophy of Education (Society of Great Britain)* 29 (1995): 168; see 166–172. See also Tomasi, "Kymlicka, Liberalism, and Respect for Cultural Minorities," 595–603, and Richard C. Sinopoli, "Associational Freedom, Equality, and Rights Against the State," *Political Research Quarterly* 47 (December 1994): 891–908, especially 902–904.

65. David Johnston, *The Idea of a Liberal Theory: A Critique and Reconstruction* (Princeton, NJ: Princeton University Press, 1994), 75; see 69–79, 22–24, and 138.

66. Tamir, *Liberal Nationalism,* 73; on the contextual individual's role as both a situated and a choosing self, see 7.

67. Geoffrey Brahm Levey, "Liberalism and Cultural Toleration: The Ineluctability of Autonomy" (paper presented at the annual meeting of the American Political Science Association, Washington, DC, August 1997), 12.

68. Adeno Addis, "On Human Diversity and the Limits of Toleration," in *Ethnicity and Group Rights: Nomos XXXIX,* ed. Ian Shapiro and Will Kymlicka (New York: New York University Press, 1997), 149, n. 37.

69. Levey, "Liberalism and Cultural Toleration," 9; see also 7 and 9–10.

4: ETHNIC AND GENDER IDENTITY

1. Joseph S. Carens, "Immigration, Political Community, and the Transformation of Identity: Quebec's Immigration Politics in Critical Perspective," in *Is Quebec Nationalism Just? Perspectives from Anglophone Canada,* ed. Joseph S. Carens (Montreal, Quebec, and Kingston, Ontario: McGill-Queen's University Press, 1995), 50.

2. Will Kymlicka, *Multicultural Citizenship: A Liberal Theory of Minority Rights* (Oxford: Clarendon Press, 1995), 66; see 60–69, 78, 95–101, and 177–178.

3. Sherene Razack, "Collective Rights and Women: 'The Cold Game of Equality Staring,'" *Group Rights,* ed. Judith Baker (Toronto: University of Toronto Press, 1994), 70.

4. Yael Tamir, *Liberal Nationalism* (Princeton, NJ: Princeton University Press, 1993), 41; see 35–42. Compare Will Kymlicka, *Liberalism, Community and Culture* (Oxford: Clarendon Press, 1991), 36–40 and 114–121.

5. Kymlicka, *Multicultural Citizenship,* 169.

6. Jeff Spinner, *The Boundaries of Citizenship: Race, Ethnicity, and Nationality in the Liberal State* (Baltimore: Johns Hopkins University Press, 1994), 47; see 37–38, 45–48, and 185–186. On pressures for conformity, see 60–62, 171–175, and David Johnston, *The Idea of a Liberal Theory: A Critique and Reconstruction* (Princeton, NJ: Princeton University Press, 1994), 155–156. On the state's purported neutrality, see Spinner, *The Boundaries of Citizenship,* 10 and 79; Tamir, *Liberal Nationalism,* 141–143;

J. Donald Moon, *Constructing Community: Moral Pluralism and Tragic Conflict* (Princeton, NJ: Princeton University Press, 1993), 11 and 55–58; Charles Taylor, *Multiculturalism and "The Politics of Recognition"* (Princeton, NJ: Princeton University Press, 1992), 43–44; and Kymlicka, *Multicultural Citizenship*, 3–4.

7. Johnston, *The Idea of a Liberal Theory*, 155. See also Spinner, *The Boundaries of Citizenship*, 75, and Tamir, *Liberal Nationalism*, 53–56.

8. Spinner, *The Boundaries of Citizenship*, 51. See also 25–26, 29–32, 49–53, and Taylor, *Multiculturalism and "The Politics of Recognition,"* 80–81.

9. L. A. Kosman, "Being Properly Affected: Virtues and Feelings in Aristotle's Ethics," in *Essays on Aristotle's Ethics*, ed. Amélie Oksenberg Rorty (Berkeley: University of California Press, 1980), 112; see 106–113.

10. Alan Wolfe, "The Return of the Melting Pot," *New Republic* 203 (December 31, 1990): 30.

11. Roberto Rodriguez and Patrisia Gonzales, "Identity Issue Is Complex for Black Latinos," *Chicago Sun-Times* (February 6, 1995), 27.

12. Roberto Rodriguez and Patrisia Gonzales, "Mestizos Denied Their Indigenous Identities," *Chicago Sun-Times* (May 27, 1995), 13.

13. Donna Britt, "Company Line Can Bind 'Purists' to Silly Extremes," *Chicago Sun-Times* (April 10, 1994), 42.

14. Iris Marion Young, "Together in Difference: Transforming the Logic of Group Political Conflict," in *The Rights of Minority Cultures*, ed. Will Kymlicka (New York: Oxford University Press, 1995), 165; see 157–166, and Iris Marion Young, *Justice and the Politics of Difference* (Princeton, NJ: Princeton University Press, 1990), 156–191.

15. Kymlicka, *Multicultural Citizenship*, 145.

16. Michael Walzer, "Pluralism: A Political Perspective," in *The Rights of Minority Cultures*, ed. Will Kymlicka (New York: Oxford University Press, 1995), 149.

17. Michael J. Sandel, *Liberalism and the Limits of Justice* (New York: Cambridge University Press, 1982), 153.

18. Felicity Barringer, "Judge Nullifies Mandatory Use of English," *New York Times* (February 8, 1990), A1.

19. Linda Greenhouse, "Justices to Review Arizona's Law Making English Its Official Language," *New York Times* (March 26, 1996), A10, and Linda Greenhouse, "Appeal to Save English-Only Law Fails," *New York Times* (January 12, 1999), A16.

20. Seth Mydans, "Pressure for English-Only Job Rules Stirring a Sharp Debate Around U.S.," *New York Times* (August 8, 1990), A10.

21. David Foster, "English-Only Rules Spur Linguistic Battles," *Chicago Sun-Times* (September 20, 1992), 65.

22. Mirta Ojito, "Bias Suits Over English-Only Rules," *New York Times* (April 23, 1997), C22.

23. Sam Howe Verhovek, "Clash of Culture Tears City," *New York Times* (September 30, 1997), A10.

24. Mydans, "Pressure for English-Only Job Rules," A10.

25. Joseph H. Carens, "Liberalism, Justice, and Political Community: Theoretical Perspectives on Quebec's Liberal Nationalism," in *Is Quebec Nationalism Just? Perspectives from Anglophone Canada*, ed. Joseph H. Carens (Montreal, Quebec, and Kingston, Ontario: McGill-Queen's University Press, 1995), 9.

26. Taylor, *Multiculturalism and "The Politics of Recognition,"* 58–59.

27. Spinner, *The Boundaries of Citizenship*, 149; see 145–160. See also Tamir, *Liberal Nationalism*, 45; Taylor, *Multiculturalism and "The Politics of Recognition,"* 54–56; and Carens, "Immigration, Political Community, and the Transformation of Identity," 56–65.

28. Norma Claire Moruzzi, "A Problem with Headscarves: Contemporary Complexities of Political and Social Identity," *Political Theory* 22 (November 1994): 653 and 658.

29. Anna Elisabetta Galeotti, "Citizenship and Equality: The Place for Toleration," *Political Theory* 21 (November 1993): 393; see 588–594.

30. Moruzzi, "A Problem with Headscarves," 659; see 657–665.

31. Alan Riding, "France Reversing Course, Fights Immigrants' Refusal to Be French," *New York Times* (December 5, 1993), A6.

32. Laurie Goodstein, "Women in Islamic Headdresses Find Faith and Prejudice, Too," *New York Times* (November 3, 1997), A14; see also A1, and Somini Sengupta, "Restaurant Faces Bias Suit for Barring Man in Turban," *New York Times* (April 25, 1997), A17.

33. Spinner, *The Boundaries of Citizenship*, 69 and 72.

34. Warren Hoge, "Marked for Death by Their Families," *New York Times* (October 18, 1997), A4.

35. Don Terry, "Cultural Tradition and Law Collide in Middle America," *New York Times* (December 2, 1996), A6; see also "Prison Terms for Two Men in Marrying Young Girls," *New York Times* (September 24, 1997), A12.

36. Celia W. Dugger, "Immigrant Cultures Raising Issues of Child Punishment," *New York Times* (February 29, 1996), A12.

37. Mirta Ojito, "Culture Clash: Foreign Parents, American Child Rearing," *New York Times* (June 29, 1997), E3.

38. Barbara Crossette, "Testing the Limits of Tolerance as Cultures Mix," *New York Times* (March 6, 1999), A15 and A17.

39. Carens, "Immigration, Political Community, and the Transformation of Identity," 53–54.

40. Kymlicka, *Liberalism, Community and Culture*, 86–87; see also 55–56.

41. Young, *Justice and the Politics of Difference*, 97. See also Martha Minow, *Making All the Difference: Inclusion, Exclusion, and American Law* (Ithaca, NY: Cornell University Press, 1990), 151.

42. Jean Bethke Elshtain, "Against Androgyny," in *Feminism and Equality*, ed. Anne Phillips (New York: New York University Press, 1987), 145; see 143–148.

43. Minow, *Making All the Difference*, 20; see also 47.

44. Nancy Fraser, *Justice Interruptus: Critical Reflections on the "Postsocialist" Condition* (New York: Routledge, 1997), 174; see 173–175 and 181–184.

45. Carole Pateman, *The Sexual Contract* (Stanford: Stanford University Press, 1988), 187. See also 6–8, 109–111, 118–119, 164–166, 184–185, 231–232, and Minow, *Making All the Difference*, 148–156 and 275–283.

46. Zillah Eisenstein, *The Female Body and the Law* (Berkeley: University of California Press, 1988), 107; see 3, 54, 67–87, 126–127, 195–200, and 204.

47. See also ibid., 201–210, and Young, *Justice and the Politics of Difference*, 175–178.

48. Minow, *Making All the Difference*, 86; see also 53–74, 110–120, and 214–215.

49. *California Savings and Loan Association et al. v. Mark Guerra et al.*, 479 U.S. 272 (1987).

50. Minow, *Making All the Difference*, 59; see 58–59 and 87–89.

51. Nancy J. Hirschmann, "Toward a Feminist Theory of Freedom," *Political Theory* 24 (February 1996): 52; see 49–52, and Nancy J. Hirschmann, "Freedom, Recognition, Obligation: A Feminist Approach to Political Theory," *American Political Science Review* 83 (December 1989): 1229–1241.

52. *E.E.O.C. v. Sears, Roebuck & Co.*, 628 F. Supp. 1264 (N.D. Ill. 1986), *affd.* 839 F. 2d 302 (7th Cir. 1988).

53. Sondra Farganis, *Situating Feminism: From Thought to Action* (Thousand Oaks, CA: Sage Publications, 1994), 58; see 53–60 and 69.

54. Susan Moller Okin, *Justice, Gender, and the Family* (New York: Basic Books, 1989), 132; see 124–133, and Fraser, *Justice Interruptus*, 41–66.

55. Fraser, *Justice Interruptus*, 16 and 21; see 11–39. For Fraser's "Universal Caregiver" model, which allows all individuals to be both workers and caregivers, see 41–66.

56. Okin, *Justice, Gender, and the Family*, 171.

57. Martha Nussbaum, "Justice for Women!" review of Okin, *Justice, Gender, and the Family*, in *New York Review of Books* (October 8, 1992), 46.

58. Young, *Justice and the Politics of Difference*, 176–177; see 165.

5: TOLERATION AND RELIGIOUS BELIEF

1. John Rawls, *Political Liberalism* (New York: Columbia University Press, 1993), xxiv–xxvii and 36–38.

2. James Davison Hunter, for example, argues that as a belief system or specific conception of moral order, secular humanism functions like a religion, even without theistic content. Overt recognition of this would carry policy implications: establishment cases would need to ensure that secularistic standards are not favored over transcendent ones, if government is to be neutral toward religious belief. The context within which we act either is or is not structured to confine the label of religion to theistic belief systems, and this structure in turn determines the meaning of neutrality within that particular context (James Davison Hunter, "Religious Freedom and the Challenge of Modern Pluralism," in *Articles of Faith, Articles of Peace: The Religious Liberty Clauses and the American Public Philosophy*, ed. James Davison Hunter and Os Guinness (Washington, DC: Brookings Institution Press, 1990), 58–71.

3. Susan Mendus, *Toleration and the Limits of Liberalism* (Atlantic Highlands, NJ: Humanities Press International, 1989), 15 and 9; see 8–18.

4. John Horton, "Toleration as a Virtue," in *Toleration: An Elusive Virtue*, ed. David Heyd (Princeton, NJ: Princeton University Press, 1996), 33; see also 35–36, and George P. Fletcher, "The Instability of Tolerance," also in Heyd, ed., *Toleration: An Elusive Virtue*, 158–159.

5. Horton, "Toleration as a Virtue," 36.

6. Bernard Williams, "Toleration: An Impossible Virtue?" in *Toleration: An Elusive Virtue*, ed. David Heyd (Princeton, NJ: Princeton University Press, 1996), 19–22.

7. David Heyd, ed., *Toleration: An Elusive Virtue* (Princeton, NJ: Princeton University Press, 1996), 15.

8. As E. A. Goerner and Walter J. Thompson remind us in the context of Thomas Aquinas, "In short, no one has been able to offer a practical alternative to the commonsensical view that every means is a means to some ends and not others, that every technique is a technique to produce this and not that. . . . In other words, politics is always a choice of ends as well as of means." Although the authors suggest that recognition of this fact may justify coercion, the fact can also stand by itself (Goerner and Thompson, "Politics and Coercion," *Political Theory* 24 [November 1996]: 643).

9. Mendus, *Toleration and the Limits of Liberation*, 149; see 75–109.

10. Heyd, ed., *Toleration: An Elusive Virtue*, 12–14. See also Alex Harel, "The Boundaries of Justifiable Tolerance: A Liberal Perspective," in *Toleration: An Elusive Virtue*, ed. David Heyd (Princeton, NJ: Princeton University Press, 1996), 116–118.

11. Mendus, *Toleration and the Limits of Liberalism*, 154–162. See also Adeno Addis, "On Human Diversity and the Limits of Toleration," *Ethnicity and Group Rights: Nomos XXXIX*, ed. Ian Shapiro and Will Kymlicka (New York: New York University Press, 1997), 117–124.

12. This point is well demonstrated by Andrew Murphy in his consideration of epistemology in Locke, Hobbes, the Massachusetts Puritans, and Roger Williams ("Tolerance, Toleration, and the Liberal Tradition," *Polity* 29 [summer 1997]: 593–623), and in his discussion of contractarianism in the Puritans, Roger Williams, William Penn, Hobbes, and Locke ("The Uneasy Relationship Between Contract Theory and Religious Toleration," *Journal of Politics* 59 [May 1997]: 368–392).

13. Rogers M. Smith, *Liberalism and American Constitutional Law* (Cambridge, MA: Harvard University Press, 1985), 14–17 and 44.

14. Ingrid Creppell, "Locke on Toleration: The Transformation of Constraint," *Political Theory* 24 (May 1996): 204–216. See also Kirstie McClure, "Difference, Diversity, and the Limits of Toleration," *Political Theory* 18 (August 1990): 370; see 365–369 on the significance of "indifferent things" or *adiaphora*, which are religious matters undetermined by biblical injunction or scriptural command as bearing on salvation.

15. George Will, "Court Refuses to Share Power," *Chicago Sun-Times* (June 30, 1997), 23.

16. Creppell, "Locke on Toleration," 227–229.

17. McClure, "Difference, Diversity," 373–381, and John Locke, *A Letter Concerning Toleration* (New York: Liberal Arts Press, 1950), 39–40; see 23–24 and 17–18 for Locke's caution that the civil authorities, who are themselves self-interested, do not use their monopoly on coercion as a pretext for imposing their own interpretations of correct belief.

18. Martha Minow, *Making All the Difference: Inclusion, Exclusion, and American Law* (Ithaca, NY: Cornell University Press, 1990), 86 and 108–120. See also Murphy, "The Uneasy Relationship," 382.

19. Patrick Neal, *Liberalism and Its Discontents* (New York: New York University Press, 1997), 34–47.

20. McClure, "Difference, Diversity," 393; see 382–383.

21. Kristin Luker, *Abortion and the Politics of Motherhood* (Berkeley: University of California Press, 1984), 158–191.

22. McClure, "Difference, Diversity," 384; see 384–386, 374–375, and 380–381. For another example of competing sets of social "facts," see Bhikhu Parekh, "The Rushdie Affair: Research Agenda for Political Philosophy," *The Rights of Minority Cultures,* ed. Will Kymlicka (New York: Oxford University Press, 1995), 312–319.

23. Will Kymlicka, "Two Models of Pluralism and Tolerance," in *Toleration: An Elusive Virtue,* ed. David Heyd (Princeton, NJ: Princeton University Press, 1996), 82; see 81–87, and Will Kymlicka, *Multicultural Citizenship: A Liberal Theory of Minority Rights* (Oxford: Clarendon Press, 1995), 152–163.

24. Kymlicka, "Two Models of Pluralism and Tolerance," 82; see 85, and Kymlicka, *Multicultural Citizenship,* 160–163 and 216, n. 23.

25. Kymlicka, *Multicultural Citizenship,* 159.

26. Mendus, *Toleration and the Limits of Liberalism,* 56; see 55–57.

27. Kymlicka, "Two Models of Pluralism and Tolerance," 89; see 87–90.

28. Moshe Halbertal, "Autonomy, Toleration, and Group Rights: A Response to Will Kymlicka," in *Toleration: An Elusive Virtue,* ed. David Heyd (Princeton, NJ: Princeton University Press, 1996), 107–108.

29. Rawls, *Political Liberalism,* 77–78, 98–99, and 199.

30. Kymlicka, "Two Models of Pluralism and Tolerance," 93; see 87–97, and Kymlicka, *Multicultural Citizenship,* 158–170.

31. Rawls, *Political Liberalism,* 185–186; see also 33–34, 185–187, and Will Kymlicka, *Liberalism, Community and Culture* (Oxford: Clarendon Press, 1991), 36–40.

32. Kymlicka, *Multicultural Citizenship,* 159.

33. Yael Tamir, "Two Concepts of Multiculturalism," *Journal of Philosophy of Education (Society of Great Britain)* 29 (1995): 168; see 166–172.

34. Josiah Conder, Hymn 706, *The Hymnal 1982, According to the Use of the Episcopal Church* (New York: Church Hymnal Corporation, 1982).

35. Andrew Murphy, "Conscience, Identity, and the Foundations of Liberal Freedom" (paper presented at the annual meeting of the Midwest Political Science Association, Chicago, April 1997), 5; see 3–5. For a contrast between the notions of identity

and conscience, see 9–10, 13–14, and Andrew Murphy, "Liberalism, Identity and the Limits of the Conscience Paradigm" (paper presented at the annual meeting of the American Political Science Association, Washington, DC, August 1997), 10–19.

36. Mendus, *Toleration and the Limits of Liberalism*, 35; see also 106, 136, and 149–151.

37. Michael J. Sandel, *Liberalism and the Limits of Justice* (New York: Cambridge University Press, 1982), 58; also see 172.

38. Michael J. Sandel, "Freedom of Conscience or Freedom of Choice?" in *Articles of Faith, Articles of Peace: The Religious Liberty Clauses and the American Public Philosophy*, ed. James Davison Hunter and Os Guinness (Washington, DC: Brookings Institution Press, 1990), 76; see 75–87. See also Sandel, *Liberalism and the Limits of Justice*, 150, and Neal, *Liberalism and Its Discontents*, 34–47.

39. Sandel, "Freedom of Conscience," 81; see 78–87.

40. *Wallace v. Jaffree*, 105 S. Ct. 2479 (1985), at 2487–2488, in Sandel, "Freedom of Conscience," 86; see 85–89.

41. Sandel, "Freedom of Conscience," 89, with reference to *Thornton v. Calder, Inc.*, 105 S. Ct. 2914 (1985).

42. Sandel, "Freedom of Conscience," 90, with reference to *Sherbert v. Verner*, 374 U.S. 398 (1963), at 409.

43. Rawls, *Political Liberalism*, 193; see 190–195.

44. *Wisconsin v. Yoder*, 406 U.S. 205 (1972), at 216 and 220. Sandel comments on this case in "Freedom of Conscience," 90–91 (I shall discuss this case further in chapter 7).

45. David A. J. Richards, *Toleration and the Constitution* (New York: Oxford University Press, 1986), 140.

46. Yael Tamir, *Liberal Nationalism* (Princeton, NJ: Princeton University Press, 1993), 37; see also 7–8 and 41–42. Compare Kymlicka, *Liberalism, Community and Culture*, 189–190 and 237–242.

47. Sandel, "Freedom of Conscience," 91, with reference to *Goldman v. Weinberger*, 106 S. Ct. 1310 (1986), at 1310 and 1313–1315.

48. Tamir, *Liberal Nationalism*, 39–40; see 35–42, and Geoffrey Brahm Levey, "Equality, Autonomy, and Cultural Rights," *Political Theory* 25 (April 1997): 232–241.

49. Halbertal, "Autonomy, Toleration, and Group Rights," 109; see 106–113.

50. Geoffrey Brahm Levey, "Liberalism and Cultural Toleration: The Ineluctability of Autonomy" (paper presented at the annual meeting of the American Political Science Association, Washington, DC, August 1997), 17–18; see 17–21.

51. Amy R. McCready, "The Ethical Individual: An Historical Alternative to Contemporary Conceptions of the Self," *American Political Science Review* 90 (March 1996): 91.

52. Sandel, *Liberalism and the Limits of Justice*, 153. On the voluntarist and cognitivist modes of agency, see 57–59 and 121–122.

53. McCready, "The Ethical Individual," 100. For a complementary view of the role of the will in both fulfilling and creating moral norms, see Heiner Bielefeldt, "Auton-

omy and Republicanism: Immanuel Kant's Philosophy of Freedom," *Political Theory* 25 (August 1997): 524–558.

54. John Bartlett, *Familiar Quotations* (Boston: Little, Brown, 1980), 155.

55. Rawls, *Political Liberalism*, 10; see 4–11 and 174–176.

56. Andrew Murphy, "Political Liberalism, Religion, and the Overlapping Consensus: Historical and Contemporary Reflections on Rawls and Liberty of Conscience" (paper presented at the annual meeting of the American Political Science Association, San Francisco, August 1996), 6–15.

57. Rawls, *Political Liberalism*, 243; see 243–244 and 335.

58. Charles Taylor, "Religion in a Free Society," in *Articles of Faith, Articles of Peace: The Religious Liberty Clauses and the American Public Philosophy*, ed. James Davison Hunter and Os Guinness (Washington, DC: Brookings Institution Press, 1990), 101-113.

59. Michael Walzer, "Response to Kukathas," in *Ethnicity and Group Rights: Nomos XXXIX*, ed. Ian Shapiro and Will Kymlicka (New York: New York University Press, 1997), 108.

60. Jeff Spinner, *The Boundaries of Citizenship: Race, Ethnicity, and Nationality in the Liberal State* (Baltimore: Johns Hopkins University Press, 1994), 74; see also 76 and 135–136. On the idea that toleration does not imply the protection of all cultural practices, see 62, 66–73, 76, 135–136, 149, 183–188, and Tamir, *Liberal Nationalism*, 37 and 48–53.

61. Locke, *A Letter Concerning Toleration*, 23–24.

62. Jeff Spinner-Halev, "The Religious Challenge to Diversity and Equality" (paper presented at the annual meeting of the American Political Science Association, San Francisco, August 1996), 4; see 1–33, and Spinner, *The Boundaries of Citizenship*, 95–105.

63. Spinner-Halev, "The Religious Challenge," 8.

64. Michael daCourey Hinds, "In Tests of Who Can Join, Scouts Confront Identity," *New York Times* (June 23, 1991), A1 and A12.

65. "Court Upholds Boy Scouts Over 'Duty to God' in Oath," *New York Times* (May 23, 1993), A11.

66. "Court Rules Wisely on Scouts," *Chicago Sun-Times* (December 9, 1993), 41.

67. William Claiborne, "Agnostic Twins Picked to Become Eagle Scouts," *Washington Post* (March 17, 1998), A03.

68. George H. Smith, "God and Boy in the Scouts," *New York Times* (January 9, 1992), A13.

69. "Girl Scouts Revising Pledge to Accept Religious Diversity," *New York Times* (October 25, 1993), A12.

70. "Judge Says Scouts Can Ban Gay Scoutmaster," *New York Times* (May 23, 1991), A13.

71. "Troop that Accepts Gay Scouts Keeps Its Charter," *New York Times* (February 23, 1992), A15.

72. "Bay Area Boy Scouts Lose Support," *New York Times* (April 10, 1992), A13.

73. Paul Farhi, "Scouts' Anti-Gay Stance Puts Donors in a Bind," *Chicago Sun-Times* (September 11, 1992), 56.

74. "Gay Issue Embroils Boy Scouts," *New York Times* (December 19, 1996), A15. The Narragansett, Rhode Island, Council issued a similar statement after an Eagle Scout on a Scout camp staff was asked to confirm rumors that he was gay, did so, and was fired. He was later reinstated with a council statement that although it does not accept known homosexuals, it also has no policy of inquiring about sexual orientation (Carey Goldberg, "Some Say Scouts Retreat in Gay Policy," *New York Times* (August 12, 1999), A11.

75. Robert Henley, "Jersey Court Rules Against Scouts' Ouster of Gay Man," *New York Times* (March 3, 1998), A18.

76. Joyce Wadler, "A Matter of Scout's Honor, Says Gay Courtroom Victor," *New York Times* (March 11, 1998), A19.

77. Dennis Byrne, "I Will . . . Obey the Scout Law," *Chicago Sun-Times* (March 4, 1998), 43.

78. "The Invisible Victory," *New York Times* (March 12, 1998), A24.

79. Todd S. Purdum, "California Supreme Court Allows Boy Scouts to Bar Gay Members," *New York Times* (March 24, 1998), A1 and A19. The two cases included both an appeal from the 1991 decision that ruled against a gay applicant for assistant scoutmaster and an appeal concerning the two agnostics who had applied for candidacy to the rank of Eagle Scout.

80. Robert Henley, "New Jersey Court Overturns Ouster of Gay Boy Scout," *New York Times* (August 5, 1999), A1 and A21. The next week, a federal appeals court in Illinois upheld a lower court ruling that barred the Boy Scouts from discriminating against applicants for employment on the basis of sexual orientation (Gary Wisby, "Scouts Can't Bar Gay Hires," *Chicago Sun-Times* (August 14, 1999), 8.

81. Richard E. Sincere Jr., "Pro-Gay Ruling in New Jersey Hurts Gay Rights," *Wall Street Journal* (August 11, 1999), A18. In June of 2000, the U.S. Supreme Court narrowly upheld the Boy Scouts on grounds that opposition to homosexuality was part of its "expressive message" (*Boy Scouts of America vs. Dale,* No. 99-699). Although the language of Scout publications is not self-defining, the fact that Scout officials interpret it to exclude homosexuals is reason enough to allow their exclusion. First, an association need not exist for the express purpose of disseminating a given message in order to be entitled to First Amendment protection. Second, a message may be conveyed by example as well as by words. Finally, the existence of disagreement within an organization's ranks does not negate official positions that may be taken on controversial matters. In sum, the forced inclusion of gay Scouts would intrude severely on the Scout right to freedom of expressive association.

82. *Roberts v. United States Jaycees,* 468 U.S. 609 (1984), at 627 and 628.

83. Boy Scouts of America, *Boy Scout Handbook* (Irving, TX: Boy Scouts of America, 1990), 5–8.

84. Troy M. Yoshino, "What Scouts Value," letter to the editor, *New York Times* (March 23, 1998), A18.

85. Nancy L. Rosenblum, *Membership and Morals: The Personal Uses of Pluralism in America* (Princeton, NJ: Princeton University Press, 1998), 198–199; see 191–203.

86. Jacob Heilbraunn, "Christian Rights: The Next Big Conservative Issue," *New Republic* 217 (July 7, 1997): 23.

87. Michael R. Gordon, "Russians Pass Bill Sharply Favoring Orthodox Church," *New York Times* (September 20, 1997), A1 and A5.

88. Cam Simpson, "Deal Severs City's Tie to Boy Scouts," *Chicago Sun-Times* (February 5, 1998), 3.

89. "New Rules Give Federal Workers More Freedom to Express Religion," *Chicago Sun-Times* (August 15, 1997), 32.

90. David Lauter, "Religious Employees Seek More Protection," *Chicago Sun-Times* (December 7, 1997), 54.

6: SEXUALITY, NEUTRALITY, AND AUTONOMY

1. As of late 1998, oral and anal sex between homosexuals was still a crime in five states; the same practice between homosexuals *or* heterosexuals was a crime in thirteen additional states (Kevin Sack, "Georgia's High Court Voids Sodomy Law," *New York Times* [November 24, 1998], A14).

2. Mary Ann Glendon, *Rights Talk: The Impoverishment of Political Discourse* (New York: Free Press of Macmillan, 1991), 154; see 151–158.

3. William A. Galston, "Public Morality and Religion in the Liberal State," *PS* 19 (fall 1986): 821–822.

4. David McCabe, "Outline for a Defense of Unreconstructed Liberalism," *Journal of Social Philosophy* 19 (spring 1998): 72; see 67–77.

5. Yael Tamir, *Liberal Nationalism* (Princeton, NJ: Princeton University Press, 1993), 41; see 35–42.

6. Karen Struening, "Privacy and Sexuality in a Society Divided over Moral Culture," *Political Research Quarterly* 49 (September 1996): 509, see 507–509. See also Kristin Luker, *Abortion and the Politics of Motherhood* (Berkeley: University of California Press, 1984), for a similar analysis of the abortion controversy. On the futility of bracketing moral beliefs because the state will always be complicit in some viewpoint, see Fred M. Frohock, "The Boundaries of Public Research," *American Political Science Review* 91 (December 1997): 840–841.

7. Steven Kautz, "Liberalism and the Idea of Toleration," *American Journal of Political Science* 37 (May 1993): 620. See also Steven Kautz, *Liberalism and Community* (Ithaca, NY: Cornell University Press, 1995), 63.

8. Kautz, "Liberalism and the Idea of Toleration," 624. See also Kautz, *Liberalism and Community*, 52–57, 67–68, and 72–75.

9. Kautz, "Liberalism and the Idea of Toleration," 629; see also 614.

10. Kautz, *Liberalism and Community*, 13; see 11–13, 56, and 68. See also Richard Sinopoli, "Thick-Skinned Liberalism: Redefining Civility," *American Political Science Review*

89 (September 1995): 613–618, for the contrasting argument that withholding equal respect will promote beneficial dialogue on the intersubjective nature of the good life.

11. Alasdair MacIntyre, *After Virtue* (Notre Dame, IN: University of Notre Dame Press, 1981), 204.

12. William R. Lund, "Communitarian Politics and the Problem of Equality," *Political Research Quarterly* 46 (September 1993): 587.

13. Patrick Neal, *Liberalism and Its Discontents* (New York: New York University Press, 1997), 197; see 185–205.

14. John Rawls, *Political Liberalism* (New York: Columbia University Press, 1993), 148; see also 134.

15. Brian Walker, "John Rawls, Mikhail Bakhtin, and the Praxis of Toleration," *Political Theory* 23 (February 1995): 121.

16. Andrew Murphy, "Tolerance, Toleration, and the Liberal Tradition," *Polity* 29 (summer 1997): 596.

17. Andrew Sullivan, *Virtually Normal: An Argument About Homosexuality* (New York: Vintage Books of Random House, 1996), 21–25. On compassion for the trapped, see also Didi Herman, *The Antigay Agenda: Orthodox Vision and the Christian Right* (Chicago: University of Chicago Press, 1997), 46–51.

18. Patricia Boling, *Privacy and the Politics of Intimate Life* (Ithaca, NY: Cornell University Press, 1996), 133; see 132–136.

19. Sullivan, *Virtually Normal*, 95; see 95–96. See also 101–106 on the perceived homosexual threat to the social fabric.

20. Andrew Sullivan, "They've Changed, So They Say," *New York Times* (July 26, 1998), WK15.

21. Tamir, *Liberal Nationalism*, 41.

22. Sullivan, "They've Changed," WK15.

23. James W. Button, Barbara A. Rienzo, and Kenneth D. Wald, *Private Lives, Public Conflicts: Battles over Gay Rights in American Communities* (Washington, DC: Congressional Quarterly Press, 1997), 12; see 12–13.

24. Button et al., *Private Lives, Public Conflicts*, 185; see also 89–90, and Sullivan, *Virtually Normal*, 151–155.

25. Sullivan, *Virtually Normal*, 153; see 151–153, and Mark Strasser, *Legally Wed: Same-Sex Marriage and the Constitution* (Ithaca, NY: Cornell University Press, 1997), 30–44.

26. Andrew Murphy, "Liberalism, Identity, and the Limits of the Conscience Paradigm" (paper presented at the annual meeting of the American Political Science Association, Washington, DC, August 1997), 16.

27. Ingrid Creppell, "Locke on Toleration: The Transformation of Constraint," *Political Theory* 24 (May 1996): 226–230.

28. Boling, *Privacy and the Politics of Intimate Life*, 146; see 146–148 and 56–59. Boling maintains that one may decide not only to reveal hitherto hidden aspects of identity but also to claim as central to identity known characteristics one previously regarded as merely contingent (134–135).

29. Sullivan, *Virtually Normal*, 137; see also 139 and 148–161 for his view overall.

30. See also ibid., 178–187 and 221–222.

31. Strasser, *Legally Wed*, 59, 91.

32. Sullivan, *Virtually Normal*, 139, 186–187.

33. Chandran Kukathas, "Liberalism and Multiculturalism: The Politics of Indifference," *Political Theory* 26 (October 1998): 691; see 690–695.

34. Albert Dzur, "Liberal Perfectionism and Democratic Participation," *Polity* 30 (summer 1998): 678; see 676–680, 668, and 671–674. On the role of debate, see 680–690.

35. *Bowers v. Hardwick*, 478 U.S. 186 (1986), 191; see 190–196. The law was invalidated by the Georgia Supreme Court in 1998 (Sack, "Georgia's High Court Voids Sodomy Law," A14). An argument parallel to Justice White's about the absence of a fundamental right to engage in homosexual sodomy appears in an Alabama case challenging a 1998 law banning the sale of vibrators and other sexual aids. Although the challengers appealed to privacy rights, the state argued that "there is no fundamental right to a product used to produce an orgasm" ("Women Fight Alabama's Sex-toy Ban," *Chicago Sun-Times* [February 18, 1999], 20).

36. Boling, *Privacy and the Politics of Intimate Life*, 103; see 85–90, 101–103, and Michael J. Sandel, *Democracy's Discontent: America in Search of a Public Philosophy* (Cambridge, MA: Belknap Press of Harvard University Press, 1996), 91–108.

37. Sandel, *Democracy's Discontent*, 93. See also Stephen Macedo, *Liberal Virtues: Citizenship, Virtue, and Community in Liberal Constitutionalism* (Oxford: Clarendon Press of Oxford University Press, 1990), 194–196.

38. Lund, "Communitarian Politics and the Problem of Equality," 595.

39. Philip Selznick, "Dworkin's Unfinished Task," *California Law Review* 77 (1989): 511–512; see 511–513.

40. Sandel, *Democracy's Discontent*, 107; see 106–107.

41. Bonnie Honig, *Political Theory and the Displacement of Politics* (Ithaca, NY: Cornell University Press, 1993), 191–192; see also 171.

42. Thomas Bridges, *The Culture of Citizenship: Inventing Postmodern Civic Culture* (Albany: State University of New York Press, 1994), 168–189.

43. Eamonn Callan, "Beyond Sentimental Civic Education," *American Journal of Education* 102 (February 1994): 209–210; see 205–211.

44. Eamonn Callan, "Common Schools for Common Education," *Canadian Journal of Education* 20 (1995): 260; see 257–260. On ways in which traditions "embody continuities of conflict," see MacIntyre, *After Virtue*, 206.

45. Boling, *Privacy and the Politics of Intimate Life*, 26; see 24–27 and 108–109. See also Struening, "Privacy and Sexuality," 510, and Frank Michelman, "Law's Republic," *Yale Law Journal* 97 (July 1988): 1533–1535.

46. *Bowers v. Hardwick*, 478 U.S. 186 (1986), 205–206.

47. *Roberts v. United States Jaycees*, 468 U.S. 609 (1984), 619.

48. Dirk Johnson, "Colorado Court Nullifies a Ban on Gay Rights," *New York Times* (October 12, 1994), A1 and A13.

49. Richard Bernstein, "Double Vision: Where One Person's Civil Rights Are Another's Moral Outrage," *New York Times* (October 6, 1994), E6.

50. *Romer v. Evans,* 517 U.S. 620 (1996), 630–631. On the possible implications of the enforcement of Amendment 2, see Linda Greenhouse, "U.S. Justices Hear, and Also Debate, a Gay Rights Case," *New York Times* (October 11, 1995), A1 and A18, and Jeffrey Rosen, "Disoriented," *New Republic* 213 (October 23, 1995): 24–26.

51. Scalia notes that if deprivation of the franchise could not stand today, it would fall only because the Court now deems the right to vote a fundamental right.

52. Struening, "Privacy and Sexuality," 510.

53. Deb Price, "Sexual Orientation Bias Ought to Be Banned," *Chicago Sun-Times* (May 27, 1994), 39.

54. *Roberts v. United States Jaycees,* 468 U.S. 609 (1984), 633.

55. Herman, *The Antigay Agenda,* 161; see 159–165.

56. Rosen, "Disoriented," 25.

57. Jonathan Rauch, "Beyond Oppression: Homosexuality and Victimology," *New Republic* 208 (May 10, 1993): 20 and 23.

58. Anthony Lewis, "Homage to Virtue," *New York Times* (June 13, 1997), A17. Attorney General Bowers prosecuted *Bowers v. Hardwick.*

59. Rauch, "Beyond Oppression," 20.

60. Sullivan, *Virtually Normal,* 153; see 153–154 for a comparison of homosexuals with slaves.

61. Vernon Jarrett, "Gay Rights, Black Struggles Are Different," *Chicago Sun-Times* (April 25, 1993), 41.

62. Button et al., *Private Lives, Public Conflicts,* 185.

63. Herman, *The Antigay Agenda,* 121; see 116–125 and 69–76.

64. Kenneth Sherrill, "The Political Power of Lesbians, Gays, and Bisexuals," *PS: Political Science and Politics* 29 (September 1996): 472. For statistics supporting the Christian Right, see Herman, *The Antigay Agenda,* 69–76.

65. Andrew Sullivan, "Three's a Crowd: The Polygamy Diversion," *New Republic* 214 (June 17, 1996): 10. See also Strasser, *Legally Wed,* 37–40, and David A. J. Richards, *Women, Gays, and the Constitution* (Chicago: University of Chicago Press, 1998), 449–453.

66. John Stuart Mill, "On Liberty," in *On Liberty and Other Writings,* ed. Stefan Collini (New York: Cambridge University Press, 1989), 84.

67. T. M. Scanlon, "The Difficulty of Toleration," in *Toleration: An Elusive Virtue,* ed. David Heyd (Princeton, NJ: Princeton University Press, 1996), 229.

68. Samuel M. Marcosson, "The 'Special Rights' Canard in the Debate over Lesbian and Gay Civil Rights," *Notre Dame Journal of Law, Ethics and Public Policy* 9 (1995): 168; see also 165, 144–145, 156, and Richards, *Women, Gays, and the Constitution,* 396–398. This is also the proper response to alarmists who fear that cracking the door to homosexual practices and commitments also opens the floodgates to polygamy, pederasty, and incest. To defend some practices as legitimate expressions of conscience does not ipso facto justify or legitimize all such practices.

69. Samuel M. Marcosson, "*Romer* and the Limits of Legitimacy: Stripping Opponents of Gay and Lesbian Rights of Their 'First Line of Defense' in the Same-Sex Marriage Fight," *Journal of Contemporary Law* 24 (1998): 230; see 229–231. See 231–234 on the connection between *Romer* and the illegitimacy of *Bowers*.

70. Richards, *Women, Gays, and the Constitution*, 275; see 155, 261, 267–287, 345–356, 365–370, 385, 408, and 458–459.

71. Kautz, "Liberalism and the Idea of Toleration," 624.

72. David Johnston, *The Idea of Liberal Theory: A Critique and a Reconstruction* (Princeton, NJ: Princeton University Press, 1994), 155.

73. Richards, *Women, Gays, and the Constitution*, 357; see also 357–370, and Strasser, *Legally Wed*, 30–44.

74. Richards, *Women, Gays, and the Constitution*, 360; see 357–360 and 377–405. For Richards's view that *Romer* invalidates *Bowers*, and therefore the military exclusion policy grounded in the illegality of homosexual sodomy, see 414–415, 430–435, and 444.

75. Jeremy Waldron, "Particular Values and Critical Morality," *California Law Review* 77 (1989): 579–581.

76. Sanford Levinson, *Constitutional Faith* (Princeton, NJ: Princeton University Press, 1988), 193.

7: EDUCATION FOR CITIZENSHIP

1. John Rawls, *Political Liberalism* (New York: Columbia University Press, 1993), 122.

2. Eamonn Callan, "Last Word," *Review of Politics* 58 (winter 1996): 49.

3. Amy Gutmann, *Democratic Education* (Princeton, NJ: Princeton University Press, 1987), 33; see also 30, 44, and 14.

4. Amy Gutmann, "Undemocratic Education," in *Liberalism and the Moral Life*, ed. Nancy L. Rosenblum (Cambridge, MA: Harvard University Press, 1989), 85.

5. Gutmann, *Democratic Education*, 44; see 30, 44–45, and 77–80.

6. Amy Gutmann and Dennis Thompson, "Moral Conflict and Political Consensus," *Ethics* 101 (October 1990): 76; see 76–81, and Amy Gutmann, "Civic Education and Social Diversity," *Ethics* 105 (April 1995): 560–565.

7. Gutmann, "Civic Education and Social Diversity," 563; see also 559–560 and 573–579.

8. Eamonn Callan, "Political Liberalism and Political Education," *Review of Politics* 58 (winter 1996): 17; see 14–18 and also 11–14 on the normative difficulties of the subsequently required bifurcation between public and private selves.

9. Eamonn Callan, "Tradition and Integrity in Moral Education," *American Journal of Education* 101 (November 1992): 22; see 16–24, and Jeff Spinner, *The Boundaries of Citizenship* (Baltimore: Johns Hopkins University Press, 1994), 93–94.

10. Callan, "Political Liberalism and Political Education," 22.

11. William A. Galston, "Civic Education in the Liberal State," in *Liberalism and the*

Moral Life, ed. Nancy L. Rosenblum (Cambridge, MA: Harvard University Press, 1989), 100; see also 153 and 130.

12. William A. Galston, *Liberal Purposes: Goods, Virtues, and Diversity in the Liberal State* (New York: Cambridge University Press, 1991), 329, n. 12. See also William A. Galston, "Two Concepts of Liberalism," *Ethics* 105 (April 1995): 523–524.

13. Galston, "Civic Education in the Liberal State," 90. See also Galston, *Liberal Purposes*, 242–243.

14. Galston, "Civic Education in the Liberal State," 96.

15. Galston, *Liberal Purposes*, 175–176; see also 253, and Galston, "Civic Education in the Liberal State," 99.

16. Galston, *Liberal Purposes*, 149; see 143–149, 277, and 259.

17. Galston, "Two Concepts of Liberalism," 524; see also 523–524, and Galston, *Liberal Purposes*, 129, 256, and 329, n. 12.

18. Galston, "Two Concepts of Liberalism," 529.

19. David Johnston, *The Idea of a Liberal Theory* (Princeton, NJ: Princeton University Press, 1994), 91; see 91–99.

20. Galston, "Two Concepts of Liberalism," 528.

21. Galston, *Liberal Purposes*, 129.

22. Galston, "Two Concepts of Liberalism," 531–534.

23. Callan, "Tradition and Integrity in Moral Education," 22.

24. Galston, *Liberal Purposes*, 280–289.

25. William A. Galston, "Public Morality and Religion in the Liberal State," *PS* 19 (fall 1986): 820–822.

26. Galston, *Liberal Purposes*, 282–283.

27. Eamonn Callan, "Beyond Sentimental Civic Education," *American Journal of Education* 102 (February 1994): 203; see 200–203.

28. Callan, "Beyond Sentimental Civic Education," 209; see 205–214.

29. Eamonn Callan, "Common Schools for Common Education," *Canadian Journal of Education* 20 (1995): 256; see 252–264.

30. Stephen Macedo, "Multiculturalism for the Religious Right? Defending Liberal Civic Education," *Journal of Philosophy of Education* 29 (July 1995): 226; see 224–229.

31. Stephen Macedo, "Transformative Constitutionalism and the Case of Religion: Defending the Moderate Hegemony of Liberalism," *Political Theory* 26 (February 1998): 58.

32. Stephen Macedo, "Liberal Civic Education and Its Limits," *Canadian Journal of Education* 20 (1995): 304. See also Stephen Macedo, "Community, Diversity, and Civic Education: Toward a Liberal Political Science of Group Life," *Social Philosophy and Policy* 13 (1996): 240–268.

33. Macedo, "Transformative Constitutionalism," 73.

34. Macedo, "Liberal Civic Education and Its Limits," 308; see 308–309.

35. Stephen Macedo, *Liberal Virtues: Citizenship, Virtue, and Community in Liberal Constitutionalism* (Oxford: Clarendon Press, 1990), 253.

36. Macedo, "Liberal Civic Education and Its Limits," 309.

37. Macedo, "Transformative Constitutionalism," 69; see 70–75.

38. Macedo, *Liberal Virtues*, 64.

39. Stephen Macedo, "Liberal Civic Education and Religious Fundamentalism: The Case of God v. John Rawls," *Ethics* 105 (April 1995): 469–470.

40. Kirstie M. McClure, "Difference, Diversity, and the Limits of Toleration," *Political Theory* 18 (August 1990): 361–391.

41. Ike Flores, "Florida County: Schools Must Teach U.S. 'Superiority,' " *Chicago Sun-Times* (May 29, 1994), 28.

42. Dennis Byrne, "Don't Fret Over Superiority Complex," *Chicago Sun-Times* (May 29, 1994), 37.

43. *Wisconsin v. Yoder*, 406 U.S. 205 (1972), 210; see 210–215.

44. Spinner, *The Boundaries of Citizenship*, 97; see 95–99 and 39–45.

45. Will Kymlicka, *Multicultural Citizenship: A Liberal Theory of Minority Rights* (Oxford: Clarendon Press, 1995), 105; see also 83, and Will Kymlicka, *Liberalism, Community and Culture* (Oxford: Clarendon Press, 1991), 165.

46. Spinner, *The Boundaries of Citizenship*, 99; see 99–108.

47. Galston, "Two Concepts of Liberalism," 534.

48. Spinner, *The Boundaries of Citizenship*, 101; see 101–102.

49. Walter Feinberg, "Liberalism and the Aims of Multicultural Education," *Journal of Philosophy of Education (Society of Great Britain)* 29 (July 1995): 205.

50. Macedo, *Liberal Virtues*, 59.

51. Feinberg, "Liberalism and the Aims of Multicultural Education," 206.

52. Spinner, *The Boundaries of Citizenship*, 104; see 103–105.

53. Jeremy Waldron, "Multiculturalism and Mélange," *Public Education in a Multicultural Society*, ed. Robert K. Fullinwider (New York: Cambridge University Press, 1996), 91.

54. Macedo, "Liberal Civic Education and Its Limits," 308.

55. Spinner, *The Boundaries of Citizenship*, 103.

56. Galston, "Two Concepts of Liberalism," 529.

57. Gutmann, *Democratic Education*, 123.

58. Galston, *Liberal Purposes*, 295.

59. *Mozert v. Hawkins County Board of Education, Mozert V*, 827 F. 2d 1058 (6th Circuit 1987).

60. Joseph Raz, *The Morality of Freedom* (Oxford: Clarendon Press, 1986), 391.

61. Susan Mendus, *Toleration and the Limits of Liberalism* (Atlantic Highlands, NJ: Humanities Press International, 1989), 106; see also 111, 144, and 156.

62. Nomi Maya Stolzenberg, " 'He Drew a Circle That Shut Me Out': Assimilation, Indoctrination, and the Paradox of Liberal Education," *Harvard Law Review* 106 (1993): 591.

63. Callan, "Political Liberalism and Political Education," 22; see also 17.

64. Stolzenberg, " 'He Drew a Circle,' " 626–627.

65. Rawls, *Political Liberalism*, 63.

66. Callan, "Political Liberalism and Political Education," 19; see 18–20.

67. Kenneth Strike, "Must Liberal Citizens Be Reasonable?" *Review of Politics* 58 (winter 1996): 44.

68. Callan, "Last Word," 50–51.

69. Alasdair MacIntyre, *After Virtue* (Notre Dame, IN: University of Notre Dame Press, 1981), 206.

70. Rawls, *Political Liberalism*, 32.

71. Stolzenberg, " 'He Drew a Circle,' " 650; see also 651–666 for discussion of the way liberal, communitarian, and civic republican traditions possess resources that clarify this conflict but do not offer a definitive solution.

72. Shelley Burtt, "Religious Parents, Secular Schools: A Liberal Defense of an Illiberal Education," *Review of Politics* 56 (winter 1994): 58; see also 62.

73. Shelley Burtt, "In Defense of *Yoder*," in *Political Order: Nomos XXXVIII*, ed. Ian Shapiro and Russell Hardin (New York: New York University Press, 1996), 418. See also Burtt, "Religious Parents, Secular Schools," 66.

74. Burtt, "Religious Parents, Secular Schools," 67.

75. Burtt, "In Defense of *Yoder*," 422; see also 419.

76. Burtt, "Religious Parents, Secular Schools," 69; see 67–70.

77. Burtt, "In Defense of *Yoder*," 426–427.

78. In a thoughtful comment, Patrick Neal has suggested that I am perhaps not completely fair to link the examined life so closely to experience with alternatives. An orthodox rabbi who spends his life studying the Talmud neither experiences life outside his community nor even considers doing so. "On the other hand, . . . he may well have lived a deeply examined life through a lifelong encounter with sacred Scriptures, indeed a life that is far more examined than the lives of 'quiet desperation' led by millions of people who 'experiment' with many different 'lifestyles' and who, in one sense, make many more 'choices' than the rabbi could even imagine. . . . Arguably it may be the rabbi who leads the genuinely examined life" (communication of January 18, 1999). I agree that a qualitative component, not merely a quantitative one, is part of this examination of alternatives. But critical reflection on alternative interpretations of the Talmud affords both quantitative and qualitative challenges that others may escape, even in the larger world.

79. Richard J. Arneson and Ian Shapiro, "Democratic Autonomy and Religious Freedom: A Critique of *Wisconsin v. Yoder*," in *Political Order: Nomos XXXVIII*, ed. Ian Shapiro and Russell Hardin (New York: New York University Press, 1996), 403; see 396–406, and Macedo, "Liberal Civic Education and Religious Fundamentalism," 488–490.

80. Burtt, "In Defense of *Yoder*," 422; see 424–429.

81. Stolzenberg, " 'He Drew a Circle,' " 652.

82. Macedo, "Liberal Civic Education and Its Limits," 311–312; Macedo, "Multiculturalism for the Religious Right?" 225; Macedo, "Transformative Constitutionalism,"

69 and 79, n. 53. See also Macedo, "Multiculturalism for the Religious Right?" 224–235, for a discussion of Stephen Carter in this context.

83. Macedo, "Transformative Constitutionalism," 72–73. See also Macedo, "Multiculturalism for the Religious Right?" 226.

84. Macedo, "Transformative Constitutionalism," 75.

85. Susan Mendus, "Toleration and Recognition: Education in a Multicultural Society," *Journal of Philosophy of Education (Society of Great Britain)* 29 (July 1995): 195–196.

86. Thomas Bridges, *The Culture of Citizenship: Inventing Postmodern Civic Culture* (Albany: State University of New York Press, 1994), 209; see also 168–189, and Anthony K. Appiah, "Culture, Subculture, Multiculturalism: Educational Options," in *Public Education in a Multicultural Society,* ed. Robert K. Fullinwider (New York: Cambridge University Press, 1996), 84–85.

Index